International Entrepreneurship

Third Edition

International Entrepreneurship

Starting, Developing, and Managing a Global Venture

Third Edition

Robert D. Hisrich
Bridgestone Chair of International Marketing
Associate Dean of Graduate and International Programs
Kent State University

Los Angeles | London | New Delhi
Singapore | Washington DC

Los Angeles | London | New Delhi
Singapore | Washington DC

FOR INFORMATION:

SAGE Publications, Inc.
2455 Teller Road
Thousand Oaks, California 91320
E-mail: order@sagepub.com

SAGE Publications Ltd.
1 Oliver's Yard
55 City Road
London EC1Y 1SP
United Kingdom

SAGE Publications India Pvt. Ltd.
B 1/I 1 Mohan Cooperative Industrial Area
Mathura Road, New Delhi 110 044
India

SAGE Publications Asia-Pacific Pte. Ltd.
3 Church Street
#10-04 Samsung Hub
Singapore 049483

Printed in the United States of America

ISBN 978-1-4833-4439-3

Acquisitions Editor: Maggie Stanley
Editorial Assistant: Nicole Mangona
eLearning editor: Katie Bierach
Production Editor: Laura Barrett
Copy Editor: Erin Livingston
Typesetter: C&M Digitals (P) Ltd.
Proofreader: Kris Bergstad
Indexer: Michael Ferreira
Cover Designer: Anupama Krishan
Marketing Manager: Liz Thornton

This book is printed on acid-free paper.

SUSTAINABLE FORESTRY INITIATIVE
Certified Chain of Custody
Promoting Sustainable Forestry
www.sfiprogram.org
SFI-01268
SFI label applies to text stock

15 16 17 18 19 10 9 8 7 6 5 4 3 2 1

Brief Contents

Detailed Contents

Preface

Starting and operating a new venture in one's own country involves considerable risk and energy to overcome all the obstacles involved. These are significantly compounded when one crosses national borders—the fate of the global entrepreneur. This book is designed to help understand all these international obstacles and to assist in starting and growing a successful international venture.

To provide an understanding of the person and the process of creating and growing an international venture, the third edition of the book, *International Entrepreneurship*, is divided into three parts—international entrepreneurship and opportunities, entering the global market, and managing the global entrepreneurial enterprise.

Part I (International Entrepreneurship and Entrepreneurship Opportunities) deals with the aspects of being a global entrepreneur and identifying global opportunities. Specific issues covered include the importance of international entrepreneurship, globalization and the international environment, the impact of a culture, the global entrepreneur and his or her venture, and the global monetary system.

The chapters describing the general nature and aspects of international entrepreneurship are followed by material on entering a global market (Part II). The three chapters in Part II are extremely important, because without a successful global market selection and entry, obtaining sales and revenues from the global effort becomes very difficult. These three chapters address the selection of international business opportunities, the development of the global business plan, and the international legal concerns that the global entrepreneur needs to address.

The final section of the book, Part III, deals with all aspects of managing the global entrepreneurial enterprise. The specific areas addressed include alternative entry strategies for entering the selected market, global marketing and research and development, global human resource management, and implementing and managing a global entrepreneurial strategy and venture.

To facilitate an understanding of the material and allow the reader to apply it in a global context, original case studies are contained in Part IV. These case studies, written by individuals from a wide range of countries, cover global entrepreneurs from these countries who are creating and growing ventures in a variety of industries. Each case study is followed by questions that will ensure that the most important aspects of the case have been covered.

Ancillaries

A companion website at **study.sagepub.com/hisrich3e** features additional materials to support teaching and learning. Students can access a sample business plan on the open-access site, and instructors can log in to find sample answers to end-of-chapter questions and teaching notes for the cases.

Acknowledgments

Many individuals—corporate executives, entrepreneurs, small business managers, professors from all over the world, and the publishing staff—have made this book possible. My special thanks goes to individuals involved with the publishing process for their detailed comments and editorial assistance at SAGE: Maggie Stanley, acquisitions editor; Nicole Mangona, editorial assistant; and Laura Barrett, senior project editor. Thanks go to my research assistant, Fiona Teerlink, who provided significant research and editorial assistance, and to Anetta Hunek, whose website provided the Cultural Stories. And my utmost appreciation goes to my administrative assistant, Carol Pacelli, without whom this book would have never been prepared in a timely manner.

Special thanks to the following reviewers for their helpful comments and suggestions:

Kayven Miri Lavassani, *North Carolina Central University*
R. Greg Bell, *University of Dallas*
Robert Linowes, *American University*
Bruce Bachenheimer, *Pace University*

I am deeply indebted to my wife, Tina; my daughters, Kary, Katy, and Kelly; my son-in-law, Rich; and my grandchildren, Rachel, Andrew, and Sarah; as well as Kaiya, for their support and understanding of my time commitment in writing this book. It is to them that this book is particularly dedicated; their world is truly global.

PART I

INTERNATIONAL ENTREPRENEURSHIP AND OPPORTUNITIES

1

Importance of International Entrepreneurship

Profile: RidingO

Each year, there are about 1.24 million road fatalities globally, yet the number of cars surpassed one billion in 2011. There have been many attempts by governments and nongovernmental organizations (NGOs) in recent years to reduce the number of motor vehicle related deaths, either by encouraging people to take public transportation or by imposing laws, including higher taxes, to make cars a less attractive mode of transportation. Other efforts emerged to encourage carpooling to reduce total CO_2 emissions and to reduce the number of cars on the road, ultimately reducing traffic and accidents. However, carpooling never became popular in India, in part due to the awkwardness of having to ask colleagues for money to share a ride. The Indian mobile and cloud-based platform RidingO is based in Bangalore and has developed a way to turn the ideal of carpooling into a reality, with both social and economic benefits for all parties.

The platform brings together car owners and passengers for relatively secure carpooling in India. Only verified members (professionals from known companies) are permitted to access the site and women are only paired up with other women, unless they specifically identify and select a male passenger to share a ride with. The benefits offered by this company are significant. Car owners have potentially great savings, as they no longer have to pay for all fuel expenses alone. Sharing rides is also greener, as it results in less traffic and fewer emissions, and sharing a ride is less stressful than driving alone. Passengers, on the other hand, benefit from higher levels of comfort than they could achieve with some other forms of transportation, much lower costs than would be incurred driving alone or taking a taxi, and more opportunities to expand their social life and network with other business professionals. RidingO's website even offers a very simple tool to calculate annual cost savings for both parties based on the number of kilometers traveled per day.

Cofounders Vardhan Koshal and Srivatsan Mohan established this business in January 2013 and had already attracted 700 users by April of that year, 250 of which were car owners. As the market has become more competitive in the past year, RidingO has shifted its focus to more specifically target professionals in the information technology (IT) industry by partnering with Electronic City. Electronic City is one of the largest tech parks in India, with 200 companies and about 150,000 people in 10,000–15,000 cars in the area daily. Since this new campaign was launched on March 11, 2014, RidingO has already attracted an additional 1,000 registered users.

The company has developed an innovative solution to the messy traffic situation in Bangalore and now seems to be perfecting its business model. Perhaps this company can become a global brand in ride sharing, as RidingO has the potential to make ride sharing a more fun and relaxed experience, even outside of its home country. After all, there are certainly more countries around the world that could use some help in solving the increasing transportation problem. However, before it might be able to do so, the company's management team will need to develop a strategy to achieve a competitive advantage when compared to other giants, including Carpooling.com (based in Munich) and Lyft.com or ZimRide (from the United States). This company has certainly decided to tackle a global issue and has determined that Bangalore is the place to start.

SOURCES: Balakrishnan, R. (2014, March 24). Carpooling tries to target better. Retrieved April 28, 2014, from http://www.business-standard.com/article/companies/car-pooling-tries-to-target-better-114032300364_1.html

RidingO [website]. (n.d). Retrieved February 10, 2015, from https://www.RidingO.com/

CHAPTER OBJECTIVES

1. To understand the fundamental importance of the global venture in today's changing world
2. To introduce the concept of entrepreneurship from a global perspective, crossing national boundaries
3. To learn the key differences in operating a business in a global versus domestic environment
4. To identify the major motivators for taking a business global or for conceiving a new business with a global focus

Introduction

Never before in the history of the world has there been such a variety of exciting international business opportunities. The movement of the once-controlled economies to more market-oriented ones, the economics of the Pacific Rim, and the markets in the Middle East and Africa provide a myriad of possibilities for entrepreneurs wanting to start a new enterprise in a foreign market as well as for existing entrepreneurial firms desiring to expand their businesses globally. The world is truly global.

As more countries become market oriented and economically developed, the distinction between foreign and domestic markets is becoming less pronounced. What was once only produced domestically is now produced internationally. For example, Yamaha pianos are now manufactured in the United States, and Nestlé chocolate (started in Europe) is made all over the world. Invacare's wheelchairs, once produced only in the United States, are now made in Germany and China. This blurring of national identities will continue to accelerate as more products are introduced outside domestic boundaries earlier in the life of entrepreneurial firms.

Organizations are increasingly attempting to redefine themselves as being truly global. The pressure to internationalize is being felt in every type of organization: nonprofit and for-profit, public and private, large and small. This need to internationalize is accelerating because of the self-interest of these organizations as well as the effect of a variety of external events. Today, more than seven eighths of the world's economic states have some form of market economy. A few large trading blocs such as the European Union (EU) and NAFTA (the North American Free Trade Agreement between Canada, Mexico, and the United States) have emerged and are growing. Once-developing countries, such as China, are economic powers.

These changes are well recognized by organizations that are investing trillions of dollars in a world economy that includes emerging markets as some of the major vehicles of future growth. About 85% of the world's population lives in developing countries, most of which are in need of major investment in infrastructure development. Just ask the potato farmers in the Chuvash Republic of Russia, who saw 26% of their crop rot because of inadequate distribution and warehousing, whether there is a need for this investment in infrastructure. Or ask the economics professor in the Czech Republic, who had to leave the university to find other employment due to the low university wages, whether massive investment in education is needed. The professor, like many human resources in these developing countries, needs training and education to provide the manpower required in the next century.

The need for physical and technological infrastructure is no more apparent than in one of the fastest-growing markets in the 2000s and early 2010s—the Pacific Rim. This area offers economically viable locations for manufacturing and trade. Over half of the world's population lives in Asia, with China containing 20% of the world's population. In terms of population, India alone is twice the size of Latin America. And then there is Japan, with its world economy ranking high particularly in the area of exporting and importing.

There are also new market opportunities in South America, Ukraine, Vietnam, Iraq, and other countries in transition throughout the world. These areas are becoming highly attractive to globally oriented companies that want to grow their business internationally and develop a strong market position as the economies of countries change through privatization and deregulation.

The globalization of entrepreneurship creates wealth and employment that benefit individuals and nations throughout the world. International entrepreneurship is exciting because it combines the many aspects of domestic entrepreneurship with other disciplines such as anthropology, economics, geography, history, jurisprudence, and language. In today's hypercompetitive world with rapidly changing technology, it is essential for an entrepreneur to at least consider entering the global market.

Many entrepreneurs find it difficult to manage and expand the venture they have created, especially into the global marketplace. They tend to forget a basic axiom: The only constant is change. Entrepreneurs who understand this can effectively manage change by continually adapting their organizational culture, structure, procedures, and strategic direction as well as their products and services in both a domestic and an international orientation. Entrepreneurs in developed countries such as the United States, Japan, the United Kingdom, and Germany need to sell their products in a variety of new and different market areas as early as possible to further the growth of their firms.

Global markets offer entrepreneurial companies new market opportunities. Since 1950, the growth of international trade and investment has often been larger than the growth of domestic economies, even those of the United States and China. This combination of domestic and international sales offers the entrepreneur an opportunity for expansion and growth that is not available solely in a domestic market.

The Nature of International Entrepreneurship

Simply stated, *international entrepreneurship* is the process of an entrepreneur conducting business activities across national boundaries. It may consist of exporting, licensing, opening a sales office in another country, or something as simple as placing a classified advertisement in the Paris edition of the *International Herald Tribune*. The activities necessary for ascertaining and satisfying the needs and wants of target consumers often take place in more than one country. When an entrepreneur executes his or her business model in more than one country, international entrepreneurship is occurring.

The term *international entrepreneurship* was introduced around 1988 to describe the many untapped foreign markets open to new ventures reflecting a new technological and cultural environment (Morrow, 1988). McDougall (1989, p. 389) defined international entrepreneurship as "the development of international new ventures or start-ups that, from their inception, engage in international business, thus viewing their operating domain as international from the initial stages of the firm's operation."

In 1997, McDougall and Oviatt introduced a broader definition of international entrepreneurship to include the study of established companies and the recognition of comparative (cross-national) analysis. They defined it as "a combination of innovative, proactive, and risk-seeking behavior that crosses or is compared across national borders and is intended to create value in business organizations" (McDougall & Oviatt, 2000, p. 903). This definition takes into account at the organizational level the notions of innovation, risk taking, and proactive behavior. It also focuses on the entrepreneurial behavior of these firms rather than only the characteristics and intentions of the individual entrepreneurs. The key dimensions of entrepreneurship—innovativeness, proactiveness, and risk propensity—can be found and developed at the organizational level.

A good definition and understanding of international entrepreneurship occurred in the introduction to an issue devoted to the topic in *Entrepreneurship Theory and Practice* (Honig-Haftel, Hisrich, McDougall, & Oviatt, 1996). The authors broadly defined international entrepreneurship as any activity of an entrepreneur that crossed a national border. This understanding was further developed in a review article (Ruzzier, Antoncic, & Hisrich, 2006). Numerous research studies and definitions have emerged, focusing on a wide variety of areas, such as the international sales of new ventures (McDougall, 1989), born-global ventures (McDougall & Oviatt, 2000), the role of national culture (McGrath, MacMillan, & Scheinberg, 1992), and the internationalization of small and medium enterprises (Lu & Beamish, 2001). It has also been applied in many geographic contexts, such as Eastern Europe (Hisrich, 1994; Hisrich & O'Cinneide, 1991), Germany (Grichnik & Hisrich, 2004), Hungary (Hisrich & Fulop, 1993, 1995; Hisrich & Szirmai, 1993; Hisrich & Vecsenyi, 1994), Ireland (Hisrich & O'Cinneide, 1989), Israel (Lerner, Brush, & Hisrich, 1997), Northern Ireland (Hisrich, 1988), Slovenia (Hisrich, Vahcic, Glas, & Bucar, 1998), the Soviet Union (Ageev, Grachev, & Hisrich, 1995), Ukraine (Hisrich, Bowser, & Smarsh, 2006), and developing economies (Antoncic & Hisrich, 1999, 2000; Hisrich & Öztürk, 1999). According to McDougall, Oviatt, and Shrader's definition (2003, p. 61), international entrepreneurship is "a combination of innovative, proactive, and risk-seeking behavior that crosses national borders and is intended to create value in organizations."

With a commercial history of only 300 years, the United States is a relative newcomer to the international business arena. As soon as settlements were established in the New World, American businesses began an active international trade with Europe. Foreign investors helped build much of the early industrial trade with Europe as well as much of the early industrial base of the United States. The future commercial strength of the United States, as well as the rest of the world, will depend on the ability of both entrepreneurs and established companies to be involved in markets outside their borders.

International Versus Domestic Entrepreneurship

Although both international and domestic entrepreneurs are concerned with revenues, costs, and profits, what differentiates domestic from international entrepreneurship is the variation in the relative importance of the factors affecting each decision. International

Table 1.1 International Versus Domestic Business: Factors That Are Different
• Economics • Stage of economic development • Balance of payments • Type of economic system • Political-legal environment • Language • Cultural environment • Technological environment • Local foreign competition • Subsidies offered by foreign governments

SOURCE: Adapted from Hisrich, R. D., Peters, M. A., & Shepherd, D. A. (2013). *Entrepreneurship* (9th ed., p. 126). Burr Ridge, IL: McGraw-Hill/Irwin.

entrepreneurial decisions are more complex due to such uncontrollable factors as economics, politics, culture, and technology (see Table 1.1).

Economics

In a domestic business strategy, a single country is the focus of entrepreneurial efforts. The entire country is almost always organized under a single economic system with the same currency. Creating a business strategy for a multicountry area means dealing with differences in levels of economic development; currency valuations; government regulations; and banking, venture capital, marketing, and distribution systems. These differences manifest themselves in each aspect of the entrepreneur's international business plan and methods of doing business.

Stage of Economic Development

The United States is an industrially developed nation with many regional variances. While he or she may need to adjust the business plan according to regional differences, an entrepreneur doing business only in the United States does not have to worry about a significant lack of such fundamental infrastructures as roads, electricity, communication systems, banking facilities and systems, adequate educational systems, a well-developed legal system, and established business ethics and norms. These factors vary greatly in other countries and significantly affect the ability to successfully engage in international business.

Balance of Payments

With the present system of flexible exchange rates, a country's *balance of payments* (the difference between the value of a country's imports and exports over time) affects the valuation of its currency and this valuation of one country's currency affects business transactions between countries. At one time, Italy's chronic balance-of-payments deficit led to a radical depreciation in the value of the lira, Italy's currency. Fiat Group Automobiles S.p.A. responded by offering significant rebates on cars sold in the United States. These rebates cost Fiat very little because fewer dollars purchased many more liras due to the decreased value of the lira. Similar exchange rate divergences have occurred for Japanese automobile manufacturers and many products made in other countries. The decreasing value of the U.S. dollar helps U.S. firms export more due to lower prices of U.S. goods in foreign currencies.

Type of Economic System

Pepsi Cola looked at the possibility of marketing in the former U.S.S.R. as early as 1959, following the visit of U.S. Vice President Richard Nixon. When Premier Nikita Khrushchev approved Pepsi's taste, East-West trade really began moving, with Pepsi entering the former U.S.S.R. Instead of using its traditional type of franchise bottler in their entry strategy, Pepsi used a barter-type arrangement that satisfied both the socialized system of the former U.S.S.R. and the U.S. capitalist system. In return for receiving technology and syrup from Pepsi, the former U.S.S.R. provided the company with Soviet vodka and distribution rights in the United States. Many such barter or third-party arrangements have been used to increase the amount of business activity in countries in various stages of development. Having to come up with appropriate bartering arrangements is just one of the many difficulties in doing business in developing and transition economies.

Political-Legal Environment

The multiplicity of political and legal environments in the international market creates vastly different business problems, opening some market opportunities for entrepreneurs and eliminating others. For example, U.S. environmental standards have eliminated the possibility of importing several models of European cars. A usual event in the political-legal environment involves price fluctuations and significant swings in prices and availability of such things as oil, other energy products, and food.

Each element of the business strategy of an international entrepreneur has the potential to be affected by the multiplicity of legal environments. Pricing decisions in a country that has a value-added tax are different from those decisions made by the same entrepreneur in a country with no value-added tax. Advertising strategy is affected by the variations in what can be said in the copy or in the support needed for advertising claims in different countries. Product decisions are affected by legal requirements regarding labeling, ingredients, and packaging. Types of ownership and organizational forms vary widely throughout the world.

CULTURAL STORIES

Story 1

"My wife and I were in Argentina having dinner at a fancy restaurant when it was time for dessert. The waiter asked my wife if she had decided and she said, "Could you bring me a portion of cajeta?" In Mexico, this is like candy-caramel made of milk. In Argentina, however, *cajeta* means something far different.

I will never forget the waiter's expression."

Often, in different countries that officially speak the same language, the same word has an entirely different meaning. In this couple's case, it would have spared them embarrassment to know beforehand how the word for caramel, or "dulce de leche," differs within Spanish-speaking countries:

Argentina, Costa Rica, Spain, El Salvador, Guatemala, Paraguay, Uruguay, the Dominican Republic, and Puerto Rico: Dulce de leche

Mexico: Dulce de cajeta

Chile and Ecuador: Manjar

Venezuela and Colombia: Arequipe

Peru, Bolivia, and Panamá: Manjar blanco

Cuba: Fanguito

Story 2

While studying in Shanghai in the summer of 1995, I would routinely drive around the city in a taxi to get to know the area and to chat with the taxi drivers (who were always very knowledgeable about the city).

One day, the driver asked me my English name. I told him it was "Phillip," and he looked puzzled. I asked him what "Phillip" meant to him and he replied, "Good reception with many channels."

So, I have that going for me . . . which is nice.

SOURCES: http://www.culturalconfusions.com (Story 1 by Bernardo Alanis; Story 2 by Phillip Graham).

The laws governing business arrangements also vary greatly, with over 150 different legal systems and national laws.

Cultural Environment

The effect of culture on entrepreneurs and strategies is also significant. Entrepreneurs need to make sure that each element in the business plan has some degree of congruence with the local culture. For example, in some countries, point-of-purchase displays are not allowed in retail stores, while they are in others (such as most stores in the United States). An increasingly important aspect of the cultural environment in some countries concerns bribes and corruption. How should an entrepreneur deal with these situations? What is the best course of action to take to maintain the needed high ethical standards? Sometimes, one of the biggest problems is finding a translator. To avoid errors, entrepreneurs should hire a translator whose native tongue is the target language and who reports directly to the entrepreneur.

Technological Environment

Technology, like culture, varies significantly across countries. The variations and availability of technology are often surprising, particularly to an entrepreneur from a developed country. While U.S. firms produce mostly standardized, relatively uniform products that meet industry standards, this is not the case in many countries, making it more difficult to achieve a consistent level of quality. New products in a country are created based on the conditions and infrastructure operating in that country. For example, U.S. car designers can assume wider roads and less expensive gasoline than European designers. When these designers work on transportation vehicles for other parts of the world, their assumptions need to be significantly altered.

Local Foreign Competition

When entering a foreign market, the international entrepreneur needs to be aware of the strength of local competitors who are already established in the market. These competitive companies can often be a formidable force against foreign entry, as they are recognized companies with known products and services. This can be particularly difficult when there is a "buy national" attitude in the country. A sustained effort stressing the unique selling propositions of the entering product or service is necessary, including a guarantee to ensure customer satisfaction, in order to compete.

Subsidies Offered by Foreign Governments

Some governments offer subsidies to attract particular types of foreign companies and investments to help further the development of the country's economy. These subsidies can take different forms, such as cash or a tax holiday for a period of time, and usually involve infrastructure development. This occurred for the U.S. oil companies that built the oil fields and delivery system in the Middle East and for the foreign banks that assisted in developing the banking system in China. Foreign governments can also offer subsidies to local firms to help them compete against foreign products. This is often called an *infant industry protection policy*.

Motivations to Go Global

Unless they are "born global," most entrepreneurs will only pursue international activities when stimulated to do so. A variety of proactive and reactive motivations can cause an entrepreneur to become involved in international business, as is indicated in Table 1.2. Profits are, of course, one of the most significant reasons for going global. Often, the profitability expected from going global is not easily obtained. In fact, profitability can be adversely affected by the costs of getting ready to go global, underestimating the costs involved, and mistakes. The difference between the planned and actual results may be particularly large in the first attempt to go global. Anything you think won't happen probably will, such as having significant shifts in foreign exchange rates.

Table 1.2 Motivations for Going Global
• Profits • Competitive pressures • Unique product(s) or service(s) • Excess production capacity • Declining home-country sales • Unique market opportunity • Economies of scale • Technological advantage • Tax benefits

SOURCE: Adapted from Hisrich, R. D., Peters, M. A., & Shepherd, D. A. (2013). *Entrepreneurship* (9th ed., p. 134). Burr Ridge, IL: McGraw-Hill/Irwin.

The allure of profits is reflected in the motive to sell to other markets. For a U.S.-based entrepreneurial firm, the fact that 95% of the world's population is living outside the United States offers a very large market opportunity. These sales can cover any significant research and development and start-up manufacturing costs that were incurred in the domestic market. Without sales to these international markets, these costs would be spread solely over domestic sales, resulting in fewer sales and smaller profits.

Another reason for going global: the home domestic market is leveling or even declining in sales or sales potential. This is occurring in several markets in the United States with its aging demographics.

Sometimes an entrepreneur moves to international markets to avoid increased regulations or governmental or societal concerns about their products or services. Cigarette companies such as Philip Morris aggressively pursued sales outside the United States, particularly in developing economies, when confronted with increased government regulations and anti-smoking attitudes of consumers. Sometimes this took the form of purchasing existing cigarette companies in foreign markets such as Russia.

When the entrepreneur's technology becomes obsolete in the domestic market or the product or service is near the end of its life cycle, there may be sales opportunities in foreign markets. One entrepreneur found new sales life for the company's gas-permeable hard contact lenses and solutions when highly competitive soft lenses negatively affected the domestic market in the United States. Volkswagen continued to sell its original VW Beetle in Latin and South America for years after stopping its sales in the United States.

Entrepreneurs often go global to take advantage of lower costs in foreign countries for labor, manufacturing overhead, and raw materials. The "Flip Watch" made by Hour-Power could not be marketed at its price point in Things Remembered and JC Penney stores without being produced in China. Waterford Crystal is manufacturing some products in Prague to help offset the higher labor costs in Ireland. This cost advantage decreases as the Czech Republic develops as a member of the European Union. There are often some cost advantages to having at least a distribution and sales office in a foreign market. Graphisoft, a Hungarian software company, found its sales significantly increased in the United States when it opened a sales office in California.

Several other motivations can motivate an entrepreneur to go global. When an entrepreneur establishes a global presence, many company operations can be internationalized and leveraged. For example, when going global, an entrepreneur will establish a global distribution system and an integrated manufacturing capability. Establishing these gives the company a competitive advantage because they not only facilitate the successful production and distribution of present products but help keep out competitive products as well. By going global, an entrepreneur can offer a variety of different products at better price points.

Traits of an International Entrepreneur

Several characteristics and traits are identifiable in international entrepreneurs, regardless of the country of origin. These include the ability to embrace change, the desire to achieve, the ability to establish a vision, a high tolerance for ambiguity, a high level of integrity, and knowing the importance of individuals.

Embraces Change

A global entrepreneur likes and even embraces differences in people as well as situations. He or she constantly seeks new and exciting things and likes to break the mold and challenge corporate orthodoxies. Living in and learning about different cultures and ways of doing things is an exciting way to live. New ways of doing things are encouraged. Employees are taught how to manage change.

Desire to Achieve

A global entrepreneur has good business savvy and a strong desire to achieve. To succeed, an entrepreneur needs to have profit/loss experience and an ability to create value in a different culture. A possession of broad business knowledge—such as transfer pricing, foreign exchange, and international customs and laws—combined with a global mind-set provides a basis for success.

Ability to Establish a Vision

A global entrepreneur needs to establish a vision that employees and customers understand. Employees should feel that they are an important part of the global organization and essential to its success. A global entrepreneur is very optimistic, assumes that everything is possible, and establishes a limited number of short-term goals to obtain the vision. He or she focuses more on outcomes than processes, works long hours, has a high energy level, and does not fear failure.

High Tolerance for Ambiguity

The passion for learning from a variety of sources and viewing uncertainty as an opportunity instead of a threat allows a global entrepreneur to develop mental maps that will lead to achieving the vision established. Incrementally moving initiatives in a variety of areas without completing one regularly is not a problem. This high tolerance for ambiguity is a key virtue of any practice at the individual or company level.

High Level of Integrity

A global entrepreneur has an extremely high standard for individual and company integrity. These established standards are used inside and outside the company. The same high ethical standards are expected from all employees and activities of the venture.

Individuals Are Important

A global entrepreneur focuses on the well-being of his or her employees and acts as a nurturing coach. He or she focuses on building and inspiring people and works effectively with others in teams. Spending more time listening than talking, a global entrepreneur values people—employees as well as customers—and wants to build a sustainable enterprise in a particular culture and country.

The Importance of Global Business

Global business has become increasingly important to firms of all sizes in today's hyper-competitive global economy. There can be little doubt that today's entrepreneur must be able to move in the world of international business. The successful entrepreneur will be someone who fully understands how international business differs from purely domestic business and is able to respond accordingly. An entrepreneur entering the international market should address the following questions:

1. What are the options available for engaging in international business?

2. What are the strategic issues in successfully going global?

3. How is managing international business different from managing domestic business?

Many factors affect how an entrepreneurial firm can become truly global. Since the cultural environment, political and legal environment, economy, and the available distribution channels vary significantly from country to country, each of these needs to be taken into account when deciding to go global, as discussed in the following summary. Change and communication are important aspects of operating in a global environment, as are market selection and entry.

SUMMARY

At no other time in history has the potential for great wealth and prosperity been accessible to so many. This first chapter introduces the concept of international entrepreneurship and the process that takes place when an entrepreneur conducts business activities across national boundaries. More businesses than ever before are deciding to go global early in their inception and some are even "born global." Entrepreneurs today have numerous opportunities from which to choose. The chapter emphasizes how economics; state of economic development; balance of payments; economic system; and political-legal, cultural, and technological environments all play a large role in the establishment of an international versus domestic company. The motives for launching an international enterprise, including a large market opportunity and potential for profit, are also examined. The chapter concludes by discussing the questions an individual or company should consider before going global.

QUESTIONS FOR DISCUSSION

1. What are some differences between domestic and international entrepreneurship?

2. What are the key characteristics to understand when moving a business from one country or region to another?

3. What potential problems might a global entrepreneur encounter when entering a new country?

4. What does a global entrepreneur need to be aware of before entering a foreign market?

CHAPTER EXERCISES

1. Define international entrepreneurship and describe an example of a global entrepreneur and his/her business.

2. Explain the differences between domestic and international entrepreneurship and how these affect a global venture.

3. What are the motivations for taking a business global? What factors influence this decision?

NOTE

Portions of this chapter are adapted from Chapter 5 of Hisrich, R. D., Peters, M. A., & Shepherd, D. A. (2013). *Entrepreneurship* (9th ed.). Burr Ridge, IL: McGraw-Hill/Irwin.

REFERENCES

Ageev, A. I., Grachev, M. V., & Hisrich, R. D. (1995). Entrepreneurship in the Soviet Union and post-socialist Russia. *Small Business Economics, 7,* 1–121.

Antoncic, B., & Hisrich, R. D. (1999, May). The role of entrepreneurship in transition economies: Insights from a comparative study. *Proceedings of the 1999 Conference on Entrepreneurship, Frontiers of Entrepreneurship Research,* pp. 214–215.

Antoncic, B., & Hisrich, R. D. (2000, April). Intrapreneurship model in transition economies: A comparison of Slovenia and the United States. *Journal of Developmental Entrepreneurship, 5*(1), 21–40.

Grichnik, D., & Hisrich, R. D. (2004). Entrepreneurship education needs arising from entrepreneurial profiles in a unified Germany: An international comparison. In A. Miettinen, L. Landoli, & M. Raffa (Eds.), *Internationalizing Entrepreneurship Education and Training Conference proceedings* (pp. 157–160). Napoli, Italy: Edizione Scientifiche Italiane.

Hisrich, R. D. (1988, July). The entrepreneur in Northern Ireland: Characteristics, problems, and recommendations for the future. *Journal of Small Business Management, 26*(5), 32–39.

Hisrich, R. D. (1994). Developing technology joint ventures in Central and Eastern Europe. In L. Dana (Ed.), *Advances in global high-technology management: International management of high technology* (pp. 111–130). Greenwich, CT: JAI.

Hisrich, R. D., Bowser, K., & Smarsh, L. S. (2006). Women entrepreneurs in the Ukraine. *International Journal of Entrepreneurship and Small Business, 3*(2), 207–221.

Hisrich, R. D., & Fulop, G. (1993, March). Women entrepreneurs in controlled economies: A Hungarian perspective. *Proceedings of the 1993 Conference on Entrepreneurship,* 590–592.

Hisrich, R. D., & Fulop, G. (1995, July). Hungarian entrepreneurs and their enterprises. *Journal of Small Business Management, 33*(3), 88–94.

Hisrich, R. D., & O'Cinneide, B. (1989, April). The entrepreneur and the angel: An exploratory cross-cultural study. *Proceedings of the 1989 Conference on Entrepreneurship,* 530–531.

Hisrich, R. D., & O'Cinneide, B. (1991, May). Analysis of emergent entrepreneurship trends in Eastern Europe: A public policy perspective. *Proceedings of the 1991 Conference on Entrepreneurship,* 594–596.

Hisrich, R. D., & Öztürk, S. A. (1999, Fall). Women entrepreneurs in a developing economy. *Journal of Management Development, 18*(2), 114–124.

Hisrich, R. D., & Szirmai, P. (1993). Developing a market oriented economy: A Hungarian perspective. *Entrepreneurship and Regional Development, 5*(1), 61–71.

Hisrich, R. D., Vahcic, A., Glas, M., & Bucar, B. (1998, May). Why Slovene public policy should focus on high growth SMEs. *Proceedings of the 1998 Conference on Entrepreneurship,* 487–489.

Hisrich, R. D., & Vecsenyi, J. (1994). Graphisoft: The entry of a Hungarian software venture into the U.S. market. In R. D. Hisrich, P. P. McDougall, & B. M. Oviatt (Eds.), *Cases in international entrepreneurship* (pp. 80–96). Homewood, IL: Irwin.

Honig-Haftel, S., Hisrich, R. D., McDougall, P. P., & Oviatt, B. M. (1996, Summer). International entrepreneurship: Past, present, and future. *Entrepreneurship Theory and Practice, 20*(4), 5–7.

Lerner, M., Brush, C., & Hisrich, R. D. (1997, July). Israeli women entrepreneurs: An examination of factors affecting performance. *Journal of Business Venturing, 12*(4), 315–339.

Lu, J. W., & Beamish, P. W. (2001). The internationalization and performance of SMEs. *Strategic Management Journal, 22,* 565–586.

McDougall, P. P. (1989). International versus domestic entrepreneurship: New venture strategic behavior and industry structure. *Journal of Business Venturing, 4,* 387–399.

McDougall, P. P., & Oviatt, B. M. (1997). International entrepreneurship literature in the 1990s and directions for future research. In D. L. Sexton & R. W. Smilor (Eds.), *Entrepreneurship 2000* (pp. 291–320). Chicago, IL: Upstart.

McDougall, P. P., & Oviatt, B. M. (2000). International entrepreneurship: The intersection of two research paths. *Academy of Management Journal, 43,* 902–908.

McDougall, P. P., Oviatt, B. M., & Shrader, R. C. (2003). A comparison of international and domestic new ventures. *Journal of International Entrepreneurship, 1,* 59–82.

McGrath, R. G., MacMillan, I. C., & Scheinberg, S. (1992). Elitists, risk-takers, and rugged individuals? An exploratory analysis of cultural differences between entrepreneurs and non-entrepreneurs. *Journal of Business Venturing, 7*(2), 115–135.

Morrow, J. F. (1988). International entrepreneurship: A new growth opportunity. *New Management, 5*(3), 59–60.

Ruzzier, M., Antoncic, B., & Hisrich, R. D. (2006). SME internationalization research: Past, present, and future. *Journal of Small Business and Enterprise Development, 13*(4), 476–497.

SUGGESTED READINGS

Akpor-Robaro, M. (2012). The impact of globalization on entrepreneurship development in developing economies: A theoretical analysis of the Nigerian experience in the manufacturing industry. *Management Science & Engineering, 6*(2), 1–10. doi:10.3968/j.mse.1913035X20120602.2551

This article examines the impact of global entrepreneurship in developing economies and focuses on economic and business globalization. For the analysis, the article critically analyzes implications and effects of global entrepreneurship in Nigeria.

Langevang, T., & Gough, K. (2012). Diverging pathways: Young female employment and entrepreneurship in Sub-Saharan Africa. *Geographical Journal, 178*(3), 242–252. doi:10.1111/j.1475-4959.2011.00457.x

The paper analyzes how entrepreneurship opportunities for young women in Sub-Saharan Africa have been affected by globalization. It contrasts the effects on hairdressers and dressmakers. The case presents a critical analysis of the complex way in which globalization is changing the landscape of opportunities in Sub-Saharan Africa.

McCann, P., & Acs, Z. J. (2011). Globalization: Countries, cities and multinationals. *Regional Studies, 45*(1), 17–32. doi:10.1080/00343404.2010.505915

The article examines the relationship between the sizes of countries and cities and the importance of scale in the modern global era. It examines how multinational companies play a critical role in global connectivity of a city and how these cities in turn power the national economy.

Morrison, J. (2012). Before hegemony: Adam Smith, American independence, and the origins of the first era of globalization. *International Organization, 66*(3), 395–428. doi:10.1017/S0020818312000148

The article examines the history of Great Britain's hegemonic ascension, suggesting they began to structure for open trade in the 1780s, contradicting the conventional story that they began to liberalize their economy in the 1820s. This view challenges the hegemonic stability theory, which suggests such liberalization would be unlikely to occur in a multipolar world. The article describes the significance of key intellectuals in influencing foreign policy at critical junctures in history. The historical perspective provides insights into the extent to which economic liberalization depends on hegemony.

Vernekar, S. S., & Venkatasubramanian, K. (2010). Celebrating the spirit of entrepreneurship and its role in international business. *Journal of Marketing & Communication, 5*(3), 46–50. *Business Source Complete*. Web. 29 Oct. 2013.

This article tells the story of a group of entrepreneurs who paved the way for multinational corporations today. The risks and challenges they faced are described and their bravery is commended. The paper describes the predecessors of today's global entrepreneurs.

2

Globalization and the International Environment

Profile: Virgin Australia Airlines

Formerly named Virgin Blue Airlines, this airline was founded in 2000 by Richard Branson and Brett Godfrey (who was the firm's CEO until 2010). Initially positioned as a relatively small, low-cost carrier, Virgin Blue was able to benefit greatly from the timing of its entry into the Australian airline industry. When Ansett Australia collapsed in September 2001, the company was able to achieve fast growth due to the gap left behind in the market by this competitor. Virgin Australia now serves 29 cities in Australia and also flies to multiple international destinations with its fleet of Boeing, Embraer, and Airbus jets. Its partnerships allow the firm to offer more destinations to its customers through code-share flights with other airlines internationally, including Delta Airlines, Singapore Airlines, and various other Virgin-branded airlines worldwide.

Virgin Blue was able to grow significantly not only due to its luck with timing but also due to its sophisticated business model. At first, the company used a model very similar to that of Southwest Airlines and Ryanair, favoring low prices over in-flight meals. After operating as a low-cost carrier initially, the airline developed a new business model: the "New World Carrier." In this model, the company offers its customer the choice between a very stripped low-cost transportation service and paying a little more for a full-service airline. This model allowed Virgin Blue to compete both with budget airlines for last-minute and leisure customers and with full-service airlines such as Qantas for business customers. With this success, the company has become Australia's second airline with a total fleet of 94 different aircraft.

In May 2010, John Borghetti, the former executive general manager at Qantas, replaced Brett Godfrey as CEO. Under his supervision, the company convinced the United States Department of Transportation to approve an agreement in which Virgin Blue and Delta Airlines would cooperate on trans-Pacific flights. In addition, former Qantas staff replaced various Virgin Blue staff, the airline was rebranded as Virgin Australia, and it proudly launched its use of Airbus A330 jets. In 2012, the company purchased a 60% stake in Tiger Airways Australia, and it acquired the regional carrier Skywest Airlines in 2013. In only 14 years, Virgin Australia was recognized with service excellence awards on five separate occasions and its frequent-flyer program, Velocity Rewards, was recognized with four consecutive Freddie Awards.

Now a significant player in the airline industry, Virgin Australia launched its pilot cadet program in November 2012. The first pilot cadets graduated from the training program in December 2013. Its frequent-flyer program has reached over four million members, the company served 19.3 million customers in 2013 alone, and its revenues surpassed four billion in 2013, up from 2.169 billion in 2007.

Virgin Australia is a proud member of the global Virgin Group. Virgin has created more than 300 branded companies worldwide since the establishment of its first company, Virgin Records, employing approximately 50,000 people in 30 countries. Industries covered by the Virgin Group include telecommunications, transportation, financial services, and media. The group even plans to launch a space tourism operation to be named Virgin Galactic. Just like the overall Virgin Group, Virgin Australia adheres to the core principles of value for money, quality, innovation, fun, and a sense of competitive challenge while constantly innovating to improve its services to customers. By focusing on improvement and customer feedback, this company is "determined to become the airline of choice for corporate and leisure travelers alike." Its strong business model, its passion for continuous innovation, and its openness to change might indeed make it possible for this airline to further develop its global brand.

SOURCES: Virgin Australia. (n.d.). Retrieved February 10, 2015, from http://www.virginaustralia.com/au/en/

Virgin Australia. (2013). Annual report 2013. Retrieved April 30, 2014, from http://www.virginaustralia.com/cs/groups/internetcontent/@wc/documents/webcontent/~edisp/annual-rpt-2013.pdf.

CHAPTER OBJECTIVES

1. To understand the implications of taking a venture global
2. To define the critical issues of taking a company global
3. To identify and define strategic issues faced by global entrepreneurs
4. To determine methods for analyzing the environment in which a venture is operating
5. To determine the key components of planning and taking a venture global

Introduction

To be a global entrepreneur, one needs to establish an international vision. The level of international skills and knowledge of the company, industry, and market will help determine the international strategy. If you have not had any international experience, you may want to find someone with this experience to provide help, particularly in a plan that needs significant overseas market involvement at the outset, such as a foreign sales office or a research and development alliance. Your success in global business will ultimately reflect how well you identify and leverage your core competencies and that of your venture.

Strategic Effects of Going Global

While going global presents a variety of new environments and new ways of doing business, it is also accompanied by a new array of problems. The mechanisms of carrying out business internationally involve many new documents, such as commercial invoices, bills of lading, inspection certificates, and shipper's export declarations, in addition to compliance with domestic and international regulations.

The proximity to customers and new distribution systems is an issue. Physical and psychological closeness to the international market affects some global entrepreneurs. Geographic closeness to the foreign market may inhibit the development of a perceived closeness to the foreign customer. Sometimes cultural variables, language, and legal factors make a foreign market that is geographically closer seem psychologically more distant. For example, some U.S. entrepreneurs perceive Canada, Ireland, and the United Kingdom to be much closer psychologically due to similarities in culture and language.

Three issues are involved in this psychological distance. First, the distance envisioned by the entrepreneur may be based more on perception than reality. Some Canadian and even Australian entrepreneurs focus too much on the similarities with the United States market, losing sight of the vast differences. Such differences are in every international market to some extent and need to be taken into account to avoid costly mistakes. Second, closer psychological proximity does make it easier for an entrepreneurial firm to enter a market. It may be advantageous for the entrepreneur to go global by first selecting a market that is closer psychologically to gain some experience before entering markets that are perceived as more distant. Finally, the entrepreneur should also keep in mind that there are more similarities than differences between individual entrepreneurs, regardless of the country. Each has gone through the entrepreneurial process, taken on the risks, passionately loved his or her business idea, and struggled to succeed.

Additionally, choosing operations in countries that not only have a physical and psychological advantage but also advantages such as trade agreements and current operations of other companies from the entrepreneur's home country often makes entering and succeeding in a country more manageable. Today, there are more than 300 regional trade agreements (RTAs) in existence, and an additional 100 are being proposed or are under negotiation. Of these, the majority are free trade agreements (FTAs) making trade across these borders much easier. Some of the most familiar include the European Union (EU), the European Free Trade Association (EFTA), the North American Free Trade Agreement (NAFTA), the Southern Common Market (Mercosur), the Association of Southeast Asian Nations (ASEAN) Free Trade Area (AFTA), and the Common Market of Eastern and Southern Africa (COMESA). These RTAs do not include additional agreements made bilaterally between nations, discussed later in the chapter.

With outsourcing becoming a reality for most all entrepreneurs, it is important to understand that FTAs—with their possible reductions in costs and duties on goods being imported—can create further opportunities. Some disputes affecting certain industries and regional trade blocs perhaps prevent, more than aid, the trade process.

Strategic Issues

Four strategic issues are important to an entrepreneur going global: (1) the allocation of responsibility between the state side and foreign operations; (2) the nature of the planning, reporting, and control systems to be used throughout the international operations; (3) the appropriate organizational structure for conducting international operations; and (4) the potential degree of standardization. Each of these issues affects a firm's organizational structure in each of three primary stages.

- *Stage* 1. When making the first movements into international business, an entrepreneur typically follows a highly centralized decision-making process. Since the entrepreneur generally has access to a limited number of individuals with global experience, a centralized decision-making approach is usually used.
- *Stage* 2. When the business is successful, it is no longer possible to use a completely centralized decision-making process. The multiplicity of environments becomes far too complex to handle from a central headquarters. In response, an entrepreneur often decentralizes the entire international operation.
- *Stage* 3. The process of decentralization carried out in Stage 2 becomes more difficult once further success is attained. Business operations in the different countries end up in conflict with one another. The U.S. headquarters is often the last to receive information about problems. When this occurs, some authority and responsibility are moved back to the home country base of operations. A balance is usually achieved with the home country headquarters having reasonably tight control over major strategic marketing decisions and the in-country operating unit having the responsibility for the tactical implementation of corporate strategy. Planning, reporting, and control systems are particularly important for international success at this stage.

Opportunities and Barriers to International Trade

Beginning around 1947 with the development of trade agreements and the reduction of tariffs and other trade barriers, there has been an overall positive atmosphere concerning trade between countries. Regardless of this positive atmosphere, the global entrepreneur needs to be aware of the risks and barriers that still exist. Understanding each market and its specific culture and environment will help in achieving success within those markets.

World Trade Organization (WTO)

One of the leading international organizations on trade, founded by one of the longest-lasting agreements, is the World Trade Organization (WTO). Begun in 1947 under U.S. leadership as the General Agreement on Tariffs and Trade (GATT), the WTO was officially established in January 1995 under the Uruguay Round (1986–1994) as a multilateral agreement among nations with the objective of liberalizing trade by eliminating or reducing tariffs, subsidies, and import quotas. WTO membership includes more than 150 nations that create policies in rounds. The WTO has had numerous rounds of tariff reductions. Mutual tariff reductions are typically negotiated between member nations.

Monitored by the Dispute Settlement Board (DSB) of the WTO, which was established in 1995 along with the WTO, member countries are able to bring disputes to this mechanism if they feel that a violation has occurred. Often, these cases are brought against more than one nation by more than one country, forming something similar to a bloc. If the investigation uncovers a violation, violating countries are asked to change their policy and conform to the agreed-upon tariffs and agreements or barriers in other sectors can be levied by prosecuting countries to compensate for lost revenues. With over 600 cases already brought before the WTO DSB with successful trials, decisions, and according actions, trade has been protected among developed and developing nations.

A case brought against the United States and its steel industry shows the WTO DSB's role and its unilateral actions against dumping. The U.S. Congress used an antidumping fine to aid U.S. steel companies under the name of the Byrd Amendment. Creating an environment solely beneficial to the U.S. steel companies, the U.S. Congress had allowed this fine to be directed solely into the coffers of U.S. companies affected as a result of dumping. With a myriad of countries claiming unfair trade practices, Japan, the EU, Mexico, South Korea, and a variety of others took the case to the DSB, and after appeal, the United States lost and the other countries were allowed to levy taxes against similar industries (World Trade Organization, 2003). Under the ruling, these nations could levy up to 72% of the money raised and distributed during the life of this amendment affecting other industries such as U.S. paper, farm goods, textiles, and machinery ("WTO Rules in Favor of EU," 2004).

Important from an entrepreneurial aspect, these types of cases can affect industries and sectors in which the entrepreneur's new venture is operating. Understanding the implications for each business venture helps guide the direction and strategy employed.

Increasing Protectionist Attitudes

Although the support for the WTO varies and was relatively low in the 1970s, it increased in the 1980s due to the rise in protectionist pressures in many industrialized countries. The renewed support reflected three events. First, the world trading system was strained by the persistent trade deficit of the United States (the world's largest economy), a situation that caused adjustments in such industries as automobiles, semiconductors, steel, and textiles. Second, the economic success of a country perceived as not playing by the rules (e.g., Japan and then China) has also strained the world's trading system. Japan's and China's successes as the world's largest traders and the perception that their internal markets are, in effect, closed to imports and foreign investment have caused problems. Finally, in response to these pressures, many countries have established bilateral voluntary export restraints to circumvent the WTO. China did this during the economic prosperity of the 1990s due to the pressures from the world, particularly the United States. The support continues at a high level today.

Trade Blocs and Free Trade Areas

Around the world, nations are banding together to increase trade and investment between nations in the group. One agreement between the United States and Israel, signed in 1985, establishes an FTA between the two nations. All tariffs and quotas, except those on certain agricultural products, were phased out over a 10-year period. In 1989, an FTA went into effect between Canada and the United States that phased out tariffs and quotas between the two countries, which are each other's largest trading partners.

CULTURAL STORY

For the Chinese New Year in 2000, my company—a pan-Asian systems integrator—wished to give each employee a *hong bao* (a traditional red packet usually containing a gift of money for a special occasion) with approximately two or three U.S. dollars. The employees would have normally considered this a very thoughtful gift, but something went terribly wrong.

The conversion came to four Singapore dollars. What the headquarters failed to realize was that four is a very unlucky number in Chinese culture. This is because the word for four and the word for death are identical except for the tone used.

Morale and productivity plummeted as staff felt Western management somehow wished them ill will. After learning eight is a lucky number in Chinese and knowing that four plus four equals eight, management attempted to resolve the situation by sending a second packet of four Singapore dollars.

The local Singaporean staff did not see it that way. They thought the management now wished them double the bad luck and to "die twice."

At this point, I am managing 15 people across seven countries, with most of them thinking that management wants them to suffer in some way. Not fun.

SOURCE: http://www.culturalconfusions.com (Story by Phillip Graham).

Many trading alliances have occurred in the Americas. In 1991, the United States signed a framework trade agreement with Argentina, Brazil, Paraguay, and Uruguay to support the development of more liberal trade relations. The United States has also signed bilateral trade agreements with Bolivia, Chile, Colombia, Costa Rica, Ecuador, El Salvador, Honduras, Peru, and Venezuela. The NAFTA among the United States, Canada, and Mexico is an agreement to reduce trade barriers and quotas and encourage investment among the three countries. Similarly, the United States, Argentina, Brazil, Paraguay, and Uruguay operate under the Treaty of Asunción, which created the Mercosur trade zone, a free trade zone among the countries.

Another important trading bloc is the EU. Unlike NAFTA and other agreements similar to it, the EU is founded on the principle of supranationality; member nations are not able to enter into trade agreements on their own that are inconsistent with EU regulations. As nations are added, the EU trading bloc becomes an increasingly important factor for entrepreneurs doing international business.

Entrepreneur's Strategy and Trade Barriers

Clearly, trade barriers pose problems for the entrepreneur who wants to become involved in international business. First, trade barriers increase an entrepreneur's costs of exporting products or semifinished products to a country. If the increased cost puts the entrepreneur at a competitive disadvantage with respect to indigenous competitive products, it may be more economical to establish production facilities in the country. Second, voluntary export restraints may limit an entrepreneur's ability to sell products in a country from production facilities outside the country, which may also warrant establishing production facilities in the country to compete. Finally, an entrepreneur may have to locate assembly or production facilities in a country to conform to the local product content regulations of the country.

Important Considerations

In addition to these outside considerations, the entrepreneur also needs to be aware of the internal features of a country that affect a business. Examining these political, economic, social, technological, and environmental factors is known as a PESTE analysis. Such in-depth consideration can protect the entrepreneur from future concerns or difficulties. When Intel Corporation wanted to expand, it was not sure where to take its operations. After negotiating with Costa Rica, Brazil, Mexico, and Chile in Latin America, the company finally decided to open operations in Costa Rica based on its political stability during government transitions, the quality of the workforce and its labor unions, and government incentives that would not handcuff the company. In making its decision, Intel dealt with all facets of the PESTE.

Regardless of the size of the company, this analysis takes careful planning and evaluation. As witnessed when Microsoft took Windows into China in 1993, a lack of careful planning and analysis can produce bad results. Not only did Microsoft have minimal sales of Windows to Chinese consumers, but in early 1994, the company was blacklisted by the Chinese government. Microsoft founder Bill Gates went to China to make a personal appeal to Chinese President Jiang Zemin. He argued that China should join much of the rest of the world in adopting Windows as its standard operating system. Gates was ignored. Instead, he was told that if he was going to sell to the Chinese customer, he needed to better understand their culture.

Microsoft faced piracy concerns as well as problems created by software that did not have full capabilities. In addition, the company did not realize that in some countries such as China, a portion of the ownership of the business would be in the hands of the Chinese government upon entry. It took a decade, but in 2006, Gates and Microsoft finally found a solution to the opposition of the Chinese government and were able to enter one of the biggest markets in the world (Khanna, 2008).

To understand what is required for effective planning, reporting, and control in international operations, the entrepreneur should consider situational analysis, strategic planning, organizational structure, and controlling the program (see Table 2.1).

Table 2.1	Requirements for Effective Planning, Reporting, and Control in International Operations

Situational Analysis

1. What are the unique characteristics of each national market? What characteristics does each market have in common with other national markets?

2. Can any national markets be clustered together for operating and/or planning purposes? What dimensions of markets should be used to cluster markets?

Strategic Planning

3. Who should be involved in marketing decisions?

4. What are the major assumptions about target markets? Are these valid?

5. What needs are satisfied by the company's products in the target markets?

6. What customer benefits are provided by the product in the target markets?

7. What are the conditions under which the products are used in the target markets?

8. How great is the ability to buy our products in the target markets?

9. What are the company's major strengths and weaknesses relative to existing and potential competition in the target markets?

10. Should the company extend, adapt, or invent products, prices, advertising, and promotion programs for target markets?

11. What are the balance-of-payments and currency situations in the target markets? Will the company be able to remit earnings? Is the political climate acceptable?

12. What are the company's objectives, given the alternatives available and the assessment of opportunity, risk, and company capability?

Organizational Structure

13. How should the organization be structured to optimally achieve the established objectives, given the company's skills and resources? What is the responsibility of each organizational level?

14. Given the objectives, structure, and assessment of the market environment, how can an effective operational marketing plan be implemented? What products should be marketed, at what prices, through what channels, with what communications, and to which target markets?

Controlling the Program

15. How does the company measure and monitor the plan's performance? What steps should be taken to ensure that marketing objectives are met?

SOURCE: Adapted from Hisrich, R. D., Peters, M. A., & Shepherd, D. A. (2007). *Entrepreneurship* (7th ed., pp. 526–527). Burr Ridge, IL: McGraw-Hill/Irwin.

Situational Analysis

Once an entrepreneur completes the situational analysis outlined in Table 2.1, several other questions need to be asked: What are the unique characteristics of each national market? What characteristics does each market have in common with other national markets? As with many regional markets, deciding between one market and another can make the difference between building and growing the business and/or facing extensive competition from similar companies. When the computer company Dell entered Latin America, the company was able to successfully leverage its knowledge of the national market in Brazil by addressing these questions. In Brazil, states are able to negotiate their own tax incentive packages to entice companies to invest. Realizing this, Dell asked each state to create the best package for the company before deciding where to locate. This understanding of the market was critical in Dell's entry and success in this market.

By beginning to cluster the markets, the entrepreneur increases his or her ability to understand how to operate within these environments. Can any national markets be clustered together for operating and/or planning purposes? What dimensions of markets should be used for this clustering? These questions should be answered as the market is chosen, as the answers could help ensure the correct market choice and the future success of the company.

Strategic Planning

After deciding on the market, the entrepreneur needs to strategically plan and carefully implement that plan. Who should be involved in marketing decisions? What are the major assumptions about target markets? Are these valid?

Defining the target market is critical to strategic planning for marketing, bringing the product to market, and pricing. A company must define and clearly delineate what the target market wants from the product. What needs are satisfied by the company's products in the target markets? What customer benefits does the product in the target markets provide? What are the conditions under which the products are used? How easy is it to purchase the product?

Analyzing the strengths and weaknesses of the company in this way makes it easier to evaluate where the company stands in comparison to its competitors and how to better extend, adapt, or invent new products, prices, advertising, and promotion programs to meet these needs.

Organizational Structure

After understanding the environment in which the entrepreneur is entering and strategically assessing how to take advantage of this, the next step is to determine the structure of the company. How should the organization be structured to achieve the established objectives, given the company's skills and resources? What is the responsibility of each organizational level? These questions assist in the company entering and growing in the global market.

Operational Planning

Just as important as the structure is the operational planning. Even with a strong organizational structure, operations need to be outlined to give the company the best chance to satisfy the target market. Given the objectives, structure, and assessment of the market environment, how can an effective operational marketing plan be implemented? What products should be marketed, at what prices, through what channels, with what communications, and to which target markets?

Controlling the Program

How does the company measure and monitor performance? What steps should be taken to ensure that marketing objectives are met? One key to successful strategic planning is understanding the market. While environmental analysis focuses on this dimension of the planning process, the first step in identifying markets and clustering countries is to analyze data on each country in the following six areas. First are the market characteristics: the size of market, rate of growth, stage of development, stage of product life cycle and saturation level, buyer behavior characteristics, social and cultural factors, and physical environment. The second area includes the marketing institutions such as the distribution systems, communication media, and marketing services to reach the customer, whether in advertising or research. The third area involves the industry conditions, focusing on competitive size and practices and technical development of the product. This can help the entrepreneur to adapt, extend, or invent new products or services. The legal environment is the fourth area, which will be covered in a later chapter. Critical resources make up the fifth area. This includes available personnel who have the skills and potential required. The sixth consideration is the political environment. An understanding of the present and future outlook of the government, especially in emerging economies, is most important before market entry.

SUMMARY

Chapter 2 focuses on the fundamental strategic questions that every entrepreneur needs to ask as he or she prepares to enter the global market. When considering international expansion, an entrepreneur needs to be able to handle the many problems that arise when dealing with multiple countries that have their own regulations, culture, and economy. Also, the entrepreneur needs to consider the effect that the physical or psychological closeness to a foreign market has on the company's decision to enter that market. This psychological closeness is based on individual perception, which may be different from reality. This chapter describes strategic issues facing the global entrepreneur, such as allocation of responsibility; nature of planning, reporting, and control systems; appropriate organizational structure; and potential degree of standardization. The evolution of the organization as it becomes international starts with highly centralized decision making; it evolves into a decentralized structure; and finally, it reorganizes into a decentralized structure in which major decision making and controls can come directly from headquarters.

QUESTIONS FOR DISCUSSION

1. What are the most critical strategic factors to consider before entering a foreign market?

2. How does the control of foreign operations change as the enterprise grows?

CHAPTER EXERCISES

1. Describe each of the major issues and considerations a global entrepreneur must address when launching his or her product or company in a new country.

2. Choose a country besides your home country and create a comparative table that describes the key environmental factors (economic, political, etc.) in that country versus your home country. What major differences exist? What is one major attribute that you must consider when doing business in the foreign country?

3. Suppose you are the CEO of a small firm that is taking its business into a new country. You are fortunate to have two gifted managers who have volunteered to handle the operational issues for this project, but you must choose just one to send to the new country. One of the managers has extensive work experience in all the operational aspects of running a business and the other manager is from the new country and previously ran a business there. Which manager will you send and why?

NOTE

Portions of this chapter are adapted from Chapter 5 of Hisrich, R. D., Peters, M. A., & Shepherd, D. A. (2013). *Entrepreneurship* (9th ed.). Burr Ridge, IL: McGraw-Hill/Irwin.

REFERENCES

Khanna, T. (2008, March 28). Microsoft's China foibles. *Forbes*. Retrieved February 10, 2015, from http://www.forbes.com/2008/03/28/entrepreneurs-microsoft-china-oped-books-cx_tk_0328khanna.html

World Trade Organization. (2003, December 10). *United States—Definitive safeguard measures on imports of certain steel products* (WTO Dispute Settlement DS248). Retrieved January 18, 2015, from http://www.wto.org/english/tratop_e/dispu_e/cases_e/ds248_e.htm

WTO rules in favor of EU in US trade row. (2004, August 31). Retrieved January 18, 2015, from http://news.bbc.co.uk/1/hi/business/3615030.stm

SUGGESTED READINGS

Cesinger, B., & Kraus, S. (2012). The pre-export model: Prospects for research on rapidly internationalizing ventures. *International Journal of Business Research, 12*(3), 17–26. *Business Source Complete*. Web. 29 Oct. 2013.

The article addresses the differences between empirical findings and traditional models of the speed of internationalization in new ventures. It focuses on the accuracy of the pre-export model presented with regard to recent empirical findings. The model's value for further research is critically evaluated.

Hagen, B., & Zucchella, A. (2011). A longitudinal look at the international entrepreneurship dimensions: Cases and predictions. *International Journal of Management Cases, 13*(3), 484–504. *Business Source Complete*. Web. 29 Oct. 2013.

This article explains how research about global entrepreneurship needs to develop a better understanding of the long-term dynamics of the internationalization process. It describes the necessity of this view to help managers and owners of small and medium-sized enterprises (SMEs) make strategy decisions. The article focuses specifically on born-global firms.

Kiss, A. N., Wade, M. D., & Cavusgil, S. T. (2012). International entrepreneurship research in emerging economies: A critical review and research agenda. *Journal of Business Venturing, 27*(2), 266–290. *Business Source Complete*. Web. 29 Oct. 2013.

This article examines the relevance, importance, and timeliness of emerging economies in considering global market opportunities. The article analyzes 88 articles published over the last 20 years to show how emerging economies are of increasing importance for international entrepreneurs. It further considers new questions for entrepreneurship and international business scholars.

Sciascia, S., Mazzola, P., Astrachan, J. H., & Torsten P. (2012). The role of family ownership in international entrepreneurship: Exploring nonlinear effects. *Small Business Economics, 38*(1), 15–31. *Business Source Complete*. Web. 29 Oct. 2013.

This article explores the pros and cons of family ownership for international entrepreneurship. A regression analysis is used in a sample of over 1,000 family businesses in the United States to suggest that international entrepreneurship is at its peak when family ownership is at moderate concentrations.

Stengelhofen, T. (2011). Impact of reduction in trade barriers on international entrepreneurship: European Union developments and the "Grande Region." *Proceedings for the Northeast Region Decision Sciences Institute (NEDSI)*, 330–339. *Business Source Complete*. Web. 29 Oct. 2013.

The paper examines entrepreneurial activity of SMEs in the "Grande Region" of the EU after investment and trade barriers were removed. It concludes that more SMEs have gone international in the region that encompasses France, Luxembourg, Belgium, and Germany. It also discusses obstacles remaining for internationalization in the EU.

3

Cultures and International Entrepreneurship

Profile: Miyako Hotels & Resorts

Among some of Japan's most stunning and iconic hotels are the 20 Miyako Hotels & Resorts in the Kinki and Tokai regions of Japan. Everything at these high-end luxury hotels has been developed to exceed guests' expectations. Although each location is different, this chain offers "today's comforts combined with true Japanese hospitality at locations of different styles, chic modern urban properties ideal for business and at relaxing romantic resorts." With the objective of appealing to a wide range of customers, each location is unique for those guests who wish to explore different styles while relying on the quality service of the same brand; Miyako Hotels & Resorts is an excellent choice.

When the firm expanded its services to the United States, it did so with the intention of bringing the traditional beauty and impeccable service of Japan to a global community. Its two new locations in California form the company's first venture outside its home country of Japan. Although much is different between these two locations, Miyako has managed to retain the beauty and high levels of service in these hotels, the qualities that make the brand so valuable in Japan. However, when entering this international environment, the company has had to keep cultural differences of not only its customers but also its employees in mind. Successfully implementing a Japanese trend in a foreign market requires a great deal of leadership and understanding: Especially because national cultures are so different, developing a deep understanding of the market one wishes to enter is critical in order to develop the best possible entry strategy.

Perhaps this company's success is in part due to its willingness to collaborate with international partners. In March 2014, Marriott International opened the first Marriott hotel in Osaka, Japan, in collaboration with Miyako. The Osaka Marriott Miyako Hotel's general manager, Masahiko Torii, intended for this hotel to become a landmark and symbol of Osaka, completely in line with Miyako's other hotels in the country. In addition, the hotel is to become an Alliance Hotel of Universal Studios Japan. This partnership has not only offered Marriott the opportunity to open its fourth hotel in Japan and benefit from Miyako's local expertise, but it has also allowed Miyako Hotels & Resorts to benefit from a deepened understanding of other cultures globally. This, in turn, could greatly support any efforts by Miyako in the future to expand further internationally. Some of the chain's other partnerships, including those with Westin and Sheraton, have also allowed the firm to benchmark and make any improvements that would further support its international growth. For this particular company, it seems that partnerships were a key part of a successful entry into a different culture. The leadership and experience gained from this can only help the company to achieve successes in other markets as well.

SOURCES: Kai, J. (2014, March 7). Marriott International opens first Marriott Hotel in Osaka. Retrieved on April 30, 2014, from http://news.marriott.com/2014/03/marriott-international-opens-first-marriott-hotel-in-osaka.html

Miyako Hotels & Resorts [website]. (2011). Retrieved February 11, 2015, from http://www.miyakohotels.ne.jp/english/index.html/

Chapter Objectives

1. To introduce the importance of culture in achieving success as a global entrepreneur
2. To describe how language—verbal or nonverbal—can influence the message of a product/service
3. To understand the effect of societal structure and religion on decisions
4. To discuss how economic and political philosophies impact the culture
5. To emphasize the importance of learning about the manners and customs of different cultures for successful venture launch

Introduction

The ever-increasing amount of international business, the opening of new markets, and hypercompetition have provided the opportunity for entrepreneurs to start or expand globally. To be successful in their global efforts, entrepreneurs need to understand the culture of each country. Strategic plans must tailor products/services to different attitudes, behaviors, and values of each culture. Clothing, for example, is a cultural product. Suits that sell well in Italy may have less success in Japan. Styling and colors vary by culture. What sells well in the United States may have a limited market elsewhere. Additionally, for continued success, the global entrepreneur needs to meet and understand the cultural needs of suppliers and the potential workforce to maintain and/or expand the business.

Nature of Culture

Probably the single most important aspect that must be considered in global entrepreneurship is crossing cultures. The word *culture* comes from the Latin word *cultura*, which means "cult or worship." Although *culture* has been variously defined, the term generally refers to common ways of thinking and behaving that are passed down by the family unit or transmitted by social organizations and are then developed and reinforced through social pressure. Culture is learned behavior and the identity of an individual and society. Most would agree that culture is adaptive (humans have the capacity to change or adapt), learned (acquired by learning and experience, not inherited), shared (individuals as members of a group share their culture), structured (culture is integrated into a structure), symbolic (culture has symbols with meaning), and transgenerational (it is passed on from generation to generation).

Culture encompasses a multitude of elements, including language, social structure, religion, political philosophy, economic philosophy, education, and manners and customs (see Figure 3.1). Each of these affects the cultural norms and values of a country and the groups within the country.

Figure 3.1   Cultural Determinants

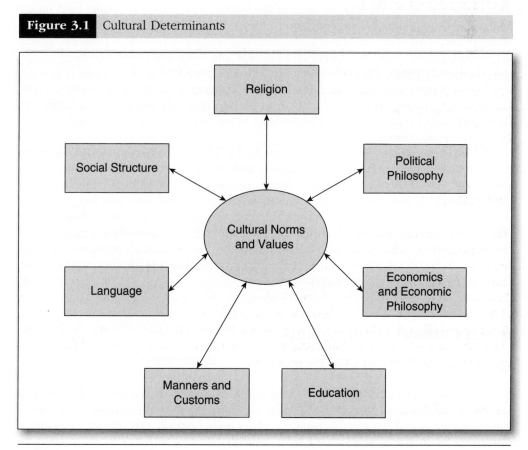

SOURCE: Hisrich, R. D., Peters, M. A., & Shepherd, D. A. (2013). *Entrepreneurship* (9th ed., p. 132). Burr Ridge, IL: McGraw-Hill/Irwin.

Values are basic beliefs individuals have regarding good/evil, important/unimportant, and right/wrong. These are shared beliefs that are internalized by each individual in the group. The more entrenched the values and norms are in a group, the less the tendency for change. In some countries, there is an overall generally positive attitude toward change. Change is viewed negatively in other countries, particularly when it is introduced by a foreign entity. For example, although change is fairly well accepted in some sectors in the United States, this is not the case in Japan, where there is stronger resistance to change.

At the same time, similarities in values exist between cultures. Research has shown that managers from four different countries (Australia, India, Japan, and the United States) have similar personal values that relate to success (England & Lee, 1974). Not only was there a reasonably strong relationship between values and success across the four countries but the value patterns could be used effectively in selection and placement decisions.

While values and culture are relatively stable and do not change rapidly, change does occur over time. This can be seen in the values of Japanese managers both inside and outside the country. One study found that Japanese managers felt that traditional attitudes and organizational values such as lifetime employment, formal authority, group orientation, paternalism, and seniority were less important than they had been in the past (Reichel & Flynn, 1984). Similarly, there is evidence that individualism is gaining traction in Japan. Instead of denouncing individualism as a threat to society, many Japanese are starting to view individualism as necessary for the country's economic well-being, which has contributed to the start of an awakened entrepreneurial attitude and spirit in the country.

Additionally, global entrepreneurs need to be aware of other cultural dimensions that will play significant roles in negotiations and the ability to succeed with local suppliers and customers. Recent studies have analyzed the five cultural dimensions of power—distance, individualism, masculinity, uncertainty avoidance, and long-term orientation. These dimensions give insight into the way the seven cultural determinants discussed next play a further role in how an entrepreneur approaches a new market (Hofstede, 2001). Additional studies have taken the five cultural dimensions one step further, focusing on the leadership of individuals within these cultural norms (Javidan, Dorman, de Luque, & House, 2005).

Seven Cultural Determinants

Language

Language—sometimes thought of as the mirror of culture—is composed of verbal and nonverbal components. Messages and ideas are transmitted by the spoken words used, the voice tone, and the nonverbal actions such as body position, eye contact, or gestures. Entrepreneurs and their teams must have command of the language of the country in which business is being done. It is important for information gathering and evaluation, for communication with all involved, and, eventually, in advertising campaigns. Even though English has overall become the accepted language of business, dealing with language almost always requires local assistance, whether it is a local translation, a local market research firm, or a local advertising agency.

One U.S. entrepreneur was having a difficult time negotiating an agreement on importing a new high-tech microscope from a small entrepreneurial firm in St. Petersburg, Russia. The problems were resolved when the entrepreneur realized that translations were not being done correctly and hired a new translator who reported to him. Examples of some very problematic translation errors by some U.S. companies are shown in Table 3.1.

Table 3.1 Potential Translation Problems

Lost in Translation		
Even the best-laid business plans can be botched by a careless translator. Here is how some of America's biggest companies have managed to mess things up.		
Kentucky Fried Chicken	English: "Finger lickin' good."	Chinese: "Eat your fingers off."
Adolph Coors Co.	English: "Turn it loose."	Spanish: "Drink Coors and get diarrhea."
Otis Engineering Corp.	English: "Complete equipment."	Russian: "Equipment for orgasms."
Parker Pen Co.	English: "Avoid embarrassment."	Spanish: "Avoid pregnancy."
Perdue Farms Inc.	English: "It takes a tough man to make a tender chicken."	Spanish: "It takes a sexually excited man to make a chick affectionate."

SOURCE: Adapted from Piech, A. (2003, June). Speaking in tongues. *Inc., 25*(6), 50.

Equally important to verbal language is the nonverbal or hidden language of the culture. This can be thought of in terms of several components—directness, expressiveness, context, and formality. From a nonverbal standpoint, the directness and contextual uses of language can play a very large role in understanding a culture. Very low-context cultures use words and language to express themselves, and very high-context cultures use body language, facial expressions, and movements to convey their meaning. Consider four countries from different parts of the world. Argentina and China tend to be very high-context cultures, requiring an entrepreneur to understand that not everything is going to be expressed with words but potentially more with actions. Doors closed to offices, copying individuals on e-mails, and preferring telephone use to talking face-to-face are examples of high-context clues that bring insight into certain cultures; in each case, subtle actions show the intentions or desires of the individuals. Germany and Denmark, on the other hand, are very low-context cultures, managing and negotiating very forthrightly. From a directness perspective, these cultures often explicitly express their wishes or desires when doing business, while others view this type of forwardness to be rude. Almost all Asian and Latin cultures tend to carry a more indirect approach to communication, preferring not to tackle issues in a confrontational manner (Training Management Corporation, 2008).

The expansion of Canada's Bank of Nova Scotia into the Mexican market through obtaining an increased stake in the Mexican bank, Grupo Financiero Inverlat, offers insight into what can happen when people from cultures with opposite communication orientations interact. With meetings being conducted in English, Canadian managers, being more direct and low context, found their manner of communication, while paramount to making decisions, was not being understood, and many of the Mexicans felt the same way. Instead of letting the Mexican managers discuss and carry on side conversations in meetings, as was necessary for a very indirect and high-context culture, the more rigid style of the Canadians led to discontent among each party involved (Campbell, 1997).

Both verbal and nonverbal language affects business relationships, and for entrepreneurs, the types of communication styles in different cultures need to be understood. In many countries, for example, it is necessary to know a potential business partner on a personal level before any transactions occur or business is even discussed. One global entrepreneur in Australia met the president, the management team, and their families, each on a different social occasion, before any business between the two companies was discussed.

Social Structure

Social structure and institutions also affect the culture facing the global entrepreneur. While the family unit in the United States usually consists of parent(s) and children, in many cultures, it extends to grandparents and other relatives. This, of course, radically affects lifestyles, living standards, and consumption patterns.

Social stratification can be very strong in some cultures, significantly affecting the way people in one social stratum behave and purchase. India, for example, is known for a relatively rigid, hierarchical social class system, which can offset the acceptance of new products/services.

Reference groups in any culture provide values and attitudes that influence behavior. Besides providing overall socialization, reference groups develop a person's concept of self and provide a baseline for compliance with group norms. As such, they significantly affect an individual's behavior and buying habits.

The global entrepreneur needs to recognize that the social structure and institutions of a culture will also affect the relationships of managers and subordinates. In some cultures, cooperation between managers and subordinates is elicited through equality, while in others, the two groups are separated explicitly and implicitly.

CULTURAL STORY

I was building a market in Mexico in the late 1980s for a privately held one-man-founded U.S. manufacturing firm. In my presentation in Spanish, I kept referring to the founder as *"El Señor."* I noticed smiles everywhere every time I said it.

I finally asked my agent what I was saying that prompted responses like that. He explained that, within the context of the presentation, "the" not only had made the founder appear like a God based on his accomplishment of founding the company, but I was actually calling him "God"—the article *"El"* before *"Señor"* implied God.

Luckily, the audiences were well educated enough and experienced enough in dealing with gringos to be understanding.

SOURCE: C., J.P. (2011, February 26). A highly-regarded founder. Retrieved January 21, 2015, from http://culturalcon fusions.com/?s=J.P.+C.

Religion

Religion in a culture defines certain ideas that are reflected in the values and attitudes of individuals and the overall society. The effect of religion on entrepreneurship, consumption, and business in general will vary depending on the strength of the dominant religious tenets and the level of these tenets' influence on values and attitudes of the culture. Religion also provides the basis for some degree of transcultural similarity, as shared beliefs and attitudes can be seen in some of the dominant religions of the world—Christianity, Islam, Hinduism, Buddhism, and Judaism. Similarly, nonreligious or secularist societies are also powerful forces affecting behavior.

Political Philosophy

The political philosophy of an area also affects culture. The rules and regulations of the country significantly affect the global entrepreneur and the way he or she conducts business. For example, embargoes or trade sanctions, tariffs, export controls, and other business regulations may preclude a global entrepreneur from doing business in a particular culture or, at the very least, will affect the attitudes and behaviors of people in that culture when business is done.

Economics and Economic Philosophy

Economics and the economic philosophy affect the culture of a country and the global entrepreneur. The country's overall view of trade or trade restrictions, attitudes toward balance of payments and balance of trade, convertible or nonconvertible currency, and overall trading policy and rules affect not only whether it is advantageous to do business in a certain market, but the types and efficiency of any transactions that occur.

Some countries use import duties, tariffs, subsidization of exports, and restrictions on the importation of certain products to protect the country's own industry—often called *infant industry protection*—and maximize the gain of more exports than imports. Think how difficult it would be to do business in a country that restricts the exportation of the profits of an international company. Or how difficult it is to do business in a culture that is antimaterialist and more equalitarian.

Education

Both formal and informal education affect the culture and the way the culture is passed on. A global entrepreneur not only needs to be aware of the education level as indicated by the literacy rate of a culture but also the degree of emphasis on particular skills or career paths. China, Japan, and India, for example, emphasize the sciences and engineering more than many Western cultures do. Slovenia has a very high literacy rate.

The technology level of a company's products may be too sophisticated, depending on the educational level of the culture. This also influences whether customers are able to use the product or service properly and understand the firm's advertising or other promotional messages.

Manners and Customs

Manners and customs, the final aspect of culture, need to be considered in any business communication and decision. Understanding names and customs is particularly important for the global entrepreneur when negotiating and giving gifts. In negotiations, unless care is taken, the global entrepreneur can come to an incorrect conclusion because the interpretations are based on his or her frame of reference instead of the frame of reference of the culture. The silence of the Chinese and Japanese has been used effectively in negotiating with American entrepreneurs when American entrepreneurs interpret this incorrectly as a negative sign. Agreements in these countries, as well as other countries in Asia and the Middle East, may take much longer because there is a desire to talk about unrelated issues. Aggressively demanding last-minute changes is a tactic used by Russian negotiators.

Probably the area that requires the most sensitivity is gift giving. Gifts can be an important part of developing relationships in a culture, but one must take great care to determine whether it is appropriate to give a gift, the type of gift, how the gift is wrapped, and the manner in which the gift is given. For example, in China, a gift is given with two hands and is usually not opened at the time of receiving but rather in privacy by the recipient.

Cultural Dimensions and Leadership

Hofstede's Five Cultural Dimensions

Having looked at the seven cultural determinants that are the basis for understanding, the five cultural dimensions described by Hofstede (2001)—power distance, individualism, masculinity, uncertainty avoidance, and long-term orientation—provide the entrepreneur with further insight into how these determinants often play out in a business setting. *Power distance,* or the hierarchical gap between the least powerful (lowest-level employee, lowest-regarded individual in society) and the most powerful, and the acceptance of this position demonstrates to the entrepreneur the level of power and inequality that a society possesses. If an entrepreneur wants to do business in South Korea, for example, it would be important for decisions to be made and discussed with only top-level individuals. Power distance is high in this culture, and these managers would be the only individuals capable of rendering and carrying out decisions in general. Without this knowledge, the entrepreneur could be stuck negotiating for months with people of little to no importance, not furthering the negotiation process in the least.

The second dimension, individualism, reflects how decisions are made. In some societies, there is a strong, integrated group mentality with typically unyielding loyalty and unquestioning authority. In other societies, there is a very individualistic mentality with the priority being the individual and the importance of the individual and his or her immediate family. In collectivistic societies, such as those in Latin America and Asia, decision making is often based on what is best for the society, group, or company as a whole.

The third dimension, masculinity, is an aspect of social structure reflecting the importance and role of gender. In many Latin American countries, women have often been viewed as important figureheads in the household, but their role in business has been limited. These roles, however, are constantly changing, as evidenced in Latin America by the election of two women presidents, Michelle Bachelet in Chile and Cristina Fernandez de Kirchner in Argentina, in 2006 and 2007, respectively. Both of these societies are regarded as being on the masculine side of the spectrum (Reel, 2007).

The fourth dimension is uncertainty avoidance. This measures the tolerance a society has for ambiguity and whether the members of society feel comfortable in situations that are not typical or structured in the usual customary way. In uncertainty avoidance cultures, the people follow strict laws, rules, and security measures and do not openly accept opinions different from their own. In cultures on the opposite side of the spectrum, the rules are few and far between and people often have difficulty expressing their emotions. In a country with a low uncertainty avoidance index, bribes are often considered not only acceptable but necessary for transacting business. This is something entrepreneurs need to be aware of before deciding to do business in a culture.

Finally, the long-term orientation of a culture is based on the values of that specific society. In a culture with a long-term orientation, thrift and perseverance are the two values that are most important, whereas a short-term-oriented individual has a respect for tradition, social obligations, and the appearance of "face." In Japan, for instance, the name of the company for which one works is the basis for respect and gives face to the individual who works there, especially if he or she is someone in a more senior level. Table 3.2 indicates the positioning of many countries on each of these dimensions.

GLOBE and Leadership

Building on Hofstede's five determinants, the Global Leadership and Organizational Behavior Effectiveness (GLOBE) project focuses on how a better understanding of cultural dimensions can improve the leadership of the entrepreneur, creating success

Table 3.2 Geert Hofstede's Five Cultural Dimensions by Country

Country	Power Distance Index (PDI)	Individualism vs. Collectivism (IDV)	Masculinity vs. Femininity (MAS)	Uncertainty Avoidance Index (UAI)	Pragmatic vs. Normative (PRA)	Indulgence vs. Restraint (IND)
Albania	90	20	80	70	61	15
Angola	83	18	20	60	15	83
Argentina	49	46	56	86	20	62
Australia	36	90	61	51	21	71
Austria	11	55	79	70	60	63
Bangladesh	80	20	55	60	47	20
Belgium	65	75	54	94	82	57
Bhutan	94	52	32	28		
Brazil	69	38	49	76	44	59
Bulgaria	70	30	40	85	69	16
Burkina Faso	70	15	50	55	27	18
Canada	39	80	52	48	36	68
Cape Verde	75	20	15	40	12	83
Chile	63	23	28	86	31	68
China	80	20	66	30	87	24
Colombia	67	13	64	80	13	83
Costa Rica	35	15	21	86		
Croatia	73	33	40	80	58	33
Czech Republic	57	58	57	74	70	29
Denmark	18	74	16	23	35	70
Dominican Republic	65	30	65	45	13	54
Ecuador	78	8	63	67		
Egypt	70	25	45	80	7	4
El Salvador	66	19	40	94	20	89
Estonia	40	60	30	60	82	16
Ethiopia	70	20	65	55		
Fiji	78	14	46	48		
Finland	33	63	26	59	38	57
France	68	71	43	86	63	48

Country	Power Distance Index (PDI)	Individualism vs. Collectivism (IDV)	Masculinity vs. Femininity (MAS)	Uncertainty Avoidance Index (UAI)	Pragmatic vs. Normative (PRA)	Indulgence vs. Restraint (IND)
Germany	35	67	66	65	83	40
Ghana	80	15	40	65	4	72
Greece	60	35	57	100	45	50
Guatemala	95	6	37	99		
Honduras	80	20	40	50		
Hong Kong	68	25	57	29	61	17
Hungary	46	80	88	82	58	31
Iceland	30	60	10	50	28	67
India	77	48	56	40	51	26
Indonesia	78	14	46	48	62	38
Iran	58	41	43	59	14	40
Iraq	95	30	70	85	25	17
Ireland	28	70	68	35	24	65
Israel	13	54	47	81	38	
Italy	50	76	70	75	61	30
Jamaica	45	39	68	13		
Japan	54	46	95	92	88	42
Jordan	70	30	45	64	16	43
Kenya	70	25	60	50		
Kuwait	90	25	40	80		
Latvia	44	70	9	63	69	13
Lebanon	75	40	65	50	14	25
Libya	80	38	52	68	23	34
Lithuania	42	60	19	65	82	16
Luxembourg	40	60	50	70	64	56
Malawi	70	30	40	50		
Malaysia	100	26	50	36	41	57
Malta	56	59	47	96	47	66
Mexico	81	30	69	82	24	97
Morocco	70	46	53	68	14	25
Mozambique	85	15	38	44	11	80

(Continued)

Table 3.2 (Continued)

Country	Power Distance Index (PDI)	Individualism vs. Collectivism (IDV)	Masculinity vs. Femininity (MAS)	Uncertainty Avoidance Index (UAI)	Pragmatic vs. Normative (PRA)	Indulgence vs. Restraint (IND)
Namibia	65	30	40	45	35	
Nepal	65	30	40	40		
Netherlands	38	80	14	53	67	68
New Zealand	22	79	58	49	33	75
Nigeria	80	30	60	55	13	84
Norway	31	69	8	50	35	55
Pakistan	55	14	50	70	50	0
Panama	95	11	44	86		
Peru	64	16	42	87	25	46
Philippines	94	32	64	44	27	42
Poland	68	60	64	93	38	29
Portugal	63	27	31	99	28	33
Romania	90	30	42	90	52	20
Russia	93	39	36	95	81	20
Saudi Arabia	95	25	60	80	36	52
Senegal	70	25	45	55	25	
Serbia	86	25	43	92	52	28
Sierra Leone	70	20	40	50		
Singapore	74	20	48	8	72	46
Slovakia	100	52	100	51	77	28
Slovenia	71	27	19	88	49	48
South Africa	49	65	63	49	34	63
South Korea	60	18	39	85	100	29
Spain	57	51	42	86	48	44
Sri Lanka	80	35	10	45	45	
Suriname	85	47	37	92		
Sweden	31	71	5	29	53	78
Switzerland	34	68	70	58	74	66
Syria	80	35	52	60	30	
Taiwan	58	17	45	69	93	49

Country	Power Distance Index (PDI)	Individualism vs. Collectivism (IDV)	Masculinity vs. Femininity (MAS)	Uncertainty Avoidance Index (UAI)	Pragmatic vs. Normative (PRA)	Indulgence vs. Restraint (IND)
Tanzania	70	25	40	50	34	38
Thailand	64	20	34	64	32	45
Trinidad and Tobago	47	16	58	55	13	80
Turkey	66	37	45	85	46	49
United Arab Emirates	90	25	50	80		
United Kingdom	35	89	66	35	51	69
United States	40	91	62	46	26	68
Uruguay	61	36	38	99	26	53
Venezuela	81	12	73	76	16	100
Vietnam	70	20	40	30	57	35
Zambia	60	35	40	50	30	42

SOURCE: Adapted from gert-hofstede.com. (n.d.) Retrieved February 11, 2015, from http://www.gert-hofstede.com/hofstede_dimensions.php

[a] Estimated values.

from the top down. This research program also includes gender egalitarianism, power distance, and uncertainty avoidance, and a future orientation (similar to Hofstede's long-term orientation) but adds assertiveness and performance and human orientation as well. Building on the idea of the determinant individualism or collectivism, the authors focus on institutional and in-group collectivism, separating to what degree individuals of society are rewarded for collective actions and to what degree individuals express pride in their organizations.

Assertive cultures are those that enjoy competition in business, such as the United States and Austria, whereas less assertive ones, such as Sweden and New Zealand, prefer harmony in relationships and emphasize loyalty and solidarity. Understanding this environment can help the entrepreneur from a marketing and competitive intelligence point of view while providing additional techniques for better managing local suppliers, customers, and the workforce.

Performance orientation and human orientation give rise to how an enterprise operates based on the rewards offered to the individuals for excellence and additionally how the collective encourages and rewards their individuals for being fair, caring, and generous. From a performance perspective, Singapore and many Western nations score very high in training and development; Russia and Greece are good examples of cultures where family and background are more important. As for human orientation, Egypt and Malaysia emphasize the collectivistic nature, whereas Germany and France are not so disposed in this way.

Global entrepreneurs can better understand how to take advantage of a market if they understand the culture. By having a better understanding, entrepreneurs can select and enter a market with less risk and a better guarantee of success, knowing they can reach the target consumers, suppliers, workforce, and understand how to manage them according to their dispositions.

This area is further elaborated upon in Chapter 10.

SUMMARY

A full understanding of the culture of the new market that a company plans to enter is vital to the venture's success. Chapter 3 outlines the important cultural considerations that each global entrepreneur needs to take into account as he or she decides to enter a new market or partner with individuals or companies from a different country. *Culture* generally refers to common ways of thinking and behaving that are passed on from parents to their children or transmitted by social organizations, developed, and then reinforced through social pressure. Every entrepreneur must keep in mind that by nature, culture is adaptive, learned, shared, structured, symbolic, and transgenerational. This chapter concludes by describing how social structure, language, religion/belief systems, political philosophy, economic philosophy/system, education, and customs and manners can affect a country's culture. A few examples show that an entrepreneur needs to be aware of and adapt to cultural differences. An entrepreneur's understanding of a different culture can make or break the success of a new venture.

QUESTIONS FOR DISCUSSION

1. Why does a global entrepreneur need to be aware of the culture of the country that he or she is entering?

2. How should a global entrepreneur act in a country with a high power distance?

3. Why do you need to be culturally aware when you receive gifts in different countries?

CHAPTER EXERCISES

1. With a partner, discuss an instance of cultural misunderstanding that has personally happened to you. Could this misunderstanding have been avoided? If so, how?

2. Choose one of the cultural scenarios in the chapter. How would you have avoided the same cultural problems that the company faced?

3. Pick a foreign country where you would like to do business. Write a brief report explaining the cultural differences between your country and that country and describe how you would handle them.

4. Find an article about a company that attributes its failure in a foreign country to misunderstanding the local culture. What could the company have done to prevent this failure?

NOTE

Portions of this chapter are adapted from Chapter 5 of Hisrich, R. D., Peters, M. A., & Shepherd, D. A. (2013). *Entrepreneurship* (9th ed.). Burr Ridge, IL: McGraw-Hill/Irwin.

REFERENCES

Campbell, D. D. (1997, February 15). *Grupo Financiero Inverlat* (Version: [A], 9497L00). Ontario, Canada: Ivey Management Services.

England, G. W., & Lee, R. (1974, August). The relationship between managerial values and managerial success in the United States, Japan, India, and Australia. *Journal of Applied Psychology, 59*(4), 411–419.

Hofstede, G. (2001). *Culture's consequences: Comparing values, behaviors, institutions, and organizations across nations.* Thousand Oaks, CA: Sage.

Javidan, M., Dorman, P. W., de Luque, M. S., & House, R. J. (2005). In the eye of the beholder: Cross cultural lessons in leadership from project GLOBE. *Academy of Management Executive, 20*(1), 67–90.

Reel, M. (2007, October 31). South America ushers in the era of the presidenta. *The Washington Post,* A12.

Reichel, A., & Flynn, D. M. (1984). Values in transition: An empirical study of Japanese managers in the U.S. *Management International Review, 23*(4), 69–79.

Training Management Corporation. (2008). *The cultural navigator—Cultural Orientation Inventory.* Retrieved January 19, 2015, from http://www.culturalnavigator.com

SUGGESTED READINGS

Marcotte, C. (2011). Country entrepreneurial profiles: Assessing the individual and organizational levels of entrepreneurship across countries. *Journal of Enterprising Culture, 19*(2), 169–200. *Business Source Complete.* Web. 29 Oct. 2013.

This article examines different entrepreneurship profiles in various countries, sorting them along the lines of how different types of entrepreneurial ventures are allocated across an array of levels and dimensions. The article attempts to compare organizational and individual indicators of global entrepreneurship activity in 22 countries of the Organization for Economic Co-operation and Development (OECD). A negative correlation is discovered between individual and corporate indicators.

Mosakowski, E., Calic, G., & Earley C. P. (2013). Cultures as learning laboratories: What makes some more effective than others? *Academy of Management Learning & Education, 12*(3), 512–526. doi:10.5465/amle.2013.0149

    This article considers whether some cultures are better suited to create a global mind-set than others. It studies inexperienced foreign business students in a U.S. university who take part in a service-learning project for veterans of the U.S. military. It further describes four aspects key to effective cross-cultural learning, which include a tight culture, high moral desirability, low context, and a moderate level of cultural difference.

Sanchez-Runde, C., Nardon, L., & Steers, R. (2013). The cultural roots of ethical conflicts in global business. *Journal of Business Ethics, 116*(4), 689–701. doi:10.1007/s10551-013-1815-y

    The authors examine world views of morality to argue that a deep understanding of moral conflicts is hindered by overemphasis on Western viewpoints. Three sources of ethical conflicts in business are considered: conflicts of preferences and tastes, importance of morality versus the rule of law, and tolerance for different values.

Schwens, C., Bierwerth, M., Isidor, R., & Kabst, R. (2011). International entrepreneurship: A meta-analysis. *Academy of Management Annual Meeting Proceedings,* 1–5. *Business Source Complete.* Web. 29 Oct. 2013.

    The paper describes a study that provides meta-analytic evidence on the relationship of internationalization and performance. The researchers examine firms based on size, age, and country of origin. They explain how international entrepreneurs aim to create a competitive advantage through sales and use of resources in foreign countries.

4

The Global
Monetary System

Profile: MTN

Celebrating its 20th anniversary in 2014, MTN has achieved great things since its inception in 1994. With business operations in countries such as Syria, Yemen, Iran, Sudan, and Afghanistan, MTN is far from risk averse and faces several challenges in the global business environment, especially regarding international sanctions. What is known by MTN managers as a "healthy appetite for risk" has translated into huge growth and has proven the idea that high-risk markets also have potential for high returns. The company now has a market cap of $40 billion and is among the top 10 global telecom providers. MTN has a presence in 22 countries in Africa and the Middle East and holds a 35%–45% market share in the South Africa market, with Vodacom as the largest competitor. In South Africa, half of its business is contracted and half is prepaid. Outside of South Africa, all of MTN's business is prepaid. In Nigeria, its market share is just under 50% and the company has a 55% margin.

With a healthy appetite for risk, MTN generates very high returns and is a company without debt, with high growth levels, and that also pays dividends. The African market presents many business opportunities: There are limited fixed-line data connections, which means there is plenty of room to serve mobile data consumers with services such as mobile banking. People penetration is also still quite low, presenting a significant opportunity.

Several trends influence MTN's business. First, infrastructure sharing is becoming more important as many competitive networks may soon have the same coverage. In India in particular, there is a major focus on this as a method to reduce costs. There is not yet a focus on this in South Africa, but it is becoming more prominent in Ghana, where a limit on licenses by the government forces infrastructure sharing. Another trend is that it is unlikely that contracts will become popular in countries other than South Africa any time soon, mainly because customers would require an ID and a bank account in order to become eligible for a contract, which many people do not have. In addition, prepaid telecommunications make people feel more in charge and in control of their expenses. For example, consumers are actually paying for electricity in advance in many locations. As prepaid is also a more profitable way of running a telecommunications business, MTN has no desire to change this consumer behavior.

A final trend is that competition, regulatory pressures, and the number of other online players, such as Netflix, are increasing. As a result, the risk of price wars is increasing, and these price wars are undesirable, as they often lead to shrinking margins and losses for all players.

U.S. sanctions against certain countries present a challenge: The business can operate there, but (at least for now) the money cannot come out of that country. Examples include Iran and Syria. The risks are threefold: (1) political risk, sometimes in the form of civil unrest; (2) financial risk, often regarding exchange rates; and (3) corruption or the threat of losing deals. Due to the prohibitively high costs associated with the security of insurance, MTN deals with currency risk in a very particular manner: The company takes out loans in the countries it does business in so that if the currency halves, so does its debt.

Although very risk tolerant, MTN will not enter countries with civil unrest or war, and the firm avoids entry into markets that are too small or have low returns. The country needs to make a difference to the portfolio and should therefore have a population of at least 20 to 50 million. The business's focus is on emerging markets, which grow fast, are underpenetrated, involve high risks, and offer great potential returns. MTN is an example of an international venture that has become very successful by tailoring its services, strategies, and creative risk management solutions to the local markets in which it operates.

SOURCES: Mobile Telephone Networks. (2013). Home page. Retrieved February 11, 2015, from https://www.mtn.co.za/Pages/Home.aspx#1

Tarjanne, E. (2014, January 16). Welcome to the new world. *2014 Thunderbird School of Global Management Winterim Class.* Presentation conducted in the Republic of South Africa, Pretoria.

Chapter Objectives

1. To understand the financial management tools available to manage exchange rate variations

2. To understand foreign exchange and the foreign exchange market

3. To understand the global capital market

4. To explain balance-of-payment concerns and the role of international organizations

5. To learn about the financial exposure in international financial transactions

Introduction

One of the most difficult aspects of doing international business for most global entrepreneurs involves understanding the global monetary system, foreign exchange, and foreign exchange rates. The purpose of this chapter is to explain the aspects of foreign exchange and the way foreign exchange rates are established and fluctuate. Following the discussion of the international monetary system and international capital markets, the chapter concludes by discussing the roles of the International Monetary Fund (IMF) and the World Bank.

Foreign Exchange

Foreign exchange, an essential aspect of doing international business, is a system of converting a national currency into another currency as well as transferring currency from one country to another. It includes deposits, credits, and foreign currency as well as bills of exchange, drafts, letters of credit, and traveler's checks.

Aspects of the Foreign Exchange Market

The foreign exchange market provides the platform for foreign transactions with national currencies being bought and sold against one another. It serves three important functions. First, the foreign exchange market transfers purchasing power from one country to another and from one currency to another. By so doing, it facilitates international commerce and trade and capital movement. Second, the foreign exchange market provides credit; this credit function plays an important role in increasing international trade. Finally, the foreign exchange market provides hedging facilities by covering export risk. This hedging facilitation provides a mechanism for exporters and importers to protect themselves against losses from wide fluctuations in the exchange rate between currencies occurring during the time of the transaction.

There are two primary types of exchange in the foreign exchange market: the *spot exchange* and the *forward exchange*. The spot exchange is a type of foreign exchange transaction that requires the immediate delivery or exchange of currencies. Usually, even though the terms of the transaction are established, the actual settlement takes place in one or two days. The rate of exchange for this type of transaction is the spot rate, and its market is called the *spot market*. The forward exchange involves a transaction between two parties where the delivery is made on a future date by one of the parties for payment in his or her domestic currency by the other party using the price agreed upon in a contract. The rate of exchange in a forward exchange transaction is called the *forward exchange rate* and the market is known as the *foreign market*. By having a forward exchange contract, the exporters and importers are protected against any exchange rate fluctuations that may occur during the time of the contract before the contract is fulfilled.

The foreign exchange market plays an important role in making global transactions possible. Because a global network of banks, brokers, and foreign exchange dealers connects electronically, the market provides easy access to a company in any country, usually through a bank in the local economy. Though it is a worldwide network, there are three primary trading centers: London, New York, and Tokyo. There are also several major secondary centers: Frankfurt, Hong Kong, Paris, San Francisco, Singapore, and Sydney. Of these, due to historical and geographic reasons, London is usually looked at as the most important trading center.

There are several interesting features of the market that are important to the global entrepreneur. First, the U.S. dollar plays a very important role because many transactions involve dollars. A manufacturer with Japanese yen wanting to buy Swiss francs will often purchase U.S. dollars to buy the needed Swiss francs. Dollars are easy to use in any transaction. Besides the U.S. dollar, other important currencies are the European euro, the Japanese yen, and the British pound.

Second, the foreign exchange market is always open. Even during the few hours that all three primary trading centers (London, New York, and Tokyo) are closed, trading continues in secondary markets, particularly San Francisco and Sydney.

Finally, all the markets, and particularly the primary and secondary trading centers, are so closely integrated and connected electronically that the foreign exchange market acts as a single market. This means there are no significant differences in exchange rates quoted in any trading center, even those outside the primary and secondary ones. Since there are so many companies involved, any exchange rate discrepancies are small and corrected immediately as dealers attempt to make a profit through *arbitrage*, buying a currency low and selling it at a higher price.

Nature of the Foreign Exchange Market

What is the foreign exchange market and its rates of exchange? The foreign exchange market is the open market for converting the currency of one country to the currency of another country at the rate of convertibility determined by the market at the time of the transaction (the foreign exchange rate). The main function of the foreign exchange market is to convert the prices of the goods and services in one country's currency into the currency of another. Each country (or group of countries) has its own currency: Australia (Australian dollars), Canada (Canadian dollars), China (renminbi), France (euro), Germany (euro), Japan (yen), United Kingdom (British pound), and the United States (U.S. dollars). Each currency is converted into another at the exchange rate operating on the date that the exchange occurs. Some hypothetical exchange rates are presented in Table 4.1.

Such exchange rates operate for foreign tourists exchanging currency in a country and are used in the currency transactions in international trade. A company converts the money it receives from sales of its exports, income from licensing agreements, and income from its foreign investments into its home country currency or the currency of another country where payments need to be made. Companies also convert home country currency into that of a country where they are interested in investing or buying goods and services. Some companies purchase foreign currencies (hedging) in case there are any significant changes in the exchange rates. Managing the exchange rate and its fluctuations is sometimes the most difficult part of the transaction.

Foreign Exchange Rate Fluctuations

The foreign exchange market can be used to provide some protection for the global entrepreneur against wide fluctuations in exchange rates. This is accomplished through three basic mechanisms: currency swaps, forward exchange rates, and spot exchange rates.

Currency swaps are used to protect against fluctuations and foreign exchange risk when there is a need to move in and out of a currency for a limited period of time. For

Table 4.1 Examples of Foreign Exchange Rates

Country	Currency	Dollar	Euro	Pound
Argentina	Argentine Peso	8.001984	11.050006	13.465812
Australia	Australian Dollar	1.078488	1.489291	1.81477
Bahrain	Bahraini Dinar	0.377099	0.520739	0.634585
Botswana	Botswana Pula	8.787308	12.134433	14.78732
Brazil	Brazilian Real	2.228751	3.079028	3.751424
United Kingdom	British Pound	0.594266	0.820596	
Brunei	Bruneian Dollar	1.255411	1.733609	2.112622
Bulgaria	Bulgarian Lev	1.416363	1.957939	2.383728
Canada	Canadian Dollar	1.095634	1.513207	1.843943
Chile	Chilean Peso	561.797753	775.790009	945.396889
China	Chinese Yuan Renminbi	6.258216	8.641943	10.531408
Colombia	Colombian Peso	1939.714025	2678.270124	3253.029311
Croatia	Croatian Kuna	5.509812	7.607445	9.269643
Czech Republic	Czech Koruna	19.873224	27.441476	33.439485
Denmark	Danish Krone	5.405556	7.464235	9.095691
United Arab Emirates	Emirati Dirham	3.673	5.072462	6.181048
European Union	Euro	0.724178		1.21855
Hong Kong	Hong Kong Dollar	7.753275	10.706538	13.047303
Hungary	Hungarian Forint	223.266273	308.303879	375.678613
Iceland	Icelandic Krona	111.944476	154.592132	188.390163
India	Indian Rupee	60.313325	83.32312	101.547853
Indonesia	Indonesian Rupiah	11523.35	15912.66565	19391.56784
Iran	Iranian Rial	25641.02537	35268.96901	42972.64227
Israel	Israeli Shekel	3.4702	4.792706	5.838017
Japan	Japanese Yen	102.563113	141.639516	172.609715
Kazakhstan	Kazakhstani Tenge	182.066454	251.414501	306.379818
Kuwait	Kuwaiti Dinar	0.28137	0.388718	0.473528

(Continued)

Table 4.1 (Continued)

Country	Currency	Dollar	Euro	Pound
Latvia	Latvian Lat	0.508952	0.7028	0.856397
Libya	Libyan Dinar	1.2363	1.707214	2.067934
Lithuania	Lithuanian Litas	2.500442	3.4528	4.207411
Malaysia	Malaysian Ringgit	3.25894	4.500076	5.484346
Mauritius	Mauritian Rupee	29.800042	41.150886	50.147479
Mexico	Mexican Peso	13.097288	18.08618	22.035157
Nepalese	Nepalese Rupee	97.228974	134.26209	163.615002
New Zealand	New Zealand Dollar	1.168984	1.614202	1.967063
Norway	Norwegian Krone	6.011272	8.300621	10.114829
Oman	Omani Rial	0.3851	0.531787	0.648049
Pakistan	Pakistani Rupee	98.430041	135.919188	165.634308
Philippines	Philippine Peso	44.458028	61.388217	74.848051
Poland	Polish Zloty	3.038322	4.195391	5.111933
Qatar	Qatari Riyal	3.641203	5.028154	6.127432
Romania	Romanian New Leu	3.22128	4.448192	5.418313
Russia	Russian Ruble	35.626599	49.201658	59.952396
Saudi Arabia	Saudi Arabian Riyal	3.7506	5.179227	6.311534
Singapore	Singapore Dollar	1.255411	1.733609	2.112622
South Africa	South African Rand	10.550327	14.569001	17.755715
South Korea	South Korean Won	1029.847084	1422.004455	1733.707921
Sri Lanka	Sri Lankan Rupee	130.60798	180.359859	219.79111
Sweden	Swedish Krona	6.564377	9.0645	11.045691
Switzerland	Swiss Franc	0.883816	1.22049	1.487194
Taiwan	Taiwan New Dollar	30.14001	41.670779	50.703566
Thailand	Thai Baht	32.245011	44.527294	54.26206
Trinidad and Tobago	Trinidadian Dollar	6.450094	8.906995	10.854285
Turkey	Turkish Lira	2.120681	2.928251	3.568475
United States of America	U.S. Dollar		1.380906	1.682806
Venezuela	Venezuelan Bolivar	6.287707	8.682723	10.58098

SOURCE: X-Rates [website]. (2014). Retrieved April 29, 2014, from http://www.x-rates.com/

example, many companies do business in the European Union, buying and selling from member countries. Let us say, for example, Alcoa buys and sells finished goods and parts with its wholly owned plant in Hungary and wants to ensure that the US$1 million that it will need to pay some bills in Hungary at euros (EUR) .76/U.S. dollars (US$)1 is available at a known exchange rate. It also will collect EUR 20 million in 75 days, when some accounts are due. If today's spot exchange rate is US$1 = EUR .76 and the forward foreign exchange is US$1 = EUR .90, Alcoa can enter into a 75-day forward exchange currency swap for converting EUR 20 million into US$. Since the euro is at a premium on the 75-day market, the company will receive US$22.2 million (EUR 20 million/.90 = US$22.2 million). Of course, this could be reversed if the euro was trading at less than EUR .76/US$1 in 75 days.

When the global entrepreneur and another company agree to execute a transaction and exchange currency immediately, the transaction is called a *spot exchange*. In this type of transaction, the spot exchange rate is the rate that the currency of one country is converted into the currency of another country on a particular day. This rate also applies when someone is traveling to London and wants to convert euros into British pounds at a London bank. The spot exchange rate may not be the most favorable exchange rate because the value of the currency is determined by the interaction of demand and supply of each country's currency with respect to the currency of other countries on that particular day.

A final form of protection for the global entrepreneur against widely fluctuating currencies is the forward exchange rate. Forward exchange can be used by two parties to exchange currency and execute a deal at some specific date in the future. The exchange rate used in this type of transaction is called the *forward exchange rate* and is usually quoted 30, 90, or 180 days into the future. Let us assume a U.S. company and a Swiss company are doing a US$5 million transaction in 90 days, where the Swiss company is purchasing US$5 million of computer software and equipment. Both companies want to enter into a 90-day forward exchange contract. Today, the Swiss franc (SF) is trading at SF.806/US$1. Since the two companies feel that in 30 days forward, it will be SF.808/US$1; in 90 days forward, it will be SF.812/US$1; and 180 days forward, it will be SF.818 /US$1, they enter into a 90-day forward contract guaranteeing that the Swiss company would not pay more than US$6.16 million (US$6.16 million = US$5 million ÷ SF.812/US$1) for the software and equipment.

For most global entrepreneurs, foreign exchange should not be a driver of profits or losses for their venture. Companies that spend too much time trying to predict or speculate on changes in foreign exchange rates usually end up losing focus on their core product/service and then lose out in the marketplace. By using the tools previously discussed, global entrepreneurs can improve the predictability of their business and reduce one of the potential risks inherent in international business.

The Global Capital Market

A global capital market benefits both borrowers and investors as it brings together those from around the world who want to invest money with those who want to borrow money better than any single domestic market. For the borrowers, the global capital market increases the funds available for borrowing and lowers the cost of capital. In a domestic market, the pool of investors is limited to those who live in the particular country, so there is an upper limit on the supply of funds available. A global capital market increases the number of investors and supply of funds available from the larger pool.

The broader pool of capital obtained in a global market eliminates the limited liquidity found in a domestic capital market; it also lowers the cost of capital. The dividend yield and expected capital gains on equity investments as well as the interest rate on loans (debt) are lower. This lower price of obtaining capital is very important to every company all over the world. It is particularly beneficial in less-developed countries, where the pool of investors tends to be smaller than in more-developed economies.

From the investor's perspective, the global capital market provides a wider range of investment opportunities than is available in any domestic market. This allows investors to reduce their risk by diversifying their portfolios over a wide range of industries that are geographically dispersed. Generally, as the number of investments increases in an investor's portfolio, the risk in the portfolio declines until the risk approaches the systematic risk of the market. *Systematic risk* is the risk associated with the value in a portfolio attributable to macroeconomic forces affecting all firms in an economy and not one specific individual firm. Because the movement of stock and interest rates is country specific and is not perfectly correlated across countries, the investor's risk is reduced by investing in various countries. By doing this, the losses incurred when an investment(s) in one country goes down can be offset by gains in investment(s) in another country. This low correlation of value and interest rates among countries reflects the different macroeconomic policies and different economic conditions on a country-by-country basis. It also reflects the capital controls in place in some countries that restrict cross-border capital flows.

Balance of Payments

A key concern today is disparity in the balance of payments between countries. The overall balance of payments measures all the international economic transactions between countries. There are hundreds of thousands of international transactions (imports, exports, repatriation of profits, grants, and investments) that occur each year; each one is recorded and classified.

By definition, the balance of payments must balance or there is an error in the counting process. While there can be an imbalance in currency or trade between two countries, the entire balance of payment of every country is always balanced. In recording all international transactions over a period of time, the balance of payments is tracking the flow of purchases and payments between each country. Two types of business transactions dominate the balance of payments: real assets (the exchange of goods and services for other goods and services through either barter or, more commonly, money) and financial assets (the exchange of financial claims such as stocks, bonds, loans, purchases, or sales for other financial claims or money). The balance of payments consists of two primary subaccounts—the current account and the capital and financial account—and two minor subaccounts—the official reserve account and the net errors and omissions account. Each will be briefly discussed in turn.

The current account includes all international economic transactions with income or payment within the year. It includes goods trade, services trade, income, and current transfers. *Goods trade* consists of the export and import of goods, the oldest form of international economic activity. Many countries attempt to keep a positive balance or, even better, a surplus of exports over imports. *Services trade* deals with the export and import of services. Significant activity in services trade involves construction services, financial services provided by banks, and travel services of airlines. *Income* is mostly current income from investments made in previous periods. Any wages or salaries paid to nonresident workers of subsidiaries of out-of-country companies are also considered income. Finally, *current transfers* are composed of any financial settlements in change of ownership of real assets or financial items as well as any one-way transfers, gifts, or grants from one country to another.

While every country has some trade, most of the trade involves merchandise (goods trade). The balance of trade, which is widely discussed in the business press, refers to the balance of imports and exports of goods trade only. This, for large industrialized countries such as Japan, the United States, and the United Kingdom, is misleading because it does not include the other three areas of the current account, particularly services trade, which can also be very large and significant.

The capital and financial account of the balance of payments measures all international transactions of financial assets and has two major subaccounts—the capital account and the financial account. The *capital account* is composed of all the transfers of financial assets and the acquisition of nonproduced and nonfinancial assets. This is a very small part of the total combined account. The *financial account* is by far the largest component of this dual account and consists of three parts: direct investment, portfolios investment, and other long-term and short-term capital transfers. Each of the financial assets is classified by the degree of control over the particular asset the claim represents. In a portfolio investment, the investor has no control, but in a direct investment, the investor exerts some degree of control over the asset.

One minor subaccount of the balance of payments—the official reserve account—is composed of the total currency and metallic reserves held by the official monetary authority of the government of each country. Most of these revenues are in the major currencies of the world used in international trade and financial transactions. Another minor subaccount of the balance of payments is the net errors and omissions account. This very small account, as the name implies, makes sure that the balance of payments is always in balance.

Role of the International Monetary Fund and the World Bank

In addition to the balance of payments, another area important for the global entrepreneur to understand is the role of the IMF and the World Bank. Both the IMF and the World Bank were established in 1944, when representatives from 44 countries met at Bretton

Woods, New Hampshire, to design a new international monetary system. The overall goal of the meeting was to design an economic order that would endure and facilitate the economic growth of the world following the end of World War II. While the IMF was established to maintain order in the international monetary system, the World Bank was established to promote general economic development. Each will be discussed in turn in terms of its importance for the global entrepreneur.

International Monetary Fund (IMF)

Due to the worldwide financial collapse after World War II, competitive currency devaluations, high unemployment, and hyperinflation (occurring particularly in Germany in 1944), the IMF was established to avoid a repetition of these events. The discipline part of the equation was achieved through the establishment of a fixed exchange rate, thereby helping to control inflation and improving economic discipline in countries. This fixed exchange rate lasted until 1976, when a floating exchange rate was formalized and established.

Some flexibility was built into the system in the form of the IMF lending facilities and adjustable parities. Most members of the IMF make available gold and currencies to lend to member countries to cover short-term periods of balance-of-payment deficits to avoid domestic unemployment in that country due to a tightening monetary or fiscal policy. The IMF funds are lent to countries to bring down inflation rates and reduce the country's balance-of-payment deficits. Because a persistent balance-of-payment deficit would deplete a country's reserves of foreign currency, a loan to reduce this deficit helps a country avoid devaluing its currency. When extensive loans from the IMF fund are given to a country, that country must submit to increasingly stringent supervision by the IMF of its macroeconomic policies.

The system of adjustable parities established by the IMF allows for the devaluation of a country's currency by more than 10% if the IMF feels that this will help achieve a balance-of-payment equilibrium in the country. The IMF, in these circumstances, assumes that without devaluation, the member country would experience high unemployment and a persistent trade deficit.

World Bank

The World Bank, officially named the International Bank for Reconstruction and Development (IBRD), was established initially to help finance the rebuilding of Europe following World War II. Because the U.S. Marshall Plan accomplished this, the World Bank focused instead on such areas as lending money to third world countries. The focus initially was on power stations and transportation as well as agriculture, education, population control, and economic development.

The World Bank makes loans for projects in developing economies through two schemes. The first one, the IBRD scheme, raises money for the project through the sale of bonds in the international capital market. The second scheme involves International Development Association (IDA) loans from money supplied by wealthier member

CULTURAL STORIES

Story 1

When we lived in Mexico, several engineering students asked us to review resumes they had written in English. Our students had excellent English skills and wanted their resumes to be perfect.

One student was concerned about reusing verbs and had used a thesaurus to help create more variety. He did well until the bullet point about "practicing intercourse" with clients. We tried to explain that "conversing" might be better, and he insisted that the thesaurus told him his choice was perfect—until we had him look it up in the dictionary.

The word was finally understood and the story spread—everyone was asking if they could get a job with him.

Story 2

I was working at a local newspaper in San Diego and one of my responsibilities was the Latino community. One year at Christmastime, I sent an e-mail to more than 50 Latino leaders in San Diego and Tijuana wishing them a Happy New Year. What I said was Feliz Ano, forgetting to include the ~ over the n.

Instead of wishing them Happy New Year, I wished them a "Happy Rear End." Boy was I embarrassed.

SOURCES: Mattson, J. (2011, March 11). Perfect resume, ideal job. Retrieved January 20, 2015, from http://cultural confusions.com/?s=Jamie+Mattson

Hisrich, R. D. (2013). *International Entrepreneurship* (2nd ed., p. 139). Thousand Oaks, CA: Sage.

nations. A global entrepreneur may have the opportunity to be involved in one of these funded projects.

Trade Financing

One of the keys to successful global expansion is having funds available. One alternative to acquiring these funds, and often the only option available to the global entrepreneur, is *bootstrap financing*. This approach is particularly important at start-up and in the early years of the venture, when capital from debt financing (i.e., in terms of higher interest rates) or from equity financing (i.e., in terms of loss of ownership) is very expensive.

In addition to the monetary costs, outside capital has other costs as well. First, it usually takes about four to six months to raise outside equity capital or to find out that there is no outside capital available. During this time of raising equity capital, the global entrepreneur may not focus enough on the important areas of marketing, sales, product development, and operating costs. A business usually needs capital when it can least afford the time to raise it. One company's CEO spent so much time raising capital for global expansion that sales and marketing were neglected to such an extent that the forecasted sales and profit figures on the pro forma income statements were not met for the first three years after the capital infusion. This led to investor concern that, in turn, required more of the CEO's time.

Second, the availability of capital increases the global entrepreneur's impulse to spend. It can cause a company to hire more staff before needed and move to larger, more costly facilities. A company can easily forget the basic axiom of venture creation: staying lean and mean.

Third, outside capital can decrease the company's flexibility. This can hamper the direction, drive, and creativity of the global entrepreneur. Unsophisticated investors are particularly a problem because they often object to a company's moving away from the focus and direction outlined in the business plan that attracted their investment; this often occurs in taking the venture into international markets. This attitude can encumber a company to such an extent that the needed change cannot be implemented or is implemented slowly after a great deal of time and effort has been spent in consensus building. This can demoralize the global entrepreneur who likes the freedom of not working for someone else.

Finally, outside capital may cause disruption and problems in the venture. Capital is not provided without the expectation of a rate of return. Sometimes equity investors pressure the global entrepreneur to continuously grow the company so that an exit (payback) can occur as soon as possible, or at least within a five- to seven-year period. This emphasis on short-term performance can be at the expense of the long-term success of the company.

In spite of these potential problems, a global entrepreneur, at times, needs some capital to finance international growth; without outside capital, this growth can be slow or nonexistent if there are not sufficient internal sources of funds available. Outside capital should be sought only after all possible internal sources of funds have been explored. And, when outside funds are needed, the global entrepreneur should not forget to stay focused on the basics of the business. Two good sources of external funds for expanding the business are from family and friends and commercial banks. A letter of credit is frequently used in an international transaction.

Family and Friends

Family and friends are a common source of capital to go international, particularly if the capital originates from the country to be entered. These individuals are most likely to invest due to their knowledge and relationship with the global entrepreneur as well as knowledge of the country. Family and friends usually provide a small amount of equity funding for the global venture. Although it is often easier to obtain money from family and friends, as with all sources of capital, there are positive and negative aspects of using this as a source of funds. Although the amount of money provided may be small, if it is in the form of equity financing, upon funding, the family member or friend will have an ownership position in the venture and may feel they have the right to significantly influence the direction and operations of the venture. This may have a negative effect on employees and facilities and distract from a strong focus on sales and profits. On the other hand, family and friends are usually more patient in desiring a return on their investment.

To avoid problems in the future, the global entrepreneur should present the possible positive and negative consequences and the nature of the risks of the investment opportunity in the international market. The business arrangements should be strictly business. Any loans or investments from family or friends should be treated in a businesslike manner, as if the financing received was from an impersonal investor. Any loan should specify the rate of interest and a proposed repayment schedule of interest and principal. If the family or friend is treated the same as an investor, future conflicts can be avoided. Everything should be in writing, as it is amazing how short memories become when money is involved.

The global entrepreneur should carefully consider the effect of the investment on the family member or friend before accepting. Particular concern should be paid to any hardships that might result should the international market not be successful and the investment not be a good one. Each family member or friend should invest because they feel it's a good international opportunity, not because they feel a family obligation to do so.

Commercial Banks

Commercial banks are a good source of funds for global expansion when collateral is available. The funds, in the form of debt financing, require some tangible guaranty or collateral—some asset with value. This collateral can be in the form of business assets (land, equipment, or the building of the venture), personal assets (the entrepreneur's house, car, land, stocks, or bonds), the assets of the cosigner of the note, or the assets of doing business (accounts receivable, inventory). There are several types of bank loans available to the global entrepreneur. To ensure repayment, these loans are based on the assets and/or the cash flow of the venture, such as accounts receivable, inventory, or equipment.

Accounts receivable provide a good basis for a loan to do international business, particularly if the customer base is well known and creditworthy. For creditworthy customers, a bank may finance up to 80% to 85% of the value of their accounts receivable. When the customer is a foreign government, a global entrepreneur can develop a factoring arrangement whereby the factor (the bank) actually "buys" the accounts receivable at a value below the face value of the sale and collects the money directly from the foreign purchaser. In this case, if any of the receivables are not collectible, the factor (the bank) sustains the loss, not the global entrepreneur. The cost of factoring the accounts receivable is, of course, higher than the cost of securing a loan against the accounts receivable, because the bank has more risk when factoring. The costs of factoring involve the interest charge on the amount of money advanced until the time the accounts receivable are collected, the commission covering the actual collection, and protection against any possible uncollectible amount.

Inventory is another of a firm's assets that is often a basis for an international loan, particularly when the inventory is more liquid and can be easily sold. Usually, the finished goods inventory can be financed for up to 50% of its value.

Equipment can be used to secure long-term financing, usually on a three- to 10-year basis, depending on its depreciation life. Equipment financing can fall into any of several categories: financing the purchase of new equipment, financing used equipment already owned by the company, sale-leaseback financing, or lease financing. When new equipment is being purchased or presently owned equipment is used as collateral, usually 50% to 80%

of the value of the equipment can be financed, depending on its salability. Given a global entrepreneur's tendency to rent rather than own, sale-leaseback or lease financing of equipment is widely used. In the sale-leaseback arrangement, the global entrepreneur "sells" the equipment to a lender and then leases it back for the life of the equipment.

The other type of debt financing frequently provided by commercial banks and other financial institutions is cash flow financing. These conventional bank loans include lines of credit, installment loans, straight commercial loans, long-term loans, ·and character loans. Line of credit financing is perhaps the form of cash flow financing most frequently used by global entrepreneurs. In arranging for a line of credit to be used as needed, the company pays a commitment fee to ensure that the commercial bank will make the loan when requested and then pays interest on any outstanding funds borrowed from the bank. Frequently, the loan must be repaid or reduced to a certain agreed-upon level on a periodic basis.

One problem for the global entrepreneur is determining how to successfully secure an international loan from a bank. Banks are generally cautious in lending money, particularly to new ventures and ventures doing business in global markets. Regardless of geographic location, commercial loan decisions are made only after the loan officer and a loan committee carefully review the borrower and the financial track record of the business.

These decisions are based on both quantifiable information and subjective judgments. The bank's lending decisions are made according to the five Cs of lending: character, capacity, capital, collateral, and conditions. Past financial statements (balance sheets and income statements) are reviewed for key profitability and credit ratios, inventory turnover, aging of accounts receivable, the global entrepreneur's capital invested, and commitment to the business. Future projections on the international market size, sales, and profitability are also evaluated to determine the ability to repay the loan. Several questions are usually raised regarding this ability: Does the global entrepreneur expect to have the loan for an extended period of time? If problems occur, is the global entrepreneur committed enough to spend the effort necessary to make the business a success? Does the business have a unique differential advantage in a growth market? What are the downside risks? Is there protection (such as life insurance on key personnel and insurance on the plant and equipment) against disasters? The intuitive factors, particularly the first two Cs, character and capacity, are also taken into account. This part of the loan decision—the gut feeling—is the most difficult part to assess. The global entrepreneur must present his or her capabilities and the prospects for the company in a way that elicits a positive response from the lender. This intuitive part of the loan decision becomes even more important when there is little or no track record, limited experience in financial management, a nonproprietary product/service (one not protected by a patent or license), or few assets available.

Some of the concerns of the loan officer and the loan committee can be reduced by providing a good loan application and an informative global business plan. Although the specific loan application format of each bank differs to some extent, generally, the application format is a mini business plan that consists of an executive summary, business description, owner/manager profiles, international business projections, financial statements, amount and use of the loan, and repayment schedule. This information provides the loan officer and loan committee with insight into the creditworthiness of the individual and the venture as well as the ability of the venture to make enough sales and profit to repay the loan and the interest.

The global entrepreneur should evaluate several banks, select the one that has had positive loan experiences in the particular business area, make an appointment, and then carefully present the case for the loan to the loan officer. Presenting a positive business image and following the established protocol are necessary to obtain a loan from a commercial bank. The global entrepreneur needs to establish a good relationship with a globally oriented bank.

Letters of Credit

The use of letters of credit in international trade has significantly increased in the past years, particularly in the United States. A letter of credit is simply a letter from one bank to another bank requesting that the second bank do something (usually pay money to someone) once certain conditions are fulfilled, such as the receiving or shipping of merchandise. Banks issue letters of credit for a fee, and some banks take the money from the customer's account or freeze that money in the account, releasing the money to another bank when the terms and conditions are met, which can be three to four months later.

Suppose a German manufacturer wants to buy some component parts from a supplier in China. How could the transaction take place? The German company could send a check along with the order or wire transfer the money to the bank of the Chinese company. In this transaction, the German manufacturer could not be guaranteed that the component parts will be received. Instead, the Chinese company could ship the component parts to the German manufacturer along with an invoice for the amount due. When doing this, the Chinese company could not be assured that payment will be received. This is where a letter of credit plays an important role. The two companies need to reach an agreement on when the seller (the Chinese company in this case) gets paid and provide that information to the bank of each company.

This is very important when the bank issuing the letter of credit (the bank of the German company) does not take control of the amount of money of the letter of credit when it is issued. In this case, the buying company (the German company) may have 60 to 90 days before the actual money is withdrawn. If the payment is specified at a certain time and condition, the selling company (the Chinese company) can usually get most of the amount of the letter of credit by drawing a draft for this amount at its receiving bank. The receiving bank will discount the draft at the prevailing discount rate. If the discount rate is 8% and the payment period is 90 days, then the discount will be 2% (90/360 on a quarter of 8%). This can be a very inexpensive way of getting money now instead of later. Some banks, often in the United States, take the money from the issuer's account (the German company) once the letter of credit is issued.

Banks vary on their application form for obtaining a letter of credit. All forms contain such information as the demographic information on the buying and selling company, the exact items being purchased, and the specific requirements of the transaction, including how payment is to be made. The agreement between the buyer and seller may specify that payment is to be made after the items have been inspected or upon shipment or the presentation of the appropriate documents. Also included may be the latest shipping date acceptable to the buyer and who is responsible for freight.

The exact cost of a letter of credit varies greatly by bank and by country. There is always a bank charge for writing the letter of credit, and it can vary from $200 to $500. There is also a percentage charge for the amount of money involved. This ranges from 0.5% to 2.5%. Even at the highest fee and percentage, letters of credit enable the global entrepreneur to more easily buy and sell internationally.

SUMMARY

The creation, use, and effects of the global monetary system are discussed in this chapter. Since there are numerous currencies in use all over the world, a global entrepreneur must understand foreign exchange rates and how the foreign exchange market works. When a product/service is sold in a foreign country, this market converts the prices of goods and services in one country into the currency of another. The global entrepreneur will use the foreign exchange market whenever making a global sale, receiving income from foreign agreements and investments, receiving payments from foreign countries, investing in a foreign country, purchasing goods or services from a foreign country, or taking part in currency speculation. Exchange rate fluctuations can affect the costs and profits of a global enterprise. There are three mechanisms to reduce the risk of currency fluctuations: currency swaps, forward exchange rates, and spot exchange rates. The U.S. dollar is the primary currency used in international transactions along with the European euro, the Japanese yen, and the British pound. The chapter concludes with an overview of two major international financial institutions, the IMF and the World Bank, both of which could be important to a global entrepreneur.

There are many sources of capital for a small company. Banks can provide letters of credit that prove the creditworthiness of a company to its potential customers in foreign markets. Letters of credit shift the credit responsibility from the individual or company to an established bank. This can prove necessary when both buying and selling in the international market, where there is often limited knowledge.

QUESTIONS FOR DISCUSSION

1. What are the potential effects of a change in the exchange rate for an Italian entrepreneur who frequently does business in New Zealand?

2. How would a weak Swiss franc benefit a Swiss entrepreneur who exports much of his product?

3. Explain the different roles of the IMF and the World Bank.

4. Mike just signed a US$1 million contract to sell small engines to a Slovenian manufacturer.

Delivery will take place in one month, but he does not expect to receive his payment in euros for three months. What are the potential risks? What are some of the ways to mitigate these risks?

CHAPTER EXERCISES

1. Choose a foreign currency and visit the XE website (http://www.xe.com) to familiarize yourself with how the exchange rate between your home currency and that foreign currency functions.

2. Pick a country that has recently dealt with severe currency devaluation and research how that devaluation has affected foreign investment and holdings in that country.

3. Select a country besides your own and see how the balance of payments works between your country and that foreign country.

4. Go to the IMF and World Bank websites (http://www.imf.org and http://www.world bank.org) to familiarize yourself with their roles in the global economic system. How do these roles differ?

SUGGESTED READINGS

Belke, A., Bernoth, K., & Fichtner, F. (2011). The future of the international monetary system. *DIW Economic Bulletin, 1*(4), 11–17.

   This article explains the challenges to the global monetary system brought about by the recent financial crisis and the current euro crisis. The authors indicate that neither free-floating nor fixed exchange rates are suitable and that a mixed system should be implemented. They further discuss improvements in the regulatory framework of financial markets that should be implemented.

Ben-Ami, D. (2012, November 5). Managing a difficult transition. *Fund Strategy,* 1. Retrieved November 19, 2013, from http://www.fundweb.co.uk/fund-strategy/issues/5th-november-2012/managing-a-difficult-transition/1060495.article

   The article details the history of the dollar's emergence as the global currency. The author further explores the possibility of a different global currency in the future. It references the book, *Exorbitant Privilege: The Rise and Fall of the Dollar and the Future of the International Monetary System,* by Barry Eichengreen.

Shelton, J. (2012). Gold and government. *CATO Journal, 32*(2), 333–347.

   This article describes how economic reform in the United States could restore the global monetary system. The author proposes the issuance of medium-term debt obligations in the form of Treasury Trust Bonds that would be zero-coupon bonds to be redeemed in either gold or dollars. The article concludes that backing the bonds with gold will show the U.S. government's intent to preserve the integrity of the dollar.

Taylor, A. M. (2013). The future of international liquidity and the role of China. *Journal of Applied Corporate Finance, 25*(2), 86–94. doi:10.1111/jacf.12017

    The article discusses the drawbacks of China's strategy of running a trade surplus and accumulating reserves. It details recent changes to this strategy in light of these drawbacks. It further analyzes the consequences of the Chinese renminbi reaching reserve currency status and how this would affect the dollar and the global economy.

Truman, E. M. (2010). The international monetary system and global imbalances. *Economics, Management & Financial Markets, 5*(4), 93–105.

    The article argues that the current international monetary system is not exceptionally prone to global current account imbalances, making the case that radical reforms are unnecessary. It states that the U.S. dollar's role as a reserve currency and an international currency does not create current account deficits in the United States. The author concludes that the system should continue to evolve but talk of radical change is misguided.

WEBSITES

http://www.imf.org

The IMF is an international organization of 185 member countries that promotes international monetary cooperation, exchange stability, and orderly exchange arrangements; fosters economic growth and high levels of employment; and provides temporary financial assistance to countries to help ease balance of payments adjustment.

http://www.worldbank.org

The World Bank is a good source of technical and financial assistance for developing countries. It is a group of entities headquartered in Washington, D.C.

http://www.xe.com

This is a currency site that provides up-to-date information on currencies as well as trading, currency education, data, and tools.

PART II

ENTERING THE GLOBAL MARKET

5

Selecting International Business Opportunities

Profile: YPlan

Named as one of the "Hottest Global Startups of 2013," YPlan is a mobile app developed for spontaneous customers looking for a fun night out. The app allows customers in San Francisco, London, and New York to browse through a list of events that are happening that same evening, pay for their tickets securely, and use the information provided by the app to redeem their ticket at the venue: No printing of tickets is required. The list of events is compiled by YPlan's team of entertainment experts, who "only work with the best venues, artists, and promoters. Partners include Beyoncé, The Royal Albert Hall, and Southbank Centre. YPlan currently works with over 550 event partners in London alone.

YPlan aims to develop such a reputable brand that its "YPlan stamp of approval" becomes trustworthy to a global audience. By offering its customers a unique deal, YPlan hopes to become the entertainment specialist. The app also offers unique "YPlan perks such as: access to a sold-out show, invitation-only events, free something with your booking, or a mouth-watering discount." Customers are offered safe checkout, can pay with various credit cards, and can purchase their event tickets from the well-known STAR (Society of Ticket Agents and Retailers).

Since its foundation, the company has received much attention from various media, including *The Wall Street Journal*, London's *Evening Standard*, and *Business Insider*. The firm's team claims that the app has a presence on one in every five smart phones in London and had over 500,000 users globally only one year after its launch in London in November 2012. Founded by two Lithuanian finance-workers-turned-entrepreneurs, Rytis Vitkauskas and Viktoras Jucikas, YPlan raised $13.7 million in funding. With London as its hub for European expansion, YPlan initially targeted the North American market, Chicago and Austin in particular. These entrepreneurs have brought some new technology to Silicon Valley and have reinforced London's position as "the digital capital of Europe."

With this exciting new business model, YPlan is a textbook example of why global companies must localize to satisfy local customers' needs and wants. It may seem obvious to a company such as YPlan that events, audience tastes, and trends are different in different locations. Companies for whom this seems less obvious, though, might benefit from the realization that tailoring products or services to local markets is essential and does take a great deal of time. Yet these localized details are precisely what make entrepreneurial ventures such as YPlan so successful: The customer feels understood and can therefore develop a connection with the brand.

SOURCES: Williams-Grut, O. (2014, February 25). London goes to Silicon Valley as YPlan launches in San Francisco. Retrieved April 28, 2014, from http://www.standard.co.uk/business/business-news/london-goes-to-silicon-valley-as-yplan-launches-in-san-francisco-9151077.html

YPlan [website]. (n.d.). Retrieved February 11, 2015, from http://yplanapp.com/

YPlan. (2013). *Forbes.* Retrieved April 28, 2014, from http://www.forbes.com/pictures/emjl45himf/yplan/

CHAPTER OBJECTIVES

1. To develop an understanding of how to select the most appropriate foreign market for each venture

2. To determine the best indicators for entry into a foreign market

3. To identify primary and secondary sources of information on foreign market industries or consumers

4. To understand how to collect country market data

5. To learn how to assess competitive strengths and weaknesses in foreign markets and determine a strategy to establish a competitive market position

Introduction

With so many potential markets and prospective countries available, a most critical issue for the global entrepreneur is foreign market selection (the focus of this chapter) and the entry strategy (the focus of Chapter 8). Should the global entrepreneur enter the top prospective country or should he or she employ a part of a country or multicountry approach? Should he or she choose the largest market possible or one that is easier to understand and navigate? Is a more-developed foreign market preferable to one that is developing?

These are just some of the questions confronting the global entrepreneur when deciding which market to enter. The market selection decision should be based on past sales and competitive positioning as well as assessment of each foreign market alternative. Data need to be systematically collected on both a regional and a country basis. A region can be a collection of countries, such as the European Union, or an area within a country, such as the southeastern part of China.

A systematic process is needed to select the best market in terms of market potential, ease of entry, and ease of doing business. This allows the global entrepreneur to avoid relying on assumptions and gut feelings. Any statistical data should be collected for at least a three-year period so any trends are evident. This collected data will also be used to develop the marketing plan and appropriate entry strategy.

Foreign Market Selection Model

Although there are several market selection models available, a good method employs a five-step approach: (1) develop appropriate indicators, (2) collect data and convert into comparable indicators, (3) establish an appropriate weight for each indicator, (4) analyze the data, and (5) select the appropriate market from the market rankings.

In Step 1, appropriate indicators are developed based on past sales, competitive research, experience, and discussions with other global entrepreneurs. Specific indicators for the new company are needed in three general areas: overall market indicators, market growth indicators, and product indicators in the business to business (BtoB). Market size indicators in the business to consumer (BtoC) generally center on population, per capita income, market for the specific product for consumer products and sales, and profits of particular companies for industrial products. In terms of market growth, the overall country growth should be determined as well as the growth rate for the particular market of the venture. Finally, appropriate product indicators, such as existing exports of the specific product category to the market and the number of sales leads and interest, should be established.

In Step 2, data for each of the indicators are collected and converted to facilitate comparison. Both primary data (original information collected for the particular requirement) and secondary data (published data already existing) need to be collected. Typically, secondary data are gathered first to establish what information needs to be collected through primary research. When collecting international secondary data, there are several problems that vary to some extent based on the stage of economic development of the country. These problems include (a) comparability (the data can be grouped differently in each country), (b) availability (some countries have much more country data than others, usually reflecting the stage of economic development), (c) accuracy (sometimes the data have not been collected using rigorous standards or are biased due to the interests of the government of the country; the latter is particularly a problem in nonmarket-oriented economies), and (d) cost of the data. The United States, with its Freedom of Information Act, makes all government-collected data that do not pertain to security or defense available to all. This is not the case in all countries. For example, one global entrepreneur was interested in opening the first Western health club in Moscow. He was going to charge two rates: a higher hard currency rate to foreigners and a lower ruble rate to Russians and other citizens of countries in the former Soviet Union. In determining the best location, he was interested in finding areas of the city where most foreigners lived. After significant searching to no avail and a high degree of frustration, he finally was able to buy the data needed from the former KGB (Soviet Union security branch).

When researching foreign markets, you will usually want economic and demographic data such as population, gross domestic product (GDP), per capita income, inflation rate, literacy rate, unemployment rate, and education levels. There are many sources for this and other foreign information at government agencies, websites, and embassies. One important source of data is the government of the country. There are also a large number of international reports—country reports, country analysis briefs (CABs), country commercial guides (CCGs), food market reports, international reports and reviews, Department of State background notes, and import/export reports. Other good sources of country data are trade associations and embassies.

The data for each selected indicator are then converted to point scores so each indicator from each country can be numerically ranked against the others. Various methods can be used to assign these values, each of which involves some judgment by the global entrepreneur. Another method is to compare country data for each indicator against global standards.

Step 3 establishes appropriate weights for the indicators that reflect the importance of each in predicting foreign market potential. For one company manufacturing hospital beds, the number and types of hospitals, the age of the hospitals and their beds, and the government expenditure on health care were the best country indicators in selecting a foreign market. This procedure results in each indicator receiving a weight that reflects its relative importance. The assignment of points and weights as well as the selection of indicators varies greatly from one global entrepreneur to another and, indeed, is somewhat arbitrary. Regardless, this requires intensive thinking and internal discussion, which results in better market selection decisions.

Step 4 involves analyzing the results. When looking at the data, the global entrepreneur needs to evaluate them carefully. A "what if" analysis can be conducted by changing some of the weights and seeing how the results vary.

Step 5 is the selection of a market to enter and follow-up markets so that an appropriate entry strategy can be determined and a market plan developed. China, India, Ireland, and Germany are countries that ICU Global, a videoconferencing provider, is targeting, according to founder and chief executive Stephen McKenzie. McKenzie feels it is easy to expand into other countries even when you are a small business as long as you can provide "the same quality assurance to end users" (Woods, 2008). He adds, "Technology allows you to provide full-support, virtual operations in other countries." The countries in question have been selected because they offer the greatest opportunities for ICU Global. "It's good to have a base in Germany because you can easily access the rest of Europe," McKenzie says. "Meanwhile, Ireland has a large number of companies from continental Europe and the United States investing in it, so there is good opportunity in the context of new technology. Then, there's a thriving technology center in India."

Developing Foreign Market Indicators

While some global entrepreneurs, especially those who have had success in their domestic markets, have an idea of the best foreign markets to enter based on sales or past experience, most do not. Thus, for those in this latter group, it is important to identify some indicators for potential success in foreign markets to assist in the selection process.

Internal Company Indicators

Several internal company indicators can be used to develop foreign market indicators, including competitive information, information from fellow global entrepreneurs, previous leads and sales, and trade show information. Foreign markets with good potential are ones that a company's competitors are entering.

Another good internal way to establish foreign market indicators is to discuss the various markets with noncompeting global entrepreneurs. These individuals can provide significant information based on their experience in specific foreign markets and advice on the potential of your company's product success in those markets. Sometimes you can even establish a mentoring relationship with a more experienced global entrepreneur.

A third source for developing marketing indicators is your company's past sales and leads. Leads and actual sales, while doing business domestically, from out-of-country markets are by far the best indicators of foreign market potential. Care needs to be taken to ensure that potential leads really are meaningful and not just distributors trying to establish product lines for their country. A sale in a foreign country signifies that at least for one customer, your product can compete.

The final sources for developing foreign market indicators are leads from domestic and foreign trade shows. These gather firms and buyers in a particular product area and provide a great opportunity to gather market information to determine market potential in various countries. They also provide an opportunity to gather competitive information on both domestic and foreign products.

Primary Versus Secondary Foreign Market Data

One of the most important aspects of any market selection decision is market and demographic information on the foreign country. This can be secondary data (data that are already published) or primary data (original data gathered specifically for the particular decision). Although primary data are generally more accurate, they are also more costly and time consuming to collect versus data that already exist and have been collected by third parties. It is usually best for the global entrepreneur to start the data-gathering process by first identifying the secondary data available about the foreign country.

Secondary Data

The first step in obtaining secondary data is to identify the classification codes associated with the company's product/service. These include the Standard Industrial Classification (SIC), the North American Industry Classification System (NAICS), the Standard International Trade Classification (SITC), and the International Harmonized Commodity Description and Coding System (International Harmonized Commodity Code), each of which will be discussed in turn.

The SIC code is appropriate for an initial appraisal of the extent and nature of the need in a foreign market, particularly for industrial products. SIC codes—the means by which the U.S. government classifies manufacturing industries—are based on the product produced or operation performed. Each industry is assigned a 2-, 3-, or, where needed for further breakdown, 4-digit code.

To determine the primary market demand using the SIC method, first determine all potential customers that have a need for the product/service being considered. Once the groups have been selected, the appropriate basis for demand determination is established and the published material on the industry groups obtained from the Census of Manufacturers. Then, the primary demand can be determined based on the size of the group and the expenditure in the product area. The website for using the SIC code is http://www.osha.gov/oshstats/sicser.html.

The NAICS is a newer system replacing the SIC system. This newer system is based on a 6-digit code versus the 4-digit code of the SIC system and has new industries, particularly in the service and technology sectors, that were not included in the SIC system. The NAICS system is used in the United States, Canada, and Mexico, allowing for greater country comparisons than previously available. The website for the NAICS system is http://www.census.gov/eos/www/naics/.

Once the global entrepreneur has obtained the codes for his or her product/service, these can be converted to the code system used in the European Union. Each NAICS Rev. 1.1 code is shown with its corresponding International Standard Industrial Classification (ISIC) Rev. 3.1 code on an easily accessible website (http://unstats.un.org/unsd/cr/regis try/regso.asp?Ci=26&Lg=1).

The final two coding systems are more useful for international data. The SITC, developed by the United Nations in 1950, is used to report international trade statistics. It classifies products and services based on a 5-digit code, but frequently, data are available at only the 2- or 3-digit code level. Each year, approximately 140 countries report their import and export trade statistics to the United Nations. The data are compiled and printed in the United Nations' *International Trade Statistics Yearbook*. The data are also available at their website (http://unstats.un.org/unsd).

The final and perhaps best system for obtaining international data is the Harmonized Commodity Description and Coding System, better known as the International Harmonized Commodity Codes. Each product or service is identified by a 10-digit number that is broken down by chapter (first two digits), heading (first four digits), subheading (first six digits), and the commodity code (all 10 digits). Here are some sample codes:

Name	International Harmonized Commodity Code
Peanut butter	2008.11.1000
Grand pianos	9201.20.0000
Farmed Atlantic salmon	0302.12.0003

Care must be taken when using the International Harmonized Commodity Codes because there may be differences between countries as well as variance within a country, depending on whether the codes are used for exporting or importing products. In the United States, for example, the purpose of the commodity codes is different for importing and exporting. For importing, the code is used to determine the import duty (if any); for exporting, the primary use of the code is for statistical reporting. This results in two sets of commodity codes in the United States: one set for importing and one set for exporting.

The exporting system of classification is labeled *Schedule B*, and the importing system of classification is called the *Harmonized Tariff Schedule*, maintained by the Office of Tariff Affairs and Trade Agreements.

Problems in Collecting Secondary Data

There are several problems in collecting international secondary data. The first, and perhaps the most troublesome one, is accuracy. Often, countries are not particularly rigorous in their data collection, resulting in data not reflective of the true situation in a country. Sometimes, particularly in more controlled countries, the data are collected to satisfy a political agenda rather than statistical reliability.

The second problem is comparability—the data available in one country may not be comparable to the data collected in another country. This may be due to the different methodologies used, errors in the data collection, or differences in applying the commodity coding system.

Lack of current data in a country is a third problem. In many growing countries, the frequency of data collection is much more sporadic than in more developed countries. In dynamically changing economies, four- to five-year-old data are obsolete and not very valuable in decision making.

The final problem in secondary data is the cost. In many countries, the data may only be available at a fairly high price.

Sources of Country Market Data

Finding useful, accurate data for your country selection decision can sometimes be challenging. Even for the global entrepreneur who has had experience collecting data in the United States, the process of collecting data in other countries is much more difficult and usually more expensive. There are several sources for both country market and industry data, discussed in the following sections.

Country Industry Market Data

Economic and country data on such things as age, population, GDP, inflation, literacy, and per capita income is often available from a variety of sources, depending on the country. The Central Intelligence Agency's *World Factbook* provides data on various aspects of a country, such as demographics of population, economic indicators, geography, military, politics, and resources available. CCGs are produced for most countries on a yearly basis. Each guide contains the following information on a country: executive summary, economic trends and outlook, political environment, marketing U.S. products and services, leading sectors for U.S. exports and investments, trade regulations and standards, investment climate, trade and project financing, and business travel. It also has numerous appendices in such areas as country data, domestic economy, trade, investment statistics, U.S. and country contacts, market research, and trade event schedules. These are invaluable to the global entrepreneur in understanding the numbers and trade possibilities in a country. Even though these data are mainly focused on the United States, the reports contain valuable information for global entrepreneurs regardless of country. The National Trade Data Bank (NTDB), maintained by the U.S. Department of Commerce, is also an important database available to the global entrepreneur at virtually no cost. The NTDB database comprises international reports, trade statistics, research, and leads on trading opportunities.

Another source of country market data is STAT-USA (Statistics USA). This international data source, managed by an agency of the U.S. Department of Commerce, is enormous and includes the just-discussed NTDB, Global Business Opportunities (GLOBUS) database, and the State of the Nation database. Contributed to by many governmental agencies, the STAT-USA has a multitude of international and national reports available, including the following:

- African Development Bank Business Opportunities
- Asia Commerce Overview
- Bureau of Export Administration (BXA) Annual Report
- Computer Markets
- CABS
- Directory of Feasibility Studies and Projects
- Fish and Fishery Product Imports and Exports
- Food Market Reports
- Foreign Labor Trends
- International Automotive Industry
- Latin American/Caribbean Business Bulletin
- Minerals Yearbook
- Steel Monitoring Report
- Telecommunications Information and Reports
- Trade Associations and Publications
- U.S. Foreign Trade Reports
- U.S. International Trade in Goods and Services
- World Agricultural Production Reports
- World Bank International Business Opportunities

Because this is just a small sampling of the reports and data available, it is important that every global entrepreneur look into STAT-USA when collecting the needed international data. Each country also has data on its STAT-(country name), such as STAT-Brazil.

One of the best sources of information is the World Bank, which uses various criteria to rank every country on the ease of doing business there. The index ranks countries (economies) from 1 to 178 and is calculated by averaging the percentile rankings on each of the 10 topics covered in *Doing Business: Economy Rankings* (2014). The criteria being ranked include ease of doing business, ease of starting a business, dealing with licenses, registering property, getting credit, protecting investors, paying taxes, trading across borders, enforcing contracts, and closing a business. The rankings for selected countries are shown in Table 5.1. Singapore, Hong Kong SAR China, New Zealand, and the United States were ranked 1, 2, 3, and 4, respectively, on the ease of doing business. New Zealand, Canada, Singapore, and Australia were ranked 1, 2, 3, and 4, respectively, on the ease of starting a business.

Table 5.1 Rankings of Countries on Various Business Criteria

Economy	Ease of Doing Business Rank	Starting a Business	Dealing with Construction Permits	Getting Electricity	Registering Property	Getting Credit	Protecting Investors	Paying Taxes	Trading across Borders	Enforcing Contracts	Resolving Insolvency
Singapore	1	3	3	6	28	3	2	5	1	12	4
Hong Kong SAR, China	2	5	1	5	89	3	3	4	2	9	19
New Zealand	3	1	12	45	2	3	1	23	21	18	12
United States	4	20	34	13	25	3	6	64	22	11	17
Denmark	5	40	8	18	7	28	34	12	8	32	10
Malaysia	6	16	43	21	35	1	4	36	5	30	42
Korea, Rep.	7	34	18	2	75	13	52	25	3	2	15
Georgia	8	8	2	54	1	3	16	29	43	33	88
Norway	9	53	28	17	10	73	22	17	26	4	2
United Kingdom	10	28	27	74	68	1	10	14	16	56	7
Australia	11	4	10	34	40	3	68	44	46	14	18
Finland	12	55	36	22	26	42	68	21	9	8	3
Iceland	13	52	41	1	12	42	52	37	50	3	11
Sweden	14	61	24	9	38	42	34	41	6	25	20
Ireland	15	12	115	100	57	13	6	6	20	62	8
Taiwan, China	16	17	7	7	31	73	34	58	18	84	16
Lithuania	17	11	39	75	6	28	68	56	15	17	44
Thailand	18	91	14	12	29	73	12	70	24	22	58
Canada	19	2	116	145	55	28	4	8	45	58	9
Mauritius	20	19	123	48	65	42	12	13	12	54	61
Germany	21	111	12	3	81	28	98	89	14	5	13

Economy	Ease of Doing Business Rank	Starting a Business	Dealing with Construction Permits	Getting Electricity	Registering Property	Getting Credit	Protecting Investors	Paying Taxes	Trading across Borders	Enforcing Contracts	Resolving Insolvency
Estonia	22	61	38	56	15	42	68	32	7	26	66
United Arab Emirates	23	37	5	4	4	86	98	1	4	100	101
Latvia	24	57	79	83	33	3	68	49	17	21	43
Macedonia, FYR	25	7	63	76	84	3	16	26	89	95	52
Saudi Arabia	26	84	17	15	14	55	22	3	69	127	106
Japan	27	120	91	26	66	28	16	140	23	36	1
Netherlands	28	14	97	70	47	73	115	28	13	29	5
Switzerland	29	104	58	8	16	28	170	16	35	20	47
Austria	30	138	94	28	36	28	98	79	19	6	14
Portugal	31	32	76	36	30	109	52	81	25	24	23
Rwanda	32	9	85	53	8	13	22	22	162	40	137
Slovenia	33	38	59	32	83	109	14	54	48	52	41
Chile	34	22	101	43	55	55	34	38	40	64	102
Israel	35	35	140	103	151	13	6	93	10	93	35
Belgium	36	49	100	90	180	73	16	76	28	16	6
Armenia	37	6	79	109	5	42	22	103	117	112	76
France	38	41	92	42	149	55	80	52	36	7	46
Cyprus	39	44	86	108	103	55	34	33	27	110	24
Puerto Rico (U.S.)	40	18	172	38	131	13	16	110	87	101	21
South Africa	41	64	26	150	99	28	10	24	106	80	82
Peru	42	63	117	79	22	28	16	73	55	105	110
Colombia	43	79	24	101	53	73	6	104	94	155	25

(Continued)

Table 5.1 (Continued)

Economy	Ease of Doing Business Rank	Starting a Business	Dealing with Construction Permits	Getting Electricity	Registering Property	Getting Credit	Protecting Investors	Paying Taxes	Trading across Borders	Enforcing Contracts	Resolving Insolvency
Montenegro	44	69	106	69	98	3	34	86	53	136	45
Poland	45	116	88	137	54	3	52	113	49	55	37
Bahrain	46	99	4	52	32	130	115	7	81	122	27
Oman	47	77	69	58	21	86	98	9	47	107	72
Qatar	48	112	23	27	43	130	128	2	67	93	36
Slovak Republic	49	108	53	65	11	42	115	102	108	65	38
Kazakhstan	50	30	145	87	18	86	22	18	186	27	54
Tunisia	51	70	122	55	72	109	52	60	31	78	39
Spain	52	142	98	62	60	55	98	67	32	59	22
Mexico	53	48	40	133	150	42	68	118	59	71	26
Hungary	54	59	47	112	45	55	128	124	70	15	70
Panama	55	25	62	16	74	55	80	175	11	127	112
Botswana	56	96	69	107	41	73	52	47	145	86	34
Tonga	57	42	35	30	146	55	115	51	63	48	118
Bulgaria	58	65	118	135	62	28	52	81	79	79	92
Brunei Darussalam	59	137	46	29	116	55	115	20	39	161	48
Luxembourg	60	103	37	66	124	170	128	15	41	1	53
Samoa	61	33	73	37	39	130	34	86	58	77	139
Fiji	62	141	74	81	63	55	52	88	111	63	50
Belarus	63	15	30	168	3	109	98	133	149	13	74
St. Lucia	64	57	11	31	129	130	34	45	104	170	56
Italy	65	90	112	89	34	109	52	138	56	103	33

Economy	Ease of Doing Business Rank	Starting a Business	Dealing with Construction Permits	Getting Electricity	Registering Property	Getting Credit	Protecting Investors	Paying Taxes	Trading across Borders	Enforcing Contracts	Resolving Insolvency
Trinidad and Tobago	66	67	77	10	178	28	22	97	73	174	114
Ghana	67	128	159	85	49	28	34	68	109	43	116
Kyrgyz Republic	68	12	66	180	9	13	22	127	182	70	132
Turkey	69	93	148	49	50	86	34	71	86	38	130
Azerbaijan	70	10	180	181	13	55	22	77	168	28	86
Antigua and Barbuda	71	92	21	20	128	130	34	151	93	65	80
Greece	72	36	66	61	161	86	80	53	52	98	87
Romania	73	60	136	174	70	13	52	134	76	53	99
Vanuatu	74	126	50	129	110	55	80	30	119	72	57
Czech Republic	75	146	86	146	37	55	98	122	68	75	29
Mongolia	76	25	107	162	27	55	22	74	181	30	133
Dominica	77	51	22	64	119	86	34	75	88	172	105
Moldova	78	81	174	165	19	13	80	95	150	23	91
Guatemala	79	145	61	34	23	13	157	85	116	97	109
Seychelles	80	118	68	147	69	170	68	19	29	82	65
San Marino	81	155	120	10	158	186	52	40	75	34	49
St. Vincent and the Grenadines	82	68	6	25	153	130	34	72	38	90	189
Zambia	83	45	57	152	102	13	80	68	163	120	73
Bahamas, The	84	83	75	45	182	86	115	45	72	125	32
Sri Lanka	85	54	108	91	145	73	52	171	51	135	59

(Continued)

Table 5.1 (Continued)

Economy	Ease of Doing Business Rank	Starting a Business	Dealing with Construction Permits	Getting Electricity	Registering Property	Getting Credit	Protecting Investors	Paying Taxes	Trading across Borders	Enforcing Contracts	Resolving Insolvency
Kosovo	86	100	136	121	58	28	98	43	121	138	83
Morocco	87	39	83	97	156	109	115	78	37	83	69
Uruguay	88	43	154	23	167	73	98	146	90	105	51
Croatia	89	80	152	60	106	42	157	34	99	49	98
Albania	90	76	189	158	119	13	14	146	85	124	62
Barbados	91	77	56	83	142	86	170	112	30	110	28
Russian Federation	92	88	178	117	17	109	115	56	157	10	55
Serbia	93	45	182	85	44	42	80	161	98	116	103
Jamaica	94	23	52	132	114	109	80	168	118	131	31
Maldives	95	71	18	131	161	109	80	115	138	90	40
China	96	158	185	119	48	73	98	120	74	19	78
Solomon Islands	97	82	81	130	172	86	52	30	78	109	127
Namibia	98	132	31	72	178	55	80	114	141	69	85
Vietnam	99	109	29	156	51	42	157	149	65	46	149
Palau	100	129	45	78	20	86	178	84	96	141	96
St. Kitts and Nevis	101	73	15	19	169	130	34	145	66	112	189
Costa Rica	102	102	82	47	46	86	170	136	44	130	124
Malta	103	161	163	115	77	180	68	27	34	122	64
Kuwait	104	152	133	59	90	130	80	11	112	119	94
Nepal	105	97	105	98	24	55	80	126	177	139	125
Belize	106	167	16	57	143	130	128	48	101	173	30
Grenada	107	72	9	71	157	130	34	90	61	166	189

Economy	Ease of Doing Business Rank	Starting a Business	Dealing with Construction Permits	Getting Electricity	Registering Property	Getting Credit	Protecting Investors	Paying Taxes	Trading across Borders	Enforcing Contracts	Resolving Insolvency
Philippines	108	170	99	33	121	86	128	131	42	114	100
Paraguay	109	113	71	50	71	86	68	125	154	102	152
Pakistan	110	105	109	175	125	73	34	166	91	158	71
Lebanon	111	120	179	51	112	109	98	39	97	126	93
Ukraine	112	47	41	172	97	13	128	164	148	45	162
Papua New Guinea	113	101	165	24	87	86	68	116	134	168	128
Marshall Islands	114	56	32	77	189	86	157	96	62	61	138
Guyana	115	94	33	155	111	170	80	110	71	73	141
Brazil	116	123	130	14	107	109	80	159	124	121	135
Dominican Republic	117	144	121	127	115	86	98	106	33	81	159
El Salvador	118	148	144	154	59	55	170	165	64	68	90
Jordan	119	117	111	41	104	170	170	35	57	133	113
Indonesia	120	175	88	121	101	86	52	137	54	147	144
Cabo Verde	121	66	135	151	64	109	138	80	95	35	189
Kiribati	122	156	133	159	73	165	52	10	77	74	189
Swaziland	123	172	51	163	130	55	128	59	127	176	68
Nicaragua	124	123	152	114	135	109	138	163	82	47	84
Ethiopia	125	166	55	91	113	109	157	109	166	44	75
Argentina	126	164	181	80	138	73	98	153	129	57	97
Honduras	127	162	83	125	94	13	170	144	84	182	136
Egypt, Arab Rep.	128	50	149	105	105	86	147	148	83	156	146

(Continued)

Table 5.1 (Continued)

Economy	Ease of Doing Business Rank	Starting a Business	Dealing with Construction Permits	Getting Electricity	Registering Property	Getting Credit	Protecting Investors	Paying Taxes	Trading across Borders	Enforcing Contracts	Resolving Insolvency
Kenya	129	134	47	166	163	13	98	166	156	151	123
Bangladesh	130	74	93	189	177	86	22	100	130	185	119
Bosnia and Herzegovina	131	174	175	164	96	73	115	135	107	115	77
Uganda	132	151	143	178	126	42	115	98	164	117	79
Yemen, Rep.	133	114	101	116	61	170	138	129	128	85	126
India	134	179	182	111	92	28	34	158	132	186	121
Ecuador	135	176	64	138	91	86	138	91	122	99	143
Lesotho	136	89	145	136	88	159	98	101	144	144	104
Cambodia	137	184	161	134	118	42	80	65	114	162	163
West Bank and Gaza	138	143	131	87	122	165	80	62	123	88	189
Mozambique	139	95	77	171	152	130	52	129	131	145	148
Burundi	140	27	126	161	52	170	34	143	175	177	164
Bhutan	141	86	132	91	86	109	147	104	172	37	189
Sierra Leone	142	75	176	179	170	86	22	128	140	149	158
Tajikistan	143	87	184	186	78	159	22	178	188	39	81
Liberia	144	31	129	142	181	86	147	42	142	165	161
Tanzania	145	119	177	102	146	130	98	141	139	42	134
Uzbekistan	146	21	159	173	136	130	138	168	189	40	63
Nigeria	147	122	151	185	185	13	68	170	158	136	107
Madagascar	148	29	157	187	155	180	68	61	115	160	157
Sudan	149	131	167	113	41	170	157	108	155	154	89
Gambia, The	150	130	104	120	117	165	178	184	99	60	108

Economy	Ease of Doing Business Rank	Starting a Business	Dealing with Construction Permits	Getting Electricity	Registering Property	Getting Credit	Protecting Investors	Paying Taxes	Trading across Borders	Enforcing Contracts	Resolving Insolvency
Iraq	151	169	20	39	108	180	128	63	179	142	189
Iran, Islamic Rep.	152	107	169	169	168	86	147	139	153	51	129
Algeria	153	164	147	148	176	130	98	174	133	129	60
Burkina Faso	154	125	60	141	123	130	147	160	174	108	117
Mali	155	136	113	118	99	130	147	157	160	140	131
Micronesia, Fed. Sts.	156	106	54	106	189	130	178	94	103	152	168
Togo	157	168	114	96	159	130	147	172	110	153	111
Comoros	158	163	44	109	79	159	138	123	146	159	189
Lao PDR	159	85	96	140	76	159	187	119	161	104	189
Djibouti	160	127	157	144	133	180	182	66	60	163	147
Suriname	161	181	49	40	173	170	186	50	105	184	160
Bolivia	162	180	136	128	144	130	138	185	126	131	67
Gabon	163	153	71	138	166	109	157	152	135	157	153
Afghanistan	164	24	167	104	175	130	189	98	184	168	115
Syrian Arab Republic	165	135	189	82	82	180	115	120	147	179	120
Equatorial Guinea	166	185	125	99	109	109	147	177	137	50	189
Côte d'Ivoire	167	115	162	153	127	130	157	173	165	88	95
Cameroon	168	132	127	62	159	109	128	180	159	175	151
São Tomé and Príncipe	169	98	103	73	165	186	157	156	102	183	166
Zimbabwe	170	150	170	157	93	109	128	142	167	118	156

(Continued)

Table 5.1 (Continued)

Economy	Ease of Doing Business Rank	Starting a Business	Dealing with Construction Permits	Getting Electricity	Registering Property	Getting Credit	Protecting Investors	Paying Taxes	Trading across Borders	Enforcing Contracts	Resolving Insolvency
Malawi	171	149	173	183	85	130	80	81	176	145	150
Timor-Leste	172	154	128	44	189	165	115	55	92	189	189
Mauritania	173	173	123	124	67	170	147	181	152	75	189
Benin	174	139	95	160	137	130	157	179	119	181	140
Guinea	175	146	155	91	140	159	178	186	136	134	145
Niger	176	159	164	123	80	130	157	162	178	143	154
Haiti	177	187	141	67	138	165	170	132	151	96	189
Senegal	178	110	165	182	174	130	170	182	80	167	122
Angola	179	178	65	170	132	130	80	155	169	187	189
Guinea-Bissau	180	159	119	188	170	130	138	153	125	148	189
Venezuela, RB	181	157	110	167	95	130	182	187	173	92	165
Myanmar	182	189	150	126	154	170	182	107	113	188	155
Congo, Dem. Rep.	183	185	90	142	133	159	147	176	171	177	167
Eritrea	184	188	189	95	184	186	115	150	170	67	189
Congo, Rep.	185	182	142	175	164	109	157	183	180	164	142
South Sudan	186	140	171	184	183	180	182	92	187	87	189
Libya	187	171	189	68	189	186	187	116	143	150	189
Central African Republic	188	177	156	177	141	109	138	188	185	180	
Chad	189	183	139	149	146	130	157	189	183	171	189

SOURCE: Doing Business. (2013). *Economy rankings*. Retrieved April 29, 2014, from http://www.doingbusiness.org/rankings

Trade Associations

Trade associations in the United States and throughout the world are also a good source for industry data about a particular country. Some trade associations do market surveys of their members' international activities and are strategically involved in international standards issues for their particular industry.

Trade Publications and Periodicals

There are numerous domestic and international publications specific to particular industries that are also good sources of information. The editorial content of these journals can provide interesting information and insights on trends, companies, and trade shows by giving a more local perspective on the particular market and market conditions. Sometimes trade journals are the best and often the only source of information on competition and growth rates in a particular country.

Competitive Positioning

One aspect of success in both international and domestic markets is competitive positioning—knowing the competition very well and being able to position your company and product in that product/market space. In positioning your company internationally, it is even more important to identify the strategy of each competitive company. The strategy will significantly affect the manner and commitment of a company in an international market, which in turn affects the nature and degree of its competitive behavior in that market. A competitive company's international strategy may not be the same as yours. If the global entrepreneur emphasizes the competitive analysis too much without taking into account the competitive company's strategy, then he or she can create a reactive strategy that can be totally ineffective and inappropriate. This is particularly important in developing economies where some companies use a "hit or miss" strategy, realizing that many of the markets will lose money and will not be viable over a long period of time.

The global entrepreneur should begin competitive positioning by first documenting the current strategy of each primary competitor. This can be organized by using the form method indicated in Table 5.2. Information on competitors can be gathered initially by using as much public information as possible and then by complementing this with a marketing research project. Newspaper articles, websites, catalogs, promotions, interviews with distributors and customers, and any other marketing or company information available should be reviewed. Articles that have been written on competitors can be found by using a computer search in any university or local library. These articles should be analyzed for information on competitor strategies and should identify the names of individuals who were interviewed, referenced, or even mentioned in the articles. Any of these individuals, as well as the author of the article, can then be contacted to obtain further information. All the information can then be summarized in the form in Table 5.3. Once the competitors' strategies have been summarized, the global entrepreneur should begin to identify the strengths and weaknesses of each competitor, as shown in the table.

Table 5.2	An Assessment of Competitor Market Strategies and Strengths and Weaknesses		

	Competitor A	**Competitor B**	**Competitor C**
Product or service strategies			
Pricing strategies			
Distribution strategies			
Promotion strategies			
Strengths and weaknesses			

SOURCE: Hisrich, R. D., Peters, M. P., & Shepherd, D. A. (2013). *Entrepreneurship: Starting, developing, and managing a new enterprise* (9th ed., p. 212). New York, NY: McGraw-Hill.

The information in Table 5.2 can then be used to formulate the market positioning strategy of the new venture. Will the new venture imitate a particular competitor or will it try to satisfy needs in the market that are not being filled by any other company? This analysis will enlighten the global entrepreneur and provide a solid basis for developing the market entry plan for the international market.

One method for analyzing a market opportunity and determining your competitive position is indicated in Table 5.3. Using this evaluation process, various elements of the opportunity are evaluated, such as (1) the creation and length of the opportunity, (2) its real and perceived value(s), (3) its risks and returns, (4) its competitive environment, (5) its industry, and (6) its fit with the personal skills and goals of the entrepreneur.

It is important that the global entrepreneur understand the nature and root cause of the opportunity. Is it technological change, market shift, government regulation, or competition? These factors and the resulting opportunity result in a different market size and time dimension. The market size and the length of the window of international opportunity form the primary basis for determining the risks and rewards involved. The amount of capital needed determines the returns and rewards.

In this evaluation, the competition is carefully analyzed. Features and potential price for the product/service need to be evaluated against those of competitive products presently in the product/market space in the country. If any major problems and competitive disadvantages are identified, modifications can be made or a new market investigated.

The relative advantages of the product/service versus competitive products can be determined through use of the following questions: How does the new idea compare with competitive products in terms of quality and reliability? Is the idea superior or deficient compared with products currently available in the market? Is this a good market opportunity? These questions and others can be used in a conversational interview. Here, selected individuals are asked to compare the idea against products presently filling that need. By comparing the characteristics and attributes of the new idea, some uniqueness of the idea can be determined.

To accurately evaluate the idea, it is helpful to define the potential needs of the market in terms of timing, satisfaction, alternatives, benefits and risks, future expectations, price-versus-product performance features, market structure and size, and economic conditions (see Table 5.3). These factors need to be evaluated in terms of the idea's competitive strength relative to each factor. This comparison with competitive products will indicate the strengths and weaknesses of the idea.

Table 5.3 Determining the Company's Competitive Position

Factor	Your Idea/ Capability	Competitive Company A's Idea/Capability	Competitive Company B's Idea/Capability	Differential Advantage	Unique Selling Proposition
Type of Need Continuing need Declining need Emerging need Future need					
Timing of Need Duration of need Frequency of need Demand cycle Position in life cycle					
Competing Ways to Satisfy Need Doing without Using present way Modifying present way					
Perceived Benefits/Risks Utility to customer Appealing characteristics Customer tastes and preferences Buying motives Consumption habits					

(Continued)

Table 5.3 (Continued)

Factor	Your Idea/ Capability	Competitive Company A's Idea/Capability	Competitive Company B's Idea/Capability	Differential Advantage	Unique Selling Proposition
Price Versus Performance Features Price-quantity relationship Demand elasticity Stability of price Stability of market					
Market Size Potential Market growth Market trends Market development requirements Threats to market					
Availability to Customer Funds General economic conditions Economic trends Customer income Financing opportunities					

SOURCE: Adapted from Hisrich, R. D. (1991). *Marketing decisions for new and mature products* (2nd ed.). Copyright 1991. Upper Saddle River, NJ: Prentice Hall.

Once the idea has been evaluated in terms of the need and the market, an initial value determination should be done. Financial issues such as cash outflow, cash inflow, contribution to profit, and return on investment need to be evaluated versus similar numbers and returns for other ideas. Using the form in Table 5.4, the dollar amount of each of the aspects can be determined as accurately as possible so that a quantitative evaluation can be performed. These figures will be revised many times as new information becomes available.

Table 5.4	Determining the Value of the Product/Service in the International Market

Value Consideration	Cost (in dollars)
Cash Outflow Research and development costs Marketing costs Capital equipment costs Other costs	
Cash Inflow Sales of new product Effect on additional sales Salvageable value	
Net Cash Flow Maximum exposure Time to maximum exposure Duration of exposure Total investment Maximum net cash in a single year	
Profit Profit from new product Profit affecting additional sales of existing products Fraction of total company profit	
Relative Return Return on shareholders' equity (ROE) Return on investment (ROI) Cost of capital Present value (PV) Discounted cash flow (DCF) Return on assets employed (ROA) Return on sales	
Comparisons Compared to other investments Compared to other product opportunities Compared to other investment opportunities	

SOURCE: Hisrich, R. D. (1991). *Marketing decisions for new and mature products* (2nd ed.). Copyright 1991. Upper Saddle River, NJ: Prentice Hall.

Finally, the product/service/international market must fit the personal skills and goals of the global entrepreneur. It is particularly important that the global entrepreneur be culturally sensitive to make the venture succeed. The global entrepreneur also needs to have the desire to go global. A global entrepreneur must believe in the idea so much that he or she will make the necessary sacrifices to develop the idea into a sound business model that will be the basis for a successful new venture in the international market.

International Competitive Information

There are many good international sources for competitive information. These include company information, databases, journals, newspapers, trade associations, and personal interviews.

Company Information

Particularly with publicly traded companies, the competitive companies provide a significant amount of data useful to the global entrepreneur. This is often the best and easiest source of competitive information and is usually very accurate, particularly for companies in developed economies. All company literature and information regarding their international activities should be collected. Sometimes this is very easily obtained at international trade shows, where more detailed information is available from the individuals staffing the company's booth. The website of the company should be thoroughly explored as well as the websites of overseas customers and distributors. Companies continually put more and more important information on their websites.

CULTURAL STORY

I was living in Colombia and one of the vice presidents from the Argentina headquarters had just arrived. It was just 10:00 a.m. and an assistant offered him a *tinto*.

In Spanish, *vino tinto* means "red wine." The VP was confused and could not understand how Colombians could start drinking so early, not to mention at work! He later discovered that *tinto* is the slang for "coffee"—at least in the city of Medellin.

SOURCE: Alanis, B. (2011, March 30). Tinto time! Retrieved January 22, 2015, from http://culturalconfusions.com/2011/03/30/tinto-time/

The international advertising of each competitive company should also be examined. This will help develop the market entry strategy and marketing campaign. This is also particularly helpful in providing much-needed pricing information. When possible, be sure to determine whether the advertisement was placed by the company or the distributor in the international market. If the advertisement mentions only one distributor as the contact and provides no details on how to reach the company or if there are products featured from more than one manufacturer, the advertisement was probably placed by the distributor. This is important because the manufacturer's direct involvement in the placement of the advertisement suggests that this particular market is a priority. Direct placement of advertisements in a market indicates a higher level of commitment and involvement in the particular market. The advertisements also provide insight into how the competitive company is competing in the particular market; a company's competitive strategies may vary from one international market to the next.

International Databases

Four primary databases provide good sources of international competitive information. These are the Directory of United States Exporters, Port Import Export Report Service (PIERS), United Nations' *International Trade Statistics Yearbook*, and United States Exports by Commodity.

The Directory of United States Exporters, published each year by the *Journal of Commerce*, is a combination of some information from PIERS and company responses to a questionnaire. The data for each company include the following:

- Address
- Telephone and fax numbers
- Number of employees
- Year established
- Bank SIC code
- Modes of transportation used
- Contact names and titles
- Commodity code and description of products exported
- Destination countries
- Annual 20-foot equivalent units (TEUs) of containers
- Annual number of shipments
- Company PIERS identification numbers

Sometimes one of the most important pieces of information—destination country—is not reported directly but simply indicated as "worldwide." The Directory of United States Exporters is available in both print and CD-ROM versions directly from the *Journal of Commerce* and can often be used at the state trade assistance center.

The second useful database is the PIERS. The information in this database comes from the manifests of vessels loading international cargo outbound from the United States as well as the manifests of all inbound shipments (imports). Although not every item is available in every situation, the information in the PIERS database includes the following:

- Product description
- PIERS product code
- Harmonized tariff code and description
- U.S. and overseas port name

- Container size, quantity, TEU count, and cubic feet
- Steamship line and vessel name
- Manifest number
- Cargo quantity and unit of measure
- Cargo weight
- Voyage number
- Estimated cargo value
- Payment type
- Bank name
- Shipment direction
- U.S. and overseas origins and destinations
- Marks and numbers
- Name and address of U.S. importer (imports only)
- Bill of lading number
- Name and address of U.S. exporter
- Container number
- Name and address of foreign shipper (imports only)
- Customs clearing district (imports only)
- Name and address of notify party
- Arrival and departure dates in U.S. ports

The PIERS database has been expanded to include the shipping activities of most ports of Latin American countries and Mexico.

Other good databases for industry, market, and competitive analysis are indicated in Table 5.5.

Table 5.5 Some Example Databases

- Industry Analysis
  - IBISWorld (http://www.ibisworld.com)
  - Business Source Complete (http://www.ebscohost.com/academic/business-source-complete)
  - Datamonitor (http://datamonitor.com)
  - Plunkett Research (http://www.plunkettresearch.com)
  - Hoovers (http://www.hoovers.com)

- Competitive Landscape and Trends
  - Mint Global (http://mintglobal.bvdinfo.com; best for private firms)
  - Frost & Sullivan (http://ww2.frost.com/)
  - Gartner (http://www.gartner.com/)
  - Trade journals
  - Trade Show News Network (http://www.tsnn.com)

> - ○ Economist Intelligent Unit (http://www.eiu.com/; country database)
> - ○ ISI Emerging Markets
>
> - Market Analysis
>
>   - ○ SRDS (http://next.srds.com/home; local market analysis)
>   - ○ Euromonitor (http://www.euromonitor.com/; consumer data by country)
>   - ○ Corporate Affiliations (http://www.corporateaffiliations.com/)
>   - ○ Census reports
>
>   - ○ http://www.factfinder.census.gov
>   - ○ http://www.census.gov/econ/cbp/ (country business patterns)
>
>   - ○ D&B Million Dollar database (http://www.mergentmddi.com/; supplies and distribution)
>   - ○ Kompass (http://kompass.com/; suppliers and databases)
>
> - Financial Ratios
>
>   - ○ RAM E-statement
>   - ○ Bizstats (http://bizstats.com)
>   - ○ IBIS World (http://ibisworld.com/)

Journals, Newspapers, and Trade Associations

Journals, newspapers, and trade associations provide another very valuable source of information on competition. Most trade journals are very industry specific and can focus on international activities in that industry. There are also industry trade journals in foreign markets. From these, competitive product and other competitive information, distribution lists, advertisements, and other industry data can be easily obtained at little or no cost through the various search and retrieval options available. Many are available on the Internet.

While not usually as valuable, newspapers can also provide competitive information, particularly the local newspaper in the city where the competitive company is headquartered. The local newspaper often provides information not found anywhere else in its coverage of the company and interviews with company managers.

Finally, trade associations in the industry often have summary data on sales and pricing in the industry. Most trade associations track international trends and data. Even just a list of association members provides information about the companies interested in a particular industry.

Personal Interviews

Probably the best and most comprehensive source of competitive information comes from personal interviews with individuals who really know the competitor company and international market. By interviewing these individuals and staff writers of journals and newspapers, the global entrepreneur can obtain up-to-date information. Even though sometimes they are not company specific, government contacts in a particular country can provide information about competitive trends and challenges. Industry experts can provide detailed information on the industry and usually on companies in that industry. And, best of all, foreign customers and distributors can provide detailed information about the local market and the activities of competitors.

While you need to analyze foreign markets and the competition and adapt your product/service to meet local market needs to expand internationally, you will also need a person to run the operation. No one knows this better than Bruce McGaw, president of Bruce McGaw Graphics, a West Nyack, New York, fine-arts poster publisher. "As smart as I am about the American market, my knowledge doesn't necessarily apply abroad," admits McGaw (Fenn, 1995). Rather than sending one of his U.S. employees to establish a London distributorship, he decided to search for a local manager to run his United Kingdom operation. Because he did not want to "run over there every other week," he began searching for "someone talented, who would take the ball and run with it." The individual needed the following:

- Significant industry experience and real marketplace intelligence
- An understanding that customer service was central to the company's success
- The ability to take charge and run the business as if it were "his own little business"

McGaw found the right individual—a customer whose business was struggling. McGaw Graphics bought the company and the individual became the UK manager. Five years later, European sales accounted for $3.5 million of the company's total $15 million in revenue; the UK operation was considered a market leader. McGaw used a similar strategy in France when he acquired a business run by an American. "Where you set up your business is not as important as finding the right person to run it," says McGaw. Although his strategic plan includes expansion into Germany, Italy, and Spain, McGaw will not move until he finds the right managers.

SUMMARY

This chapter discusses researching and selecting the best foreign market(s) to launch a company internationally. Finding the best market is only possible with thorough research using multiple resources. The chapter describes an effective five-step foreign market selection process: (1) develop appropriate indicators, (2) collect data and convert into comparable indicators, (3) establish an appropriate weight for each indicator, (4) analyze the data, and (5) select the appropriate market from the market rankings. A global entrepreneur must determine the best indicators for whether or not the company will do well in the foreign market and then collect information based on those indicators from federal and international commerce and trade institutions as well as from competitors and other global entrepreneurs that are working in the same market. At least three years of detailed information needs to be collected and analyzed to develop a trend. The information will be either from primary sources, which is a more costly and time-consuming process, or secondary sources, which normally take much less time to access. The main problems that a global entrepreneur will find with secondary data are the comparability between countries/regions and lack of specificity. Analyzing the strengths and weaknesses of the competitors' strategies can provide guidelines for developing the best strategy and determining the most appropriate market.

QUESTIONS FOR DISCUSSION

1. What types of information should global entrepreneurs seek out before deciding which foreign market to enter?

2. What are the different types and sources of information that are available?

3. What are some potential problems with data collected in another country?

4. Jean-Marie is considering expanding her bakery business from France into Croatia. What information would help her determine a good location to start her business there?

CHAPTER EXERCISES

1. Pick a business and create the key indicators that you will use to analyze the new market.

2. Using the same business you chose for Exercise 1, outline the information that you will need to collect about the new market.

3. Finally, create a list of competitors in the new market and identify primary sources to interview about these competitors.

REFERENCES

Doing Business. (2014). *Economy rankings.* Retrieved April 29, 2014, from http://www.doingbusiness .org/rankings

Fenn, D. (1995, June). Opening up an overseas operation. *Inc., 17*(8), 89.

Woods, C. (2008, April 8). ICU Global grabs international opportunities. *Real Business.* Retrieved January 21, 2015, from http://realbusiness.co.uk/article/737-icu_global_grabs_international_ opportunities

SUGGESTED READINGS

Butler, J. E., Doktor, R., & Lins, F. A. (2010). Linking international entrepreneurship to uncertainty, opportunity discovery, and cognition. *Journal of International Entrepreneurship, 8*(2), 121–134. *Business Source Complete.* Web. 29 Oct. 2013.

   This article presents a cognitive model for realizing opportunities and dealing with uncertainty in international entrepreneurial ventures. Cognitive processes of international entrepreneurs, along with cultural differences, are described in terms of how they influence the global entrepreneur's ability to identify opportunities as well as to tolerate risk.

Chandra, Y., Styles, C., & Wilkinson, I. F. (2012). An opportunity-based view of rapid internationalization. *Journal of International Marketing, 20*(1), 74–102. *Business Source Complete*. Web. 29 Oct. 2013.

> The authors suggest using an "opportunity-based view" (OBV) rather than a firm-based view to better comprehend rapid internationalization patterns. They describe historical patterns of dynamic entrepreneurial processes to show how path-dependent opportunity developments are influenced by international and domestic networks.

Liesch, P., Welch, L., & Buckley, P. (2011). Risk and uncertainty in internationalisation and international entrepreneurship studies. *Management International Review (MIR), 51*(6), 851–873. *Business Source Complete*. Web. 29 Oct. 2013.

> This article explains risk and uncertainty in international expansion. In international entrepreneurship literature, high levels of risk and uncertainty restrain forward momentum. The article aims to describe concepts of "risk accommodation and uncertainty acclimatization" in order to appreciate how uncertainty and risk change over time.

Reuber, A. R., & Fischer, E. (2011). International entrepreneurship in Internet-enabled markets. *Journal of Business Venturing, 26*(6), 660–679. *Business Source Complete*. Web. 29 Oct. 2013.

> The article describes the latent potential for using the Internet to pursue global opportunities. It explains how online reputation, technological capabilities, and Internet-brand communities are correlated to success in the pursuit of global opportunities in online markets.

6

Developing the Global Business Plan

Profile: Aentropico

As companies both large and small become able to collect more information about their customers, people seem to become overwhelmed with the amount of data available. Many different departments within one company collect data not only about their current customers but also about their past and potential future customers. Then there are also outside organizations that collect data simply so others do not necessarily have to. Technology has become so advanced in recent years that companies must now deal with a mountain of data and are often unsure how to actually acquire the answer to a specific question or concern. The Latin American company Aentropico was founded to provide global businesses with the opportunity to tackle the issue of big data: The company was established to "turn messy data into crisp decisions."

Aentropico was founded by Sebastián Pérez Saaibi (CEO) and Juan Pablo Marín Díaz (CIO) in Colombia in February 2012. Although some large corporations are already in possession of and making use of the solutions provided, this company aimed to offer applications to sort through big data to any other company that could benefit from it. The company has developed various DataApps, which transform vast amounts of data into valuable insights for decision makers. This data transformation has the ability to save managers time and provide them with an easy and user friendly way to utilize any data they have available. In essence, this firm's mission is to be a new player in this fast-growing market, which is also becoming highly competitive very fast, by democratizing "access to high quality predictive analytics for decision makers." Its objective is to become the "top Predictive Analytics platform in Latin America" within only three years.

Selected as one of twelve "Latin American startups to look out for in 2014," the firm was initially backed by Fundación Bavaria and INNpulsa, and received start-up capital from Start-Up Chile and Argentina's NXTP Labs. The company has also taken part in 21212's acceleration program in Rio de Janeiro. "In addition, Aentropico's founders received support from Boston-based accelerator, MassChallenge, and Massachusetts-based open innovation company, Innocentive." Still a very young company, Aentropico has set several aggressive growth objectives and could perhaps become one of the top Latin American companies to keep an eye on. The team definitely seems to have the motivation and passion to move their company forward. Breaking through in this highly competitive industry will certainly prove challenging, though. The quality of Aentropico's global business plan will be likely to determine whether this company can achieve its aggressive short-term goals.

SOURCES: Aentropico [website]. (n.d.). Retrieved February 11, 2015, from http://www.aentropi.com

Heim, A. (2013, December 28). 12 Latin American startups to look out for in 2014. Retrieved April 26, 2014, from http://thenextweb.com/la/2013/12/28/12-latin-american-startups-look-2014/.

Chapter Objectives

1. To know the internal and external purposes of a global business plan
2. To be able to identify all the parts of the business plan and the direction for each department or organizational function of the company
3. To be able to create a global business plan from the outline and sample provided

Introduction

In today's highly competitive business environment, there is perhaps nothing more important than developing a business plan. In any organization, there are many different types of plans, such as financial, human resource, marketing, production, and sales. These plans may be short-term or long-term, strategic or operational, and may vary greatly in scope. In spite of the differences in scope and coverage, each plan has a common purpose: to provide guidance and structure on a continuing basis for managing the organization in a rapidly changing, hypercompetitive environment. This chapter will first look at an opportunity assessment plan. Then the purpose and aspects of a global business plan will be discussed. The chapter will conclude with a discussion of the do's and don'ts of a plan.

Opportunity Assessment Plan

Every innovative idea and opportunity needs to be carefully assessed by the global entrepreneur. A good way to do this is by developing an opportunity assessment plan. An opportunity assessment plan is *not* a business plan, as it focuses on the idea and the market (the opportunity) for the idea, not on the venture. It also is shorter than a business plan and does not contain any formal financial statements of the business venture. The opportunity assessment plan is developed to serve as the basis for the decision to either act on the opportunity or wait until another, better opportunity comes along. A typical opportunity assessment plan has four sections: (1) a description of the idea and its competition, (2) an assessment of the domestic and international market for the idea, (3) an assessment of the entrepreneur and the team, and (4) a determination of the steps needed to make the idea the basis for a viable business venture.

The Idea and Its Competition

This section focuses on one of the major areas of the opportunity assessment plan: the idea itself and the competition. The product or service first needs to be described in as much detail as possible. A prototype or schematic of the product is often helpful in fully understanding all its aspects and features. All competitive products and competitive companies in the product (service) market space need to be identified and listed. The new product/service idea should be compared with at least three of the most competitive products/services that are most similar in filling the same identified market need. This analysis will result in a description of how the new product/service is different and unique and will indicate its unique selling propositions. If the idea does not have at least three to five unique selling propositions versus competitive products/services on the market, the global entrepreneur needs to more carefully examine whether the idea is really unique enough to compete and be successful in the market. The competitive products/ services available can be found through the use of the counting system of the country used to determine the country's gross domestic product (GDP). This is the North American Industry Classification System (NAICS) country code system for the United States, the Standard Industrial Classification (SIC) for Korea, and a different SIC system for China.

The Market and the Opportunity

The second section of the opportunity assessment plan addresses the size and the characteristics of the market. Market data should be collected for at least the past three years so that a trend is apparent for the overall industry, the overall market, the market segment, and the target market. This can be done by gathering as much secondary (published) data as possible. For example, if you had an idea for a motorized wheelchair for small children that was shaped like a car, you would get market statistics on the health care industry (overall industry), wheelchairs (overall market), motorized wheelchairs (market segment), and children needing wheelchairs (target market). This funnel approach indicates the overall industry market size as well as the size of the specific target market.

In the consumer market, data on one of the three most widely used consumer demographic variables—age, income, or gender—for the geographic area should be collected for the last three years.

Not only should the size of these markets be determined but also their characteristics. Is the market made up of a few large companies or many small ones? Does the market respond quickly or slowly to new entrants? How many (if any) new products are introduced each year in the market? How geographically dispersed is the market? What market need is being filled? What social conditions underlie this market? What other products might the company also introduce into this market? Based on this section of the opportunity assessment plan, the entrepreneur should be able to determine both the size and the characteristics of the market and whether it is large enough and suitable enough to warrant the time and effort required to proceed and perhaps actually enter the market.

Entrepreneur and Team Assessment

Next, both the entrepreneur and the entrepreneurial team need to be assessed. At least one person on the team needs to have experience in the industry area of the new idea. This is one characteristic that correlates to the probability of success of the venture. Several questions need to be answered, such as why does this idea and opportunity excite you? Will this idea and opportunity sustain you once the initial excitement has worn off? How does the idea and opportunity fit your personal background and experience? How does it fit the personal background, experience, and skills of the entrepreneurial team? This section of the opportunity assessment plan is usually shorter than the previous two sections and allows the entrepreneur to determine if indeed he or she is really excited and suited to successfully move the idea into the market.

The Next Steps

This final section of the opportunity assessment plan delineates the critical steps that need to be taken to make the idea a reality in the marketplace. The steps need to be identified and put in sequential order, and the time and the money needed for each step needs to be determined. If the idea cannot be self-financed, then sources of capital need to be identified. The entrepreneur should always keep in mind that most entrepreneurs tend to underestimate both the costs and the time needed for each step by about 30%.

Some questions to answer when developing an opportunity assessment plan are listed in Table 6.1.

Purpose of a Global Business Plan

Given the hypercompetitive environment and the difficulties of doing business outside your home country, a global business plan is an integral part of strategically managing an organization. A global business plan is a written document prepared by the entrepreneur that describes all the relevant external and internal elements in going global. By describing all the relevant external and internal elements involved in starting and managing a global organization, the business plan integrates the functional plans (such as finance, marketing, and organizational plans), thereby providing a road map for the future of the organization.

Often, a global business plan is read by a variety of stakeholders and can have several different purposes. It needs to be comprehensive enough to address the issues

Table 6.1	Questions for the Development of an Opportunity Assessment Plan

Description of the Product or Service Idea and Competition

- What is the market need for the product/service?
- What are the specific aspects of the product/service (including any copyright, patent, or trademark information)?
- What competitive products are already available and filling this need?
- What are the competitive companies in this product market space? Describe their competitive behavior.
- What are the strengths and weaknesses of each of your competitors?
- What is the country code(s) for this product/service?
- What are the unique selling propositions of this product or service?
- What patents might be available to fulfill this need?
- What are total industry sales in this country code category for the past five years?
- What is anticipated growth in this industry?
- What, if any, new products have been recently introduced in this industry?

An Assessment of the Market

- What market need does the product/service fill?
- What are the size and past trends over the last three years of this market?
- What are the future growth prospects and characteristics of this market?
- What does the international market look like?
- What is the profile of your typical customers?

Entrepreneurial Self-Assessment and the Entrepreneurial Team

- Why does this opportunity excite you?
- What are your reasons for going into this business?
- Will this opportunity sustain you once the initial excitement subsides?
- How does this opportunity fit into your background, experience, and skills?
- What experience will you need to successfully implement the business plan?
- What are the skills, experiences, and backgrounds of other members of your team?

Next Steps for Translating This Opportunity Into a Viable Venture

- What are the critical steps to go forward?
- What is the sequence of activities (steps) to launch the venture?
- What is the amount of time and the amount of money needed at each step?
- Where will the money needed come from?

and concerns of advisers, bankers, consultants, customers, employees, investors, and venture capitalists. It can also serve such purposes as to obtain financial resources, obtain other resources, develop strategic alliances, or provide direction and guidance for the organization. Although a global business plan can serve these various purposes, its most frequent use is to obtain financial resources. Bankers, investors, and venture capitalists will not take an investment possibility seriously without a comprehensive global business plan. Some will not even meet with a global entrepreneur without first reviewing the global business plan. A well-developed global business plan is important because it (1) provides guidance to the entrepreneur and managers in decision making and organizing the international direction of the company, (2) indicates the viability of an organization in the designated global market(s), and (3) serves as the vehicle for obtaining financing.

Aspects of a Global Business Plan

Given the importance and purpose of a global business plan, it is important that it be comprehensive and covers all aspects of the organization. The plan will be read by a variety of individuals, each of whom is looking for a certain level of detail (Taylor, 2006). As is indicated in Table 6.2, the global business plan can be divided into several areas, each of which has several sections.

Table 6.2 Outline of an International Business Plan

I. Title Page, Table of Contents, and Executive Summary

- Three-page description of the project

II. Introduction

- The type of business proposed and an in-depth description of the major product/service involved, a description of the country proposed for market entry, the rationale for selecting the country, identification of existing trade barriers, and identification of sources of information

III. Analysis of the International Business Opportunity

A. Economic, Political, and Legal Analysis of the Trading Country

   1. The trading country's economic system, economic information important to the proposed product/service, and the level of foreign investment in that country

   2. The trading country's governmental structure and stability and how the government regulates trade and private business

   3. Laws and/or governmental agencies that affect the product/service, such as labor laws and trade laws

B. Trade Area and Cultural Analysis

    1. Geographic and demographic information, important customs and traditions, other pertinent cultural information, and competitive advantages and disadvantages of the proposed business opportunity

IV. Operation of the Proposed Business

A. Organization

- Type of ownership and rationale; start-up steps to form the business; personnel (or functional) needs; proposed staffing to handle managerial, financial, marketing, legal, and production functions; proposed organizational chart; and brief job descriptions

B. Product/Service

    1. Product/service details include potential suppliers, manufacturing plans, and inventory policies

    2. Transportation information: costs, benefits, risks of the transportation method, documents needed to transport the product

C. Market Entry Strategy

D. Marketing Strategy Plan

    1. Pricing policies: what currency will be used; costs; markups; markdowns; relation to competition; factors that could affect the price of the product, such as competition, political conditions, taxes, tariffs, and transportation costs

    2. Promotional program: promotional activities, media availability, costs, and a one-year promotional plan outline

V. Financials

A. Projected Income and Expenses

    1. Pro forma income statements for first three years operation

    2. Pro forma cash flow statements for first three years of operation

    3. Pro forma balance sheet for the end of the first year

B. Sources and Uses of Funds Statement

    1. Country statistics

    2. Partner information

    3. Relevant laws

VI. Appendix (Exhibits)

Executive Summary

The first area, although the shortest, is perhaps the most significant, particularly when the purpose is to secure financing. This area consists of the title page, table of contents, and executive summary. The title page should contain the following information: (1) the name, address, telephone and fax numbers, and e-mail address of the organization; (2) the name and position of the principal individuals in the organization; (3) three to four sentences briefly describing the nature of the organization and the purpose of the business plan; and (4) a statement of confidentiality, such as "This is confidential business plan number 3, which cannot be reproduced without permission." This statement is important, as each numbered business plan needs to be accounted for by recording the person and organization of the individual receiving it and the date of receipt. When trying to obtain financing, this is particularly essential, as follow-up can be scheduled at the appropriate time, which is about 30 days from the receipt date and then in regular 30-day intervals. As one venture capitalist commented, "One way I get a feel for the hunger and drive of the entrepreneur is by waiting to see if he or she initiates follow-up at the appropriate time."

The table of contents is perhaps the easiest part of the business plan to develop. It should follow the standard format, with major sections and appendixes (exhibits) indicated along with the appropriate page numbers.

The final part of this first primary area of the global business plan—the executive summary—is the most important, particularly when the purpose of the plan is to secure financing or other resources. The executive summary should be no more than three pages. It is frequently used by upper-level managers, investors, venture capitalists, and bankers to determine if the entire business plan is worth reading and analyzing. The executive summary becomes the screen or hurdle that determines whether more detailed attention will be given to the plan. Imagine a typical venture capitalist who receives more than a hundred 150-page business plans per month. He or she needs to employ some mechanism for screening this large number down to perhaps 10 to 15 plans for more focused initial attention.

Given its importance, the executive summary should be written last and be written and rewritten until it highlights the organization in a concise and convincing manner, covering the key points in the business plan. The executive summary should emphasize the three most critical areas for the success of the organization. In order of importance, these are the characteristics, capabilities, and experiences of the entrepreneur and management team; the nature and degree of innovativeness of the product or service and its market size and characteristics; and the expected results in terms of sales and profits over the next five years.

Introduction

The second section of the global business plan is the introduction, where the focus is on the new global initiative, the product/service to be offered, and the country to be entered. A detailed description of the global initiative provides important information on the size and scope of the opportunity. Besides delineating the mission and purpose of the initiative, an in-depth discussion of the product/service to be offered should be provided. The questions in Table 6.3 will help the global entrepreneur prepare this section.

The introduction also needs to discuss the proposed country, the selection process, existing trade barriers, and sources of information (This is discussed in Chapter 5). Even though these terms are further developed in later sections of the global business plan, they should be summarized in this introductory section. Some key questions that should be considered by the global entrepreneur concerning the needed environmental and industry analysis in developing this section are provided in Table 6.4.

Table 6.3	Describing the Venture

1. What is the mission of the new venture?
2. What are your reasons for going into business?
3. Why will you be successful in this venture?
4. What development work has been completed to date?
5. What is your product(s) and/or service(s)?
6. Describe the product(s) and/or service(s), including patent, copyright, or trademark status.
7. Where will the business be located?
8. Is the building leased or owned? (State the terms.)
9. What office equipment will be needed?
10. Will this equipment be purchased or leased?

SOURCE: Adapted from Hisrich, R. D., Peters, M. A., & Shepherd, D. A. (2013). *Entrepreneurship* (9th ed., p. 198). Burr Ridge, IL: McGraw-Hill/Irwin.

Table 6.4	Issues for Environmental and Industry Analysis

1. What are the major economic, technological, legal, and political trends on a national and an international level?
2. What are total industry sales over the past five years?
3. What is anticipated growth in this industry?
4. How many new firms have entered this industry in the past three years?
5. What new products have been recently introduced in this industry in the last three years?
6. Who are the competitive companies?
7. What are the competitive products/services?
8. Are the sales of each of your major competitors growing, declining, or steady?
9. What are the strengths and weaknesses of each of your competitors?
10. What trends are occurring in your specific market area?
11. What is the profile of your customers?
12. How does your customer profile differ from that of your competition?

SOURCE: Adapted from Hisrich, R. D., Peters, M. A., & Shepherd, D. A. (2013). *Entrepreneurship* (9th ed., p. 197). Burr Ridge, IL: McGraw-Hill/Irwin.

Analysis of the International Business Opportunity

The third section of the global business plan addresses the international business opportunity. Since this area, to some extent, has been addressed in Chapter 3 (Cultures and International Entrepreneurship) and will be covered in Chapter 8 (Alternative Entry Strategies), only an overview will be presented here. Two focus areas should be addressed in this section—the target country's culture and the overall economic, political, and legal environment of the country. It is important to understand the economic system operating in the country, including the various financial institutions and, particularly, the banking system. Frequently, especially in developing countries, it can be difficult to get funds transferred in and out of a country. In one country where one of the author's companies was doing business, currency needed to be hand carried into the country, with transactions taking place in cash because the banking system operated very slowly at a very high cost per transaction; funds were not available in a timely manner.

The government structure and its stability as well as the various laws affecting trade and businesses need to be examined. This is particularly important in deciding the best organizational structure, which is discussed in section four of the global business plan (see Table 6.2). Also, trade and labor laws often affect a country entrance decision as well as the effect of doing business there. McDonald's, when entering Hungary in 1988, needed to get special dispensation from labor law from the Hungarian government (then under control of the Soviet Union) to be able to fire workers who were not performing to its standards. Some countries have very high legally mandated severance costs, making it less desirable to do business there. As is indicated in Figure 6.1, while there are 0 weeks in pay in severance costs legally mandated in the United States, labor laws require 8.6 weeks in Japan, 55.9 weeks in India, 91.0 weeks in China, 186.3 weeks in Egypt, and 446.3 weeks in Zimbabwe. Even though Indonesia should be well positioned to attract manufacturing because of the country's low wages and high productivity, its labor law requiring 108.3 weeks of pay in severance costs is a major deterrent to companies investing in manufacturing facilities there. One factory producing Lee Cooper brand jeans facing a cash-flow problem found it more economical to declare bankruptcy with all its workers losing their jobs rather than downsizing and laying off enough of the 1,500 employees to keep the business going at a lower level of output.

The second part of this section—cultural analysis—is equally important. The customs and traditions of the country need to be analyzed as well as any competitive products or services available. This will lead the global entrepreneur to identify the competitive advantages and disadvantages of the particular business opportunity.

The fourth section of the global business plan—the operation of the proposed business—is a most significant one. The organization, product/service, market entry strategy, and overall marketing strategy all need to be delineated.

Operation of the Proposed Business

The organizational plan is the part of the business plan that describes the venture's form of ownership—such as proprietorship, partnership, or corporation in the United

Figure 6.1 Legally Mandated Severance Costs in Select Countries (in Weeks of Pay)

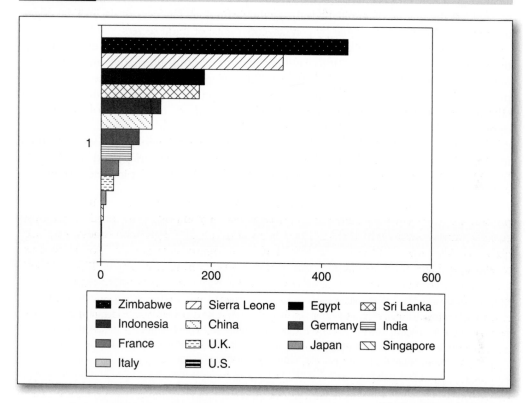

States. If the venture is a partnership, the terms of the partnership should be included. It is also important to provide an organizational chart indicating the line of authority and the responsibilities of the members of the organization. Some of the key questions the entrepreneur needs to answer in preparing this section of the business plan are listed below:

- What is the form of ownership of the organization?
- If a partnership, who are the partners and what are the terms of agreement?
- If incorporated, who are the principal shareholders and how much stock do they own?
- How many shares of voting or nonvoting stock have been issued and what type?
- Who are the members of the board of directors?
- Who are the members of the management team and what are their backgrounds?
- What are the roles and responsibilities of each member of the management team?
- What are the salaries, bonuses, or other forms of payment for each member of the management team?

This information provides a clear understanding of who will run and manage the organization and how other members will interact when performing their management functions.

The product/service to be produced and/or offered needs to be succinctly described. For technology-based products, this section should provide information on the nature of the technology; the unique differential advantage the technology has over rivals; and the degree that the technology is protectable by patents, copyrights, or trade secrets.

This section of the global business plan also describes the market entry strategy, the focus of Chapter 8. Suffice it to say here that the various alternative entry strategies need to be carefully considered by the global entrepreneur and the one most appropriate for the country/product/market situation selected. The entry strategy needs to take into account potential suppliers, manufacturing plans, inventory policies, and an operations plan.

The operations of the proposed business section of the business plan goes beyond the manufacturing process (when the new venture involves manufacturing) and describes the flow of goods and services from production to the customer. It might include inventory or

CULTURAL STORIES

Story 1

Two colleagues and I were invited to speak at a conference in Amman. At the conclusion of the program, the host invited us to dinner at a beautiful Lebanese restaurant. An extensive English-language menu was brought out from which we were to make our food selections. As I thumbed through the pages, I noticed that the desserts preceded the entrees in the menu, and being naturally curious about the culture, I asked if eating dessert before the main meal was traditional practice in Lebanon.

Everyone laughed, naturally, since it is well known that Arabic is read in the opposite direction than English. The host kindly jumped in and selected a wonderful variety of dishes for us, and we ended up having a delightful evening.

Story 2

Twenty-five years ago when my family first moved to the United States from Poland, my mom heard it was popular for kids to celebrate their birthdays at McDonalds, and decided that's where she would have my third birthday party.

She picked up the phone book, looked up "McDonald," selected a location that was closest to our house, and called the number. When a woman answered the phone, my mom informed her, "I would like to have my daughter's birthday party at your place." The woman finally understood what was going on and responded, "I would love to host a birthday party here, but my house is just too small."

It turns out that my mom, not realizing the difference between the white pages and the yellow pages, had attempted to schedule a party at someone's house with the last name of McDonald rather than the fast-food chain!

SOURCES: Frazier, G. (2011, April 12). Eating dessert in Lebanon. Retrieved January 24, 2015, from http://culturalcon fusions.com/2011/04/12/eating-dessert-in-lebanon/

Hunek, A. (2011, March 7). McDonalds. Retrieved January 24, 2015, from http://culturalconfusions.com/2011/03/07/mcdonalds/

storage of manufactured products, shipping, inventory control procedures, and customer support services. A non-manufacturer such as a retailer or service provider would also need this section in the business plan to explain the chronological steps in completing a business transaction. For example, an Internet retail sports clothing operation would need to describe how and where the products offered would be purchased, how they would be stored, how the inventory would be managed, how products would be shipped, and how a customer would log on and complete a transaction. In addition, this would be a convenient place for the entrepreneur to discuss the role of technology in the business transaction process. For any Internet retail operation, some explanation of the technology requirements needed to efficiently and profitably complete a successful business transaction should be included in this section.

It is important to note here that the major distinction between services and manufactured goods is that services involve intangible performances. This implies that they cannot be touched, seen, tasted, heard, or felt in the same manner as manufactured products. Airlines, hotels, car rental agencies, theaters, and hospitals—to name a few—rely on business delivery or quality of service. For these firms, performance often depends on location, facility layout, and personnel, which can in turn affect service quality (including such factors as reliability, responsiveness, and assurance). The process of delivering this quality of service is what distinguishes one new service venture from another and thus needs to be the focus of its operations plan. Some key questions or issues for both the manufacturing and nonmanufacturing new venture include the following:

- Will you be responsible for all or part of the manufacturing operation?
- If some or all of the manufacturing is outsourced, who will do this?
- What are the costs of manufacturing?
- What will be the layout of the production process?
- What equipment will be needed immediately for manufacturing?
- What raw materials will be needed for manufacturing?
- Who are the suppliers of new materials and what are the appropriate costs?
- What are the costs of manufacturing the product?

Market Entry Strategy

The market entry strategy is such an important part of the business plan that it is covered in a separate chapter (Chapter 8).

Marketing Strategy Plan

The marketing strategy plan is an important part of the business plan because it describes how the product(s)/service(s) will be distributed, priced, and promoted. Data supporting any of the critical marketing decision strategies, as well as for forecasting sales, should be described in this section. Specific forecasts for product(s)/service(s) are indicated to project the profitability of the venture. Budget and appropriate controls needed for marketing strategy decisions are also needed. Potential investors regard the marketing strategy plan as critical to the success of the new venture. The global entrepreneur should prepare a comprehensive, detailed plan so that investors can be clear as to the sales, revenue, and profit goals of the venture and the marketing strategies to be implemented to effectively achieve these goals. Marketing planning will be an annual requirement, with careful monitoring and changes made on a weekly or monthly basis, and will provide the road map for short-term decision making.

Financials

The final area of the global business plan covers the financials. Like the other aspects, the financials are an important part of the plan. They determine the potential investment commitment needed for the new venture and indicate whether the business plan is economically feasible.

Generally, three financial areas are discussed in this section of the business plan. First, the global entrepreneur should summarize the forecasted sales and the appropriate expenses for the first next five years, with the first year's projections provided monthly. It includes the forecasted sales, cost of goods sold, and the general and administrative expenses. Net profit after taxes can then be projected by estimating income taxes.

The second major area of financial information needed is cash flow figures for five years, with the first year's projections provided monthly. Since bills have to be paid at different times of the year, it is important to determine the demands on cash on a monthly basis, especially in the first year. Remember that sales may be irregular and receipts from customers also may be spread out, thus necessitating the borrowing of short-term capital to meet fixed expenses, such as salaries and utilities.

Next is the projected balance sheet, which shows the financial condition of the business at a specific time. It summarizes the assets of a business, its liabilities (what is owed), the investment of the entrepreneur and any partners, and retained earnings (or cumulative losses). Any assumptions considered for the balance sheet or any other item in the financial plan should be listed for the benefit of the potential investor.

Finally, there is the sources and uses of funds statement, which indicates the amount of money needed to run the business and how it will be spent.

Appendix (Exhibits)

The appendix of the business plan generally contains any backup material that is not necessary in the text of the document. Reference to any of the documents in the appendix should be made in the plan itself. Letters from customers, distributors, or subcontractors are examples of information that should be included in the appendix. Any documentation of information—that is, secondary data or primary research data used to support plan decisions—should also be included. Leases, contracts, or any other types of agreements that have been initiated also may be included in the appendix. Finally, price lists from suppliers and competitors may be added.

Do's and Don'ts of the Global Business Plan

The global business plan needs to carefully articulate all aspects of the global venture. Some of the do's and don'ts of preparing this important document are listed in Table 6.5. Two do's focus on the all-important executive summary—write it last and make sure it is a powerful statement focused on the recipient and objectives of the global business plan. The market entry strategy, marketing plan, and market research data are also important.

Table 6.5 Do's and Don'ts of a Global Business Plan

Do	Don't
• Write the executive summary last and revise it until it is a succinct and powerful statement of you, your company, and its goals. • Tailor the executive summary to each recipient of the business plan. • Include a dated and numbered statement of confidentiality to create a proper follow-up schedule. • Include information about the potential economic, legal, and political hurdles your company may face in a foreign market. • Clearly delineate the ownership of the company and its organizational structure. • Present multiple market entry strategies and assess each proposed strategy. • Describe in full the operations plan, including costs, from manufacturing or acquiring inventory to sales and shipment. • Strengthen your marketing plan by referring to in-depth market research. • Provide detailed sales and expense forecasts as well as projected cash flows and a balance sheet.	• Write the executive summary first and make minimal revisions. • Treat the business plan as a one-time report instead of a living document that should be constantly reviewed and updated. • Skip any of the sections of the business plan. • Use outdated data and figures when creating the operations plan and the financial projections. • Ignore market research when defining your market plan. • Limit your company to only one form of market entry strategy. • Hastily prepare the sales and expense forecasts and other financial data. • Be the only editor of the business plan.

Sample Global Business Plan

A sample global business plan created by a student, Joseph Naaman, for his company, Maktabi, can be found at **study.sagepub.com/hisrich3e**.

SUMMARY

This chapter takes an entrepreneur through the important process of creating a business plan, which is integral in strategically managing an organization. Business plans are used by global entrepreneurs to examine the internal and external factors that affect a company's decision to go global. A well-developed global business plan provides guidance in decision making and organizing the international direction of the company, indicates the viability of an organization in the designated global market(s), and serves as the vehicle for obtaining financing. Each section of the business plan is described, including each section's necessary content. The primary sections of the business plan are the executive summary; introduction; political, legal, and economic aspects of the new opportunity; operational plan; financials; and appendix.

QUESTIONS FOR DISCUSSION

1. What role does a business plan play for a global entrepreneur?

2. What are the key sections of the plan?

3. What additional information is needed for a global plan that would not be needed for a strictly domestic business?

CHAPTER EXERCISES

1. Create a table containing each section of the business plan, its primary audience, and its primary function and importance.

2. Explain the role of the financial section of the business plan, including where the information comes from, who the primary audience is, and what internal planning function this section serves.

3. Suppose you are an American donut company that has decided to launch a donut bakery and café in Shanghai, China. The company grosses $25 million per year from donut and café sales, $5 million of which is attributed to its bakery/cafés in Australia and New Zealand. Create an executive summary to convince a Chinese venture capitalist to invest in this project.

4. Consider your own business or business idea and outline a business plan for it. Identify which areas of the business plan will need more research, brainstorming, and calculations and what steps are needed to address these areas.

REFERENCES

Hisrich, R. D., Peters, M. A., & Shepherd, D. A. (2013). *Entrepreneurship* (9th ed.). Burr Ridge, IL: McGraw-Hill/ Irwin.

Taylor, M. (2006, May 27). Healthy living to be made out of wellness: Investors will only be interested if you have a business plan with significant room for growth. *South China Morning Post,* p. 8.

SUGGESTED READINGS

Baum, M., Schwens, C., & Kabst, R. (2013). International as opposed to domestic new venturing: The moderating role of perceived barriers to internationalization. *International Small Business Journal, 31*(5), 536–562. *Business Source Complete.* Web. 29 Oct. 2013.

The article contrasts founder-based and firm-based determinants of domestic and international entrepreneurship. It further analyzes historical events in a sample of technology companies to show how perceived financial constraints influence a firm's growth orientation.

Casillas, J. C., Moreno, A. M., & Acedo, F. J. (2010). Internationalization of family businesses: A theoretical model based on international entrepreneurship perspective. *Global Management Journal, 2*(2), 16–33. *Business Source Complete.* Web. 29 Oct. 2013.

The authors develop a new model to understand internationalization of family businesses. By comparing six multinational family businesses over their lifetime, the study identifies knowledge and family commitment as key determinants of global entrepreneurship for these types of firms. The model also includes a number of other external and internal contingent variables.

Etemad, H., Wilkinson, I., & Paul, D. L. (2010). Internetization as the necessary condition for internationalization in the newly emerging economy. *Journal of International Entrepreneurship, 8*(4), 319–342. *Business Source Complete.* Web. 29 Oct. 2013.

This article focuses on the role the Internet has played in creating a global market. It argues that "Internetization" has become necessary for internationalization of a firm. It explains the challenge of integrating a firm's Internet strategy with its international strategy.

Ignatius, A. (2013). Strategy for a world in flux. *Harvard Business Review, 91*(6), 12.

This article introduces the June 2013 edition of the *Harvard Business Review,* which focuses on business strategy in the global economy. It describes how entrepreneurs can create a competitive advantage in a global environment as well as strategies for corporate growth.

7

International Legal Concerns

Profile: Spotify

Originally founded in Stockholm, Sweden, in 2006 by Daniel Ek and Martin Lorentzon, Spotify was officially launched in October 2008 and has since achieved a customer base of about 24 million users worldwide. Spotify offers its customers the opportunity to listen to any music they want, whenever and wherever they want it. By providing users with an online profile, the music becomes available across multiple devices, from desktops and laptops to tablets and smart phones. Spotify's mobile app is now available on a variety of devices, including iPhone, Samsung, and BlackBerry. The company's objective is to allow its customers to "soundtrack your life with Spotify."

Although most user accounts are free, the firm now offers customers the opportunity to upgrade to a premium account, which allows them to listen to high-quality music offline, download their favorite songs, and avoid advertising. At $9.99 per month, no commitment is required and customers can cancel this premium account at any time. Under the free account, advertising is an essential component of Spotify's business model. Customers may access music for free, which is made possible by the many advertisers who wish to target specific audiences. Spotify offers detailed information about its customers, making targeting easy, and most customers do not seem to mind these ads, as they are aware that the advertisements make the streaming of music possible. In total, Spotify users streamed about 4.5 billion hours of music in 2013 alone.

In addition, Spotify offers a platform to artists, both world renowned and emerging, to connect with global audiences. These artists can work with Spotify directly and can even utilize the online platform as a marketing medium to announce new releases or concerts. Spotify's partnerships have been essential to its success and growth. It has allowed retailers to attract more shoppers by offering Spotify gift cards, and it has allowed large companies to "Bring Music to Your Business, and Reach the World's Largest Music Audience." The firm was also in the news regularly in the first months of 2014 due to its potential deal with Sprint to offer discounted premium accounts to Sprint users on "framily" plans, providing Spotify with a wider reach and Sprint with more exciting deals and offers to attract more customers. Spotify's approach to partnerships has been based on a positive-sum mind-set and has resulted in mutually beneficial deals for all parties involved.

This privately held Swedish firm operates as Spotify Ltd. from its headquarters in London, the city that was identified as one of the best cities in Europe to launch global businesses, along with Amsterdam, Frankfurt, Stockholm, and Paris. Research and development still takes place in Stockholm through parent company, Spotify AB. Initially, a limit was placed on the number of songs users could listen to, but after Spotify closed deals with some of the largest record companies in the United States, streaming has now become unlimited not only in the U.S. but also in France and in the United Kingdom, where restrictions were most limiting.

Spotify launched its U.S. service in July 2011 after establishing partnerships with major music producers including Sony, EMI, Universal, and Warner Music Group. With these deals, Spotify is a legal music platform and has become the long-awaited legal connection between music producers and customers. As copyright plays a significant role in this industry, just as it does in film and television, Spotify's successful licensing agreements and contracts have inspired multiple entrepreneurial ventures globally. Legal issues may still be "daunting" now, but Spotify has made an important first step toward changing the perception of legal issues to opportunities rather than threats for entrepreneurs.

SOURCES: Jardine, N. (2014). The 20 best European cities for business. Retrieved April 8, 2014 from http://www.businessinsider.com/europes-20-best-cities-for-business-2011-10#and-in-at-1london-20.

Murphy, D. (2014). Report: Sprint teaming up with Spotify to offer "framily" discount. *PC Magazine*. Retrieved April 13, 2014, from http://www.pcmag.com/article2/0,2817,2456479,00.asp.

Spotify [website]. (2015). Retrieved February 1, 2015, from https://www.spotify.com/us/

Spotify AB. (2014). Spotify partners. Retrieved April 8, 2014 from https://partners.spotify.com.

❖❖❖

CHAPTER OBJECTIVES

1. To determine methods for operating in a country with respect to its legal and political system
2. To understand the impact of morality and ethics in global business
3. To understand the various types of legal and regulatory systems
4. To assess the level of corruption and bribery in a foreign country
5. To learn the elements of political risk

Introduction

The legal and political systems confronting the global entrepreneur vary significantly around the world. Generally, the political system needs to be analyzed according to its degree of collectivism versus individualism and the degree of democracy versus totalitarianism. Some countries have a mixture of collectivism and individualism.

In collectivism, a system stressing the primacy of communal goals, the needs of a society as a whole are more important than the needs of the individual. An individual does not have the right to do something if it is counter to the good of society. Socialism and Marxism are two examples of collectivism. Individualism, the other end of the continuum from collectivism, is a system where the individual has the freedom to pursue his or her own economic and political activities. The interests of the individual usually take precedence over the interests of society. In terms of the political spectrum, democracy and totalitarianism are on both sides of the continuum. While a democracy is a political system with government by the people, exercised either directly or through elected representatives, totalitarianism is a system of government where one person or political party exercises absolute control and no opposing political parties are allowed.

Although most global entrepreneurs prefer to do business in stable and freely governed countries, good business opportunities often exist in different conditions. It is important to assess each country's policies as well as its stability. This assessment is referred to as *political risk analysis*. There is some political risk in every country, but the degree of risk varies from country to country; even in a country with a history of stability and consistency, these conditions could change. There are three major types of political risk that might be present: operating risk (risk of interference with the operations of the venture), transfer risk (risk in attempting to shift assets or other funds out of the country), and the biggest risk of all—ownership risk (risk where the country takes over the property and employees). Conflicts and changes in the solvency of the country are major risks to a global entrepreneur in particular countries. This can take such forms as civil warfare, civil disturbances, and even terrorism, where the global entrepreneur's company and employees can even be the target. Just look at the protests and violence in various countries in the Middle East. International terrorists and demonstrators can target business interests in and out of the country.

The legal system of a country also affects the global entrepreneur doing business in the country. The legal system comprises the rules and laws that regulate business behavior as well as the process by which the laws are enforced. A country's laws regulate the business practices in the country, the manner in which business transactions are executed, and the rights and obligations of the parties involved in any business transaction.

Political Activity

There are two primary areas of political activity that can affect the global entrepreneur: trade sanctions and export controls and regulations of global business behavior.

Trade Sanctions and Export Controls

The term *trade sanction* refers to a government action against the free flow of goods and services, or even ideas, for political purposes. Sanctions can be used to influence the type and amount of trade in a particular category and can even be extended to prohibit all trade in that category—a *trade embargo*. The United States, for example, has a trade embargo on Cuba prohibiting most trade except humanitarian aid.

Trade sanctions and embargoes have been used by countries as a foreign policy tool for centuries. The purposes of such actions have ranged from upholding human rights to stopping nuclear proliferation and terrorism to forcing countries to open their home markets.

Export controls are used to restrict the flow of specified goods and services to a country. The United States and other industrialized nations have established strong export controls to deny or at least limit the sale of strategically important goods. In the United States, these controls are based on the Export Administration Act and the Munitions Control Act. A list of commodities needing approval in the form of an export license has been established by the Department of Commerce working with such government agencies as the Defense, Energy, and State departments.

Given the increase in availability of products of all types, the rapid dissemination of information and innovation on a global basis, and the speed of change and new technology advancement, the denial of any product has become much more difficult to enforce. Export controls based on capacity criteria, which once occurred in computer technology, are today mostly irrelevant as the technology changes so quickly, obsolescing previous capacity constraints. For example, about 75% of sales in the data processing industry each year are from new products and services introduced in the previous two years. Given the rapidly changing technology and worldwide information dissemination via the Internet, export controls are becoming less and less enforceable.

Political Risk

Given these conflicts and differences in the political environments in countries, the global entrepreneur must manage the *political risks* involved. Generally, political risk tends to be lower in countries that have a history of stability and consistency. Political risk has three major components: ownership risk, operating risk, and transfer risk.

Ownership risk is the possibility of loss of property and life. International terrorists frequently target business facilities, operations, and personnel.

Operating risk refers to interference in the ongoing operations in a foreign country. Countries can impose new controls in prices and production or restrict access to resources or labor markets. These can disrupt or even close down the foreign operations of the global entrepreneur. The operating risk is reflected in the rules for severance of an employee and the bankruptcy laws of the country.

The final aspect of political risk—*transfer risk*—affects the movement of funds within a country or between countries. Transfer risk can result in currency and remittance restrictions that can be problematic to the foreign entrepreneurial venture (this is elaborated on in Chapter 4).

The global entrepreneur must manage these risks. One way to reduce the risk of government intervention is to demonstrate a concern for the society of the host country and to be a good global citizen. This attitude is reflected in such actions as the level of pay, good working conditions, good hiring and training practices, contributing to the economic development of the region, and having partnerships with local and national business that will share in the sales and profits of the venture. The global entrepreneur needs to monitor political developments so appropriate action can be taken.

Finally, the global entrepreneur should consider purchasing insurance that covers some possible losses. In the United States, the Overseas Private Investment Corporation (OPIC) provides three types of risk insurance for currency inconvertibility, expropriation of resources, and political violence at a cost that is not particularly prohibitive. Of course, the best risk management is good country selection, as was discussed in Chapter 5.

Legal Considerations and Regulations

Among the main difficulties confronting the global entrepreneur are the challenges of the different legal and regulatory environments. Even though there are a variety of legal and regulatory systems, each is based on one of four foundations: common law, civil law, Islamic law, and socialist law.

The common law system, stemming from English law, is the foundation of the legal system in such countries as Australia, Canada, the United Kingdom, and the United States. The civil law system, stemming from Roman law, is the basis of law in such countries as France and some countries in Latin America. Derived from the Qur'an and the teachings of the Prophet Mohammed, Islamic law prevails in most Islamic countries. Finally, social-ist law is derived from the Marxist socialist system and influences, to some degree, the law and regulations in China, Cuba, North Korea, and Russia.

These foundations result in a variety of different laws and regulations of business, which are modified by the treaties and conventions in each country. To handle this facet of going international, the global entrepreneur needs to have an overall sense of the legal system of a country. When a U.S. firm needs legal counsel, ideally, the legal firm hired would have its headquarters in the United States and an office in the host country. Several key legal areas important to every global entrepreneur are property rights, contract law, product safety, product liability, and employment laws.

Countries vary in the degree to which their legal systems protect the property rights of individuals and businesses. The property rights of a business are the resources owned, the use of those resources, and the income earned from their use. Besides buildings, equipment, and land, the protection of intellectual property is also a concern. Intellectual property, such as a book, computer software code, a music score, a video, a formula for a new chemical or drug, or another unique idea, ideally should be protected when going outside the United States. The three major ways of protecting intellectual property in the United States are patents, copyrights, and trademarks. Few countries have strong enforce-able laws protecting intellectual property. For example, videos can be purchased in China at 10% of the cost in the United States, sometimes even before being officially released. Even the ninth edition of the *Entrepreneurship* book (by Hisrich, Peters, and Shepherd, published in 2013) has legal editions in several languages including Arabic, Chinese, Hungarian, Indonesian, Portuguese, Russian, Serbian, Slovenian, and Spanish and has one illegal edition in the Iranian language because Iran does not recognize world corporate copyright laws. Before entering a country, the global entrepreneur needs to assess the country's protection of any intellectual property involved and the legal costs of defense if copied illegally.

Another area of concern is the contract laws of the country and their enforcement. A contract specifies the conditions for an exchange and the rights and duties of the parties involved in this exchange. Contract law varies significantly from country to country, in part reflecting two types of legal tradition—common law versus civil law—previously discussed. Common law tends to be relatively nonspecific, so contracts under this law are longer and more detailed, with all the contingencies spelled out. Because civil law is much more detailed, contracts under it are much shorter.

In addition to the law itself, the global entrepreneur needs to understand how contract law might be enforced and which judicial system is responsible for securing this enforcement. If the legal system of the country does not have a good track record of enforcement, the contract can contain an agreement that any contract disputes will be heard in the courts of another country. Because each global entrepreneur might have some advantage in his or her home country, a third country is usually selected. This aspect is very important for global entrepreneurs operating in developing economies with little or even a bad history of enforcement and other antibusiness countries. One company exporting Hungarian wine into Russia made sure that any disputes in all its Russian contracts were heard in the Finnish court system instead of the court system of Russia.

Another area of concern is the law of the country regarding product safety and liability. Again, the laws have significant variance between countries, from very high liability and damage awards in the United States to very low levels in Russia. When doing business in a country where the liability and product safety laws are not as stringent as in one's home country, you need to decide whether you will follow the more relaxed local standards or adhere to the stricter standards of your home country, perhaps with the risk of not being competitive and losing the business.

Perhaps the least considered yet one of the most important areas is that of employment laws. In the United States, the laws and procedures for hiring and firing employees as well as what needs to occur when there is a case of bankruptcy are established with the minimum severance periods and appropriate compensation specified. In most other countries, these minimums are significantly longer and have higher costs. The length of time severance pay can be required can easily be six to twelve weeks. The costs of paying someone for this length of time for not working are significant and can impact the operations of the company. And, in some countries, it is almost impossible to ever fire someone. If a company needs to leave a country and file bankruptcy in a country other than the United States, there are also significant punitive costs involved.

Intellectual Property and Organizational Form

Intellectual property, which includes patents, trademarks, copyrights, and trade secrets, represents important assets to the global entrepreneur. Often, global entrepreneurs, because of their lack of understanding of intellectual property, ignore the steps needed to try to protect these assets.

Because all business is regulated by the laws of the country a global business locates in, the global entrepreneur needs to be aware of any regulations that may affect the venture in that country. At different stages of the start-up, the global entrepreneur will need legal advice, which will vary based on such factors as whether the new venture is a franchise, an independent start-up, or a buyout; whether it produces a consumer product versus an industrial product; whether it is nonprofit or for-profit; and whether it involves exporting or importing.

The effect on the global entrepreneur and the venture, particularly in the case of intellectual property, reflects the disparity in laws of various countries, particularly emerging ones. For example, China, since entering the World Trade Organization (WTO) in 2001, has strengthened the rights of the owners of intellectual property and is continuing to do so. Even though China's intellectual property laws and the laws of other industrialized nations are not fully harmonized, a global entrepreneur can often receive and enforce intellectual property rights in China, depending to some extent on the region of China.

The form of company as well as the type of franchise agreement offers many options to consider. The global entrepreneur should understand the advantages and disadvantages of each type of organization as it relates to such issues as liability, taxes, continuity, transferability of interest, costs of setting up, and attractiveness for raising capital in the country of interest.

Patents

A *patent* is a contract between the government of a country and the global entrepreneur. In exchange for disclosure of the invention, the government grants the inventor exclusivity regarding the invention in the country for a specified amount of time. At the end of this time, the patent protection can be extended or the invention becomes part of the public domain.

The patent gives the global entrepreneur a *negative right* because it prevents anyone else from making, using, or selling the defined invention. Even if the global entrepreneur has been granted a patent, he or she may find during the process of producing or marketing the invention that it infringes on the patent rights of others. Sometimes, the final product or service has changed so much that the original patent does not fully cover the final offering. There are usually several types of patents:

- *Utility patents.* A utility patent grants the global entrepreneur protection from anyone else making, using, and/or selling the identified invention; it usually protects new, useful, and unobvious processes such as film developing; machines such as photocopiers; compositions of matter such as chemical compounds or mixtures of ingredients; and articles of manufacture such as the toothpaste pump. A utility patent in the United States has a term of 20 years, beginning on the date of filing with the Patent and Trademark Office (PTO). The time period and filing process varies by country.
- *Design patents.* These patents cover new, original, ornamental, and unobvious designs for articles of manufacture. A design patent reflects the appearance of an object and is granted for a 14-year term in the United States. Again, this time period varies by country. Similar to the utility patent, the design patent provides

the global entrepreneur with a negative right, excluding others from making, using, or selling an article having the ornamental appearance given in the drawings included in the patent. Companies such as Reebok and Nike are very interested in obtaining design patents as a means of protecting their original designs. These types of patents are valuable for global ventures that need to protect molded plastic parts, extrusions, and product and container configurations.

- *Plant (factory) patents.* These are issued under the same provisions as utility patents and are for new varieties of plants. Few of these types of patents are issued in the United States.

Patents in the United States are issued by the PTO. In addition to patents, the PTO administers other programs such as the Disclosure Document Program, whereby the inventor files disclosure of the invention, gaining recognition that he or she was the first to develop or invent the idea. In most cases, the inventor will eventually patent the idea. A second program is the Defensive Publication Program. This gives the inventor the opportunity to protect an idea for which he or she does not wish to obtain a patent. It prevents anyone else from patenting this idea but gives the public access to the invention.

With international trade increasing each year, the need was recognized for an international patent law to protect firms from imitations by providing some short-term protection in global markets. In response, the Patent Cooperation Treaty (PCT) was established in June 1970 to facilitate patent filings in multiple countries in one office rather than filing in each separate country. Administered by the World Intellectual Property Organization (WIPO) in Geneva, Switzerland, it provides a preliminary search that assesses whether the filing firm will face any possible infringements in any country. The company can then decide whether to proceed with the required filing of the patent in each country. There is a 20-month time frame to file for these in-country patents. There are some significant differences in patent laws in each country. For example, patent laws in the United States allow computer software to receive both patent and copyright protection. In the European Union, patent protection is not extended to software (Pike, 2005).

In China, patent applications are filed with the State Intellectual Property Office (SIPO) in Beijing. The enforcement varies throughout the country because the local SIPO offices are responsible. Since China is a signatory of the PCT, the country can be designated when a patent is filed in the United States or anytime within 12 months after this filing. Unlike the United States and the European Union, where each patent application is examined based on its merits, Chinese patent applications are examined only if the applicant makes a request for examination. Otherwise, if no request is made, the application will be abandoned.

The use of business method patents has emerged with the growth of Internet and software development. Amazon.com owns a business method patent for the single-clicking feature used by a buyer on its website to order products. Priceline.com claims a patent regarding its service whereby a buyer can submit a price bid for a particular service. Expedia was forced to pay royalties to Priceline.com after being sued for patent infringement. Many firms that hold these types of patents have used them to competitively position themselves as well as provide a steady stream of income from royalties or licensing fees.

CULTURAL STORY

At a division of General Motors in Dayton, Ohio, Kathleen was responsible for a specific product line and I was the business development person for the division.

Prior to our arrival, the division had entered into a joint venture in Japan. We had just hired a marketing person in Japan named "Hirofumi" to watch out for our interests there. Everyone just called him Hiro.

One day, the Japanese joint venture partners came to the U.S. for a meeting. Kathleen's boss, Bob, was at the head of the table with Kathleen on his left. The Japanese were on his right facing Kathleen. I was against the wall behind the Japanese.

Bob started to explain that we had hired "Hiroshima" to help us out in Japan. Kathleen's eyes got as wide as saucers while I was unabashedly aghast at the faux pas but had no need to hide my reaction as I was behind the Japanese. After our initial eye contact, Kathleen refused to look at me as I was laughing, albeit silently. Then the boss called him "Hiroshima" a second time! We were totally incredulous and embarrassed. The picture of Kathleen trying to hold it together in front of the Japanese is a priceless memory.

Needless to say, the joint venture failed.

SOURCE: Katz, J. (2011, February 25). His name was Hirofumi. . . . Retrieved January 25, 2015, from http://cultural confusions.com/2011/02/25/his-name-was-hirofumi/

Trademarks

A *trademark* is a word, symbol, design, slogan, or even a particular sound that identifies the source or sponsorship of certain goods or services. Unlike a patent, a trademark can last indefinitely, as long as the mark continues to be used in its indicated function. For all registrations in the United States, the trademark is given an initial 10-year registration with 10-year renewable terms. In the 5th year, the global entrepreneur needs to file an affidavit with the PTO indicating that the mark is currently in commercial use. If no affidavit is filed, the registration is canceled. Between the 9th and 10th years after registration, and every 10 years thereafter, the global entrepreneur must file an application for renewal of the trademark. If this does not occur, the registration is canceled. Trademark law in the United States allows the filing of a trademark solely on the intent to use the trademark in interstate or foreign commerce. The filing date often is the first date of use but this varies by country.

Generally, throughout the world, there are four categories of trademarks: (1) a *coined mark* denotes no relationship between the mark and the goods or services (e.g., Mercedes, Kodak) and offers the possibility of expansion to a wide range of products; (2) an *arbitrary mark* is one that has another meaning in the language of the United States (e.g., Apple) and is applied to a product or service; (3) a suggestive mark is used to suggest certain features, qualities, ingredients, or characteristics of a product or service (e.g., Halo shampoo) and suggests some describable attribute of the product or service; and (4) a descriptive mark must have become distinctive over a significant period of time and gained consumer recognition before it can be registered. Registering a trademark can offer significant advantages or benefits to the global entrepreneur in each country.

In China, trademark applications are filed with the China Trademark Office. Registered trademarks have more protection in China than unregistered ones, in a situation similar to the United States. Unlike the United States, however, China has a "first to file" trademark system that does not require evidence of prior use or ownership of the trademark. Early filing and a good Chinese translation of the trademark are essential, based on input from a native Chinese speaker familiar with the goods or services. Without this accurate translation, often-unintelligible trademarks result in the Chinese language.

Copyright

A *copyright* protects original works of authorship. The protection in a copyright does not protect the idea itself and thus allows someone else to use the idea or concept in a different manner. Copyright law has become especially relevant because of the tremendous growth in the use of the Internet, especially in downloading music, literary work, pictures, videos, and software.

Copyrights in the United States are registered with the Library of Congress and usually do not require an attorney. To register a work, the global entrepreneur sends a completed application (available online at http://www.copyright.gov), two copies of the work, and the required filing fees (the initial filing fee). The term of the copyright is the life of the global entrepreneur plus 70 years in the United States. This time period also varies by country.

Besides computer software, copyrights are desirable for books, scripts, articles, poems, songs, sculptures, models, maps, blueprints, printed material on board games, data, and music. In some instances, several forms of protection may be available.

Chinese copyrights are registered at the National Copyright Administration (NCA) in Beijing. Even though China recognizes protection for original works of authorship from countries belonging to the international copyright conventions without the works being specifically registered in China, to adequately enforce the copyright, the global entrepreneur should register the copyright with the NCA. Two of the author's books in the Chinese language are registered with the NCA, protecting these well-selling Chinese editions.

Trade Secrets

The global entrepreneur may prefer to maintain an idea or process as confidential and to keep it as a *trade secret*. The trade secret will have a life as long as the idea or process remains a secret.

A trade secret is not covered by any laws but is recognized under a governing body of common laws in some countries. Employees involved in working with an idea or process may be asked to first sign a confidential information agreement that will protect the global entrepreneur against the employee giving out the trade secret either while employed or after leaving the global venture. A simple example of a trade secret nondisclosure agreement is illustrated in Figure 7.1.

The amount of sensitive information to provide to employees is a difficult decision. Usually, global entrepreneurs tend to protect sensitive or confidential company information from anyone else by simply not making the information available.

| **Figure 7.1** | A Simple Nondisclosure Agreement |

WHEREAS, New Venture Corporation (NVC), Anywhere Street, Anyplace, U.S.A., is the Owner of information relating to; and
WHEREAS, NVC is desirous of disclosing said information to the undersigned (hereinafter referred to as "Recipient") for the purposes of using, evaluating, or entering into further agreements using such trade secrets as an employee, consultant, or agent of NVC; and
WHEREAS, NVC wishes to maintain in confidence said information as trade secrets; and
WHEREAS, the undersigned Recipient recognizes the necessity of maintaining the strictest confidence with respect to any trade secrets of NVC,
Recipient hereby agrees as follows:

1. Recipient shall observe the strictest secrecy with respect to all information presented by NVC and Recipient's evaluation thereof and shall disclose such information only to persons authorized to receive same by NVC. Recipient shall be responsible for any damage resulting from any breach of this Agreement by Recipient.

2. Recipient shall neither make use of nor disclose to any third party during the period of this Agreement and thereafter any such trade secrets or evaluation thereof unless prior consent in writing is given by NVC.

3. Restriction on disclosure does not apply to information previously known to Recipient or otherwise in the public domain. Any prior knowledge of trade secrets by the Recipient shall be disclosed in writing within (30) days.

4. At the completion of the services performed by the Recipient, Recipient shall, within (30) days, return all original materials provided by NVC and any copies, notes, or other documents that are in the Recipient's possession pertaining thereto.

5. Any trade secrets made public through publication or product announcements are excluded from this Agreement.

6. This Agreement is executed and delivered with the State of _____ and it shall be construed, interpreted, and applied in accordance with the laws of that State.

7. This Agreement, including the provision hereof, shall not be modified or changed in any manner except only in writing signed by all parties hereto.

SOURCE: Adapted from Hisrich, R. D., Peters, M. P., & Shepherd, D. A. (2013). *Entrepreneurship* (9th ed., p. 164). Burr Ridge, IL: McGraw-Hill/Irwin.

Most global entrepreneurs, particularly those with limited resources, can choose not to protect their ideas, products, or services, relying instead on market protection—their strong position in the market. This strategy should be used with caution, as obtaining competitive information legally is easy to accomplish. It is usually easy to obtain competitive information through trade shows, transient employees, media interviews or announcements, and websites.

Under China's Unfair Competition Law (UCL), protection is available for trade secrets as well as unregistered trademarks and packaging. The Fair Trade Bureau of the State Administration for Industry and Commerce (SAIC) in Beijing enforces the law. The enforcement of this law by the Chinese courts and administrative agencies, however, varies greatly from province to province.

Licensing

Licensing is an arrangement between two parties, where one party has proprietary rights on some information, process, or technology protected by a patent, trademark, or copyright. This arrangement, specified in a contract (discussed later in this chapter), requires the licensee to pay a royalty or some other specified sum to the holder of the proprietary rights (licensor) in return for permission to use the patent, trademark, or copyright. Licensing has significant value as a marketing strategy to holders of patents, trademarks, or copyrights to grow their businesses in new markets when resources or experience in those markets is lacking. It is also an important marketing strategy for global entrepreneurs who want to start a new venture but need permission to incorporate the patent, trademark, or copyright with their ideas.

Although licensing opportunities are often plentiful, they must be carefully considered as part of the global entrepreneur's business model. Licensing is an excellent option for the global entrepreneur to increase revenue in a global market without the risk and costly start-up investment. To be able to license requires the global entrepreneur to have something to license, which is why it is so important to seek protection for any new product, information, or name with a patent, trademark, or copyright.

Contracts

When starting a new venture, the global entrepreneur will be involved in a number of negotiations and contracts with vendors, property owners, and clients. A contract is a legally enforceable agreement between two or more parties as long as certain conditions are met. It is very important for the global entrepreneur to understand the fundamental issues regarding contracts.

Often, business deals are concluded with a handshake. Ordering supplies, lining up financing, or reaching an agreement with a partner are common situations in which a handshake consummates the deal. When things are operating smoothly, this procedure is sufficient; if disagreements occur, the global entrepreneur may find that because there is no written contract, he or she is liable for something he or she never intended. The global entrepreneur should never rely on a handshake if the deal cannot be completed within a short period of time (no more than one year).

Nearly five years after bringing its popular ice cream to Russia, Ben & Jerry's Homemade Inc. pulled out. The same legal, tax, and management problems that plagued many Western investors in Russia forced the South Burlington, Vermont, ice cream maker to rethink a production and sales joint venture that started in 1992 in the spirit of a "social mission" with the northern province of Karelia, according to Bram Kleppner, Ben & Jerry's manager of Russian operations (McKay, 1997).

Kleppner said the company's financial loss on Russian operations had been minimal, under $500,000, but the real drain was executive time spent trying to resolve, among other problems, a court case with one of its partners. Operations were also partly financed through an $850,000 grant from the U.S. Agency for International Development. "We simply don't have the people and resources to run a business in Russia," Kleppner said by telephone from Vermont. "We're a small company. You tie up two or three senior managers and you end up having a measurable effect on the company's performance" (McKay, 1997).

Ben & Jerry's started the joint venture, Iceverk, as a goodwill gesture to prove that high-quality ice cream could be made by Russian employees using mostly local ingredients. The ice cream, including the company's signature flavors such as Chunky Monkey and Cherry Garcia, quickly became a local hit. Three "scoop shops" in the Karelia region, next to Finland, were among the busiest in Ben & Jerry's entire chain. Employing 100 local employees, the joint venture also distributed ice cream to Moscow and St. Petersburg, had five franchisees, and posted sales of $1 million a year.

But the venture never turned a profit, according to Kleppner. Expansion led to quality control problems, with shipments of ice cream often arriving melted and refrozen. An unexpected change in the tax status for joint ventures sent tax liabilities soaring, with the venture unable to meet the increased tax burden. And, similar to scores of other joint ventures in Russia, this one went bad when a local financial institution, PetroBank, successfully sued Ben & Jerry's for the return of a 20% stake the U.S. partner insisted it had legally bought back.

Ben & Jerry's turned over its 70% equity stake in the venture to a third partner, Karelia's capital city of Petrozavodsk. The company also donated installed equipment and did not collect the debts of about $150,000 owed to the joint venture. The venture now makes and sells ice cream under a new trademark, said Alexander Mukhin, head of the Petrozavodsk municipal-property committee (McKay, 1997).

Business Ethics in a Global Setting

A global entrepreneur must consider how to conduct business in an ethical manner throughout the world. By operating ethically, a global venture will be better able to secure repeat business and make a profit while also adding value to the consumer. Consumers want to have a clear conscience about the type of company that their purchases support; knowing that a company has high ethical standards guarantees this peace of mind.

Ethics are the principles that guide an entrepreneur's decision making and should be based on three basic values: integrity, transparency, and accountability. Integrity requires the global entrepreneur to conduct all operations and transactions with honesty and respect for the law, including refraining from bribery and other forms of corruption. Transparency demands that the global entrepreneur undertakes internal and external functions in an open manner and does not try to hide or disguise the firm's actions. Finally, accountability requires the firm to accurately record all transactions and take responsibility for its decisions and actions. Conducting business in foreign markets should not change or alter the ethical principles that the global entrepreneur follows. In short, while the global entrepreneur must continue to grow the firm's bottom line, he or she must also make sure that these decisions are made with integrity, transparency, and accountability.

Countries often establish laws and regulations to ensure that the business activities of foreign firms are within moral and ethical boundaries considered appropriate. Of course, what is considered morally and ethically appropriate ranges from one country to the next, resulting in a wide range of laws and regulations as well as enforcement activities. A global entrepreneur must consider a country's laws and regulations while conducting business activities in an ethical manner. Sometimes this causes the global entrepreneur to have to choose between paying substantial fines and losing business.

One particular regulatory activity that affects global entrepreneurship is antitrust laws. These laws empower government agencies to closely oversee and regulate joint ventures with a foreign firm, acquisition of a domestic firm by a foreign entity, or any other foreign business activity that can restrain competition or negatively affect domestic companies and their business activities. Some countries use these laws to protect their infant industries as they attempt to establish and grow this area of business.

Global entrepreneurs are also affected by laws against bribery and corruption. In many countries, payments or favors are expected in return for doing business or gaining a contract. To establish a foreign operation, obtain a license, or even access electricity and water, global entrepreneurs are often asked to pay bribes to government officials at all levels. Due to the increased incidence of this, the United States passed the Foreign Corrupt Practices Act in 1977, making it a crime for U.S. executives of publicly traded companies to bribe a foreign official to obtain business. Although this act has been very controversial and its enforcement varies, the global entrepreneur must carefully distinguish between a reasonable way of doing business in a particular country and illegal bribery and corruption. The work of the nonprofit Transparency International provides a good resource for judging the level of corruption, real and perceived, in a foreign country. Table 7.1 provides the rankings for the level of perceived public sector corruption for a selection of countries based on Transparency International's annual survey. While Denmark and New Zealand are ranked 1 (not corrupt), Egypt is ranked 114, Argentina 106, and Iraq 171. While the United States is ranked 19, Mexico is ranked 106.

Finally, the global entrepreneur is confronted with the general standards of behavior and ethics. Is it all right to cut down trees in the rain forest or employ people at above national wages? Can you manufacture a product under different working conditions than those that occur in the United States yet pay wage levels higher than average in the country? Can you fire employees in a country? Some countries severely restrict this, even

Table 7.1 Public Sector Corruption Perceptions Index (2013)

Economy/Country	Rank	Score
Denmark	1	91
New Zealand	1	91
Finland	3	89
Sweden	3	89
Norway	5	86
Singapore	5	86
Switzerland	7	85
Netherlands	8	83
Australia	9	81
Canada	9	81
Luxembourg	11	80
Germany	12	78
Iceland	12	78
United Kingdom	14	76
Barbados	15	75
Belgium	15	75
Hong Kong	15	75
Japan	18	74
United States of America	19	73
Uruguay	19	73
Ireland	21	72
The Bahamas	22	71
Chile	22	71
France	22	71
Saint Lucia	22	71
Austria	26	69
United Arab Emirates	26	69
Estonia	28	68
Qatar	28	68
Botswana	30	64
Bhutan	31	63
Cyprus	31	63
Portugal	33	62

Economy/Country	Rank	Score
Puerto Rico	33	62
Saint Vincent and the Grenadines	33	62
Israel	36	61
Taiwan	36	61
Brunei	38	60
Poland	38	60
Spain	40	59
Cape Verde	41	58
Dominica	41	58
Lithuania	43	57
Slovenia	43	57
Malta	45	56
South Korea	46	55
Hungary	47	54
Seychelles	47	54
Costa Rica	49	53
Latvia	49	53
Rwanda	49	53
Mauritius	52	52
Malaysia	53	50
Turkey	53	50
Georgia	55	49
Lesotho	55	49
Bahrain	57	48
Croatia	57	48
Czech Republic	57	48
Namibia	57	48
Oman	61	47
Slovakia	61	47
Cuba	63	46
Ghana	63	46
Saudi Arabia	63	46
Jordan	66	45

(Continued)

Table 7.1 (Continued)

Economy/Country	Rank	Score
Macedonia FYR	67	44
Montenegro	67	44
Italy	69	43
Kuwait	69	43
Romania	69	43
Bosnia and Herzegovina	72	42
Brazil	72	42
Sao Tome and Principe	72	42
Serbia	72	42
South Africa	72	42
Bulgaria	77	41
Senegal	77	41
Tunisia	77	41
China	80	40
Greece	80	40
Swaziland	82	39
Burkina Faso	83	38
El Salvador	83	38
Jamaica	83	38
Liberia	83	38
Mongolia	83	38
Peru	83	38
Trinidad and Tobago	83	38
Zambia	83	38
Malawi	91	37
Morocco	91	37
Sri Lanka	91	37
Algeria	94	36
Armenia	94	36
Benin	94	36
Colombia	94	36
Djibouti	94	36
India	94	36

Economy/Country	Rank	Score
Philippines	94	36
Suriname	94	36
Ecuador	102	35
Moldova	102	35
Panama	102	35
Thailand	102	35
Argentina	106	34
Bolivia	106	34
Gabon	106	34
Mexico	106	34
Niger	106	34
Ethiopia	111	33
Kosovo	111	33
Tanzania	111	33
Egypt	114	32
Indonesia	114	32
Albania	116	31
Nepal	116	31
Vietnam	116	31
Mauritania	119	30
Mozambique	119	30
Sierra Leone	119	30
East Timor	119	30
Belarus	123	29
Dominican Republic	123	29
Guatemala	123	29
Togo	123	29
Azerbaijan	127	28
Comoros	127	28
Gambia	127	28
Lebanon	127	28
Madagascar	127	28
Mali	127	28

(Continued)

Table 7.1 (Continued)

Economy/Country	Rank	Score
Nicaragua	127	28
Pakistan	127	28
Russia	127	28
Bangladesh	136	27
Ivory Coast	136	27
Guyana	136	27
Kenya	136	27
Honduras	140	26
Kazakhstan	140	26
Laos	140	26
Uganda	140	26
Cameroon	144	25
Central African Republic	144	25
Iran	144	25
Nigeria	144	25
Papua New Guinea	144	25
Ukraine	144	25
Guinea	150	24
Kyrgyzstan	150	24
Paraguay	150	24
Angola	153	23
Republic of the Congo	154	22
Democratic Republic of the Congo	154	22
Tajikistan	154	22
Burundi	157	21
Myanmar	157	21
Zimbabwe	157	21
Cambodia	160	20
Eritrea	160	20
Venezuela	160	20
Chad	163	19
Equatorial Guinea	163	19
Guinea Bissau	163	19

Economy/Country	Rank	Score
Haiti	163	19
Yemen	167	18
Syria	168	17
Turkmenistan	168	17
Uzbekistan	168	17
Iraq	171	16
Libya	172	15
South Sudan	173	14
Sudan	174	11
Afghanistan	175	8
North Korea	175	8
Somalia	175	8

SOURCE: Transparency International. (2013). *Transparence International Corruption Perceptions Index.* Retrieved January 25, 2015, from http://www.transparency.org/cpi2013/results

NOTE: This index measures the perceived levels of public sector corruption in a given country from the opinions of both businesspeople from that country as well as country analysts from various international and local institutions. The scores fall on a scale of zero to 10 for each country, with 10 implying a highly clean public sector and zero implying a highly corrupt public sector. These data are useful for global entrepreneurs as they choose new markets to enter and assess the costs, risks, and ethical issues that they might face in doing business in a foreign market. Transparency International produces this index annually and publishes the results on its website (http://www.transparency.org).

though the individual has not been working hard or, even worse, has been stealing from the company. These are just some of the issues confronting the global entrepreneur as he or she does business in certain foreign countries. The global entrepreneur needs to assert leadership and establish high moral standards that help promote a high quality of life throughout the world.

Ethics and expectations of ethics do vary by country, depending in part on whether the country is based on the philosophies of Aristotle and Plato or Confucius, for example. In developing countries without a codified system of business laws that has been in place and enforced for a period of time, there is a great temptation to use bribes (also known as *facilitation payments*) to expedite the business deal. Warner Osborne, chairman and CEO of Seastone LC, in working with thousands of companies during his 20-plus years of experience in China and other countries, advises, "We make sure all partners we work with know we won't tolerate that [facilitation payments/bribes]." He says that when dealing with foreign firms, "We begin by establishing the ground rules—including the ethical rules that are critical to us—one-on-one verbally" (Dutton, 2008). These rules need to be fully understood by each employee.

SUMMARY

An understanding of a country's political and legal system is vital to the success of a new venture in a foreign country. This chapter provides an overview of the major political and legal considerations that a global entrepreneur needs to understand before entering a new foreign market. A political system, which governs a country, needs to be analyzed according to its degree of collectivism versus individualism and the degree of democracy versus totalitarianism. A country will use certain political tools, such as trade sanctions and export controls and regulations, to impact the business in that country. Also, different political systems allow (and expect) different levels of corruption and bribery. Conducting a political risk analysis assesses threats to the ownership, operation, and finances of a global entrepreneur's organization based on a country's political system and stability. A country's legal system and, in particular, its protection of both intangible and tangible property rights must also be understood by the global entrepreneur. Four different traditions of law influence the legal systems around the world: common law, civil law, Islamic law, and socialist law. Legal counsel can be particularly useful to the global entrepreneur in interpreting and enforcing contracts, property rights, liability, and product safety.

QUESTIONS FOR DISCUSSION

1. How can a global entrepreneur mitigate potential political and legal risks prior to them happening?

2. What are the four different types of legal systems, and which countries follow each of these systems?

3. How should a contract be structured differently in a country with common law compared to one with civil law?

CHAPTER EXERCISES

1. Pick one of the BRIC countries (Brazil, Russia, India, China) and analyze its political structure (collective vs. individual and democratic vs. totalitarian) compared with your home country. What is the greatest difference that exists? What is your assessment of the political risk to a business entering that country?

2. Research and explain the difference between outright bribery and corruption versus a facilitation payment.

3. Find an article describing a legal dispute that a multinational corporation has had outside its home country. What is the legal tradition of the foreign company? What is

the major legal issue of the dispute, and is there a different understanding of that issue in the home country versus the foreign country?

REFERENCES

Dutton, G. (2008, May). Do the right thing. *Entrepreneur, 36*(5), 92.

McKay, B. (1997, February 7). Ben & Jerry's post-cold war venture ends in Russia with ice cream melting. *Wall Street Journal* (Eastern ed.), p. A14.

Pike, G. H. (2005, May). Global technology and local patents. *Information Today, 22*(5), 41–46.

SUGGESTED READINGS

Barbu, M., Dunford, M., & Liu, W. (2013). Employment, entrepreneurship, and citizenship in a globalised economy: The Chinese in Prato. *Environment & Planning A, 45*(10), 2420–2441. doi:10.1068/a45484

This article presents the case of how international competition has affected the domestic textile industry for Prato. It examines the anxiety the Chinese textile industry has created for the Italians and how they are perceived to be in operation illegally. The article further examines the different regulatory frameworks and strategies for public authorities to address these tensions.

Casero, J., González, M., de la Cruz Sánchez Escobedo, M., Martínez, A., & Mogollón, R. (2013). Institutional variables, entrepreneurial activity and economic development. *Management Decision, 51*(2), 281–305. doi:10.1108/00251741311301821

The article presents a study that shows which institutional variables that impact entrepreneurship in each type of country are critical to that country's progress. It suggests that developing nations should focus on the "size of the business sector" as well as "health and primary education," while transitioning economies should focus more on "fulfilling contracts" and "integrity of the legal system." The "credit available to the private sector" and the "size of government" are determined to be the critical variables for developed economies.

Du, Q., & Vertinsky, I. (2011). International patterns of ownership structure choices of start-ups: Does the quality of law matter? *Small Business Economics, 37*(2), 235–254. doi:10.1007/s11187-009-9237-z

The authors examine how the concentration of enterprise ownership is influenced by different legal systems. A framework is developed to explain the effect the quality of shareholder and debt holder protection has on start-up founders' decisions regarding partnerships versus sole ownership. A positive correlation is found between legal system quality and ownership concentration for start-ups using data from the Adult Population Survey of Global Entrepreneurship Monitor project.

Kingsley, A. F., Vanden Bergh, R. G., & Bonardi, J. (2012). Political markets and regulatory uncertainty: Insights and implications for integrated strategy. *Academy of Management Perspectives, 26*(3), 52–67.

The article describes how managers should create an integrated strategy based on their assessment of regulatory uncertainty. It connects coalition breadth, profile level, and pivotal target to regulatory uncertainty in an effort to demonstrate how nonmarket strategies should be crafted. As an example, the article analyzes market entry strategies for firms in the telecommunications industry entering into foreign markets.

Troilo, M. (2011). Legal institutions and high-growth aspiration entrepreneurship. *Economic Systems, 35*(2), 158–175. doi:10.1016/j.ecosys.2010.08.001

This article examines the influence of contracting institutions and property rights institutions on high-growth aspiration entrants. It concludes that property rights are more important for market expansion, whereas the rule of law has a stronger effect on job growth. In addition, it states that procedural steps and number of days to start a business most negatively correlate with high-growth aspiration entrepreneurship.

PART III

MANAGING THE GLOBAL ENTREPRENEURIAL ENTERPRISE

8

Alternative Entry Strategies

Profile: vente-privee

Based on the concept of outlet malls, the French online shopping mall vente-privee.com offers customers the opportunity to acquire fashion products from internationally renowned brands at discounts of up to 70%. Products can only be purchased by website members, but membership is free and available to anyone. This allows the company to acquire valuable customer information to tailor its products and services to its customers. Online sales events are held on a regular basis and are only open for a predetermined period of time, generating buzz among the customer base and making customers feel "special" if they manage to acquire certain branded items.

Jacques-Antoine Granjon founded the business in 2001 to assist well-known brands with the sale of excess inventory. The firm's unique "limited-time sales event approach" has created a more dynamic environment, and its wide variety of partnerships with global brands has attracted over 19 million members in eight different European countries. vente-privee.com partners with more than 1,500 major international brands and had annual sales of over $2 billion in 2013. With its unique and attractive business model, vente-privee.com has achieved seventh place in Business Insider's Top 100 Internet Start-Ups, just after firms such as Facebook, Skype, and Twitter and above many others, including LinkedIn, Hulu, and Yelp.

The company pioneered the business model of online "flash sales" or event sales, and since its inception, many other companies have entered this space. Competitors have greatly focused recent efforts on expansion into high-growth markets such as China. In contrast, this firm has focused its efforts in its home market and the United States in order to maintain its profit margin, which was about 5% in 2013.

The company's funding deal with Summit Partners, which acquired a 20% stake in the company, allowed it to expand quickly into other European countries, including Spain, Germany, and The Netherlands. The firm's site was launched in the United States in 2011 through a joint venture with American Express. Future opportunities for market entry may be presented by Qatar Holding, which acquired a minority stake in vente-privee.com in December 2013. It seems that a variety of investors are interested in this business model and believe that it may hold great potential in the future. Although still a privately held firm and although CEO Jacques-Antoine Granjon seems to have no intention of changing this in the near future, partnerships have been essential to the firm's expansion. It is likely that partnerships will continue to be the main mode of entry into new markets: The timing of these partnerships will greatly influence when and how vente-privee.com expands.

Headquartered in one of Europe's best cities for start-ups, Paris, vente-privee.com now employs about 1,800 people and has diversified its product offerings to include travel, entertainment tickets, and music. With its diverse and exciting event sales model, vente-privee.com attracts about 80 million visitors per month. In 2013, the company sold 60 million products in Europe. As a result, the firm has become an important partner for global brands. This firm is proof that a successful business model may turn a potentially risky entrepreneurial venture into a desirable partner.

SOURCES: Roberts, A., & Mawad, M. (2014). vente-privee seeks 11 billion revenue with flash sales online. Retrieved April 13, 2014, from http://www.bloomberg.com/news/2014-02-09/vente-privee-seeks-11-billion-revenue-with-flash-sales-online.html

Silicon Alley Insider. (Ed.). (2014). The digital 100: The world's most valuable start-ups. Retrieved April 8, 2014, from http://www.businessinsider.com/digital-100/7-vente-privee-7.

vente-privee [website]. (n.d.). Retrieved February 11, 2015, from https://us.venteprivee.com/main/#/about

CHAPTER OBJECTIVES

1. To determine the best overall strategy for bringing a venture to market
2. To understand and be able to implement each market entry strategy
3. To understand the benefits of entrepreneurial partnering with home-country entrepreneurs
4. To understand how to select a partner in a foreign market

Introduction

Once the product/service idea and the market opportunity have been selected, it is important to develop a strategy to go international. This global strategy outlines the actions the company will take to obtain the international goals established and successfully enter the international market(s) selected. To be profitable (making sure that total revenues are greater than total costs), the global entrepreneur needs to be competitive and offer something that has value to customers at a price that they are willing to pay. This requires being attentive to the value of what is being offered for sale as well as controlling the costs of the offering.

Formulating the Global Strategy

To develop a global strategy, a global entrepreneur usually undertakes the following steps: (1) scan the external environment, (2) determine the strengths and weaknesses of the entrepreneur and the company, and (3) develop the goals and strategy. Each of these will be discussed in turn.

Scan the External Environment

Environmental scanning is a way to develop a good idea about the geographic area being considered for the global business. Two aspects of environmental scanning were the focus of Chapters 5 and 7: selecting the international business opportunity and understanding international legal concerns. Other areas of environmental scanning, particularly when forecasts are also needed, include competitive analysis, consumer data, the overall economy, and the political stability. A typical environmental scan will evaluate and forecast the following:

- Markets for the products/services
- Per capita income of the population
- Labor and raw material availability
- Exchange rates, exchange controls, and tariffs
- Inflation rate
- Competitive products/services available
- Positioning
- Political risk

The resulting forecasts and assessments provide the global entrepreneur with a risk profile and the profit potential of each geographic area investigated. This will help in making a good decision on which global market(s) to enter.

Determine the Strengths and Weaknesses of the Entrepreneur and the Company

Along with environmental scanning, it is important for the global entrepreneur to assess the strengths and weaknesses of his or her company. This assessment provides an understanding of the venture's financial, managerial, marketing, and technical capabilities as well as the critical factors for success that could affect how well the venture will perform. The goal of this analysis is for the global entrepreneur to match as closely as possible the external opportunities identified through the scanning of the environment with the internal strengths of the global entrepreneur and the venture. When the people and resources are present to develop and maintain the critical factors for success, the correct market entry strategy can be more successfully implemented.

Develop the Goals and Strategy

Although a global entrepreneur already has some general objectives that initiated the environmental scanning, more-specific goals and objectives based on both the external and internal analysis need to be established. Goals are usually established in the areas of finance, human resources, marketing, and profitability.

Profitability is key in going global; in general, a venture should achieve higher profitability from its international business than its domestic activities to compensate for the additional effort, management costs, and risk. For those ventures having significant success in their domestic markets, achieving additional market share at home is often very costly and difficult. Global markets offer an ideal alternative for increasing growth and profitability. Based on the established strategic goals, the global entrepreneur will need to develop specific operational goals and controls, which will help ensure that the overseas group operates in a way that supports the strategic goals of the plan.

Timing of Market Entry

Once the market(s) has been selected and the global strategy formulated, it is important to determine the timing of the market entry. One consideration is whether to enter a market before other foreign firms—first mover advantage—or after other foreign businesses have been established in the market—second mover advantage. First mover advantages associated with early market entry include (1) preempting competitive firms and capturing sales by establishing a strong brand name; (2) creating switching costs tying customers to your company's products or services; and (3) building a sales volume that provides an experience curve and cost advantages over later market entrants.

There are also some disadvantages, often referred to as *pioneering costs*, in being the first entrant into a foreign market. Pioneering costs can be somewhat avoided or minimized by late entrants into the foreign market. Because these costs can be particularly problematic and high when the business system in the foreign market is very different from the firm's home market, considerable effort, expense, and time are needed to successfully enter the new market situation. The highest cost is business failure due to a lack of understanding of doing business in the foreign market. Other pioneering costs include the cost of educating the foreign market customer about the product through promotion and advertising. In developing economies where the rules and regulations governing businesses are still evolving, the first mover may have extra costs of reformulating the company's strategy to take into account any changes in rules and regulations that occur. Sometimes these changes can invalidate the entire business model used in market entrance.

The second mover has the advantage of observing and learning from the entrance and mistakes made by early entrants. The later entrant can use a business model that takes these mistakes into account as well as any changes in the business laws and regulations of the foreign market. The reduction in liability and costs and the increase in learning raise the probability of success for global entrepreneurs entering a foreign market after several other foreign firms have already entered.

Scale of Entry

A final issue that a global entrepreneur needs to address before selecting an entry mode into a foreign market is the scale of entry. Entering a market on a large scale involves a significant amount of time and resources with significantly increasing risks. This requires a strategic commitment to the market that has long-term effects on the global entrepreneur and enterprise and is a decision that is very difficult to reverse.

It also signals to the competition the firm's commitment and can influence the nature and reaction of incumbent firms. This strategic commitment to a foreign market will make it easier to attract customers and establish a base of sales and may also make other companies deciding to enter the market at least reconsider this decision, because they will have to compete with the firms in the market in addition to this first entry. A full-scale commitment will alert incumbent firms and could elicit a vigorous competitive response.

The strategic commitment to enter a foreign market on a large scale decreases the flexibility of the global entrepreneur. Committing heavily to one market leaves fewer resources available to support entrance and expansion in other markets. Few firms have the resources needed to have many large-scale market entries.

Although large-scale market entries are neither always good nor always bad, it is important for the global entrepreneur to think through carefully the implications of such a decision because it will definitely impact the competitive landscape. It is important to identify the nature of the competitive reactions, realizing that large-scale entry will increase sales substantially and provide economies of scale of production and distribution while providing some barriers to entry due to the company's presence and/or switching costs.

A small-scale market entry allows the global entrepreneur to learn more about a foreign market with limited resource exposure. Information can be obtained about the foreign market before significant resources are committed. This increases the venture's flexibility and reduces the risk. The potential long-term rewards are likely to be lower, however, because it will be more difficult and time-consuming to build market share and capture all the first mover advantages.

Foreign Market Entry Modes

There are various ways a global entrepreneur can market products internationally. The method of entry into a market and the mode of operating overseas are dependent on the goals of the global entrepreneur and the company's strengths and weaknesses. The modes of entering or engaging in international business along with some of their advantages and disadvantages are indicated in Table 8.1.

Exporting

Usually, a global entrepreneur starts doing international business through exporting. Exporting normally involves the sale and shipment of products manufactured in one country to a customer located in another country. There are two general classifications of exporting: indirect and direct.

Table 8.1 Various Entry Modes

Entry Mode	Advantage	Disadvantage
Exporting	• Ability to realize location and experience curve economies	• High transport costs • Trade barriers • Problems with local marketing agents
Turnkey contracts	• Ability to earn returns from process technology skills in countries where Foreign Direct Investment (FDI) is restricted	• Creates efficient competitors • Lack of long-term market presence
Licensing	• Low development costs and risks	• Lack of control over technology • Inability to realize location and experience curve economies • Inability to engage in global strategic coordination
Franchising	• Low development costs and risks	• Lack of control over quality • Inability to engage in global strategic coordination
Joint ventures	• Access to local partner's knowledge • Sharing development costs and risks • Politically acceptable	• Lack of control over technology • Inability to engage in global strategic coordination • Inability to realize location • Will not be able to enter certain markets
Wholly owned subsidiaries	• Protection of technology • Ability to engage in global strategic coordination • Ability to realize location and access local and country markets	• High costs and risks

SOURCE: Hisrich, R. D., Peters, M. P., & Shepherd, D. A. (2013). *Entrepreneurship* (9th ed., p. 139). Burr Ridge, IL: McGraw-Hill/Irwin.

Indirect Exporting

Indirect exporting involves having a foreign purchaser in the local market or using an export management firm. For certain commodities and manufactured goods, foreign buyers actively seek out sources of supply and have purchasing offices in markets throughout the world. A global entrepreneur wanting to sell into one of these overseas markets can deal with one of these buyers. When this occurs, the entire transaction is handled as though it were a domestic transaction, with the goods being shipped out of the country by the foreign buyer. This method of exporting involves the least amount of knowledge and risk for the global entrepreneur.

Export management firms, another avenue of indirect exporting, are located in most commercial centers. These firms provide representation in foreign markets for a fee. Typically, they represent a group of noncompeting manufacturers from the same country with no interest in becoming directly involved in exporting. The export management firm handles all the selling, marketing, and delivery of the global entrepreneur's products/ services, in addition to any technical problems, in the export process to the foreign country.

One method for indirect exporting is using the Internet. This is exemplified in Green & Black's decision to open an online shop to expand its operations internationally. The organic chocolatier's retail site went live on November 15, 2006, enabling both United States and United Kingdom consumers to buy its products online for the first time. Products include gift items ranging from dinner party to birthday selections as well as Green & Black's flagship bar products. Customers tailor their gift by picking their own assortment of bars, which is presented in a ribbon-wrapped gift box. The products are also tailored for occasions such as Christmas and Mother's Day.

Green & Black's senior brand manager, Katie Selman, indicated that the launch of the online shop was the first time the company had offered a gifting service to customers. "The online shop allows customers to create tailor-made gifts, which shows they put that little bit more thought into them." The brand is entering a competitive arena. Hotel Chocolat, which launched more than 10 years ago, originally as a catalogue retailer, has been selling products online for the last five years (Charles, 2006).

Another form of indirect exports for the global entrepreneur, particularly in the United States, is through home shopping networks. TV shopping on networks such as QVC and Home Shopping Network (HSN) has resulted in products getting instant brand recognition as well as selling thousands of units. QVC and HSN reach nearly 200 million homes in the United States with the following viewer demographics: 75% women between the ages of 25 and 54 with an average household income of $60,000. These home shopping networks conveniently provide quality at an affordable price and sometimes even feature celebrities.

Home shopping networks are particularly open to global entrepreneurs with innovative new products and a background and a story that is interesting to their viewers. Both QVC and HSN attend relevant trade shows to find new product/service opportunities; QVC also accepts online submissions at its website (http://www.qvcproductsearch.com). Both networks look for unique products/services that are usually recognizable and have broad appeal. One entrepreneur who invented a cleaning compound for outdoor furniture was amazed when 100,000 18-oz. bottles of his cleaning compound sold in one session on QVC. Laurie Feltheimer, founder of Hot in Hollywood, a company in California specializing in trendy clothes and accessories modeled on Hollywood fashions, recently called HSN's CEO to set up a personal meeting to present her concept to the network. Now, supplying HSN alone is a multimillion-dollar business. According to Feltheimer, who appears on HSN six to eight times each year, "At this point, I am really happy with my business at HSN. It is growing, it's keeping me busy and interested, and I don't see any reason to complicate my life any further" (Wilson, 2008).

Direct Exporting

If the global entrepreneur wants more involvement without any financial commitment, direct exporting through independent distributors or the company's own overseas sales office is a way to enter a foreign market and get involved in international business. Independent foreign distributors usually handle products for firms seeking relatively rapid entry into a large number of foreign markets. This independent distributor directly contacts potential foreign customers and takes care of all the technicalities of arranging for export documentation, financing, and delivery for an established rate of commission.

Global entrepreneurs can also open their own overseas sales offices and hire their own salespeople to provide market representation. When starting out, the global entrepreneur may send a domestic salesperson to be a representative in the foreign market. As more business is done in the overseas sales office, warehouses are usually opened, followed by a local assembly process when sales reach a level high enough to warrant the investment. The assembly operation can eventually evolve into the establishment of manufacturing operations in the foreign market. Global entrepreneurs can then export the output from these manufacturing operations to other international markets.

Dieter Kondek, a German-born entrepreneur, was talking with friends at a dinner party, expressing his distaste for the lighting designs of the hotel and resort developments opening around his home in Cape Coral, Florida. At that point, a friend mentioned a German company, Moonlight, that manufactures glowing orbs that can light a room, illuminate a path, or float in a pool.

"They create light like the moon," says Kondek. "This is what was fascinating to us." He researched the company and found that the polyethylene globes can withstand temperatures from minus 40° to 170° Fahrenheit, range in size from 13 to 30 inches in diameter, and are powered with rechargeable batteries or hardwired into an outlet. Kondek also found out that Moonlight's products were decorating wealthy homes in Europe, Asia, and the Middle East but were not in the United States. So, after 30 years in the high-tech field, Kondek, along with his wife and two friends, launched Moonlight U.S.A. and became the exclusive U.S. distributor. Worldwide, Moonlight has sold more than 10,000 balls, which cost from $325 to $1,000, and Kondek believes that the United States can eventually make up half the company's sales (Centers, 2008).

Nonequity Arrangements

When market and financial conditions warrant, a global entrepreneur can enter into international business by one of three types of nonequity arrangements: licensing, turnkey projects, and management contracts. Each of these arrangements allows the global entrepreneur to enter a market and obtain sales and profits without a direct equity investment in the foreign market.

Licensing

Licensing involves a global entrepreneur who is a manufacturer (licensor) giving a foreign manufacturer (licensee) the right to use a patent, trademark, technology, production process, or product in return for the payment of a royalty. The licensing arrangement is most appropriate when the global entrepreneur has no intention of entering a particular market through exporting or direct investment. Since the process is low risk yet provides a way to generate incremental income, a licensing agreement can be a good method for the global entrepreneur to engage in international business. Unfortunately, some global entrepreneurs have entered into these arrangements without careful analysis and later found that they have licensed their largest competitor into business or that they are investing large sums of time and money to help the licensee adopt the technology or knowledge being licensed.

Wolverine World Wide, Inc., opened a Hush Puppies store in Sofia, Bulgaria, through a licensing agreement with Pikin, a local country combine. Similar arrangements were made a year later in the former U.S.S.R. with Kirov, a shoe combine. Stores in both countries are doing well.

Turnkey Projects

Another method by which the global entrepreneur can do international business without much risk is through turnkey projects. The underdeveloped or lesser-developed countries of the world have recognized their need for manufacturing technology and infrastructure and yet do not want to turn over substantial portions of their economy to foreign ownership. One solution to this dilemma has been to have a foreign entrepreneur build a factory or other facility, train the workers, train the management, and then turn it over to local owners once the business is operational, hence the name *turnkey operation*.

Global entrepreneurs have found turnkey projects an attractive alternative. Initial profits can be made from this method, and follow-up export sales can result. Financing is provided by the local company or the local government, paying the global entrepreneur for work completed over the life of the project.

Management Contracts

The final nonequity method the global entrepreneur can use in international business is the management contract. Several global entrepreneurs have successfully entered international business by contracting their management techniques and skills. The management contract allows the purchasing country to gain foreign expertise without giving ownership of its resources to a foreigner. For the global entrepreneur, the management contract is a way of entering a foreign market without a large equity investment. It is used extensively in the seminar/training business.

Direct Foreign Investment

The wholly owned foreign subsidiary has been a preferred mode of ownership for global entrepreneurs using direct foreign investment for doing business in international markets. Joint ventures, minority and majority interest positions, and mergers and acquisitions are also methods for making direct foreign investments. The percentage of ownership obtained in the foreign venture by the global entrepreneur is related to the amount of money invested, the nature of the industry, and the rules of the host government.

Joint Ventures

Another direct foreign investment method used by global entrepreneurs to enter foreign markets is the joint venture. Although a joint venture can take many forms, in its most traditional form, two firms (for example, one U.S. firm and one German firm) get together and form a third company in which they share the equity.

Joint ventures have been used by global entrepreneurs most often in two situations: (1) when the global entrepreneur wants to purchase local knowledge as well as an already-established marketing or manufacturing facility and (2) when rapid entry into a market is needed. Sometimes the joint venture is dissolved for a lack of performance or when the global entrepreneur assumes 100% ownership.

Even though using a joint venture to enter a foreign market is a fundamental strategic decision, the keys to its success have not been well understood. The reasons for forming a joint venture today are also different from those of the past. Previously, joint ventures were viewed as partnerships and often involved firms whose stock was owned by several other firms. Joint ventures in the United States were first used by mining concerns and railroads as early as 1850. The use of joint ventures, mostly vertical joint ventures (described below), started increasing significantly during the 1950s. Through the vertical joint venture, two firms could absorb the large volume of output when neither could afford the diseconomies associated with a smaller plant.

What has caused this increase in the use of joint ventures, particularly when many have not worked? The studies of success and failure of joint ventures have found many different reasons for their formation. One of the most frequent reasons a global entrepreneur forms a joint venture is to share the costs and risks of a project. Projects where costly technology is involved frequently require resource sharing. This can be particularly important when a global entrepreneur does not have the financial resources necessary to engage in capital-intensive activities. Another reason for forming a joint venture is to obtain a competitive advantage. A joint venture can preempt competitors, allowing an entrepreneur to access new customers and expand the market base. Joint ventures are frequently used by global entrepreneurs to enter markets and economies that pose entrance difficulties or to compensate for a company's lack of foreign experience. This has been the case for the transition economies of eastern and central Europe and Russia.

Minority Interests

Japanese companies have been frequent users of the minority equity position in making their direct foreign investment. A minority interest can provide a firm with a source of raw materials or a relatively captive market for its products. Global entrepreneurs have used minority positions to gain a foothold or acquire experience in a market before making a major commitment. When the minority shareholder has something of strong value, the ability to influence the decision-making process is often far in excess of the amount of ownership.

Majority Interests

Another equity method for the global entrepreneur to enter international markets is to purchase a majority interest in a foreign business. In a technical sense, anything over 50% of the equity in a firm is a majority interest. The majority interest allows the global entrepreneur to obtain managerial control while maintaining the acquired firm's local identity. When entering a volatile international market, some global entrepreneurs take a smaller position, which they increase up to 100% as sales and profits increase.

Mergers

A global entrepreneur can obtain 100% ownership to ensure complete control. Many U.S. entrepreneurs desire complete ownership and control in cases of foreign investments. If the global entrepreneur has the capital, technology, and marketing skills required for successful entry into a market, there may be no reason to share ownership.

Mergers and acquisitions have been used significantly to engage in international business as well as domestically within the United States. During periods of intense merger activity, a global entrepreneur may spend significant time searching for a firm to acquire and then finalize the transaction. Any merger should reflect basic principles of any capital investment decision and make a net contribution to shareholders' wealth. Often, the merits of a particular merger are difficult to assess. Not only do the benefits and cost of a merger need to be determined, but special accounting, legal, and tax issues must also be addressed. The global entrepreneur needs a general understanding of the benefits and problems of mergers as a strategic option as well as an understanding of the complexity of integrating an entire company into present operations.

There are five basic types of mergers: horizontal, vertical, product extension, market extension, and diversified activity. A *horizontal merger* is the combination of two firms that produce one or more of the same or closely related products in the same geographic area. They are motivated by economies of scale in marketing, production, or sales. An example is the acquisition of convenience food store chain Southland Stores by 7-Eleven Convenience Stores.

A *vertical merger* is the combination of two or more firms in successive stages of production that often involve a buyer-seller relationship. This form of merger stabilizes supply and production and offers more control of these critical areas. Examples are McDonald's acquiring its store franchises and Phillips Petroleum acquiring its gas station franchises. In each case, these outlets become company-owned stores.

A *product extension merger* occurs when acquiring and acquired companies have related production and/or distribution activities but do not have products that compete directly with each other. Examples are the acquisitions of Miller Brewing (beer) by Philip Morris (cigarettes) and Western Publishing (children's books) by Mattel (toys).

A *market extension merger* is a combination of two firms producing the same products but selling them in different geographic markets. The motivation is that the acquiring firm can economically combine its management skills, production, and marketing with that of the acquired firm. An example of this type of merger is the acquisition of Diamond Chain (a West Coast retailer) by Dayton Hudson (a Minneapolis retailer).

The final type of merger is a *diversified activity merger*. This is a conglomerate merger involving the consolidation of two essentially unrelated firms. Usually, the acquiring firm is not interested in either using its cash resources to expand shareholder wealth or actively running and managing the acquired company. An example of a diversified activity merger is Hillenbrand Industries (a caskets and hospital furniture manufacturer) acquiring American Tourister (a luggage manufacturer).

Mergers are a sound strategic option for a global entrepreneur when synergy is present. Synergy is the qualitative effect on the acquiring firm brought about by complementary factors inherent in the firm being acquired. Synergy in the form of people, customers, inventory, plant, or equipment provides leverage for the joint venture. The degree of the synergy determines how beneficial the joint venture will be for the companies involved. Several factors cause synergy to occur and make two firms worth more together than apart.

The first factor, economies of scale, is probably the most important reason for a merger. Economies of scale can occur in production, coordination, and administration; sharing central services such as office management and accounting; financial control; and upper-level management. Economies of scale increase operating, financial, and management efficiency, thereby resulting in lower costs, fewer employees, and better earnings.

The second factor is taxation or, more specifically, unused tax credits. Sometimes a firm has had a loss in previous years but not enough profits to take tax advantage of the loss. Corporate income tax regulations allow the net operating losses of one company to reduce the taxable income of another when they are combined. By combining a firm with a loss with a firm with a profit, the tax-loss carryover can be used.

The final important factor for mergers is the benefits received in combining complementary resources. Many entrepreneurs will merge with other firms to ensure a source of supply for key ingredients, to obtain a new technology, or to keep the other firm's product from being a competitive threat. It is often quicker and easier for a firm to merge with

CULTURAL STORIES

Story 1

A friend of mine from Poland bought an expensive watch in a big, respected department store. Sometime later, the watch stopped working. He immediately took it back to the store and explained that the watch did not function properly.

An elegant salesperson, after examining the watch, stated with an expert's confidence while nodding her head, "Second hand."

My friend, infuriated, raised his voice and stated, "No, I bought it here!"

Story 2

My friend was traveling around small towns throughout Russia, developing contracts and purchasing textiles from local factories.

(Continued)

(Continued)

Together with several Russians, we were discussing (in Russian) his job at a Canada Dry party in Moscow, and he mentioned that he frequently had to attend banquets with local mayors and other dignitaries. Somebody asked him what he discussed with these dignitaries, to which he replied, "Politiki, Sport, Ekonomiki, Pollutsya."

There was a stunned silence at the table, and it fell to me to enlighten him on the finer points of Russian (his was quite good, but not quite good enough).

"Pollutsya" in Russian, does not mean pollution, but something very, very different. He had been using this conversational gambit for quite a while, including with several female mayors!

SOURCES: Bozena, H. (2011, March 31). Tick tock. Retrieved January 27, 2015, from http://culturalconfusions.com/2011/03/31/tick-tock/

Rovetta, B. (2011, March 1). Politics, sports, economy, and pollution. Retrieved January 27, 2015, from http://cultural confusions.com/2011/03/01/politics-sports-economy-and-pollution/

another that already has a new technology developed—combining the technological innovation with the acquiring firm's engineering and sales talent—than to develop the technology from scratch.

Entrepreneurial Partnering

One of the best methods for a global entrepreneur to enter an international market is to partner with an entrepreneur in that country. These foreign (in-country) entrepreneurs know the country and culture and therefore can facilitate business transactions while keeping the global entrepreneur current on business, economic, and political conditions.

There are several characteristics of a good partner. A good partner helps the global entrepreneur achieve his or her goals, such as market access, cost sharing, or core competency obtainment. A good partner also shares the global entrepreneur's vision and is unlikely to try to opportunistically exploit the partnership for his or her own benefit.

How do you select a good partner? First, you need to collect as much information as possible on the industry and potential partners in the country. This information needs to be collected from embassy officials, members of the country's chamber of commerce, firms doing business in that country, and customers of the potential partner. The global entrepreneur will need to attend any appropriate trade shows. References for each potential partner should be checked and each reference asked for other references. Finally, it is most important that the global entrepreneur meet several times with a potential partner to get to know the individual and the company as well as possible before any commitment is made.

SUMMARY

This chapter discusses developing a market entry strategy, choosing the right time for market entry, defining the scale of entry, and finally, establishing the best mode of entry. To develop a sound entry strategy, a global entrepreneur needs to (1) scan the external environment, (2) determine the strengths and weaknesses of the entrepreneur and the company, and (3) develop the goals and strategy. The global entrepreneur needs to always keep in mind that the international business should be more profitable than the domestic business to compensate for the higher risk involved. The timing for market entry centers on whether the global entrepreneur is the first to enter the foreign market or enters after other competitors have already established their businesses. The primary advantages for first movers are preempting competitors and gaining market share; creating switching costs that tie the customer to the entrepreneur's product/services; and building sales volume to maintain profitability after competitors enter the market. A later entry into a foreign market allows a global entrepreneur to learn from the mistakes of the first entrant while also reducing some of the pioneering costs. The global entrepreneur needs to then weigh the advantages and disadvantages of entering a market on a large scale to command the market or on a small scale to make sure the foreign market is right for the product/service. Finally, the best mode for entering the market needs to be determined. Market entry falls into three categories: exporting (indirect or direct), nonequity arrangements (licensing, turnkey projects, and management contracts), and direct foreign investment (wholly owned foreign subsidiaries, joint ventures, majority and minority equity positions, and mergers). The chapter concludes by discussing one final option for entry into a foreign market—partnering with an entrepreneur from that country.

QUESTIONS FOR DISCUSSION

1. Discuss the different ways to enter a foreign market. What are the advantages and disadvantages of each?

2. Discuss factors a global entrepreneur should consider when deciding on an entry strategy.

3. Anastasia is considering introducing her new line of high-end food products into Mexico. She has heard through a friend that one of her competitors is planning to do the same. Give arguments as to why it can be better to be the first mover into the market and why it might be better to be the second.

CHAPTER EXERCISES

1. Using your own company or business idea, choose a new market for your product/ service. Define the external environment, your own and your company's strengths and weaknesses, and a basic strategy to enter that market.

2. What are the advantages of a first-mover strategy? What are the best market conditions in which to use this strategy?

3. Imagine that you are the inventor of unique, robotic dolls that have been very successful and popular in your home country. You see a great opportunity in bringing this product to Germany. Conduct a basic analysis of the German market and suggest the best entry mode (exporting, nonequity arrangements, or direct foreign investment) for your product.

NOTE

Portions of this chapter are adapted from Chapter 5 of Hisrich, R. D., Peters, M. A., & Shepherd, D. A. (2013). *Entrepreneurship* (9th ed.). Burr Ridge, IL: McGraw-Hill/Irwin.

REFERENCES

Centers, J. (2008, April 1). Great balls of light. *Fortune Small Business, 18*(3), 25.

Charles, G. (2006, October 18). Green & Black's in web shop. *Marketing,* 12. Retrieved January 27, 2015, from http://www.marketingmagazine.co.uk/news/rss/599139/Green—Blacks-web-shop/

Wilson, S. (2008, May). Big break. *Entrepreneur, 36*(5), 102–108. Retrieved January 27, 2015, from http://www.entrepreneur.com/article/192754

SUGGESTED READINGS

Chan, A. (2012). Breaking into the international jewelry market: Legitimacy strategies and entrepreneurship of Hong Kong small businesses. *International Journal of China Marketing, 2*(2), 89–106. *Business Source Complete.* Web. 29 Oct. 2013.

Through narrative analysis, this article contrasts the "craftsman entrepreneurs" with the "opportunistic entrepreneurs" in their strategies for entering the global jewelry market. The article describes the craftsman entrepreneurs' weaknesses and how these could be overcome. It concludes by explaining in a context-dependent way how varying entrepreneurial strategies can maximize chances of success.

Cox, K. A. (2011). Learn to expect the unexpected in global retail expansion. *Graziadio Business Review, 14*(4), 1–7.

This article examines the successes and failures of businesses using international retail expansion as a method of entering a global market. It discusses Wal-Mart's success and Best Buy's failure using this approach. It also considers Tesco PLC's challenges in maintaining its world market share.

Harms, R., & Schiele, H. (2012). Antecedents and consequences of effectuation and causation in the international new venture creation process. *Journal of International Entrepreneurship, 10*(2), 95–116. *Business Source Complete.* Web. 29 Oct. 2013.

The article shows how a process-based view is useful for selecting an entry mode for international entrepreneurship. By framing international market entry as a process, the study contrasts causation and effectuation analysis in deciding on an entry mode. The article suggests that effectuation, as opposed to causation, tends to influence decisions made by more experienced entrepreneurs.

Rundh, B. (2011). Linking flexibility and entrepreneurship to the performances of SMEs in export markets. *Journal of Manufacturing Technology Management, 22*(3), 330–347. *Business Source Complete.* Web. 29 Oct. 2013.

The article presents a study of small and medium-sized enterprises' (SMEs) export marketing strategies. The study suggests different marketing approaches for exporting SMEs and the significance of the quality of exports and a flexible approach to local export markets. It has implications for managers, as it promotes a highly flexible market entry approach.

9

Global Marketing and Research and Development

Profile: Nando's

When Portuguese explorers visited Africa and "bumped" into the peri-peri spices in Mozambique in the 1600s, they decided to use these spices to marinate their chicken. Hundreds of years later, Fernando Duarte and Robbie Brozin fell in love with the recipe at a small restaurant in Rosettenville, South Africa. "It was love at first bite!" These two entrepreneurs started what is now a global brand: a chain with a presence in 24 countries, which has been voted the best business to work for in the United Kingdom (UK).

Although sometimes mistakenly thought of as Portuguese, Nando's is a proudly South African company that lives on the edge of marketing ethics; greatly values its human capital; and offers a very relaxed, collaborative, and friendly workplace environment. The company's headquarters are still based where the Nando's adventure started, in Rosettenville, Johannesburg. Nando's is the number-one exported brand out of South Africa and has a presence of 1,100 restaurants worldwide, even though the business is only 27 years old.

It is just as "big" in the UK as it is in South Africa, although the business is run very differently in the different locations. The Nando's business model is based on the idea of "my home is your home": The environment is inviting, homey, welcoming, sharing, and warm. In South Africa and Australia, the business is take-away style, but in the UK and now also in the U.S., there is a "hosted cockerel style," in which customers place their order, pay, and sit down; the food is then brought to your table. In Dubai, Nando's is a normal sit-down restaurant.

With passion, pride, courage, integrity, and family as its core values, training and human capital development is a key pillar of this business. Arts and "giving back" are the other two pillars of the business. Nando's purchases at least 10 works of South African art per restaurant and initiated a "chicken run" program, purchasing art from galleries in townships. The Creative Block Program also employs 250 artists to create small square "blocks" of art for use in the many restaurants worldwide. The firm believes in giving back to the local community and thus has quite a large program to fight malaria, which includes the distribution of mosquito nets.

The firm's marketing efforts have supported its success globally. Nando's ads are, in a way, the voice of the people and present responses to public events. The ads are controversial and must pass through several regulating bodies in South Africa. Nando's is currently moving toward making its corporate marketing more enabling for franchised markets. Key campaigns are designed at headquarters and can be modified or local-ized for different markets, but approval is necessary. Despite several challenges, the company has achieved impressive global brand awareness and has developed its start-up "chicken place" into a global chain.

SOURCES: Nando's [website]. (2014). Retrieved February 12, 2015, from http://www.nandos.com/

Ransom, S. (2014, January 16). *Corporate culture and marketing at Nando's*. Presentation at 2014 Thunderbird School of Global Management Winterim Class to the Republic of South Africa, Pretoria.

CHAPTER OBJECTIVES

1. To understand how increasing changes in the telecommunications technology will affect the global entrepreneur

2. To understand the importance of and role of innovation

3. To learn how to adapt a new product/service to the market it is entering

4. To understand and be able to use the product life cycle and to understand how to plan and develop this process

5. To learn how to evaluate new products for suitability to enter a market

6. To understand the global marketing mix and its key components

Introduction

The four major problems in the areas of marketing and research and development facing the global entrepreneur when entering or expanding in an international market(s) are (1) the technological environment, (2) product policy and the total quality issues, (3) adopting the best research and development strategy, and (4) developing and implementing the best marketing strategy. Each of these problems has become at the same time easier and yet more difficult due to rapidly changing technologies, shorter and shorter product life cycles, chang-ing consumer tastes, and changing economies, particularly in emerging markets. Depending on the nature of the global market, there can be significant problems in any of these four areas, particularly in the short run. When General Electric (GE) purchased a controlling inter-est in Tungstrum, the Hungarian light bulb manufacturing company, it expected to turn the company around, solve the total quality issue, and start to sell light bulbs to the countries in the European Union (EU) in a much shorter period of time than actually occurred. The GE manager in charge of changing the Tungstrum operation was continually heard saying, "In six months, we will have light bulbs for Europe." Six months turned into three years before the product was at a quality level acceptable to the European market. In spite of this time delay, in 2005–2006, GE moved much of its research and development in light bulbs to Tungstrum in Hungary, recognizing the quality of the science and scientists.

Technological Environment

The technological environment varies greatly from country to country and can change significantly. There are several ways in which technology will affect the global entrepreneur in the next decade. First, and perhaps foremost, is the use of social media. The Internet allows individuals from around the world to obtain information from millions of sources and often be able to purchase the product/service. Second, automatic translation in various media is available, allowing people to communicate in their own language with individuals all over the world. Third, satellites as well as the cloud play an ever increasing role in communication, learning, and storage, enabling people in even very remote areas to receive voice messages and data through handheld telephones. Fourth, there is the increasing use of nanotechnology to create products on a micro level. Fifth, advances in biotechnology constantly transform agriculture and its output and the level of medicine. And, sixth, more and more people have purchasing power as more countries move into market economies. These result in issues in telecommunication and e-business, discussed in the following sections.

Telecommunications

One of the biggest obstacles in global business, particularly in less-developed and emerging markets, used to be telecommunications, but this is rapidly changing. Since it is no longer necessary to hardwire phone lines, economies are leapfrogging from phones being unavailable to cellular phones being available everywhere, even in the remotest parts of China and Africa. Because of the quick and relatively inexpensive installation of this new infrastructure and the merging technology of the cloud, computer, and telephone, a growing number of people, even in rural areas of Asia, are accessing the web through cell phones, allowing business transactions to take place in the remotest of areas. During the next decade, the further merger of wireless technology and the Internet will radically change the way people communicate and will open even more markets in less-developed countries and rural areas. Cellular phones are also making an impact in developed countries such as Finland, Norway, and Sweden, where more than 80% of each country's population are cellular subscribers.

With telecommunication services providing a better communication system, it is felt that this helps support economic development and the attraction of foreign direct investment. Some telecommunication operations are state run, such as many in the Asia-Pacific region, but an increasing number are private-sector companies. Some former state-owned companies that have been privatized, often with the help of foreign companies, include Korea Telecom, Philippines Global Telecom, and Thailand's Telecom Asia. Most of the investment needed to privatize and expand the telecommunication systems in developed and developing countries will come from outside the country itself.

E-Business

As the number of individuals and companies having access to the Internet expands, the role of e-business in international commerce will be similarly impacted. This will occur in both the business-to-business and the business-to-consumer markets. Two areas of e-business will have a significant effect on global consumers: retailing and financial services. Eventually, there will be a convergence of business transactions, money, and personal computers, allowing the use of electronic cash to become more widely used. The forerunner of this is in existence already: prepaid smart cards. Twenty-four-hour buying and selling throughout global worldwide markets is now a regular event and will continue to grow.

This worldwide e-commerce system (both business-to-business and business-to-consumer) has affected the role of financial institutions. For example, companies today do not have to wait as long for their money after a sales transaction occurs, substantially reducing the days in accounts receivable and the funding required.

This speed in cash obtainment in turn affects the foreign currency markets. Today, if a company in China buys goods in the United States and wants to pay in Chinese renminbi (RMB), a system is used for converting RMBs to U.S. dollars. This is easily done through regulated foreign exchange markets as discussed in Chapter 4. The system's move to a single common exchange market using the prevailing exchange rates makes the transaction seamless and much faster.

Product Policy and Total Quality Issues

Goods and/or services are the core of a global entrepreneur's international operations; success depends on how well the goods or services offered satisfy the wants and needs of the targeted market and how they are seen as different (their unique selling proposition) from competitive products and services available. This process will be looked at in terms of product adaptation and total quality.

Product Adaptation

There are two major factors that affect the degree to which a domestic product/service needs to be altered to be a success in the global market: the domestic product/service itself and the characteristics of the international market on both a country and local basis. The needed changes can range from minor ones (such as translating the label) to major ones (such as physical product changes). Changes needed generally include such things as brand names, instructions-on-use labels, logos, measurement units, packaging, and product features and design.

Aspects of the Domestic Product/Service

The type and characteristics of the domestic product/service significantly affect the degree of modifications needed for an international market. A global entrepreneur needs to ensure that the product does not contain ingredients that violate the legal requirements or religious or social customs of a country. For example, in Islamic countries, vegetable shortening needs to be used rather than animal fats. In Japan, it is illegal to have any formaldehyde in hair and skin products. In India, mutton needs to be used instead of beef. In some countries, the product may not be operable due to the differences in the current and disruptions in electric power systems and the outlets.

A major difficulty confronting the global entrepreneur is making available the needed parts, repairs, or servicing for a product. If there are problems with the product/service and repairs and service are not up to standard, then the product/service and company image suffer and future sales will be difficult. Sometimes a product/service designed for use in one way in the domestic market will be used for entirely different purposes in the global market. It is important that the global entrepreneur provide good training for the individuals providing the repairs and service. This is usually most easily accomplished through outsourcing to a local firm under a contract reflecting the laws of the country.

Brand names and aesthetics provide another challenge. Since the brand name conveys the image of the product/service, it is important to standardize it as much as possible across global markets. Standardizing the name is particularly difficult due to translation problems, especially when a variety of products are going to many different countries. Sometimes other elements such as colors, packaging, and symbols also need to be standardized.

Packaging is an area where modifications almost always occur in entering a global market. This in part reflects the longer time that the product remains in the distribution system and the differences in the channel members of the distribution itself. Usually, the international package uses more expensive materials, such as the airtight, reclosable containers that are used in the global distribution of food products.

The labeling of the packaging usually needs modification. Sometimes this means conforming to a legal requirement to list all text bilingually, such as in French and English in Canada and in Finnish and Swedish in Finland. Some country regulations often require more informative labeling concerning the content and percentage of ingredients, particularly on food products. This information provides for better consumer understanding and protection. Not conforming to the content, language, or laws of the country will often cause a product to be held up in customs, such as occurred when the author was importing wine from Hungary that did not have the alcohol content of the wine correctly provided on the label.

Characteristics of the International Market

Typically, the characteristics of the global market(s) mandate some product/service modifications. These often result from government regulations, some of which may be protecting domestic industry or responding to political controversies among countries. The global entrepreneur must be aware of not only the present regulations but also the exceptions and possible future changes. Products entering some global markets, such as the EU, must comply with the product standards established by the EU as well as adopt the overall system approved by the International Standards Organization.

Tariff and nontariff barriers also affect product adaptations. If tariffs are so high that the domestic product is not price competitive, then a less costly version may have to be developed. Nontariff barriers—such as bureaucratic red tape, product standards, required testing or approval procedures, or domestic product subsidies—can also affect product adaptation. Because some nontariff barriers may be intended to protect domestic products and industries, they may be the most difficult to overcome.

Competitive products and features often affect the product adaptation needed. Already established in their domestic market, these competitive products need to be analyzed to determine any product changes needed for competitive positioning. Ideally, the changes made will not only establish a strong competitive market position but will be hard to duplicate by any domestic product manufacturers.

The stage of economic development of the foreign market and the economic status of potential users can also affect the product. As the economy of a country becomes stronger, buyers are usually better able to afford and demand higher-quality product alternatives, as has been occurring in China over the last years. Sometimes the economic stage of a country requires that the product be significantly simplified or downgraded due to the lack of purchasing power or usage conditions.

Purchase decisions are also affected by the attitudes, behavior, beliefs, and traditions of the purchaser in the global market. The global entrepreneur must be very aware of how these cultural aspects affect the changes needed in the product to gain customer approval and result in sales. Such cultural aspects particularly affect the product's positioning in the market and the perception of the consumers of the global product with respect to competitive products. For instance, Coke entered the Japanese and EU markets using the name Coke Light instead of Diet Coke so as not to confront consumers with the idea of weight loss. The promotional theme behind Coke Light was not weight loss but rather figure maintenance.

Training the Global Managers   Training global managers for overseas assignments is very important. Proper training can help global managers understand the culture, customers, and work habits of the specific market situation. The most common topics covered in this cultural training include business etiquette, customs, economics, history, politics, and social etiquette of the country.

The type of training also reflects the global entrepreneur's overall philosophy of international management. Some global entrepreneurs prefer to send their own people to fill an overseas position; others prefer to use host-country locals. The management philosophy of global entrepreneurs tends to be one of the following: (1) ethnocentric philosophy (putting home-country people in key international positions), (2) geocentric philosophy (integrating diverse regions of the world through a global approach to decision making), or (3) polycentric philosophy (using local host-country nationals in key international positions). The venture with the ethnocentric philosophy usually does the training at the headquarters in the home country, while the polycentric philosophy has the local key managers do the training in the host country. One company, when entering the EU, wanted its facility in Germany to mirror the facility and operations of the company in the United States.

Leadership in an International Context The leadership style of a global entrepreneur tends to fall in one of three categories: (1) authoritarian (focuses on work-centered behavior to ensure task accomplishment), (2) paternalistic (uses work-centered behavior along with a protective employee-centered concern), or (3) participative (uses both a work-centered and a people-centered approach). Different approaches to each of these occur in various parts of the world.

Of course, an outstanding global entrepreneurial leader is a transformational one—a visionary leader with a sense of mission who is able to motivate employees to embrace the vision, goals, and new ways of doing things. These global leaders have several things in common, regardless of the culture of the operation. First, the transformational global leader is charismatic and has the admiration of employees. He or she builds confidence, loyalty, and pride at all levels of the organization. Second, a global transformational leader gets employees to question old paradigms and accept new ways of doing things, effectively articulating the vision and mission. Finally, a transformational global leader determines the needs of employees and further develops these individuals so they are more effective and efficient.

The leadership in a particular country needs to reflect the culture of the country. This has been the focus of the Global Leadership and Organizational Behavior Effectiveness (GLOBE) project, which evaluated the cultural dimensions of performance orientation, assertiveness, future orientation, humane orientation, institutional collectivism, in-group collectivism, gender egalitarianism, power distance, and uncertainty avoidance across many countries. As indicated in Table 9.1, countries vary on each of these dimensions. While the United States and Russia (individualistic countries) scored high on performance improvement, Singapore and Sweden (collectivistic countries) scored high on institutional collectivism. In terms of power distance (the degree to which members of an organization should expect power to be distributed equally), entrepreneurial companies in high-power-distance countries such as Brazil, France, and Thailand tend to have more hierarchical decision-making processes with limited participation and communication. A good global entrepreneurial leader takes into account the country dimensions in the leadership style employed in the particular country.

Total Quality Issues

One major issue for the global entrepreneur is the total quality of the product/service offered; international customers need to have their expectations met or exceeded regardless of the provider. This is true even in developing economies where some products/services provided in the past have not been of sufficient quality. To accomplish this, the global entrepreneur needs to focus on quality, cost, and innovation.

| Table 9.1 | Cultural Clusters Classified on Societal Culture Practices |

Cultural Dimension	High-Score Clusters	Mid-Score Clusters	Low-Score Clusters
Performance Orientation	Confucian Asia Germanic Europe Anglo	Southern Asia Sub-Saharan Africa Latin Europe Nordic Europe Middle East	Latin America Eastern Europe
Assertiveness	Germanic Europe Eastern Europe	Sub-Saharan Africa Latin America Anglo Middle East Confucian Asia Latin Europe Southern Asia	
Future Orientation	Germanic Europe Nordic Europe	Confucian Asia Anglo Southern Asia Sub-Saharan Africa Latin Europe	Middle East Latin America Eastern Europe
Humane Orientation	Southern Asia Sub-Saharan Africa	Middle East Anglo Nordic Europe Latin America Confucian Asia Eastern Europe	Latin Europe Germanic Europe
Institutional Collectivism	Nordic Europe Confucian Asia	Anglo Southern Asia Sub-Saharan Africa Middle East Eastern Europe	Latin Europe Latin America
In-Group Collectivism	Southern Asia Middle East Eastern Europe Latin America Confucian Asia	Sub-Saharan Africa Latin Europe	Anglo Germanic Europe Nordic Europe

(Continued)

Table 9.1 (Continued)

Cultural Dimension	High-Score Clusters	Mid-Score Clusters	Low-Score Clusters
Gender Egalitarianism	Eastern Europe Nordic Europe	Latin America Anglo Latin Europe Sub-Saharan Africa Southern Asia Confucian Asia Germanic Europe	Middle East
Power Distance		Southern Asia Latin America Eastern Europe Sub-Saharan Africa Middle East Latin Europe Confucian Asia Anglo Germanic Europe	Nordic Europe
Uncertainty Avoidance	Nordic Europe Germanic Europe	Confucian Asia Anglo Sub-Saharan Africa Latin Europe Southern Asia	Middle East Latin America Eastern Europe

SOURCE: Javidan, M., Dorfman, P., de Luque, M. S., & House, R. J. (2006, February). In the eye of the beholder: Cross-cultural lessons in leadership from project GLOBE. *Academy of Management Executive, 20*(1), 67.

China, India, Ireland, and Germany are countries that ICU Global (a video conferencing provider) targeted, according to founder and chief executive Stephen McKenzie. The company had six people in the UK with an anticipated turnover of £3 million. McKenzie feels it is easier for a small business to expand into other countries, as you can provide "the same quality assurance to end users." He adds, "Technology allows you to provide full-support, virtual operations in other countries" (Woods, 2008).

The countries that offer the greatest opportunities are selected for expansion. "It's good to have a base in Germany because you can easily access the rest of Europe," McKenzie states. "Then, there's a thriving technology center in India." McKenzie also has taken advantage of being born in Germany and the possibilities in India due to a former employee returning home to the subcontinent. "Therefore, there was an opportunity to move into the main cities in India," he says. ICU Global started in China by doing research and development with a Chinese company. McKenzie notes, "It's a situation that will only grow" (Woods, 2008).

Some global entrepreneurs falsely believe that by increasing the quality of their product/service to a very high level, the accompanying costs would increase, resulting in a need to have a very high price. Companies measuring quality in terms of defective parts per million have found that as the error rate (expressed in terms of sigma) fell (the level of sigma increased), so did the cost of producing the product. In other words, quality and cost are inversely related. A global entrepreneur can produce quality at a lower cost per unit when producing with low error rates than when producing with higher error rates.

A similar false belief surrounds technology. Many global entrepreneurs falsely think that the best way to exploit any new technology is to get to the international market first and charge a premium price. Often, the best way to exploit the advantage of a new high technology is to enter the international market at a lower price. This allows the company to grow its market share as quickly as possible, driving less efficient competition from the market while increasing overall revenues and profits. Paradoxically, some high-tech global entrepreneurs can thrive at the same time their prices are falling the fastest. Because this usually results in significantly reduced margins and lower return on investment (ROI), these global entrepreneurs are generating more revenues through increased sales.

The hypercompetitive, shorter product life cycles today require a global entrepreneur to outsource more and more of their manufacturing and focus on developing new technologies. They also need to continually add features that increase the value to keep their product/service from becoming generic or sold almost strictly on price. This requires an effective use of benchmarking—identifying what leading-edge competitors are doing and using this to produce improved products or services. Whenever possible, a global entrepreneur should employ mass customizations—tailor-making mass production products to meet the expectations of the customer. Indeed, offering quality goods and services for the right market price always pays off.

Adopting the Best Research and Development Strategy

Developing a good international research and development process requires focus on three areas: (1) defining what innovation is to the company, (2) performing opportunity analysis, and (3) understanding the product life cycle.

CULTURAL STORIES

Story 1

My husband and I met a guy named Nacho in a sports bar in Argentina. We got to talking about Nacho's cousin who was in "jail." We told him we were sorry to hear that. Nacho looked at us with a confused face and said, "But it's a good school." That's when we realized he meant "Yale."

(Continued)

(Continued)

Story 2

When my Chinese was pretty elementary, I told my girlfriend's father that I used to deliver furniture in high school. I did not know the word for deliver, so looked up "send" and used the word "tou" (ÿ)—but instead I had informed him that, in high school, I was a furniture thief.

SOURCES: Reser, Jessica (2011, May 19). Nacho's cousin. Retrieved January 29, 2015, from http://culturalconfusions .com/2011/05/19/nachos-cousin/

Schulte, S. (2011, March 10). Chairs, tables, and sofas. Retrieved January 29, 2015, from http://culturalconfusions .com/2011/03/10/chairs-tables-and-sofas/

Innovation

Innovation is the key to the future of any global or even domestic company. As technologies change, old products decrease in sales and old industries decrease in volume and sometimes die. Inventions and innovations are the building blocks of the future of any international organization. As Thomas Edison reportedly said, "Innovative genius is 1% inspiration and 99% perspiration."

There are a variety of views regarding what constitutes innovation. To some, it is a new technological breakthrough. For others, it is a new invention or way of doing things. Still for others, innovation is a new design or new business model. For some, it is managing chaos or turbulence. The only commonality among these many views is "new." Indeed, while innovation requires something new and involves creativity and invention, true innovation requires one more thing—delivering customer value. Until the innovation is on the market delivering some new value to customers, it is not really an innovation. In the marketplace, an innovation can take a variety of forms, such as a new design, a new delivery system, a new package, a new production process, a new invention, or a radical new technological breakthrough.

Types of Innovation

There are various levels of innovation based on the uniqueness of the idea. Figure 9.1 presents three major types of innovation in decreasing order of uniqueness: breakthrough innovation, technological innovation, and ordinary innovation. As you would expect, the rarest innovations are of the breakthrough type. These extremely unique innovations often establish the platform on which future innovations in an area are developed. Given that they are often the basis for further innovation in an area, these innovations should be protected as much as possible by strong patents, trade secrets, or copyrights. Breakthrough innovations include such ideas as penicillin, the steam engine, the computer, the airplane, the automobile, the Internet, and nanotechnology.

Figure 9.1 Types of Innovation and Their Frequency

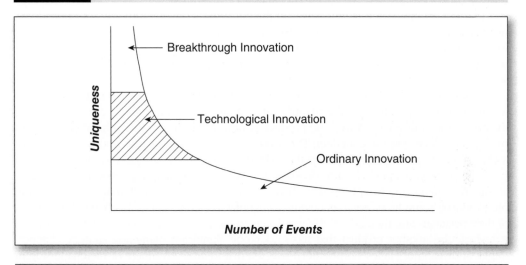

SOURCE: Hisrich, R. D., Peters, M. P., & Shepherd, D. A. (2013). *Entrepreneurship* (9th ed., p. 99). Burr Ridge, IL: McGraw-Hill/Irwin.

The next type of innovation—technological innovation—occurs more frequently than breakthrough innovation and in general is not at the same level of scientific discovery and advancement. Nonetheless, these are very meaningful innovations, because they do offer advancements in the product/market arena. As such, they usually need to be protected. Such innovations as the personal computer, the flip watch for containing pictures, voice and text messaging, and the jet airplane are examples of technological innovations.

The final type of innovation—ordinary innovation—is the one that occurs most frequently. These more numerous innovations usually extend a technological innovation into a better product/service or one that has a different—usually better—market appeal. These innovations often come from market analysis and market pull, not technology push. The market has a stronger effect on the innovation (market pull) than the technology (technology push). One ordinary innovation was developed by Sara Blakely, who wanted to get rid of unsightly panty lines while also being able to wear open-toed shoes and sandals. To do this, she cut off the feet of her control-top pantyhose to produce footless pantyhose. Investing all of her total money available (US$5,000), Sara Blakely started Spanx, an Atlanta-based company, which in five years had annual earnings of US$20 million.

Defining a New Innovation (Product or Service)

One of the dilemmas facing global entrepreneurs is defining a "new" product or identifying what is actually new or unique in an idea. Fashion jeans became very popular, even though the concept of blue jeans was not new. What was new was the use of names such as Sassoon, Vanderbilt, and Chic on the label of the jeans. Sony made the Walkman one of the most popular new products of the 1980s, although the concept of cassette players had been in existence for many years.

In these examples, the newness was in the consumer concept. Other types of products, not necessarily new in concept, have also been defined as new. When coffee companies introduced naturally decaffeinated coffee, the initial promotional campaigns made definite use of the word *new* in the copy, even though the only change in the product was it being without caffeine.

Other products have simply been marketed in new packages or containers but have been identified as new products by the manufacturer. When soft drink manufacturers introduced the can, some consumers viewed the product as new, even though the only difference from previous products was the container. The invention of the aerosol can is another example of a change in the package or container that added an element of newness to old, established products such as whipped cream, deodorant, and hair spray. Flip-top cans, plastic bottles, aseptic packaging, and the pump have also contributed to a perceived image of newness in old products. Some firms, such as detergent manufacturers, have merely changed the colors of their packages and then added the word *new* to the package and their promotional copy. Pantyhose are another product that has undergone significant marketing strategy changes. L'eggs (a division of Hanes Corporation) was the first to take advantage of merchandising in supermarkets using special packaging, lower prices, and a new display.

In the industrial market, firms may call their products "new" when only slight changes or modifications have been made in the appearance of the product. For example, improvements in metallurgical techniques have modified the precision and strength of many raw materials that are used in industrial products, such as machinery. These improved characteristics have led firms to market products containing the improved metals as "new."

In the process of expanding their sales volume, many companies add products to their product line that are already marketed by other companies. For example, when a drug company added a cold tablet to its product line and a longtime manufacturer of soap pads entered the dishwasher detergent market, both advertised their products as new. In both cases, the product was new to the manufacturer but not new to the consumer. With the increased emphasis on diversification in the world economy, this frequently occurs today. Firms are constantly looking for new markets to enter in order to increase profits and make more effective use of their resources. Other firms are simply changing one or more of the marketing mix elements to give old products a new image.

Classification of New Products

New products may be classified from the viewpoint of either the consumer or the firm. Each of these points of view should be considered as both establish product objectives; the consumer perception of these objectives can determine the success or failure of any new product in the new or current market.

From a Consumer's Viewpoint There is a broad interpretation of what actually is a new product from the consumer's viewpoint. One attempt to identify new products classifies the degree of newness according to how much behavioral change or new learning is required by the consumer to use the product. This technique looks at newness in terms of its effect on the consumer rather than whether the product is new to a company, is packaged differently, has changed physical form, or is an improved version of an old or existing product.

The continuum proposed by Thomas Robertson (shown in Figure 9.2) contains three categories based on the disrupting influence that product innovation has on established consumption patterns. Most new products tend to fall at the *continuous innovations* end of the continuum. Examples are annual automobile style changes, fashion style changes, package changes, or product size or color changes. Products such as compact discs, Sony cellphones, and iPods tend to be in the middle of the continuum. Truly new products, called *discontinuous innovations*, are rare and require a great deal of new learning by the consumer because these products perform either a previously unfulfilled function or an existing function in a new way. The Internet is one example of a discontinuous innovation that has radically altered our society's lifestyle. The basis for identifying new products according to their effect on consumer consumption patterns is consistent with the marketing philosophy that satisfaction of consumer needs is fundamental to a venture's existence.

Figure 9.2 Continuum for Classifying New Products

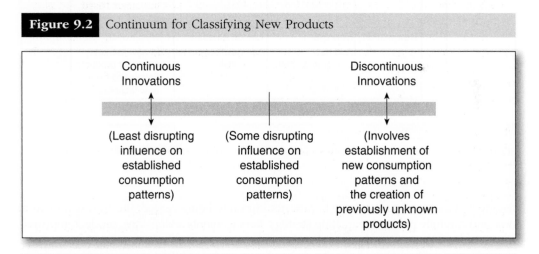

SOURCE: Adapted from Robertson, T. (1967, January). The process of innovation and the diffusion of innovation. *The Journal of Marketing, 31*(1), 14–19.

From a Firm's Viewpoint Another way to classify the objectives of new products is indicated in Figure 9.3. In this figure, an important distinction is made between new products and new markets (i.e., market development). New products are defined in terms of the amount of improved technology, whereas market development is based on the degree of new segmentation.

The situation in which there is new technology *and* a new market is the most complicated and difficult—and it has the highest degree of risk. Since the new product involves

Figure 9.3 New Product Classification System

Market Newness	Product Objectives	No Technological Change	Improved Technology	New Technology
	No market change		Reformation Change in formula or physical product to optimize costs and quality	Replacement Replace existing product with new one based on improved technology
	Strengthened market	Remerchandising Increase sales to existing customers	Improved product Improve product's utility to customers	Product life extension Add new similar products to line; serve more customers based on new technology
	New market	New use Add new segments that can use present products	Market extension Add new segments modifying present products	Diversification Add new markets with new products developed from new technology

Technology Newness ⟶

SOURCE: Hisrich, R. D., Peters, M. P., & Shepherd, D. A. (2013). *Entrepreneurship* (9th ed., p. 102). Burr Ridge, IL: McGraw-Hill/Irwin.

new technology and customers who are not currently being served, the firm will need a new and carefully planned marketing strategy. Replacements, extensions, product improvements, reformulations, and remerchandising involve product and market development strategies that will range in difficulty, depending on whether the firm has had prior experience with a similar product or with the same target market.

Opportunity Analysis

Opportunity Recognition

Some entrepreneurs have the ability to recognize a business opportunity—a skill that is fundamental to the entrepreneurial process as well as growing a business.

A business opportunity represents a possibility for the global entrepreneur to successfully fill a large enough unsatisfied need that sufficient sales and profits result. Significant research has yielded several models of the opportunity recognition process.

Recognizing an opportunity often results from the knowledge and experience of the individual global entrepreneur and, when appropriate, the entrepreneurial business. This prior knowledge results from a combination of education and experience; the relevant experience could be work-related or could result from a variety of personal experiences or events. The other important factors in this process are entrepreneurial alertness and entrepreneurial networks. The interaction between entrepreneurial alertness and the global entrepreneur's prior knowledge of markets and customer problems has a significant effect on success. Those global entrepreneurs who have the ability to recognize meaningful business opportunities are in a strategic position to successfully complete the product planning and development process and launch new ventures.

Opportunity Assessment Plan

The global entrepreneur should carefully assess every innovative idea and opportunity. One good way to do this is to develop an opportunity assessment plan, as discussed in Chapter 6. An opportunity assessment plan is *not* the business plan; it focuses on the idea and the market (the opportunity) for the idea—not on the venture. It also is shorter than a business plan and does not contain any formal financial statements of the business venture. The opportunity assessment plan is developed to serve as the basis for the decision to either act on the opportunity or wait until another (and one hopes better) opportunity comes along. A typical opportunity assessment plan has four sections: (1) a description of the idea and its competition; (2) an assessment of the domestic and international market for the idea; (3) an assessment of the entrepreneur and the team; and (4) a discussion of the steps needed to make the idea the basis for a viable business venture (see Chapter 6).

Understanding the Product Life Cycle

Once ideas emerge from idea sources or creative problem solving, they need further development and refinement. This refining process—the product planning and development process—is divided into four major stages: idea stage, concept stage, product development stage, and test marketing stage, which then results in commercialization and the start of the product life cycle (see Figure 9.4).

Establishing Evaluation Criteria

At each stage of the product planning and development process, criteria for evaluation need to be established. These criteria should be all-inclusive and quantitative enough to screen the product carefully in the particular stage of development. Criteria should be established to evaluate the new idea in terms of market opportunity, competition, the marketing system, financial factors, and production factors.

A market opportunity in the form of a new or current need for the product/service idea must exist. The determination of market demand is by far the most important criterion of a proposed new product idea. Assessment of the market opportunity and size needs to consider the characteristics and attitudes of consumers or industries that may buy the

Figure 9.4 The Product Planning and Development Process

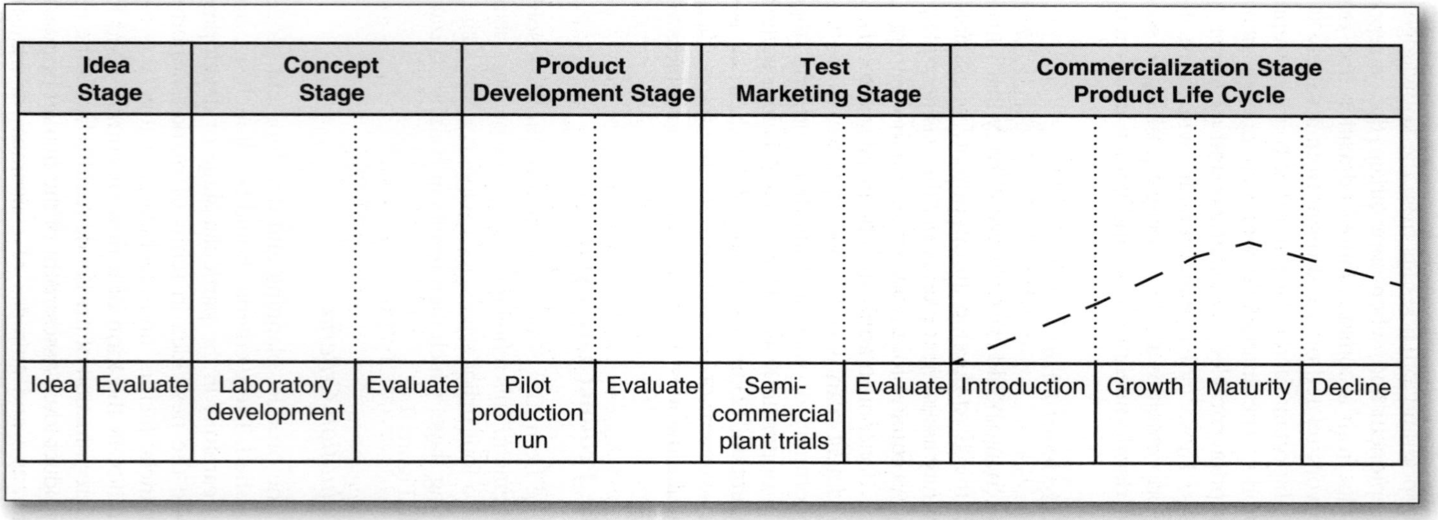

Idea Stage		Concept Stage		Product Development Stage		Test Marketing Stage		Commercialization Stage Product Life Cycle			
Idea	Evaluate	Laboratory development	Evaluate	Pilot production run	Evaluate	Semi-commercial plant trials	Evaluate	Introduction	Growth	Maturity	Decline

SOURCE: Hisrich, R. D. (1991). *Marketing decisions for new and mature products* (2nd ed.). Copyright 1991. Upper Saddle River, NJ: Pearson Education, Inc.

product, the size of this potential market in dollars and units, the nature of the market with respect to its stage in the life cycle of the product/service (growing or declining), and the share of the market the product/service could reasonably capture.

Current competing producers, prices, and marketing efforts should also be evaluated, particularly in terms of their effect on the market share of the proposed idea. The new idea should be able to compete successfully with products/services already on the market by having features that will meet or overcome current and anticipated competition. The new idea should have some unique differential advantage based on an evaluation of all competitive products/services filling the same consumer needs. At least three to five things need to be different from products/services on the market (the unique selling propositions).

The new idea should have synergy with existing management capabilities and marketing strategies. The firm should be able to use its marketing experience and other expertise in this new product/service effort. For example, GE would have a far less difficult time adding a new lighting device to its line than Procter & Gamble. Several factors should be considered in evaluating the degree of fit: the degree to which the ability and time of the present sales force can be transferred to the new product/service, the ability to sell the new product/service through the company's established channels of distribution, and the ability to piggyback the advertising and promotion required to introduce the new product/service.

The proposed product/service should be supported by and contribute to the company's financial well-being. The manufacturing cost per unit, the marketing expense, and the amount of capital need to be determined along with the breakeven point and the long-term profit outlook for the product/service.

The compatibility of the new product's production requirements with existing plant, machinery, and personnel should also be evaluated. If the new product/service idea cannot be integrated into existing manufacturing processes, additional plant and equipment costs will need to be taken into account. All required materials for production need to be available and accessible in sufficient quantity.

Global entrepreneurs need to formally evaluate an idea throughout its evolution. They must be sure that the product/service can be the basis for a new venture. This can be done through careful evaluation that results in a go or no-go decision at each of the stages of the product/service planning and development process: the idea stage, the concept stage, the product development stage, and the test marketing stage.

Idea Stage

Promising new product/service ideas should be identified and impractical ones eliminated at the idea stage, allowing maximum use of the company's resources. One evaluation method successfully used at this stage is the systematic market evaluation checklist, where each new idea is expressed in terms of its primary values, merits, and benefits. Consumers are presented with clusters of new product/service values to determine which, if any, new product service alternatives should be pursued and which should be discarded. A company can test many new alternatives with this evaluation method;

promising ideas can be further developed and resources will not be wasted on ideas that are incompatible with the market's values.

It is important to determine both the need for the new idea as well as its value to the company. If there is no need for the suggested product/service, its development should not be continued. Similarly, the new product/service idea should not be developed if it does not have any benefit or value to the firm. To accurately determine the need for a new idea, it is helpful to define the potential needs of the market in terms of timing, satisfaction, alternatives, benefits and risks, future expectations, price-versus-product performance features, market structure and size, and economic conditions. A form for helping in this need determination process is shown in Table 9.2. The factors in this table should be evaluated not only in terms of the characteristics of the potential new product/service but also in terms of the new product/service's competitive strength relative to each factor. This comparison with competitive products/services will indicate the proposed idea's strengths and weaknesses and, more importantly, its unique selling propositions.

Table 9.2 Determining the Need for a New Product or Service Idea

Factor	Aspects	Competitive Capabilities	New Product Idea Capability
Type of Need Continuing need Declining need Emerging need Future need			
Timing of Need Duration of need Frequency of need Demand cycle Position in life cycle			
Competing Ways to Satisfy Need Doing without Using present way Modifying present way			
Perceived Benefits/Risks Utility to customer Appeal characteristics Customer tastes and preferences Buying motives Consumption habits			

Factor	Aspects	Competitive Capabilities	New Product Idea Capability
Price versus Performance Features Price–quantity relationship Demand elasticity Stability of price Stability of market			
Market Size and Potential Market growth Market trends Market development requirements Threats to market			
Availability of Customer Funds General economic conditions Economic trends Customer income Financing opportunities			

SOURCE: Hisrich, R. D. (1991). *Marketing decisions for new and mature products* (2nd ed.). Copyright 1991. Upper Saddle River, NJ: Pearson Education, Inc.

The need determination should focus on the type of need, its timing, the users involved with trying the product/service, the importance of controllable marketing variables, the overall market structure, and the characteristics of the market. Each of these factors should be evaluated in terms of the characteristics of the new idea being considered and the aspects and capabilities of present methods for satisfying the particular need. This analysis will indicate the extent of the opportunity available.

In determination of the value of the new product/service to the firm, financial scheduling—such as cash outflow, cash inflow, contribution to profit, and ROI—needs to be evaluated in terms of other product/service ideas as well as investment alternatives. With the use of the form shown in Table 9.3, the dollar amount of each of the considerations important to the new idea needs to be determined as accurately as possible so that a quantitative evaluation can be made. These figures can then be revised as better information becomes available and the product/service continues to be developed.

Concept Stage

After a new product/service idea has passed evaluation at the idea stage, it is further developed and refined through interaction with customers. In the concept stage, the

Table 9.3 Determining the Value for a New Product/Service Idea

Factor	Cost (in $)
Cash Outflow Research and development costs Marketing costs Capital equipment costs Other costs	
Cash Inflow Sales of new product Effect on additional sales of existing products Salvageable value	
Net Cash Flow Maximum exposure Time to maximum exposure Duration of exposure Total investment Maximum net cash in a single year	
Profit Profit from new product Profit affecting additional sales of existing products Fraction of total company profit	
Relative Return Return on shareholders' equity (ROE)	
Return on Investment (ROI) Cost of capital Present value (PV) Discounted cash flow (DCF) Return on assets employed (ROA) Return on sales	
Compared to Other Investments Compared to other product opportunities Compared to other investment opportunities	

SOURCE: Hisrich, R. D. (1991). *Marketing decisions for new and mature products* (2nd ed.). Copyright 1991. Upper Saddle River, NJ: Pearson Education, Inc.

refined idea is tested to determine consumer acceptance. Initial reactions to the concept are obtained from potential customers or members of the distribution channel when appropriate. One method of measuring consumer acceptance is the conversational interview in which selected respondents are exposed to statements that reflect the physical characteristics and attributes of the product/service. Where competing products (or services) exist, these statements can also compare their primary features. Both favorable and unfavorable features can be discovered by analyzing consumers' responses. Favorable features can then be incorporated into the new product/service.

Features, price, and promotion need to be evaluated for both the concept being studied and any major competing products by asking the following questions:

- How does the new concept compare with competitive products or services in terms of quality and reliability?
- Is the concept superior or deficient compared with products and services currently available on the market?
- Is a good market opportunity available?

Similar evaluations should be done for all aspects of the marketing strategy.

Product Development Stage

In the product development stage, consumer reaction to the physical product/service is determined. One tool frequently used at this stage is the consumer panel, in which a group of potential consumers is given product samples. Participants keep a record of their use of the product and comment on its virtues and deficiencies. This technique is more applicable for product ideas and works for only some service ideas.

The panel of potential customers might also be given a sample of the product and one or more competitive products simultaneously. Then one of several methods—such as multiple brand comparisons, risk analysis, level of repeat purchases, or intensity of preference analysis—can be used to determine consumer preference.

Test Marketing Stage

Although the results of the product development stage provide the basis of the final marketing plan, a market test can increase the certainty of successful commercialization. This last step in the evaluation process, the test marketing stage, provides actual sales results, which indicate the acceptance level of consumers. Positive test results indicate the degree of probability of a successful product launch and company formation. This is not frequently done by a global entrepreneur due to the significant time and costs involved.

Developing and Implementing the Best Marketing Strategy

Once an international market is selected, the global entrepreneur needs to develop the appropriate marketing mix—product, price, distribution, and promotion. A first step is to determine the extent to which these elements can be standardized.

Standardization

This critical decision on the degree of standardization will affect the global entrepreneur when entering international markets. Should a cross-national strategy rather than a fully localized strategy be adopted? Some factors that favor standardization include a shrinking world marketplace; the increasing use of English as the language of business; economies of scale in production; and economies in research, development, and marketing. Other factors favor a more localized (market-specific) strategy, such as different buyer behavior patterns, different uses, government regulations, and severe local market differences and distinctiveness. Generally, a flexible marketing strategy that is based globally but acts locally yields the best results. This approach incorporates differences into the overall global marketing strategy that can be implemented locally, reflecting the local market conditions.

Pricing Decisions

Pricing decisions are much more complicated in international versus domestic markets due in part to currency and cost differences and government regulations and policies. Two critical issues involved in pricing decisions are foreign market pricing and transfer (intracompany) pricing.

Foreign Market Pricing

The factors affecting the price in a particular market (costs, competitive prices, customer price sensitivity and behavior, market structure and conditions, and objectives of the company) vary from market to market, requiring pricing decisions to vary as well. Having a uniform pricing policy should be avoided; instead, price should be used as a competitive factor in the marketing program in each country. Although individual prices should reflect the specific conditions of a market, prices should also be coordinated on a worldwide basis, particularly when economic integration is occurring across markets. One way to do this is to set maximum and minimum prices within which the local countries' price can be established. This approach allows flexibility in pricing to reflect local market conditions but does not allow so much price deviation, so a price–quality relationship can be established and cross-border shopping can be discouraged.

Every global entrepreneur has to deal with the issue of export pricing. Export pricing generally uses a standard worldwide price, different prices for domestic and export products, or market-differentiated pricing. When the global entrepreneur uses standard worldwide pricing, domestic and export products are priced the same based on average unit costs of fixed, variable, and export cost. When using dual pricing that differentiates between domestic and export prices, the global entrepreneur can use either cost plus pricing or marginal cost pricing. *Cost plus pricing* means that a margin is put on top of the full allocation of domestic and foreign costs. While this ensures that a margin or return occurs, the result can be a price too high for the market. The *marginal cost* method for pricing exports uses the direct costs for producing and selling for export as the floor of the pricing decision. Any research and development costs and domestic production and marketing costs are not used. A margin is then added to this floor cost.

Generally, export pricing methods focus on costs, not demand. One demand-oriented pricing method—market-differentiated pricing—focuses on competitive prices in a market to establish an export price. Unique export costs, such as any cost for modifying the product, costs of the export operation, and any costs for entering the foreign market, are taken into consideration.

Transfer Pricing

Transfer pricing is pricing items for sale to other members of the company. It is often referred to as *intracompany pricing*. The pricing of intracorporate sales can have a significant effect on the price of the product in the international market and therefore on global sales and profits. Various factors affect both the method and the level of transfer pricing, such as import duties, taxes, tariffs, government regulations, and rules concerning repatriation of profits. A low transfer price on goods shipped to a subsidiary and a high transfer price on goods imported from it results in a maximum tax liability for the subsidiary, which is beneficial if the tax in the subsidiary country is substantially lower than the tax in the home country of the company.

Generally, one of four methods is used for transfer pricing: (1) transfer at the price that unrelated parties would have reached on the transaction, or *arm's length pricing*; (2) transfer at the price of direct cost; (3) transfer at the price of direct cost plus any additional expenses; or (4) transfer at a price derived from the end-market price. Often, a company can have its price challenged by either the home country tax authority, who thinks that the price is too low, or the tax authority in the foreign country, who thinks the price is too high. Companies win these challenges only 50% of the time. Given this incident rate, it is far safer for the global entrepreneur to use the arm's length pricing method when establishing the company's transfer price. This also helps establish the company's image as a good global citizen.

Distribution Decisions

One of the most difficult aspects of international business is understanding and using the channel of distribution in the international market, because each country varies significantly in this aspect. Distribution decisions can be the hardest to change and may require the global entrepreneur to give up some degree of control over the product being sold.

Establishing the Channel

The selection of the best channel members is very important to being successful in international business. This process is called *determining the channel design*—the length and width of the channel. The best channel design is influenced by a number of factors, the most important ones being the culture of the market, the type of product, the competition, and the customer.

The global entrepreneur needs to carefully examine the overall culture of the market and the culture of the existing distribution system. Of all of the marketing activities, the distribution systems have the most variance from one culture to another. This in part reflects the country's legislation and regulations, which directly affect the distributors and agents operations there. In some countries, only a few selected distributors are permitted to distribute for foreign companies. In other countries, only distributors 100% locally owned can do this distribution. In others, no dealers are allowed.

The type of product/service to be distributed and its price point is the second factor affecting channel design. A short channel is usually best for bulky, expensive, perishable, or specialized products or those that require after-sale service, as well as services themselves. Stable items can have a longer channel. The positioning and price point also affect channel choice because the channel itself helps create an image for the product or service being offered. The channel member also absorbs some of the risk for the customer who is dealing with a known home-court entity, not a foreign company.

Of course, competition affects the channel design decision. The channels used by competitors need to be carefully evaluated. These channels may be the best or even the only ones accepted by both the trade and customers alike. When this occurs, these same channels should be used, but more effectively and efficiently. Whenever possible, a totally unique distribution approach is better, because it will become a unique selling proposition of the company that is difficult to replicate.

The final and by far the most important factor in the channel design is the customer. The demographic composition of the target market should be the basis for the channel design because it is the essential link between the foreign company and the customers in the target market. The buying process of the customer and the many aspects of the buying decision affect how the product/service should be made available for purchase. Sometimes two or more different channels of distribution are needed to effectively reach customers with different characteristics.

Selecting and Managing the Channel

Once the channel design has been determined, it is important to carefully select the channel members that will represent the company. This selection process is as important as hiring and recruiting within the company. An ineffective or bad distribution decision can set the company back for years, or even permanently, in a foreign market. Trade directories (such as Dun & Bradstreet), telephone directories, and the U.S. Department of Commerce can be used to identify possible company representatives that might be suitable.

Each identified prospect should be carefully screened on both performance and professional criteria; as much information as possible should be collected on each prospect. Once the channel members are in place and the channel is operating, it needs to be carefully managed. A good cooperative channel relationship will establish the best possible link between the foreign company and the local customer.

Promotion Decisions

The final decision that needs to be made in conjunction with pricing and distribution decisions is the promotion mix decision—selecting and implementing the right combination of advertising, publicity, personal selling, and sales promotion that will expedite sales in the selected target market.

Started in 1994, Blue Tomato is a snowboard company based in Austria founded by a former champion in the sport. From the beginning, the company used its roots in the sport to keep close to its customers and followed its young customer profile onto the Internet in 1999. Success followed rapidly, and within seven years, Internet sales accounted for 90% of total revenues.

The adoption of an online sales presence immediately provided the company with almost every international market. One barrier to this can be language. Since Blue Tomato's biggest market was Germany, the company's first website presence was correctly done in the firm's native German. The Internet also led to certain other developments for Blue Tomato that affected its international growth. It enabled the company to increase the sales mix by keeping more products available and reducing its dependence on seasonal markets. The Internet also enabled the company to vary and refine its service offerings through different languages and pricing strategies.

Blue Tomato again used many available options in the networked world to access international markets with an effective multichannel strategy:

- a snowboard catalog distributed to customers and stockists in two languages in addition to a regular newsletter;
- direct contact with customers by e-mail and telephone, with customer service lines staffed by experienced snowboarders;
- promotions at various snowboarding events;
- partnerships with other related websites;
- sponsorship of top snowboarding professionals; and
- sponsorship of snowboarding facilities.

Internally, communications and structure seem to work well. The company makes the most of the casual snowboarding lifestyle and work ethic, while it splits the operations of the retail and training centers. Although many sports companies that are created by people intimately involved in the sport have done well initially, many fail as the initial surge of interest in product offerings wanes. Blue Tomato is still achieving significant growth in sales in international markets (Foscht, Swoboda, & Morschett, 2006).

Advertising

The important issues in establishing a good advertising campaign for the foreign market are the advertising budget, the media strategy, and the message. The global entrepreneur needs to first establish an overall promotion budget for all areas of the promotion mix (advertising, publicity, personal selling, sales promotion, and social media) and then determine the amount that should be allocated to advertising. This budgeted amount for advertising should be enough to accomplish the sales objectives of the firm. Often, a percentage of the sales objective (somewhere around 3% to 7%, depending on the industry) is used to establish the first year's advertising budget.

The type of media to use is very dependent on the market being entered. For example, if entering Peru or Mexico, a higher percentage of the advertising budget will be allocated to television. If entering Bolivia, outdoor advertising would be used more often. If entering Kuwait or Norway, concentration will be more in print media.

Probably the most errors come in the third sphere of planning a good advertising campaign—the message. Careful consideration needs to be given to culture, language, economic development, and lifestyles when creating the best message for a specific global market. Although it is nice if a single world brand can be established throughout the foreign markets of the venture, many global entrepreneurs abandon identical campaigns for more localized ones, making sure that the advertising message is customized to the particular local global market.

Publicity

Strong publicity can be helpful in entering a foreign market by portraying the foreign company as a good global citizen interested in the well-being of a particular culture or country. The global entrepreneur should consider partnering with a nongovernmental organization (NGO) in the country to work on issues in the country such as diversity, energy, or health care. Any way that a solid company image can be established greatly benefits sales in a foreign market.

Personal Selling

In the early stages of market entry, most global entrepreneurs rely heavily on personal contacts. Personal selling is particularly important in high-priced industrial goods. Usually, a local country salesperson, when properly trained, can be more effective than someone from outside the country, especially in those countries with high levels of nationalism.

Sales Promotion

Sales promotion activities such as trade shows, coupons, samples, premiums, point-of-purchase materials, and giveaways can be especially effective when tailored to the specific product/service being offered and to the culture of the company. To be effective, the sales promotion campaign must be accepted and used by the channel members. When carefully crafted and implemented, a well-designed sales promotion effort can be very cost effective when entering and developing a foreign market.

Social Media

Social media marketing refers to marketing through a group of Internet-based applications that allow the creation of user-generated content. Social media include a wide range of online word-of-mouth marketing tools that can be divided into several categories: social networking sites (Facebook, MySpace, Google+, Badoo), creativity/works sharing sites (YouTube, Flickr), collaborative websites (Wikipedia), virtual worlds (Second Life), company-sponsored websites and blogs (Apple.com, Vocalpoint by P&G), user-sponsored blogs (unofficial Apple Weblog), company-sponsored cause or help sites (click2quit.com), invitation-only social networks (ASmallWorld.net), business networking sites (LinkedIn), and commerce communities (eBay, Amazon) (Konečnik Ruzzier, Ruzzier, & Hisrich, 2013).

Social networking sites have become the most rapidly growing communications media in the world. Social networking first emerged in 1997 with a social networking site called Six Degrees. A general characteristic of social networking sites is that they allow social networking between friends as well as making new friends. Currently, several social networking sites exist in the online environment. Among them, Facebook is the most extensively used and, at the end of 2012, was in 127 of the 137 countries worldwide. The milestone of 1 billion monthly users was reached in September 2012.

SUMMARY

This chapter discusses how effective international research and development and marketing can help the global entrepreneur handle the challenges of rapidly changing technology, shorter product life cycles, changing consumer tastes, and changing economies. Advances in telecommunications—such as cellular technology, the Internet, social media, and e-business—are allowing greater connectivity between producers and consumers. To satisfy consumer needs and wants and to be unique, products/services need to be adaptable to changing consumer tastes and preferences. Products/services need to be customized to the local culture to be successful. The global entrepreneur needs to employ a good international research and development process, including defining what innovation is to the company, performing opportunity analysis, and understanding the product life cycle. When entering a new market or launching a new product/service, each global entrepreneur must deal with (1) the technological environment, (2) product policy and the total quality issue, (3) adopting the best research and development strategy, and (4) developing and implementing the best marketing strategy. The product planning and development process (idea stage, concept stage, product development stage, test marketing stage) results in commercialization and the start of the product life cycle. To successfully commercialize in a global market, the best marketing mix (pricing, distribution, and promotion) needs to be used. Identifying the best distribution channel, as well as selecting the best in-country representatives in the foreign market, are important decisions for the global entrepreneur. The promotion of the product/service consists of identifying the right mix of advertising, publicity, personal selling, sales promotion, and social media within the promotion budget established. The global entrepreneur needs to identify the best types of media to use in the foreign market and carefully craft an advertising message that resonates with the local culture.

QUESTIONS FOR DISCUSSION

1. What are the three types of innovation? Give an example of each.

2. What is the purpose of creating an opportunity assessment plan? How does it differ from a business plan?

3. What factors should be considered when a global entrepreneur sets a price for a product/service in a foreign market?

CHAPTER EXERCISES

1. Pick a foreign market and a product. Research the alterations that are necessary for the product to be allowed in that market (e.g., package design, labeling).

2. Using that same product, find research that indicates that the product will be successful in the country that you are choosing to enter.

3. Take one of your product ideas and outline how that product will be carried through from the idea stage to commercialization.

4. You are a paper clip holder manufacturer launching your product in a new market. Identify how you will have to alter your product, pricing, distribution, and communication. What is the best distribution channel for this product? How will you develop the channel distribution?

NOTE

Portions of this chapter are from Hisrich, R. D. (1991). *Marketing decisions for new and mature products* (2nd ed.). Upper Saddle River, NJ: Pearson Education, Inc.

REFERENCES

Foscht, T., Swoboda, B., & Morschett, D. (2006). Electronic commerce-based internationalization of small niche-oriented retailing companies: The case of Blue Tomato and the snowboard industry. *International Journal of Retail & Distribution Management, 34*(7), 556–572.

Konečnik Ruzzier, M., Ruzzier, M., & Hisrich, R. D. (2013). *Marketing for entrepreneurs and SMEs.* Cheltenham, UK: Edward Elgar Publishing Ltd.

Woods, C. (2008, April 8). *ICU Global grabs international opportunities.* Retrieved January 29, 2015, from http://realbusiness.co.uk/article/737-icu_global_grabs_international_opportunities

SUGGESTED READINGS

Kumar, N., & Steenkamp, J. M. (2013). Diaspora marketing. *Harvard Business Review*, *91*(10), 127–150.

> The article addresses the marketing challenge for emerging market corporations to establish brands in Western markets. The article describes how some emerging market corporations have been able to create global brands on a small budget by outsmarting their competition. These strategies are described.

McManus, J., Ardley, B., & Floyd, D. (2012). Fostering Chinese firms through entrepreneurship, globalization, and international finance. *Strategic Change, 21*(3/4), 179–191. *Business Source Complete*. Web. 29 Oct. 2013.

> This article describes the success of nontraditional marketing strategies for international ventures of Chinese companies. The article argues for a variety of forward-thinking practices to be the starting and ending points for these companies' approach to international marketing.

Slonimski, A., & Pobol, A. (2010). Scientific and technical entrepreneurship and the international R&D market: Underpinning the sustainable development of transitive economies. *Human Resources: The Main Factor of Regional Development, 3*, 176–182. *Business Source Complete*. Web. 29 Oct. 2013.

> The article discusses the institutional and technological basis of sustainable development for economies bordering the EU. The degree of, and obstacles to, technological and scientific entrepreneurship on the global research and development market for these regions are addressed. The article considers institutional shortcomings that hinder the diffusion of technological knowledge across the regions.

Stojanovic, A., & Meulen, R. (2012). If you launch it, they will come: Bridging global and local marketing to extract the greatest value from that rare product launch. *Journal of Brand Strategy, 1*(1), 15–24.

> The article considers how the changing global market environment has necessitated a need to connect global and local marketing. It focuses on the pharmaceutical industry's launch of new products. The paper cites examples of how the best people, tools, and processes enable a free flow of information from the local markets to an international research and development project to prepare the products for a successful launch.

10

Global Human Resource Management

Profile: Haier

While China was still a large importer of technological appliances in the 1980s, there were many local companies that decided to start manufacturing these appliances for sale to the local market. Many of these companies focused on producing as many units as possible to meet the rapidly growing demand. During this process, these companies paid less attention to quality. When the market became saturated, there was one company that was determined to deliver high-quality products. This strategy of "either not in it or in it for the win" allowed the company to grow quickly, as it was positioned with a strong competitive advantage. Originally founded in China in 1984 as Qingdao Refrigerator Co., Haier is now a global brand with operations in 28 different countries on six continents around the world.

Haier's history can be summarized in five distinct stages: (1) the brand-building strategy, which was prominent from 1984 until 1991, focused on positioning Haier products as high-quality and reliable; (2) the diversification strategy that followed until 1998 was dedicated to the development of a wider range of products, including but not limited to air conditioners, televisions, and washing machines; (3) from 1998 until 2005, Haier adopted an internationalization strategy and the company managed to sell its products internationally; (4) after 2005, the company focused on building a global brand; and (5) from 2012 until now, Haier has adopted a networking strategy, which is focused on developing the company's win-win model of individual goals and further developing the company's culture.

The fifth and most recent stage has shifted the company's focus to its human resources and all its stakeholders. Employee, customer, and general stakeholder involvement is very prominent at this firm. As Haier is so focused on driving innovation in the household appliance market, it strongly encourages the entrepreneurial spirit of its employees. It is essential to Haier that all employees "carry our two spirits of entrepreneurship and innovation [which] makes each employee actively and independently create innovations to realize achievement by establishing changeability in changeability." Through innovation and a passion for constant change, the firm manages to achieve its key goal: to deliver value to its customers.

With the user at the center of its business and employees closely connected to users to drive change on their behalf, Haier presents valuable opportunities for professionals worldwide. Not only do employees have the opportunity to experience a global company, but they can also drive intrapreneurial ideas through the decision-making power they gain at this company. As users are central to Haier's growth and development, local staff must connect to the local customers. Therefore, management of Haier's global human resources is both extremely challenging and rewarding. Developing the most effective selection criteria, means of motivation, and performance evaluation are different across cultures and thus very complex yet they play a significant role in this firm's potential to succeed. When employee-user relationships do become strong, the payoff is significant.

With about 300 patent applications per year, Haier is one of the most innovative companies of the 21st century. Its CEO, Zhang Rulmin, was named 2012 Innovator of the Year and was selected as one of the most influential business leaders in China. Haier employs over 16,500 people worldwide and earned annual revenue of about 29.5 million USD in 2013. This company has certainly already achieved great things and, with its passion for development and people, it is likely that even greater things are still to come.

SOURCE: Haier [website]. (2014). Retrieved February 12, 2015, from http://www.haier.net/en/

❖❖❖

CHAPTER OBJECTIVES

1. To discuss the importance of motivating employees and the methods to accomplish this across cultures
2. To illustrate the importance of hiring global-minded employees for the success of a venture and training these employees to succeed
3. To discuss the leadership necessary to inspire and recruit personnel
4. To understand the critical role of proper human resource management in a successful global enterprise
5. To identify the major sources of potential employees and how to access them

Introduction

The importance of having good global managers and a quality international workforce cannot be overemphasized. Although the focus of the venture does change when doing international business, this importance and need does not.

In the early stages of going global, the focus is on understanding cultural differences, the political risks, and the best way to enter the international market. Typically, this first stage involves selecting a market and beginning some export activities. Often, an export manager with a very small staff with international experience is hired externally. This group handles the paperwork and facilitates the international transaction and documentation. As the level of global business progresses, the global human resource activity involves assessing and hiring personnel and handling all the needed global markets and functions. Plans are developed and implemented for the recruitment, selection, and training of employees for the needed positions.

Clear career paths for managers assigned overseas are established and a system of human resource management becomes operant. This provides promotion benchmarks and criteria and eliminates some problems that may occur in motivating home-country managers to accept foreign assignments. This also allows management of the global venture to more easily determine which individuals in the company are best suited for overseas assignments. This can be addressed by looking at motivation across cultures, sources and types of human capital, selection criteria and procedures, the global mind-set, compensation policies, and the hiring process.

Motivation Across Cultures

Motivation is a psychological process by which unsatisfied needs lead to drives that attempt to achieve goals or incentives that at least partially satisfy these needs. As such, the process has three elements: needs, drives, and goal attainment. Although the process is universal in nature, the specific content needs and goals that are pursued are significantly influenced by the local culture. For example, in the United States, personal achievement is an important need and individual success through promotion and money is an important goal. In China, on the other hand, group affiliation is an important need and harmony a desired goal. While a key incentive for individuals in the United States is money; key incentives are respect and power for individuals in Japan; and respect, family considerations, and a good personal life in Latin America.

The effect of culture on motivations changes over time, particularly with any significant changes in the economic or political environment of the country. As countries move toward market economies, the ways in which individuals in these countries are motivated continually change as well.

Culture also significantly affects the view of quality of life in a country, which directly affects the view of work and the type of work. In Sweden, there is a fairly high degree of individualism, which is reflected in the emphasis on individual decision making on the job. Conversely, in Japan there is a high degree of uncertainty avoidance, which is reflected in the structured tasks of most jobs in which individuals can have security and know what is to be done and how it is to be done.

The importance of work in an individual's life (work centrality) also varies by culture. Japan has the highest level of work centrality, followed by Israel with a moderately high level. There are average levels of work centrality in Belgium and the United States and moderately low levels in Germany and the Netherlands. This means, depending on the country, other areas of interest such as church, family, or leisure are more important than work to some extents.

Sources and Types of Human Capital

The location and nationality of the candidates for a particular job can be a significant issue in global human resources. This frequently changes as the global venture moves through the stages of internationalization. In the start-up stage, outside expertise is usually hired;

as the venture expands and gains more foreign operations, it starts to develop more of its own personnel in the international operations. As staff continues to expand and grow, the venture will rely less on home-country personnel and have more host-country nationals in management positions. The goal should be to be as fully staffed as possible with host-country personnel as soon as possible.

There are four basic sources of personnel for global ventures: home-country nationals (expatriates), host-country nationals, third-country nationals, and inpatriates.

Home-Country Nationals (Expatriates)

Home-country nationals, often called *expatriates* or *expats*, are citizens of the country where the venture of the global entrepreneur is headquartered. These individuals are willing to work for the global venture in a foreign country for a period of time. The major advantages of using expats in a foreign country are that they know the culture of the venture, relate easily and efficiently to corporate headquarters, have the particular technical or business skills needed, place the venture ahead of the country and will promote the interests of the venture, and are less likely to take the venture's knowledge and set up a competing business.

There are many disadvantages to using expats. Firms often have reintegration and retention problems because a high percentage of expats leave the venture after an overseas experience. The costs of relocation, housing, education, and overseas living allowances are usually high. Some expats return early before completion of the assignment. Using expats results in longer start-up and wind-down times and a shortsighted focus.

Host-Country Nationals

Host-country nationals, or local managers hired by the company, are a particularly good source of middle- and lower-level managers. Some foreign governments, and even customers, expect and can even stipulate that a firm hire host-country nationals to further the country's employment and training. Most global ventures use home-country managers to start the operation in a country and turn this position over to a host-country manager as soon as he or she is trained and ready to assume the position. The decision to use host-country nationals depends on such factors as the nature of the industry, the complexity and life cycle of the product, the functional areas that need staffing, and the availability and level of training of a country's human resources. The service sector typically uses the largest number of host-country nationals.

Third-Country Nationals

A third source of managers is third-country nationals. These managers are citizens of a country that is not the home country of the venture or the host country of operation. These managers are typically used in the later stages of the internationalization process of the venture or when there are no host-country nationals with the needed expertise. These third-country managers have the technical expertise or are from cultures similar to the culture of the host country.

Third-country managers tend to build a career with the company in the host country and are often lured away by competitive companies needing management talent in that particular market. These third-country national managers, particularly if they have been with the venture in a different country, are often able to achieve corporate objectives more quickly and more effectively than either expats or host-country nationals. They also bring a broader more culturally diverse perspective to the management position.

CULTURAL STORY

I arrived in the U.S. in the early '80s and was still a freshman in college, studying English. I went to the library on campus one morning and asked for the person who had been helping me the previous night.

The librarian looked at me and said "So-and-so is in the John."

I looked at her very puzzled and wondered if she had meant to say, "in a meeting with John," so I asked, "Do you know how long he's going to be in a meeting?"

She said "No, he's not in a meeting; he's in the John."

I asked, "Where is John?"

Then she said, "Oh, the women's restroom is on the left." And that's when I guessed that "the John" is probably another word for the restroom. Still to this day, I wonder why the women's restroom is not "the Mary" or "the Margaret."

SOURCE: Shawky, S. (2011, April 4). The women's restroom is on the left. Retrieved January 31, 2015, http://cultural confusions.com/2011/04/04/the-womens-restroom-is-on-the-left/

Inpatriates

Recently, a fourth type of manager has emerged—an inpatriate. This is an individual from the host country or a third-country national who works in the home country. These managers are a group that can really manage across borders and are thus truly global managers. They are very good at developing the global core competency of the venture.

Selection Criteria

Making an appropriate selection decision for an overseas assignment can be a challenge for the global entrepreneur. Traits that are used in this process range from the ideal to the real. Over time, a venture establishes more defined, accurate international selection criteria based on experience. Normally, the selection criteria include technical knowledge; experience; knowledge of the area, culture, and language; enjoying and appreciating overseas work and the specific culture; adaptability of the family; and demographics such as age, education, sex, and health.

Technical knowledge in the functional area needs to be at a high level, because an overseas manager typically has far more responsibility and less support than a domestic manager. The individual selected needs to be self-sufficient in making decisions and running the business. This technical competence is usually reflected in outstanding past performance and diverse experience with the company and industry. Experienced corporate managers going overseas also help ensure that the company culture will be established in the overseas location.

Although knowledge of the area, culture, and language are important, the ability to speak and understand the language of the host country is by far the most important. A manager who does not know the language of the country may get by with the help of associates and translators but still will never fully understand or be a part of the culture. This is still the case even though knowledge of English is widespread and, in most cases, English is the language of international businesses regardless of country.

Another factor in the selection is the manager's interest in an international assignment and appreciation of the culture of the specific country. This desire, knowledge, and adaptability to change are important for success in the overseas assignment. Some managers go through an "exhilaration curve"—they are very excited at the beginning of the overseas assignment, but after a time, frustration and confusion with the new environment set in like a delayed culture shock. An appreciation and knowledge of the particular culture allows the overseas manager to more easily become a part of the new culture and operation. This allows for total integration and a much more successful experience in the new position.

This ability to integrate into the culture also depends on the manager's family situation, because living overseas usually puts more strain on other family members than on the manager. If the family is not happy, the manager often performs poorly and is frequently terminated or leaves the company. The characteristics of the family as a whole are important. Is the marriage stable? Does the family work together? Are there any behavioral problems with the children? Most firms today are interviewing both the spouse and the manager before deciding on an overseas assignment. A family that has successfully lived abroad previously is usually a less risky choice.

Finally, demographic characteristics are very important selection criteria in an overseas assignment. Needing a minimum age and experience requirement, many overseas assignments are filled by managers at least in their mid-30s. Although the number of women in overseas assignments is increasing, it is still somewhat lower than the number of men, reflecting the view of the role of women in some countries and cultures. Any overseas manager must also be in good physical and emotional health. Many host countries have radically different environmental conditions than the home country that could aggravate existing health problems or cause new ones to occur. The author got lead poisoning after living in a country with very polluted air. An overseas manager needs to be independent and self-reliant. He or she must be able to make decisions and work at various levels in the organization without the support staff usually available in the home country.

The Global Mind-Set

The globalization of the business world has brought individuals and organizations from many different parts of the world together as customers, suppliers, partners, or creditors.

The success of global corporations is increasingly dependent on their ability to bridge cultural gaps and work effectively in environments different from their home country.

To succeed in their roles, global entrepreneurs need to influence individuals and groups inside and outside their organization in different parts of the world to achieve their organizational goals. A global mind-set is a set of individual attributes that facilitate the influence process. Global entrepreneurs who have a global mind-set are better able to influence individuals, organizations, and systems different from their own. They are also better able to understand and interpret global issues and more effectively understand the viewpoints of people from different parts of the world.

What are the components of global mind-set? A global mind-set consists of three major groups of individual attributes: intellectual capital, psychological capital, and social capital. Intellectual capital consists of the following:

- Knowledge of the global business and industry
- Knowledge of the global political and economic systems
- Ability to build and manage global value networks
- Ability to build and manage global teams
- Ability to understand and manage the tension between corporate requirements and local needs and challenges
- Understanding of other cultures and histories
- Understanding cultural similarities and differences
- Knowledge of other languages
- Ability to adapt, learn, and cope with complex cross-cultural and global issues

Psychological capital consists of the following:

- Self-confidence and self-efficacy
- Resiliency
- Curiosity
- Fearlessness and risk-taking propensities
- Quest for adventure
- Desire and passion for learning about and being in other cultures
- Openness and ability to suspend judgment
- Passion for cultural diversity
- Adaptability
- Ability to connect with people from other parts of the world
- Collaborativeness
- Ability to generate positive energy in people from other parts of the world and to excite them

Social capital is the ability to work with people from different parts of the world, the ability to generate positive energy in these people, and, most importantly, the ability to build trusting relationships with people from other cultural backgrounds. Trust is the most critical factor in building long-term relationships with others, whether they are employees, colleagues, supervisors, customers, or partners. Building trust in a cross-cultural setting is more complex because even the definition of trust is somewhat culture specific.

The combination of intellectual, psychological, and social capital composes the global mind-set, which enables global entrepreneurs to be successful. It helps them develop behavioral tools to influence those from different sociocultural systems to contribute to the achievement of organizational goals. A measuring instrument has been developed that allows an organization to determine the extent of the global mind-set of any of its employees (http://globalmindset.thunderbird.edu/).

Selection Procedures

In addition to establishing the appropriate selection criteria, the global entrepreneur also needs to establish the best selection procedure for hiring employees. The selection procedure usually employs interviewing, testing procedures, and reference checking.

Most global firms use interviews to screen and select managers for overseas assignments. Sometimes, both the manager and the spouse are interviewed. The interview should be conducted by several people in the venture to ensure that the responses are heard correctly and that all the needed information is obtained. Developing and using standard interview questions and formats assist in the process and provide a basis for comparisons.

There are many different testing procedures available. One test, for example, determines the nature and extent of the global mind-set. A few of the over 2,000 employment tests available are listed in Table 10.1. These tests generally are either cognitive tests or personality tests used by many global companies. Care must be taken to use the right test, because using the wrong test can result in the selection of the wrong person or pass over some very qualified individuals. The results of the test used and the performance of the individual should be recorded and compared to develop a good testing instrument.

Table 10.1	Testing Procedures for International Managers

Global Personality Inventory
This 300-question test is used to test executives, mid- to senior-level managers, and senior salespeople. The cost is around $40 to $50 per individual tested.

Hogan Personality Inventory
This test, using true or false responses to attitude and biographical questions, measures individuals on personality areas such as ambition and prudence and occupational scales such as clerical potential or service orientation. The cost per individual tested is $25 to $175, depending on the amount of detail in the report.

Multidimensional Aptitude Battery II
This 303-question test measures the ability to reason, plan, and solve problems of technical, managerial, and professional individuals. The cost is $190 for a 25-test kit.

(Continued)

Table 10.1	(Continued)

Occupational Personality Questionnaire

This test asks candidates to choose the statement that is most and least like them from a set of 104. The test can measure a general profile or specific leadership or sales potential traits. The cost is $30 or higher, depending on the measurement desired.

NEO Personality Inventory

This test measures executives or managers on five scales: agreeableness, conscientiousness, extroversion, neuroticism, and openness to experiences. The test costs $245 for a 25-test kit.

Personality Research Form

This 352-question test is appropriate for any level of employee. It measures 22 job-relevant personality traits. The cost is $80 for a 5-test kit.

Watson-Glaser Critical Thinking Appraisal

This test of 40 rather difficult questions appraises such things as creativity and problem-solving skills of all levels of executives and managers. The test costs between $10 and $20 per individual.

Wesmann Personnel Classification

This test uses a combination of verbal and numerical questions to predict on-the-job performance and the ability of managers at all levels to learn. The cost is $7 to $15 per individual tested.

16PF

This test of 185 questions measures 16 personality factors of managers in leadership positions. The cost is $8 to $20 per individual tested.

In many global situations, one of the most difficult aspects is accurate reference checking. Each individual contacted should be asked to provide the name of another person who knows the candidate. This new individual should also be contacted until the nature and experience and the abilities of the candidate have been verified.

Virtual Teams

Companies with an international presence, as well as those with only a domestic one with multiple locations, need to have virtual collaboration to be successful in today's hypercompetitive environment. Through global virtual teams, an international business can use the knowledge and skills of people around the world. Increasingly faster, cost-effective (if any cost at all) technology with increasing widely accessible connectivity make virtual teams easy to use and effective. Care still must be taken to help overcome the possible lack of visual communication and the difficulty in reading nonverbal cues as well as the differences in culture, work styles, and, of course, the timing of the communication when various time zones are involved.

There are several things a global entrepreneur can do to maximize the results of using virtual teams. First, there should be a time zone notation to spread the inconvenience of attending a meeting at abnormal hours among the participants. For example, if the company has participants in the virtual team from Beijing (China), San Francisco (U.S.), and Vienna (Austria), the good meeting time should be rotated between the three cities so that the meeting is at a convenient time for participants in each city at least every third meeting. Second, take time to develop relationships and trust among participants in the virtual team. This can be best accomplished by each participant sharing some personal information, such as travel destinations, vacations, sports activity, and/or hobbies. Third, make sure guidelines are established to overcome any language barriers and facilitate good interaction. Participants in the virtual team should feel free to ask for clarification of any point made and know the expectations of being a team member, the decision-making process to be employed, the method(s) for expressing disagreement, and the method(s) for finding a resolution. Finally, each meeting should have an agenda and a written summary of the major aspects of the meeting. Whenever possible, the agenda should also have backup material such as PowerPoint slides and graphics and tables.

Compensation Policies

The global venture's compensation policy and program needs to provide an incentive to leave the home country and take the foreign assignment, maintain an established standard of living in that country (including family needs), and facilitate return to the home country. Salaries and costs of global managers can be three to five times higher than their home-country counterparts. While the overall compensation package will vary from country to country as well as from company to company, the compensation of most managers overseas includes base salary, salary-related allowances, nonsalary-related allowances, and taxes. Similarly, most country managers need to be appropriately compensated to compete with other available opportunities.

The base salary of the manager, of course, is dependent on the responsibilities and duties of the position. The foreign position salary should have equity and comparability with the domestic position, reflecting the normal salary received in the home country. For example, a manager in a German venture would receive a base salary for working in Spain that reflects the salary structure of the venture in Germany.

In addition to the base salary, there is usually a foreign-service premium, valued at 10% to 25% of the base salary. Sometimes the percentage decreases each year the manager is abroad, such as 20% for the first year and 15% for the second. Sometimes the percentage slides in salary increments such as 25% of the first $50,000 base salary, 20% for the second $50,000, and 10% for any base salary over $100,000. Sometimes a ceiling is set for the total amount of foreign-service premium received.

There are several nonsalary allowances paid, such as benefits, cost-of-living allowances, housing allowances, and hardship allowances. The benefit packages are usually 25%–30% of the base salary for health care and insurance and need to be carefully evaluated in the international setting. The cost-of-living allowance makes sure that the global manager can maintain as closely as possible the same standard of living as he or she would have in the home country. This is usually calculated by selecting a percentage of base salary that would be spent at the foreign location. Almost all firms provide a housing allowance that is commensurate with the global manager's salary level and position. Because this is usually a significant cost, most firms establish a range for the housing. Most ventures pay for utilities in the housing unit outright. Finally, in some instances, there are hardship allowances to account for working and living in a very difficult environment; the percentage paid varies by the degree of difficulty.

Nonsalary-related allowances typically include (1) allowances related to housing, such as a home sale, rental protection, and shipment and storage of household goods or household furnishings in the host-country location; (2) automobile coverage, including selling a car in the home country and purchasing a car in the host country; (3) travel expenses to the host country and one or two trips each year for the manager and his family to return to the home country (called *home leave*); (4) temporary living expenses; and (5) a relocation allowance to pay for any additional expenses of the move.

The final aspect of the compensation package is taxes. A global manager may have two tax bills—one for the host country and one from the home country. It is usually good to have in place a tax-equalization plan in which the global venture pays the difference if the tax rate in the host country is higher than what would be paid in the home country or keeps the difference if the tax rate is lower. The plan would take into account differences (higher or lower) if taxes are paid in both the home and host country.

Basic economic and noneconomic compensation options are indicated in Figures 10.1 and 10.2.

The Hiring Process

The global entrepreneur needs to establish a standardized hiring process that can be used in various countries. This includes having an established system for selecting and hiring that can be used repeatedly. Some entrepreneurs do not feel hiring can be reduced to a series of processes and instead rely more on feeling and judgment. In hiring for global positions, a more established systematic approach will provide a better, more balanced view of the candidates and the basis to hire the best individual.

The systematic approach includes developing a standardized interview format and testing procedures. Because a traditional interview can result in a subjective, narrow view of a candidate in which most interviewers prefer candidates similar to themselves, a more structured behavioral interview should be established. A behavioral interview involves several interviewers defining qualities needed, asking the same questions of each candidate to give past examples of how they demonstrated those qualities, and taking copious notes. How the candidate has responded on a past job is indicative of how he or she will respond in a future job—the principle of historicity. Eventually, a standard template for what is needed for a global manager is established that can be modified for various managerial levels.

Figure 10.1 Compensation Options: Employee Economic Reward Package

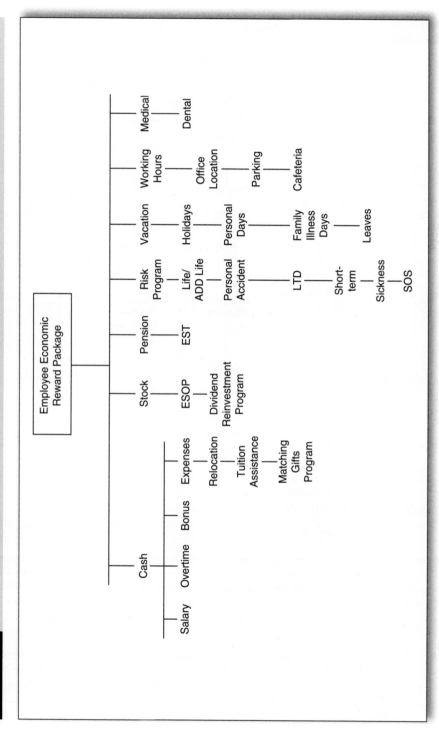

SOURCE: Hisrich, R. D. (2004). *Small business solutions: How to prevent and fix the 13 biggest problems that derail business.* New York, NY: McGraw-Hill.

Figure 10.2 Compensation Options: Employee Noneconomic Reward Package

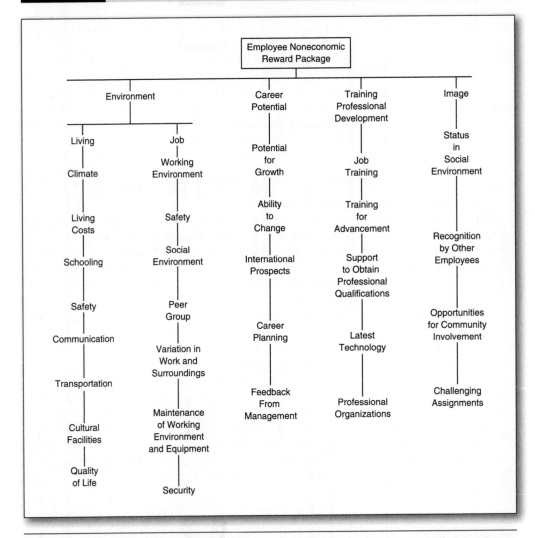

SOURCES: Adapted from material from Girard Torma, director of compensation and international human resources, Nordson Corporation

Behavioral interviews need to be combined with some tests, which can often be administered online. It is usually better to use both a cognitive test and a personality test. Table 10.1 contains examples of each type of test. Cognitive tests generally have a slightly closer correlation with job success than personality tests.

SUMMARY

This chapter focuses on how to identify and recruit the right employees for the global venture. In selecting these, the global entrepreneur needs to understand the impact of cultures on motivation. What motivates individuals in one country—whether wealth, status, or group membership—varies greatly from other countries. The global entrepreneur could decide to staff the overseas venture with individuals from the home country (expatriates), individuals from the host country (local or host-country managers), individuals from neither the host nor home countries (third-party nationals), or individuals from host or third-party countries in the home country (inpatriates). The choice of manager or employee is based on what the firm believes is needed to be successful—such as a deep understanding of the firm's culture and vision (expatriate) or the ability to motivate individuals from different cultures (third-party nationals) or thorough knowledge of the local country and culture (home-country nationals).

For the sake of consistency and easing the hiring process, a global entrepreneur needs to establish specific hiring criteria and a process that should involve a mixture of interviews and tests to understand better both the cognitive abilities and personality of prospective managers. The principle of historicity states that how a candidate performed and acted in a past job is indicative of how he or she will act and perform in a future job. The manager in the overseas venture must be able to handle varying amounts of support staff differently than his or her home-country counterparts. In addition, because the overseas ventures normally contain a mix of expatriate and third-party national managers, a global entrepreneur must keep in mind the need to interview spouses when determining if the overseas position fits the candidate. As the global entrepreneur builds the overseas workforce, particular attention needs to be paid to compensation of the international manager, including maintaining the same base pay between the home-country managers and host-country managers while also covering relocation costs and perhaps offering a foreign-service premium. Once the best managers have been selected by the global entrepreneur, providing the proper training is fundamental to the manager's success in the overseas position. The global entrepreneur needs to provide the visionary leadership to inspire, train, and guide the managers for success.

QUESTIONS FOR DISCUSSION

1. Why would an expatriate manager be better in one situation but a host-country manager better in another?

2. What traits in a manager make him or her a good candidate for a foreign assignment?

3. What components, besides salary, are important parts of a compensation package for an expatriate assignment?

4. How can you train and prepare a manager for a role in a different country?

CHAPTER EXERCISES

1. Imagine that you are leading a small company and need to find someone to handle your operations in the new market that you are entering. What characteristics are the most desirable for this employee to have? Why?

2. What are the advantages and disadvantages of relying on an expatriate, a third-country national, an inpatriate, or a host-country national to oversee your operations in a new market?

3. Choose one of the management styles and analyze how that style works well for a multi-country operation.

SUGGESTED READINGS

Ananthram, S., & Chan, C. (2013). Challenges and strategies for global human resource executives: Perspectives from Canada and the United States. *European Management Journal, 31*(3), 223–233. doi:10.1016/j.emj.2012.12.002

    The article describes the difficulties of global human resource executives. It explains which strategies to use at the macro and micro levels of the organization and cites interviews from 26 North American human resources executives.

Haworth, N. (2013). Compressed development: Global value chains, multinational enterprises and human resource development in 21st century Asia. *Journal of World Business, 48*(2), 251–259. doi:10.1016/j.jwb.2012.07.009

    This article describes how a new compressed development approach is challenging the classic late development model that has been the core of the "new competitive order" in Asia since the 1960s. The article analyzes human resource development in this new approach using an Asia-Pacific Economic Cooperation case study. The analysis provides important implications for human resource development for those working in the Asian region.

Soylu, A., & Thomas, B. S. (2010). Strategic human resource management in the global environment. *International Journal of Management Perspectives, 2*(1/2), 1.

    The article details the changes to human resource management practices in the global environment. It discusses how corporations have cut costs and increased operational quality to address the challenges of creating maintaining strategic global human resource management.

Thite, M. (2012). Strategic global human resource management: Case study of an emerging Indian multinational. *Human Resource Development International, 15*(2), 239–247. doi:10.1080/13678 868.2011.646896

    The author uses a case study of a multinational information technology company in India to exhibit the increasing importance of emerging markets. He explains the need to consider an integrative approach to non-Western models of management. The author suggest using an adaptive approach to global human resources.

Vidaković, T. (2013). Human resources management in the global environment. (English). *Zbornik Radova Ekonomskog Fakulteta u Istocnom Sarajevu, 7,* 361–370. doi:10.7251/ZREFIS1307361V

    This article explains how to organize and manage employees in a global environment. The author highlights the importance of human resources management and further explains what role human resources management should play, depending on the extent and type of internationalization.

11

Implementing and Managing a Global Entrepreneurial Strategy

Profile: Globant

Identified by Fast Company as one of South America's top ten companies for innovation in 2014, software developer Globant brings together innovation, design, and engineering to develop software solutions for giants including Google, American Express, and Coca-Cola. The company has been in the news often in the first half of 2014 as investors speculated about its registration with the Securities and Exchange Commission. "If the Buenos Aires-based Globant launches its reported $86 billion initial public offering this year, it would be the first Argentine technology company listed on the New York Stock Exchange." This exciting firm might become a global leader in software development.

With the mission of developing software solutions based on the newest technologies and latest trends in digital design, Globant was founded in 2003 by Martín Migoya (CEO), Guibert Englebienne (CTO), Martín Umarán (Chief of Staff), and Nestor Nocetti (EVP of Corporate Affairs). Its unique approach to serving its clients is rooted in its "studio model." The company's eight studios are all tailored to client's needs and are thus not industry specific. The following studios provide services to a variety of clients: consumer experience, gaming, big data/high performance, quality engineering, enterprise consumerization, creative and social, mobile, and cloud computing. With this wide range of offerings, Globant has become a reliable one-stop shop for clients to acquire innovative solutions for the whole organization, aligned across different media and functional areas.

Globant has received a variety of awards and has been recognized for its innovation on multiple accounts. In 2011, the firm acquired Nextive, based in San Francisco, to further increase the value of its mobile studio. In 2012, the company made many moves to increase its level of expertise in the global business environment: It received investment from Endeavor Catalyst; acquired the Brazilian company Terra Forum; and welcomed Reid Hoffman, cofounder of LinkedIn, to its board of advisors. Leveraging expertise from a variety of sources allowed for further effective implementation of Globant's vision to "challenge the status quo . . . [and become] the leader in the creation of innovative software products that appeal to global audiences."

In just over 10 years, Globant expanded from a small start-up in Argentina to a well-known business partner for many large corporations in many countries, including Argentina, Colombia, Uruguay, Brazil, England,

and the United States. The firm now employs over 3,000 people and achieved revenue of $129 million in 2012. This company has not only established a global business in a short period of time but it has also developed a global business culture within the company. With a focus on an entrepreneurial mind-set and flexibility, Globant relies heavily on its internal teams. As a means of putting the company, as well as its home country, on the map, employees are encouraged to "act ethically, be a team player, constantly innovate, aim for excellence, think big, and have fun." It seems that, for Globant employees, the sky should not be the limit at all. Excitement, strong internal relationships, and strategic mergers and acquisitions fueled this company's rapid growth.

SOURCES: Globant [website]. (n.d.). Retrieved February 12, 2015, from http://www.globant.com/

Weiss, J. (2014). The top 10 most innovative companies in South America. Retrieved April 22, 2014, from http://www.fast company.com/3026319/most-innovative-companies-2014/the-worlds-top-10-most-innovative-companies-in-south-america.

❖❖❖

CHAPTER OBJECTIVES

1. To analyze the various organizational structures that best meet the needs of the enterprise in different cultures

2. To understand the need for performance evaluation and benchmarking as solid techniques for controlling a global venture

3. To understand global organizational structures and the benefits and drawbacks of each structure

4. To learn how to control the global venture by using the best needed measurements and evaluation techniques appropriate for the country

Introduction

The changes in the world marketplace have been significant. More and more countries are moving toward market-oriented economies. Competition is at a very high level, with companies needing to remain competitive by matching or implementing competitive moves. There is a growing scale and mobility in the world's capital markets. Given these opportunities and challenges in the global marketplace, a global entrepreneur needs to establish a strategic planning process to match the products/services of the venture with markets and maximize the employment of company resources to strengthen the venture's long-term competitive advantage in a way that is sustainable.

Global Strategic Planning

The global strategic planning process has three important stages: (1) developing the core global strategy, (2) developing the global program, and (3) implementing and controlling the global effort.

Developing the Core Global Strategy

The global strategic plan needs to start with a clear definition of the business model and the core strategy of the venture. An assessment of the characteristics and economics of the global market almost always modifies both. To establish a global strategy on a country-by-country basis, the global entrepreneur needs to start by identifying the underlying forces that impact whether or not his or her business will be successful in the global marketplace. Planning across a broad range of markets balances the risks and resource requirements and develops a long-term position for profitability. To develop this plan, the common features of consumer needs and benefits desired and buying processes as well as the competition need to be understood.

The resources of the venture need to be taken into account to determine the capacity for creating and sustaining a competitive position in the global marketplace. Although significant resources are not a necessity, a realistic view of the costs and a long-term time frame of at least five years are important.

Key decisions need to be made about the nature of the competitive strategy for market entrance after the market(s) to enter have been selected. Several basic strategy options are available: cost leadership, differentiation, and a hybrid approach. When employing a cost leadership strategy, a global entrepreneur offers a very similar product/service at a lower cost than the competitors. This strategy does not mean that the product/service is a commodity but rather that the venture has some efficiencies that allow the product/service to be offered at a lower price. A differentiation strategy focuses on some unique aspect of the product/service (its unique selling proposition) that clearly separates it from competitive products/services presently on the market. A hybrid strategy for global market entrance and expansion combines a strong differentiation strategy with cost leadership. This can be accomplished through economies of scale in both production and marketing activities.

The first country chosen (discussed in Chapter 5) is particularly important because it serves as a vehicle for market entrance and expansion. This decision takes into account the internal strengths of the venture as measured by resources available, market share, product fit, and contribution margin and country attractiveness as measured by market size and growth rate, degree of competition, and the economic and political environment of the country. Combining the original country market choice and the internal strengths of the company along with synergies for expansion and future market entries provides a solid strategy for the global venture. Care needs to be taken to ensure that there are sufficient company resources for the expansion, which was not the case for GU Sports, even though GU Sports developed another strategy to get around this apparent weakness.

GU Sports (Sports Street Marketing) was founded in Berkeley, California, in the early 1990s by Dr. William Vaughan. The mission from day one was to provide athletes the best exercise-specific nutrition products available. After formulating the world's first energy bar, Vaughan was disappointed that the bar, due to its high level of fat, fiber, and protein, did not work for athletes while they were training and racing. "How can we call it an energy bar for athletes when all it does is shut down the system for 45 minutes or so while the body digests all those useless-to-athletes ingredients?" asked a frustrated Vaughan (Malik, n.d.). So, in the late 1980s, he began experimenting with carbohydrates in gel form. Because gels did not require any ingredients for solidity (fat, fiber, and protein), they could transport energy to working muscles within minutes without any stomach distress. The perfect food for athletes during workouts, training, and racing was invented. After extensive testing and trial use by all types of athletes, in 1991, GU Energy Gel was perfected (https://guenergy.com/gu-story). The 1- or 1½-ounce foil packets of gel offered carbohydrates combined with electrolytes, sodium, and/or amino acids that quickly dissolve into the bloodstream (Malik, n.d.).

Sold primarily through specialty shops or online to top high-endurance competitors, GU needed to enter the mainstream consumer market to reach other athletes preparing for triathlons, marathons, and other adventure sports. Malik (n.d.) reported that in the increasingly competitive landscape of energy-gel sales, GU Sports found itself having an unusual entrepreneurial problem: How could it grow the market size while still keeping its dominant market share position? One way was to encourage rival sports-nutrition companies to emerge.

When $15 million in U.S. gel sales would be achieved, GU would have a strong market position with a 50% share, PowerBar (acquired by food giant Nestlé SA in 2000) would have a 35% market share, and Clif Bar Inc. would have a 15% market share, according to Matt Powell, analyst at industry data source Sports-OneSource.

Nestlé increased distribution and marketing campaigns for Power-Bar Gels, which GU's Will Garratt, Jr., the vice president of marketing for GU, felt would "definitely create a better awareness" to the general public (Malik, n.d.). This type of market expansion had both potential and risks for a small company such as GU.

GU implemented many strategies to remain competitive with the larger companies, such as developing new products with different tastes. With 25 employees, it manufactured its own product in a six-hour process that produced 18,000 units selling for $1.25 each. Approximately 90% of its sales were in the United States, but other areas where the product was increasing market share included South America, South Africa, Australia, and New Zealand. According to Garratt, the company's gel sales increased "about 20% in each of the past 5 years along with the gel market," but with increased competition, it "had to fight a lot more for the same growth by increasing spending on grass-roots advertising and sponsorships" (Malik, n.d.).

Developing the Global Program

Once the core global strategy is established, the overall global program needs to be developed and implemented. This process actually occurs in concert with the strategy formulation. Although the core product/service or technology used to produce the product/service may be standardized, the product/service itself still needs to reflect local market conditions to the greatest extent possible. Localization is particularly needed in the marketing program. The overall marketing plan and position needs to be global, but the tactical elements of the plan should be market specific (very localized). Production, customer service activities, and warehousing need to be concentrated as much as possible to obtain any cost savings; this does not require being present in each country. Frequently, resources in one global market are used to fight competitive advances in other global markets to maintain the venture's competitive advantage.

Implementing and Controlling the Global Effort

Successful global entrepreneurs understand the need to balance local and global concerns. Local differences need to be taken into account when standardizing programs and policies; as much autonomy as possible needs to be given to the local country organization. Over-standardization and inflexibility in planning and implementing are the two biggest problems in executing a global program. Good local market research helps ensure that the product/service launch in a specific country reflects the characteristics and market conditions in that country. Without this understanding, the launch could fail. Sometimes too much local customization can cause the venture to lose its ability to achieve a successful worldwide presence. A successful global entrepreneur carefully balances the local needs and overall global strategy. This means that neither headquarters nor local country managers are totally in charge. Without the local managers and their commitment, no global program can be successful.

This success in part depends on the flow of information between each country and headquarters as well as among country organizations themselves. In this way, ideas are exchanged and the overall venture and its values strengthened. This can also be accomplished through periodic meetings of the global managers or worldwide conferences.

Any personnel interchange facilitates this. The more experience each manager has in working with others from different nationalities, the better the integration and working relationships become. Managers become familiar with different markets and people. This is particularly important for managers at headquarters, who will then become more sensitive in developing and implementing global policies. Once a global strategy or program has been developed, it is usually better to allow local managers to develop and implement their own specific local programs within specified parameters, subject to approval. This develops a spirit of cooperation and trust that does not occur when local managers are forced to strictly adhere to a set global strategy.

This openness and understanding also helps prevent the not-invented-here syndrome from occurring, which can accompany any local resistance. The global entrepreneur can take some proactive actions as well to help minimize the possibility of this occurring. One way is to make sure that local managers participate in creating and developing the venture's global strategies and programs. Another way is to give local managers a discretionary budget that they can use to respond to local competition and customer needs. A final way is to encourage local managers to submit ideas for consideration at the corporate level. Establishing this balance between headquarters and local country managers can help the organization achieve sustainability and allows the global entrepreneur to establish a truly global culture that favors no specific country and has managers with a global mind-set.

Sustainability

One key issue that needs to be addressed in the global venture is sustainability. There is significant consumer interest in the sustainability movement, making it a global concern for organizations all over the world; most are integrating sustainability into their strategic visions.

The level of concern about sustainability and the greening of the environment varies by country. In countries such as Germany, where the population density is much higher than in the United States, consumers became concerned about environmental concepts much faster than in the United States, which resulted in government mandates and resolutions. While there still are degrees of concern, the number of concerned people is getting larger in every country in the world.

Endorsing green movements as well as the issues of sustainability makes a global venture more profitable, sometimes even in the short run. Sustainability can involve making money. Dial Corporation is producing concentrated detergents to reduce packaging wastes. Intel Corporation is developing microchips that cut the amount of energy needed in home electronics. Arizona Public Service encourages employees to shut down energy-wasting computer monitors when they are not in use. Walmart is using hybrid-diesel trucks for its massive fleet. The U.S. Postal Service is using energy-saving delivery vans.

Global Organizational Structure

As a venture moves from a totally domestic orientation to a global one, its organizational structure must change to reflect the new orientation. The organizational structure needs to vary depending on the stage of internationalization of the venture and the countries that the venture will do business in. The type of organization that is appropriate is one that facilitates the development of worldwide strategies while maintaining flexibility in implementation at the local market level. This concept is captured in the phrase that should be adopted: Organize to think and plan globally, but act locally.

Overall Organizational Structure

Important factors in choosing and implementing a specific organizational structure include the focus of decision making (where decision-making authority within the organization will reside), the roles of the different entities in the organization, the needed coordination and communication, and the needed controls. These factors form the basis for the decision to use one of the following three organizational approaches: (1) placing little emphasis on the international activities of the venture, (2) recognizing the ever-growing importance of international activities taking place, and (3) being a truly global organization with no domestic/international split.

In the early stage of international development, the company's international activities are usually coordinated by the domestic operation. Because these early activities tend to be of such a small size, they have no significant impact on the organizational structure of the venture. Often, the transactions are actually facilitated using entities outside the organization, such as an export management company or freight forwarder, as discussed in Chapter 8. As international sales increase and become more important to the venture, export operations are often separated from domestic operations into a separate entity in the overall organizational structure, such as an export department. This is the first step toward internationalizing the venture. At this stage, most of international licensing activities occur in the research and development and legal areas. The faster the growth in international sales, the more quickly the export department becomes obsolete.

The amount of coordination and control needed at some point will require a more formal international organizational structure, which often results in the establishment of an international division.

The international division centralizes all the non-home-country activities of the venture to better serve the global customers. While this division oversees and has responsibility for the sales, market information, and other market opportunities, manufacturing and other functional activities remain in the domestic division. To avoid conflict, coordination between the divisions is necessary. This coordination is often achieved through a joint group (usually a virtual team, discussed in Chapter 10) that interacts regularly to discuss problems and develop the strategic plans for the venture.

As the international sales grow in size, diversity, and complexity, the international division also tends to become obsolete, requiring a new organizational structure to be implemented. There are several structural formats available, which are discussed below.

Types of Organizational Structures

There are several types of global organizational structures available for implementation. These include area structure, customer structure, product structure, mixed structure, or the matrix structure. The *global area structure* is a widely used approach that uses geographical areas as its basis. For example, a U.S. entrepreneurial company could organize its activities into four areas: Asia-Pacific, Europe, North America, and South America. The areas can be determined based on cultural similarity (such as Asia) or historical connections between the countries (such as the Balkans). No funding preference should be given; personnel in each of the areas support and monitor the activities and develop the companywide global strategy. The increased use of the global area structure reflects such regionalization activities as the North American Free Trade Agreement (NAFTA) and the European Union. The area approach aligns itself well with having one marketing concept in general or per area because each geographic area defined has similar characteristics and can be given similar marketing attention. It works particularly well for those entrepreneurial ventures that have narrow product lines with similar end users and uses that are closely related. When there are many diverse product lines or diverse end users and uses, the global area approach may not be the best one to employ.

The *global customer structure* is used when the customer groups served are dramatically different. This is often called *verticals*. Customer groups can include consumer, governmental, and industrial customers. Another grouping could be along the lines of industry, such as the automobile industry, the printing industry, or the mining industry. Even though the products for each customer group may be similar or even identical, the buying process is so different that a specific marketing and service approach is needed. Some groups may require industry specialists.

The *global product structure* is the organizational form most often used by global entrepreneurs. This approach places the responsibility for global activities in each product area. This approach allows improved cost efficiency through the centralization of manufacturing. It is frequently used by consumer-product firms, where the world market share of a product helps determine its competitive position. The global product structure balances functional input to the product with the ability to quickly respond to any specific product problems. This allows each product to be adapted to the extent needed for each foreign market. Coordination between the product groups in each market is essential, as well as having managers who have adequate country market experience. Problems can occur particularly when a customer buys multiple products from the venture.

The *global mixed structure*, as the name implies, uses two or more of the possible global structures, providing significant attention to the area, customer, and/or product. It is often used in a transition period following a merger or acquisition or before implementing the final global organizational structure—the global matrix structure.

The *global matrix structure* is a complex structure adopted mainly by large entrepreneurial corporations for planning and controlling many independent businesses, resources, and geographic areas. The matrices developed vary in the number of dimensions and allow for better cooperation between business managers, product managers, and area managers, as each person must work with the others to obtain the company's objectives. Problems and conflicts can occur because most managers report to at least two people. Often, even minor problems have to be solved through committee discussion, which seriously reduces the reaction time of a venture. This is particularly a problem in today's hypercompetitive environment, which requires a quick response time. Some companies using a matrix organization have changed to one of the other four global organizational structures (area, customer, product, or mixed) to avoid the problem of multiple reporting systems.

CULTURAL STORIES

Story 1

On a bus with my friend in Japan, we saw an older woman board. The bus was crowded and my friend decided to offer her his seat. He stood up and said, in his newly learned Japanese, *"Sawatte kudasai."* The lady looked puzzled.

He should have said *suwatte kudasa*—"please sit." Instead, he had asked her something else. She finally understood what he meant, laughed, and sat down.

Story 2

The first time I lived in Mexico City, after several weeks of tacos, I treated myself to a good 'ol American hamburger and chocolate malt at Sanborn's. Upon finishing, the waitress asked me if I wanted anything more, *"Quiere algo mas?"* I replied, in a loud and confident tone, *"No, yo estoy lleno"*—"No, I'm full."

She started laughing and told the other waitresses what I had said, and they also began to laugh and point at me. After inquiring, I learned that I had said to them that I was pregnant. And, I am a man.

SOURCES: Johnon, D. (2011, February 23). On a bus in Japan . . . Retrieved February 1, 2015, from http://culturalconfusions.com/2011/02/23/on-a-bus-in-japan/

Wilson, M. (2011, May 23). A full meal in Mexico City. Retrieved February 1, 2015, from http://culturalconfusions.com/2011/05/23/a-full-meal-in-mexico-city/

Organizational Structure and Degree of Centralization

Although the organizational structure is important, it does not necessarily indicate where the authority for decision making and control resides. This is a critical decision for the global entrepreneur and usually is referred to as the *degree of centralization* of the venture. Many global entrepreneurs prefer a high degree of centralization in which all the strategic decisions are made at headquarters (often by them) with significant controls. This high degree of centralization occurs in such functions as finance, human resources, and research and development, while in other functions, such as marketing, it does not. The more autonomy each domestic and international unit is given and the fewer the controls, the more decentralized the entire venture becomes. Since each unit is its own profit center, most of the information flow between the structural units is financial—sales, costs, and profits.

The more a venture is decentralized, the better its global units are able to market effectively and react quickly, reflecting the local conditions. This decentralization encourages a high level of participation at the local level and usually results in better corporate morale and operations.

Because a high degree of decentralization modifies the amount of control of headquarters, some companies are now using coordinated decentralization. In this hybrid model, the overall company strategy is developed at headquarters and each international unit is allowed to adjust and implement this strategy with country-specific aspects within agreed-upon parameters.

Controlling the Global Venture

In today's hypercompetitive environment, it is important that the global venture establish a system for evaluating the performance of each operating unit and the entire venture as well as for providing the necessary controls for the venture. This usually involves some form of internal and external benchmarking. External benchmarking, when the data are available, allows the global entrepreneur to evaluate his or her company performance against competitors of similar size in the same industry. The problem is that frequently the data are not available to do this, as many firms are privately held and limited firm and industry data are available in some countries.

Every venture can regularly do internal benchmarking. This provides needed information for control purposes and for sharing best practices throughout the company. This is most important for growing a successful, sustainable global organization.

The control of both the outputs of the international activities (sales, output, costs, and profits) and behavior (culture, employee behavior, management capabilities) of the company can be accomplished through bureaucratic, formalized control or through cultural control.

Formalized Versus Cultural Control

While formalized control relies on rules and regulations that indicate the activities and output, cultural controls rely on shared beliefs and expectations of personnel in the venture. A formalized control system usually features a standardized budget, reporting system, and policy manuals. The budget and reporting system is the major control mechanism for the local country operation; these establish the nature of the relationship and reporting between these local entities and headquarters. As much uniformity as possible should occur without sacrificing the ability of the local country unit to customize, grow, and respond in a timely manner. Establishing the appropriate manuals for each major function facilitates uniformity and reduces report preparation time.

When focusing on the values and culture of the venture, which is cultural control, evaluations are based on the overall company norms and the extent of the fit between the individual and the entire unit. This requires extensive informal personal interaction and regular training on the overall corporate culture and the way things are done. Sound cultural control requires that good selection and training programs are established in the venture. Regardless of the focus and positioning on the formalized, cultural continuum, it is good for the global entrepreneur to understand and use some of the control techniques discussed in the next section.

Measurement and Control Techniques

There are several useful overall important performance measures: financial performance, personnel performance, and quality performance. Financial performance of a local country operation is based on sales, profit, and return on investment (ROI). Profit is affected by management capabilities as well as external, uncontrollable factors, such as currency value, exchange rates, and competitive activities. For example, if a local country's currency value decreases (*devaluation*), sales will increase because the price of the products will be lower for foreign buyers. The opposite occurs when the value of the local currency increases.

Control using personnel performance as a measure should be done periodically. This appraisal of each manager's output and behavior is done differently, reflecting to some extent the different cultural and market conditions. Turnover among global managers needs to be minimized, but no turnover may indicate that evaluations are too infrequent or standards and expectations are too low. The last control technique, based on quality performance, makes sure the goods and services and the operation of the local country unit and the entire company are at the highest possible level of quality. This can be controlled and evaluated by using total quality management techniques, quality circles, and employee reward and recognition systems. A well-run global venture will employ performance measures in each of these three areas to ensure it has operational a sound reporting and control system.

Managing Chaos

Chaos and change are two dimensions confronting every global entrepreneurial venture. Change is an opportunity as well as a challenge for global entrepreneurs who can live with chaos. The scale and complexity of change and chaos are even greater for global entrepreneurs than their domestic counterparts, particularly in today's hypercompetitive business environment. To monitor and better understand change and be better able to manage any chaos, it is important for the global entrepreneur to understand the dynamics that occur according to Prigogine's concept of far-from-equilibrium dynamics, Heisenberg's uncertainty principle, and Zadeh's fuzzy logic.

Ilya Prigogine's concept of far-from-equilibrium dynamics reflects his comprehensive understanding of the history of science (Prigogine & Stengers, 1984). He felt that the paradigm of Newton, particularly its treatment of change and chaos, did not apply to many important phenomena. According to Prigogine, while the state of a system stabilizes around its equilibrium, fluctuations disturb this equilibrium, making its behavior unpredictable before the system returns to equilibrium and again becomes predictable. While true for some systems, many important systems are so far-from-equilibrium that they can be destructive. Still, some order forms at the edge of this chaos. In these conditions, the process of self-organization can occur and proliferate, not by imposing order on the chaos but by negotiating it and creating a new complex form of order.

Heisenberg's uncertainty principle (1950) proposes that it is not possible to measure with precision the position and the momentum of a quantum element. Although mainly applicable to the quantum world, it also applies to the macroworld of organizations when the position and movement are interdependent and change rapidly and unpredictably, sometimes resulting in things becoming the opposite when at the extreme. The new resulting position and momentum cannot be predicted from the previous states of each, making uncertainty more the norm in many systems.

Zadeh views this chaos dynamic through *fuzzy logic*, in which categories are opposites and multivalent (Zadeh & Yager, 1987). Both Z and not-Z can coexist to some degree, according to Zadeh, particularly when the complexity of the system increases. When this occurs, managers do not have the ability to make precise and relevant statements and predictions until a threshold is reached. "It is then that fuzzy statements are the only bearers of meaning and relevance" (Zadeh & Yager, 1987, p. 14). Fuzzy logic provides an understanding of change for managers when they do not attempt to achieve absolutely exact precision.

These three principles, as well as the art of managing chaos, are illustrated particularly well in the cases of two very different companies—Google and Enron. Larry Page and Sergey Brin, Google's founders, introduced the concept on Stanford University's internal website in 1996, and Google became a commercial enterprise in 1998. Today, with the majority of the world's Internet users using Google as their search engine, it's no wonder that the company has increased in sales, profits, and value and handles more transactions every day than the combination of the New York, London, Frankfurt, and Paris stock exchanges. Google embraces chaos and even profits from it by having a work environment employees often call the "Google way of working," where mistakes are viewed as tools for learning and employees are encouraged to come up with outrageous ideas. The informal environment, with no strict dress code or rules for behavior, recognizes that the most valuable resource of the company is the mind and thought processes of its employees. Google indeed thrives by managing the resulting chaos that occurs.

Enron is another classic example of managing chaos from another perspective. At Enron, change was continuous, sometimes going as intended but more often than not producing paradoxical outcomes. The company was a constantly changing entity on an exponential growth curve that was accelerating over time. The change blurred boundaries, with the potential for great success and catastrophic losses coexisting for many years. Enron can be viewed from each one of the previously discussed theoretical perspectives on managing chaos. It became a company driven by steep growth curves and expectations that needed to hit quarterly targets expected by Wall Street in a culture far from any degree of equilibrium. This unmanaged chaos, however, eventually led to the company using illegal accounting practices and, finally, to the company's bankruptcy. Many of the top management team actually went to jail and the company's accounting firm, Arthur Andersen, no longer exists.

SUMMARY

This chapter focuses on the need for a global entrepreneur to define and execute a strategic plan, establish an appropriate international organizational structure, and use benchmarking and control techniques to realize the full potential of the company. An international strategic plan is often not established before the business is launched and is almost always a continuous work in progress, with the global entrepreneur using numerous indicators and techniques to adjust and refine the strategy. The basis for the strategic plan is defining the core strategy of the venture through the careful examination of the underlying forces that affect the business's success in the global marketplace, taking into account the resources of the business. Two overall basic strategies that can be employed are differentiation and cost leadership. Once the strategy has been chosen, the global entrepreneur institutes a global program in which he or she takes the standardized product and adapts it to the local market(s), taking into consideration the culture and conditions of the particular locality. As the global venture grows, the global entrepreneur usually needs to reorganize and adapt the organization to handle the greater demands of more markets and products/services. First, the global entrepreneur needs to address (1) how much emphasis to place on the international activities of the venture, (2) how much effort the ever-growing international activities require, and (3) what a truly global organization with no domestic/international split entails. The answers to these questions help the global entrepreneur decide which type of organizational structures to use—a global area structure, global customer structure, global product structure, global mixed structure, or global matrix structure. Finally, the global entrepreneur needs to establish whether a centralized or decentralized decision-making and control structure is best for the firm. Regardless of which control structure is employed, financial performance, personnel performance, and quality performance need to be evaluated using such things as internal and external benchmarks to measure the success of the firm.

QUESTIONS FOR DISCUSSION

1. In which situations is a cost leadership strategy better suited? Under what conditions would a differentiation strategy be better?

2. Describe the different organizational structures and at what stage in the venture they might be best employed in an entrepreneurial enterprise.

3. How does organizational control change as a venture achieves more success in a foreign market(s)?

CHAPTER EXERCISES

1. Find some articles on a company that attributes its success to meeting the goals set forth in its strategic plan. What is the company's core strategy? Identify its indicators of success beyond profitability.

2. Suppose you are the owner of a successful electric-powered, environment-friendly scooter company and plan to launch your product in India. Pick either the cost leadership or differentiation strategy and explain how you would bring the scooter to market in India. Will you have to alter the design? What difficulties could the market in India pose? How will your strategic plan deal with these and other issues?

3. Create a table listing the common organizational structures for a global firm and find examples of multinational companies that use each type of structure.

4. Discuss with someone the best way to lead a global firm. Which method do you think is better—formalized or cultural leadership? Why?

REFERENCES

Heisenberg, W. (1950). *The physical principles of the quantum theory.* New York, NY: Dover.

Malik, N. S. (n.d.). *Risky business: GU Sports could benefit from Nestle energy gels, but competition stiffens.* Retrieved from http://wsjclassroomedition.com/monday/mx_06nov13.pdf (Reprinted from *The Wall Street Journal: Monday Extra,* November 13, 2006).

Prigogine, I., & Stengers, I. (1984). *Order out of chaos: Man's new dialogue with nature.* New York, NY: Bantam.

Zadeh, L. A., & Yager, R. R. (1987). *Fuzzy sets and applications: Selected papers.* New York, NY: Wiley.

SUGGESTED READINGS

Andersson, S., & Florén, H. (2011). Differences in managerial behavior between small international and non-international firms. *Journal of International Entrepreneurship, 9*(3), 233–258. *Business Source Complete.* Web. 29 Oct. 2013.

    The article contrasts the activities of managers of small firms that operate internationally with those that work only domestically. It attempts to identify the differences and consider their implications for the internationalization of small firms. It examines differences in operating activities, networking behavior, and strategic planning for small firms operating internationally versus domestically.

Casillas, J. C., Moreno, A. M., & Acedo, F. J. (2010). Internationalization of family businesses: A theoretical model based on international entrepreneurship perspective. *Global Management Journal, 2*(2), 16–33. *Business Source Complete*. Web. 29 Oct. 2013.

This article develops a new model to understand internationalization of family businesses. By comparing six multinational family businesses over their lifetime, the study identifies knowledge and family commitment as key determinants of global entrepreneurship for these types of firms. The model also includes a number of other external and internal contingent variables.

Nini, Y. (2012). Small businesses and international entrepreneurship in the economic hard time: A global strategic perspective. *International Journal of Entrepreneurship, 16*, 113–131. *Business Source Complete*. Web. 29 Oct. 2013.

The article describes international entrepreneurship strategies for small to medium-sized enterprises (SMEs). It examines unique characteristics of SMEs and social institutional variables that influence an entrepreneur's ability to internationalize. The study develops practical implications for managers and owners of SMEs to acquire resources and develop capabilities to exploit global markets.

Roudini, A., & Osman, M. H. M. (2012). The role of international entrepreneurship capability on international performance in born global firms. *I-Business, 4*(2), 126–135. *Business Source Complete*. Web. 29 Oct. 2013.

This paper is about an academic investigation that aims to describe how the dimensions of international entrepreneurial capability influence international performance in global firms. It provides a guide for born-global management.

Trąpczyński, P., & Wrona, T. (2013). From going international to being international—Strategies for international competitiveness. *Poznan University of Economics Review, 13*(1), 89–114. *Business Source Complete*. Web. 29 Oct. 2013.

The authors argue that the extent of a firm's advancement is a determining factor in the impact internationalization will have on its competitiveness in the market. The article analyzes four cases that show a correlation between a firm's commitment to international markets and the impact of internationalization. It further describes the strategy adaptations required to effectively manage a competitive international firm.

PART IV

CASES

Business Incubator Subotica

Ildiko Zedi

Introduction

While the number of business incubators in the world is about 5,000, 1,000 of these are in Asia, 1,000 in North America, and less than 900 in Europe. In Europe, the business incubators have been grouped into 60 national and regional associations. The European Business and Innovation Centre Network, the biggest association of business incubators in Europe, has more than 240 members from the European Union and 11 members from other countries (Miljašić, 2011, p. 10). The Business Incubator Network of Serbia includes all 23 business incubators (Miljašić, 2011, p. 13.).

Geographic Background

Southeastern Europe is a geographical and political region located primarily in the Balkan Peninsula (Southeast Europe, n.d.). This region includes the sovereign states of Albania, Bosnia and Herzegovina, Bulgaria, Croatia, Cyprus, Greece, Kosovo, Moldova, Montenegro, Cyprus, Romania, Serbia, Slovenia, and Turkey

The Republic of Serbia, in the center of the Balkan Peninsula, borders Romania in the northeast, Bulgaria in the east, in the south with Macedonia, in the west with Bosnia and Herzegovina and Croatia, and finally with Hungary in the north and has an area of 77,474 km^2, as indicated in Figure 1.

Serbia was one of six republics that made up the country of Yugoslavia, which broke up in the 1990s. In February 2003, Serbia and Montenegro were the remaining two republics of Yugoslavia, forming a loose federation. In 2006, Montenegro split from Serbia (Infoplace Serbia, *Geography Serbia*, 2014b).

The general economic data of the country are: GDP/PPP: $80.47 billion; per capita: $11,100; real growth rate: 2%; inflation: 2.2%; unemployment: 20.1%; arable land: 37.28%; agriculture: wheat, maize, sunflower, sugar beets, fruits (raspberries, apples, sour cherries), vegetables (tomatoes, peppers, potatoes), beef, pork, and meat products, milk and dairy products, grapes/wine; labor force: 1.703 million, agriculture 23.9%, industry 16.5%, services 59.6%; industries: automobiles, base metals, furniture, food processing, machinery, chemicals, sugar, tires, clothes, pharmaceuticals; natural resources: oil, gas, coal, iron ore, copper, zinc, antimony, chromite, gold, silver, magnesium, pyrite, limestone, marble, salt, arable land; exports: $14.61 billion; and imports: $20.54 billion (Infoplace Serbia, *Economic Summary*, 2014a).

Subotica, a city in northern Vojvodina, Serbia, is the second largest city in the province, following Novi Sad, and the fifth largest city in Serbia. According to the 2011 census, the city has a population of 97,910 (Subotica, n.d.).

| Figure 1 | Map of Serbia |

SOURCE: Infoplace.rs

Subotica has a very important geostrategic position, with a location on the major traffic crossroads. The city is about 100 km north of Novi Sad, 190 km northwest of Belgrade, and 190 km south of Budapest.

The Company

Business Incubator Subotica was established on June 21, 2006, within the Vojvodina Autonomous Province Economic Development Programme and the Strategy of Economic Development of Municipality of Subotica to create a business environment that provided early stage businesses with the necessary tools for development, growth, and success. The Business Incubator Subotica offers consulting and support in equipping for production as well as business support services, technical assistance, business training, and favorable rental prices for corporate premises, reflecting the

Incubator's strategy to eventually develop into an industrial park. The goal of the Incubator is to support the businesses so that they can become medium-sized companies and increase employment and self-employment of young people and entrepreneurs in Subotica and its neighborhood. Business Incubator Subotica is registered as a limited liability company wherein the shareholders are the City of Subotica (60%), the Regional Centre for SMEs (small and medium-sized enterprises) Development (10%), Technical College Subotica (10%), Vojvodina Investment Promotion (VIP) Fund (10%), and ATB SEVER (10%).

Reasons for Starting

One reason for the founding of the Business Incubator Subotica was to help provide jobs for the unemployed in the city as well as in the wider region (Zedi & Obradovic, 2008, p. 4). The priority of founding this business incubator was based on these two documents:

- *The Strategy of Economic Development of Municipality of Subotica*
- *The Autonomous Province of Vojvodina Economic Development Programme*

These documents indicated that this would be an important tool of economic development in Vojvodina and in the Subotica municipality.

The industrial structure of the municipality was somewhat diversified with industrial areas such as the process industry, electric and metal industry, chemical industry, textile and footwear industry, and leather industry and new technology-based services. A picture of part of the Business Incubator is indicated in Figure 2.

The state-level data indicated that the establishing process for SMEs has been successful and has even increased over the last 15 years. In 1990, about 20,000 SMEs were registered in Serbia, and this number almost tripled by 2000, amounting to about 60,000 SMEs. The number continued to grow, reaching 69,000 SMEs in 2004.

Figure 2 Part of the Business Incubator

SOURCE: Business Incubator Subotica

The general process of SME start-up and development in Serbia, especially after the embargo was lifted, caused many large industrial companies to disappear. Subotica increased more rapidly than the rest of municipalities in Vojvodina and Serbia and went through a faster industrial restructuring process. In the Subotica municipality, 2,344 companies have been registered, well over the Vojvodina average. The number of employees in small businesses was 41% of the total number of employees in the municipality and 30% in Vojvodina. Large companies employed 34% of the employees in Subotica and 43% in Vojvodina. The gross domestic product (GDP) share of large companies was 40% in Subotica and 19% in Vojvodina. Medium-sized companies created 24% of the GDP in Subotica and 16% of the GDP in Vojvodina.

A strengths, weaknesses, opportunities, and threats (SWOT) analysis of the SME sector in Subotica indicated they had weaknesses in

- a lack of financial assets,
- a low level of innovation,
- a lack of entrepreneurial spirit, and
- high production expenses.

These weaknesses were to be addressed by the general business incubator as a part of the priorities of the Strategy of Economic Development of Municipality of Subotica and the Economic Development Programme, adopted in 2006, to

- encourage successful SME establishment,
- create new jobs,
- support start-up businesses going through their most vulnerable phase, and
- contribute to the process of the municipality's and its citizens' long-term and sustainable economic growth and progress.

Conditions and Services for the Tenants

The Business Incubator leases premises to individuals who intend to establish a company, or who have already established one within the last year, for up to three years. The first year is free of charge; the second year, the rent is 40% of market value; and in the third year, the rent is 80% of market value. After three years, tenants should pay normal rent and be able to pursue their activities independently from the Incubator. Pictures of the tenant company's fairs and a training and coaching session are indicated in Figures 3 and 4.

One of the basic benefits of the Business Incubator Subotica is the rent of physical space to tenant companies. A company in the Business Incubator receives part of the necessary working equipment and the right to use common facilities (meeting and presentation rooms, the cafeteria, and the parking lot) as well as the basic business infrastructure (telephone, fax, Internet access, and postal service). Recently, an incubator motor van was added so that the tenant companies do not have to pay for transportation services to their production facilities in the nearby industrial service sector. Eighteen companies in the incubator operate their production there.

In addition to these services, Business Incubator Subotica offers training programs to improve the level of knowledge and skills of its entrepreneurs. Training programs strengthen the competitive advantage of Incubator tenants. Starting in 2013, the Business Incubator also offered a virtual incubator for those start-ups that already had physical space but needed some of the soft services provided by the incubator.

Figure 3 Fairs for Tenants

SOURCE: Business Incubator Subotica

Figure 4 A Training and Coaching Session

SOURCE: Business Incubator Subotica

Of the 28 tenant companies in the incubator from 2006–2013, 10 are post incubation (have graduated), 16 are still active members of the incubator, and two failed—a fairly successful track record.

The Role and Characteristics of Business Incubators and Clusters

Incubators

Business incubators accelerate the development of successful entrepreneurial companies by providing hands-on assistance and a variety of business and technical support services during their vulnerable early years. Typically, incubators provide space for a number of businesses under one roof with flexible space and leases; office services and equipment on a pay-as-you-go basis; an on-site incubator manager as a resource for business advice; orchestrated exposure to a network of outside business and technical consultants; accounting, marketing, engineering, and design expertise; assistance with financing; and opportunities to network and transact business with other firms in the same facility. Incubators reduce the risk involved in a business start-up and their young tenant companies by providing access to facilities and equipment that might otherwise be unavailable or unaffordable. Differences in stakeholder objectives for incubators, admission and exit criteria, the knowledge intensity of projects, and the precise configuration of facilities and services distinguish one business incubator from another.

One definition of business incubation is as follows:

> *Business incubation* is a dynamic process of business enterprise development. Incubators nurture young firms, helping them to survive and grow during the start-up period when they are most vulnerable. Incubators provide hands-on management assistance, access to financing, and orchestrated exposure to critical business or technical support services. They also offer entrepreneurial firms shared office services, access to equipment, flexible leases and expandable space—all under one roof. (National Business Incubation Association [NBIA], 2001)

Business incubators provide entrepreneurs with a supportive environment to help establish and develop their projects. By providing services on a one-stop basis and enabling overhead costs to be reduced by sharing facilities, business incubators can significantly improve the survival and growth prospects of start-ups and small firms in their early stage of development. Business incubators can be technology centers and science park incubators, business and innovation centers, organizations that have no single physical location and concentrate instead on managing a network of enterprise support services ("incubators without walls"), "new economy" incubators, and a variety of other models (European Commission Enterprise Directorate General, 2002). By locating the incubators in scientific and technological parks, the geographic proximity of firms and institutions (universities, venture capitalist associations, and other organizations in high-tech and knowledge-based sectors) provides some distinct advantages. In general, incubators can be defined as "companies whose main task is to provide and to rent available office space, and to provide administrative, technical, and other services to newly-formed enterprises or innovative organizations" (Morača, Mihalj, Lanji Hnis, & Kirchweger, 2011). Their role in economic development and society is indicated in Figure 5.

Clusters

Business incubators can provide clustering opportunities for firms. In comparison to incubators that are typically targeted at business support in the early stages of the firm's life cycle or to technological parks that are larger in size and serve a broader range of firms, clusters can involve established

| Figure 5 | The Role of Incubators in Society's/Stakeholders' Roles and Effects |

Stakeholders	Expected effects
Residents of the incubator	– Increases the chances of success – Raises credibility – Helps to improve skills – Increases the synergy between the tenants – Facilitates access to mentors, information, etc.
Government	– Addresses the shortcomings of the market – Promotes regional development – Generates new jobs – Increases revenues and fees – Demonstrates of political commitment to small businesses
Research institutions and universities	– Strengthens the interaction among universities, research institutions, and practices – Promotes research – Provides an opportunity for graduates and students to develop their knowledge and skills
The business community	– Strengthens the possibility of introducing innovations – Manages the supply chain – Shows the assumption of social responsibilities
The local community	– Develops a culture of entrepreneurship and self-assessment – Retains revenues within the community
The international community	– Creates opportunities for trade and technology transfer between companies and customers incubator hosts – Allows a better understanding of the business culture – Allows an exchange of experiences through associations

SOURCE: Paunovič, B., Du Pont, M., Dobrilović, M., Šenk, V., Ivanić, V., & Vukov, D. (2011). *Development strategy of business incubators in Vojvodina in the period from 2011 to 2015*, p. 15. Novi Sad, Serbia: Center for Strategic Economic Studies "Vojvodina-CESS."

and more mature businesses (Berbel, Rocha, Sá, & Carneiro, 2011). According to a basic typology of the World Bank, business incubation targets start-up firms and SMEs with high growth potential while industrial clusters support businesses and other organizations linked by a shared value chain (vertical) or shared final market (horizontal) concentrated in technology industries (World Bank, 2010, p. 14).

According to Michael Porter, "Clusters are geographical concentrations of interconnected companies and institutions in . . . an array of linked industries" (1998). As noted by Sforzi, the concepts of industrial district (ID) and cluster are sometimes confused, as both use the sector as a unit of economic analysis. According to Sforzi, "the concepts of ID and cluster do not share the same DNA"—the unit of analysis in industrial district is local community, and industry is its economic component (Sforzi, 2009, pp. 332–333). An industrial district differs from a "manufacturing town" by "merging" communities and firms, and it differs from an "economic region" by the dominance of industrial activity. An industrial district is a "socioterritorial entity . . . characterized by the active presence of both of [the] community of people and [the] of population of firms in one naturally and historically bounded area" (Becattini, 2004, p. 19).

Business Incubators and Clusters in Serbia

Eight business incubators in Serbia have been set up on the territory of the Vojvodina region and are located in the following towns and municipalities: Novi Sad, Subotica, Zrenjanin, Bački Petrovac, Pančevo, Senta, Kanjiža, and Beočin. These establishments are successful due in part to the large investments in the development of this sector by the Vojvodina government. Seven incubators have been set up in the region of east and southeast Serbia in Niš, Vranje, Zaječar, Bor, Knjaževac, Prokuplje, and Medveđa. There is an initiative to establish two new incubators in this region, one in Majdanpek and the other one in Kladovo. Six incubators are located in the region of Šumadija and western Serbia: Kragujevac, Rača, Kruševac, Užice, Valjevo, and Kraljevo. There are two incubators in the region of Belgrade, situated in the Zvezdara and Rakovica municipalities. The largest incubator is in Vranje (2,700 m²), the second largest in Subotica (2,000 m²), and the third largest is in Nis (1,650 m²) (Miljašić, 2011, p. 13).

Setting up business incubators in a particular place usually boosts the economic development of the entire region, since they attract new investments and are considered to be economic growth engines. Also, they can create specialized knowledge centers and increase production based on the competitive advantage they focus on.

Networking

In order to improve the coordination of work and represent the common interests of business incubators in Vojvodina, each will be connected to a common association as well as with other national and international organizations and associations. This process should develop a partner network of business incubators and local authorities, financial institutions and other sources of funding, educational institutions, research organizations, and other companies.

Facilitation of the information exchange of founders within the individual incubators of Vojvodina, as well as across Serbia, needs to be initiated. In addition, the incubators' alumni need to be involved to a greater extent and networked. As a result, knowledge and know-how can be transferred from experienced business people to start-up ventures and potential entrepreneurs. Networking with other organizations (such as, for example, investment funds, VIP funds, clusters, and trade associations) with respect to complementary services and synergies must be checked and pursued. The results of this participation are indicated in Figure 6.

Figure 6 Participants in the Network

Level	1. Incubator—Cluster Network	2. Local, Regional, and National Institutions (Regulators, Decisions)	3. Institutions that Provide Financial Support[1]	4. Scientific Research and Education Institutions	5. Other Partners
Local	• Business Incubator Subotica • Wellness Tourism Cluster • Tourist Cluster Fund Micro Palic	• Municipal Secretariat for Economic Affairs • Local Economic Development Agency		• Secondary Technical School • Technical College	
Regional	• Cluster Fund Micro Palic Subotica • Cluster Vojplast, Hajdukovo • Fruitland Subotica • Association of Bio Research Cluster • Cluster Agribusiness	• Provincial Secretariat for Economy • Provincial Secretariat for Labour and Employment • Provincial Secretariat for Science and Technology Development • Provincial Department of Education • Provincial Secretariat for Regional Development • Provincial Secretariat of Finance	**Regional Level (Directly)** • Capital Investment Fund • The Development Fund of AP Vojvodina • Development Bank of Vojvodina **Regional Level (Indirectly)** • Foundation for European Affairs VIP Fund • Guarantee Fund APV	• Faculty of Engineering Novi Sad • Faculty of Economics Subotica • Faculty of Science Novi Sad • Faculty of Technology Novi Sad • Institutes (Database of Experts from Universities) • Vojvodina Centre for Strategic Economic Studies (CESS) • BSC Center for Standardization and Certification • Center for Competitiveness and Cluster Development	• Department of Employment Agency for Development of SMEs Subotica • Regional Clusters • Businesses

Level	1. Incubator—Cluster Network	2. Local, Regional, and National Institutions (Regulators, Decisions)	3. Institutions that Provide Financial Support[1]	4. Scientific Research and Education Institutions	5. Other Partners
National		• Ministry of Economy and Regional Development • Ministry of Science	• Ministry for the National Investment Plan • National Agency for Regional Development • Republican Fund for Innovation • Commercial banks		• National Employment Service • Clusters • Multinationals
International			• European Commission (IPA Funds, FP7, CIP, TEMPUS) • GIZ (GTC) • United States Agency for Investment and Development (USAID) • UNIDO • World Bank		

SOURCE: Morača, S., Mihalj, S., Lanji Hnis, I., & Kirchweger, D. (2011). *Cooperation platform.factor of economic development* (pp. 38–40). Novi Sad, Serbia: Authors.

[1]All institutions of the state, regional, and local governments that have the financial resources to improve the competitiveness of the economy

While activities concerning the establishment of cooperation between business incubators and clusters and support of their joint actions are specific for each region, local authority, and institution, these can generally be classified into the following categories:

- The transfer of ideas, innovative solutions, and technologies from universities, public research institutes, and clusters to entrepreneurs and new ventures through business incubators
- Fostering joint industry/academic community projects
- Revitalizing and developing existing companies in clusters and incubators using the existing professionalism of universities, business incubators, and clusters
- Strengthening of professional, scientific, and technical-technological capacities through joint education and the procurement of modern equipment and further develop economic capacities in order to enable balanced economic development without wasting money through
- Providing support of *greenfield* and *brownfield* investments

NOTE

Ildiko Zedi has been the managing director of Business Incubator Subotica, Serbia since 2006, when the business incubator was established.

REFERENCES

Becattini, G. (2004). *Industrial districts. A new approach to industrial change.* Cheltenham, UK: Edward Elgar.

Berbel, A., Rocha, A., Sá, L., & Carneiro, J. (2011). *Clustering effects and the internationalization of high-tech new ventures in technology parks and incubators.* Rio de Janeiro, Brazil: Anais do XXXV Enanpad.

European Commission Enterprise Directorate General. (2002, February). *Final report benchmarking of business incubators.* Brussels, Belgium: Centre for Strategy & Evaluation Service.

Infoplease Serbia. (2014a). *Economic summary.* Retrieved February 12, 2015, from http://www.infoplease .com/country/serbia.html?pageno=9#ixzz3G6rWIhZH

Infoplease Serbia. (2014b). *Geography Serbia.* Retrieved February 12, 2015, from http://www.infoplease .com/country/serbia.html#ixzz3G6qfnQmG

Miljašić, D. (2011). *Analysis of the situation of business infrastructure in Republic of Serbia.* National Agency for Regional Development.

Morača, S., Mihalj, S., Lanji Hnis, I., & Kirchweger, D. (2011). *Cooperation platform factor of economic development.* Novi Sad, Serbia: Authors.

National Business Incubation Association (NBIA). (2001). *Best practice in action: Guidelines for implementing first-class business incubation programs.* Athens, OH: NBIA Publications.

Porter, M. E. (1998). Clusters and the new economics of competition. *Harvard Business Review, 76*(6), 77–90.

Sforzi, F. (2009). Empirical evidence. In G. Becattini, M. Bellandi, & L. D. Propris (Eds.), *A handbook of industrial districts* (pp. 323–342). Cheltenham, UK: Edward Elgar.

Southeast Europe. (n.d.). In *Wikipedia.* Retrieved February 3, 2015, from http://en.wikipedia.org/wiki/ Southeast_Europe

Subotica. (n.d.) In *Wikipedia.* Retrieved February 3, 2015, from http://en.wikipedia.org/wiki/Subotica

World Bank. (2010, October). *Global good practice in incubation policy development and implementation.* Washington, DC: The International Bank for Reconstruction and Development.

Zedi, I., & Obradovic, K. (2008). *Business Incubator Subotica as a tool of fostering development of SMEs and entrepreneurship.* Presentation at International Conference, The European Entrepreneurship in the Globalizing Economy Challenges and Opportunities, held in Varna, Bulgaria.

Mayu LLC

Kate Robertson

Introduction

After graduating from college with a BS in business administration, Kate Robertson was not seeking a traditional office job. Instead, she was looking for an adventure, one that would fulfill her never-ending wanderlust and allow her to unleash her entrepreneurial spirit. She joined the Peace Corps as a Small Business Development Volunteer and was sent to a rural community high in the Andes Mountains of Peru. During the 2 1/2 years that Kate lived in Peru, she became enamored with the country. After months of teary-eyed goodbyes, she returned to Chicago in early 2010 with an idea. Kate would create Mayu LLC, a company that would sell hand-knit fashion accessories made with pure Peruvian alpaca fiber by the artisans with whom Kate worked in the Peace Corps. Kate believed that by establishing this small social enterprise, she could remain connected to her Peace Corps community. The company would not only provide additional income to Peruvian women, but also fulfill a market need for knitwear that was both one-of-a-kind and stylish.

To test the waters, Kate returned from the Peace Corps with two giant rice sacks full of alpaca shawls, scarves, and blankets. Seeing the positive reactions of friends and family, Kate decided that starting Mayu was indeed an excellent idea. As the demand was there and the weather was cold, she dove in head first without creating a formal business plan. One year later, as Mayu was growing, Kate was faced with a number of challenges and realized she had better answer a couple of questions before moving ahead.

1. Assuming demand continued to grow, how would she scale operations in Peru? She had already accepted a full-time job in Chicago and would be working on Mayu on a part-time basis.

2. How would she take Mayu from an in-person, event-based company to a successful online store if people could not see and feel the alpaca fiber? She needed an online marketing strategy.

3. Admitting that finance was not her strong suit, Kate worried that the pro forma financial data she had calculated were missing something. She was looking for feedback on what she had done.

4. What fraction of equity would need to be given up assuming outside capital would be sought for expansion?

5. Should she partner with several individuals who had asked her to help them also import knitwear from Peru? She wanted to protect her "trade secret"—the artisans who she had worked hard to train.

SOURCE: Used by permission from Kate Robertson.

Company and Product

Mayu, which means river in Quechua, the native language of Mayu's Peruvian artisans, imports and sells alpaca accessories including hand-knit scarves, hats, shawls, wraps, gloves, and blankets. Mayu's pro bono attorney incorporated the company as an LLC and Mayu is now a registered trademark. Kate developed the following mission for the company:

> Mayu strives to be the industry leader in the sale of high-quality, one-of-a-kind, ultra-classic alpaca accessories. Mayu offers social value by increasing the livelihood and contributing to the personal and professional development of their female producers in Peru. At the same time, Mayu transparently and honestly educates American consumers about the origins of Mayu's ethical fashion accessories. Superb customer service, mutual-respect, and triple bottom line initiatives (people, planet, profit) are the elements guiding Mayu's business activities.

After many shopping excursions in Lima's markets and Internet research on alpaca accessories currently offered in the market, Kate defined the unique selling propositions of Mayu's products. The exclusive, stylish designs were handmade with eco-friendly alpaca fiber, were fairly traded (Mayu is a member of the Fair Trade Federation), and were of the highest quality, lasting a lifetime. This product offering was different from the mass-produced, machine made accessories found in brick-and-mortar and Internet-based shops in Peru and the United States. Kate also noticed that most of these products were not actually knit with pure alpaca yarn. Instead, they were typically a combination of alpaca and other wools of lesser quality. Another uniqueness was that Mayu's products used purely Peruvian materials and labor and had an interesting story behind them. The story reflected Kate's Peace Corps experience and direct relationship with the artisans.

Industry and Current Trends

Clothing and Accessories

Kate's research indicated that the demand for clothing and accessories was driven by personal income and fashion trends and that women purchased approximately 64 items of clothing per year. According to 2010 IBISWorld Clothing & Accessories stores industry forecasts, the industry was valued at $7.0 billion with profits of $772.8 million and of all the accessory products sold, 18% involved neckwear, scarves, and hats. The accessories market had seen annual growth of 5.1% over the previous 5 years and was expected to reach 7% annual growth from 2010 to 2015. The market size of the women's outerwear and clothing industry had consistent growth between 2003 and 2008. Although the recent economic downturn had impacted the accessories market as the consumer sentiments index fell by 4.1% during the preceding years, the index was expected to rise by 13.6% in 2010. Per capita disposable income in the United States was also on the rise from its lowest values in 2008. As a result, Kate thought that her target market would not be severely impacted. Studies showed that even in times of economic downturn, consumers shifted buying behavior to more classic, forever pieces, which is precisely what Mayu offered.

E-Commerce

The e-commerce industry was growing steadily, having annual growth of 6.6% from 2005 to 2010 and annual revenues over $93.8 billion. Fortunately, online sales were expected to continue growing at an even faster rate of 10.5% from 2010 to 2015. Looking at these statistics, it was clear that online retailing was a growing medium for the purchase of specialty items such as those knit by Mayu's artisans in Peru. Of all online businesses in 2010, 15% were clothing and accessories retailers. Due to increased connectivity, positive perceptions of online security, and ease of conducting transactions, online companies such as Mayu could be expected to benefit from this growth.

Trends

Kate knew that growing awareness of fair trade and ethical fashion and the recent signs of a "green revolution" would be beneficial to Mayu. There was no doubt that consumers were becoming more responsible shoppers, and Mayu offered a solution to the market's increasing demand for products that offered social value. With that, the consumer market was developing a need for transparency and traceability throughout supply chains, especially for products from the developing world. The implementation of corporate social responsibility programs and establishment of not-for-profit advocacy organizations was proof that the 21st-century business environment was changing, and companies would be unable to survive without considering the consequences of their behaviors. The Mayu website contained information about the Mayu product life cycle, and Kate intended to further expand the site to allow for even greater transparency.

According to surveys administered by the Fair Trade Federation, the trend toward fair trade shopping in the United Sates was growing quickly. By 2010, 71.4% of American consumers knew about fair trade and 88% considered themselves conscious consumers. In 2009, fair trade organizations averaged annual sales of $517,384, compared to $499,892 in 2006, and 72.4% of these organizations were for-profit entities, showing that social, mission-driven businesses were valid substitutes for the traditional "charity-based" not-for-profits. Established fair trade companies were growing with increasing numbers of employees and volunteers and increasing impact in the countries where the production of their goods took place.

As for consumer trends, A.T. Kearney indicated that in 2009, the market for sustainable products was estimated at $118 billion, while, according to the Boston Consulting Group, firms with a "true commitment to sustainability" outperformed industry peers, especially in the retail sector. These trends reiterate American society's desire to create positive change through purchasing habits.

The concept of ethical fashion was also gaining momentum, which would also benefit Mayu's eco-friendly products. The 2009 Cone Consumer Environmental Survey, which was conducted by Opinion Research Corporation, indicated that 34% of American consumers were likely to buy environmentally responsible products and 25% more Americans had greater interest in the environment today than they did one year ago. As a result, there was an increased expectation for companies to produce and sell environmentally conscious products. Seventy percent of Americans indicated that they were paying attention to what companies were doing with regard to the environment. This interest indicates that the "green revolution" is more than just a passing trend.

A 2008 study by Conscious Innovation claimed that products and services that help customers live a sustainable life and fulfill their "help me to be a conscious consumer" desire would also thrive. Consumer behaviors for purchasing clothing and gifts have changed from previous years and are expected to continue being influenced by conscious choices.

Competition

A broad range of competition existed in the industry including both online and brick-and-mortar shops selling accessories, and while some items were handmade, most were machine made. All were available in a variety of raw materials, including alpaca, cashmere, wool, and cotton.

Kate defined direct competition as online retail stores selling alpaca accessories and clothing. There were a number of e-commerce sites selling alpaca accessories but none of them sold products as unique as Mayu's. The following websites were good examples of the competition:

- Peruvian Connection—www.peruvianconnection.com
- Alpaca Direct—www.alpacadirect.com
- Purely Alpaca—www.purelyalpaca.com
- Alpaca Boutique—www.alpacaboutique.com

Mayu differentiated itself from this primary competition because of the quality and uniqueness of its products. Kate thought that the Mayu website was a higher caliber and appealed to a more fashion-forward and conscious clientele. Once customers landed on the Mayu site, they were attracted to the stylishness, sleekness, and simplicity. The site was professional, personalized, aesthetically pleasing, and most important, up-to-date with current social media and "green" shopping trends. While Mayu's prices were comparable to the competition, customers received greater value when purchasing from Mayu. Mayu provided excellent and timely customer service and a personalized touch to potential and past customers. Ease of communication with Mayu created a positive shopping experience, despite the online nature of the business.

Kate defined secondary competition as online and brick-and-mortar retail stores selling knitwear made from raw materials such as cotton, cashmere, silk, or wool. Most of these companies have an advantage over Mayu in that they are more established and therefore had greater brand awareness and Internet presence. These larger companies have excess capital and budgets to spend on marketing and other business development activities. Mayu differentiated itself through its personal story and social mission. Kate wanted Mayu to appeal to shoppers interested in supporting independent and local companies as opposed to those who purchased from "big-box" retailers who often lacked transparency, originality, personality, and ethical behavior. The following companies are among those considered secondary competition:

- Anthroplogie—www.anthropologie.com
- Nordstrom—www.nordstrom.com
- Neiman Marcus—www.neimanmarcus.com

Marketing

Target Market

Based on her research, Kate planned to target educated women between the ages of 32 and 62, who make up 67% of the accessories market. This range allowed Mayu to target a majority of women aged 15 to 65, who represent 90% of total consumer spending. Kate expected that this market would be more socially aware and understanding of global issues and would be consumers that were more responsible. It was shown that luxury shoppers, defined as consumers who earn over $100,000 per year, are more educated and demanding so workmanship, longevity, and artistry play a large role in their purchasing behaviors.

Because Mayu is striving to become an Internet business, it has access to the entire world. In order to narrow its online marketing, Kate thought she should focus on three Standard Metropolitan Statistical Areas (SMSAs)—Chicago, New York City, and San Francisco. The reasons for choosing these particular cities are that they have appropriate weather and large populations of educated and affluent female consumers. Chicago was a natural starting point, as it is Mayu's home base with existing relationships. San Francisco has a high concentration of socially conscious female consumers and New York City's inhabitants are fashion forward and the country's trendsetters.

Price

Mayu's pricing structure is cost-based pricing. Kate used the traditional industry markup of between 200% and 250% to calculate both wholesale and retail prices. The base price that Mayu pays its artisans in Peru covers labor, raw materials, and transportation in Peru. Once the products arrive in the United States, Kate added on international shipping from Peru and customs duties to generate the total cost of each item (cost of goods sold). In some instances, however, Mayu receives slightly lower or slightly higher margins than the industry standard, depending on the product and what she thought the market could pay for each item.

Distribution

Distribution will be discussed in terms of in-person events, online, and wholesale.

In-Person Events

Until now, Mayu's greatest source of revenue had been from high-end, in-person weekend holiday events. Mayu had been invited to at least 10 such events and sales ranged from $0 to $2,500 per event. Participation fees were usually 10% of revenues. Because Kate worked full time, one of her family members or her future part-time employee would staff weekday events in the fall and spring. Mayu would make itself available for private "shopping parties" throughout the Chicago area. During a party like this, the host would invite friends over for an evening of Mayu shopping. To entice hosts to have a party, items would be offered at a 10% discount from online prices and hosts would be compensated with a generous Mayu gift card.

Online

Although the majority of Mayu's sales took place during holiday shopping events, Kate's goal was to increase online sales and decrease her reliance on labor intensive and sometimes "hit-or-miss" events. She knew it would be a challenge to sell high-end products through a website, especially without a well-established brand. The beauty of the alpaca was most apparent when customers could touch the materials and try on the products. She did offer swatches of the alpaca to interested consumers but overall, the biggest problem was driving customers to her website with a limited marketing budget and convincing them that the higher-priced items were worth the investment.

Kate purchased a social media platform at $1,000 per year. Through the platform, Mayu could efficiently target numerous social media websites with the click of a button. This was an excellent strategy to build links and increase an online presence. Kate also managed a blog, which was part of the Mayu website. There, she blogged about topics related to Peru, alpaca, fair trade, and the Mayu story; photos, videos, articles, and other prose made up the content. In addition, Kate knew that Google AdWords would provide direction in terms of online marketing. She paid $250 per month on a seasonal basis to a group of professionals who would create an AdWords account and she would have to start with a $500 monthly budget for the actual pay-per-click ads.

Kate planned to buy certain advertising banners on websites during the winter months and especially before the holidays. The cost of such ads would be about $100 per month; this was for second-tier publications that had some type of an eco-fashionista following. She budgeted $500 per month for the ads.

Kate already had a functioning website created at a very reasonable price of $1,000, including six months of site adjustments and modifications. Website logistics such as domain names, security encryption, payment services, and other related costs were low and thus led to very low start-up costs. These monthly costs totaled about $50.

Wholesale

Kate received inquiries from retailers who were interested in stocking Mayu products, but during the first year, the orders were small and margins were even smaller. The minimum order was $500 and lead time was typically no more than 6 weeks, depending on the time of year. By slightly changing her prices, Kate believed she could increase wholesale orders and therefore benefit from sales volume. The question remained, though, whether the artisans would be able to keep up with the increased demand. The chance of decreasing the price she paid the knitters in Peru was slim so costs savings had to be found elsewhere on the value chain.

To increase wholesale accounts, Mayu planned to hire three sales representatives, one to cover the West Coast, another for the East Coast, and one for the Midwest. Research indicated that the sales representatives would be compensated at least 10% of total sales. She had heard nightmarish stories from her friends about their experiences with sales representatives, so it was important to find the perfect ones who would best represent the Mayu line. An additional middleman would decrease Mayu's profits further, but to gain brand recognition, get the products distributed, and start striving for volume, the investment in a team of sales reps was necessary, especially because Kate could not "pound the pavement" on her own.

Mayu would also continue to open drop-ship arrangements (affiliate marketing) with online boutiques that posted Mayu's products on their sites. When a product is sold, Mayu ships the item from the Chicago warehouse and is compensated a defined price, generally 55% to 60% of the retail sales price. These drop-ship relationships are convenient, risk free, and without cost to Mayu.

Eventually, Kate planned to participate in trade shows such as Chicago's StyleMax to place Mayu's alpaca accessories in front of thousands of retailers. These events cost at least $5,000 for 4 days and profitability is not guaranteed. Kate decided to wait on these events for the first couple of years unless she could partner with a similar small business to share a booth and costs.

Promotion

During its short life, Mayu had received free publicity, which directly boosted sales. The company was mentioned on reputable blogs and in print publications, and was covered in local magazines. Publicists seemed to enjoy the Mayu story and readers were intrigued by what Kate had accomplished in the Peace Corps. The publicity did lead to additional sales but on a small scale. Kate considered hiring her friend, a PR specialist. The rate for the season would be $3,000 with the objective to get Mayu featured in fashion publications' holiday gift guides. There was, of course, no guarantee that editors would choose to feature the Mayu brand.

Mayu implemented a referral program to help spread needed word-of-mouth sales. Past Mayu customers were given a $25 Mayu gift card each time they referred someone who purchased something from Mayu.

Operations

Peru

Kate knew that it would be difficult to manage Mayu from her home base in Chicago without frequent visits to Peru. Fortunately, she was able to communicate with the producers via telephone and occasionally by e-mail. The fact that the artisans were not computer literate and did not have consistent access to cellular phones (not to mention the frequent power outages) made communication a challenge. By living in Peru, Kate had learned to be both flexible and adaptable to the Peruvian operating environment. She placed orders and dealt with logistical issues with the designated group leader, Maria Rosemberg de Huerta. Another obstacle Kate faced was ensuring that the products had a certain level of quality and consistency. The Peruvians were less demanding and had different ideas of what constituted high quality. In addition, the artisans were frequently dishonest, claiming certain products would arrive on a certain date, when in reality, they had not even been knit yet.

The nearest regional city is 3 hours by bus and Lima, the capital of Peru, is an 8-hour trip from the village where the knitters reside. This means that Mayu's artisans have to travel long hours to access their bank accounts and to send shipments to Kate from the Federal Express office. They are always faced with the risk that large quantities of cash or finished products could be stolen during the journey. Similarly, raw materials have to be ordered via the Internet and delivered to the community by overnight bus from Lima. The cost of the raw material ranges from US$27 to $30 per kilogram for pure alpaca wool and is paid for by the artisan group. The price variation depends on whether the fiber is dyed or natural and prices are slightly susceptible to general economic conditions in Peru. Kate and the artisans jointly decide the pricing structure of the products and Kate compensates the artisans per unit produced. This price includes labor and material costs. Kate pays the artisans via wire transfer at a rate of US$11 to $85 per item knit. Typically, Kate would pay for the products up front so the artisans would be able to purchase the raw materials.

When it became necessary to scale, Kate knew that quality control, logistics, and creating a solid organizational structure would be the biggest challenges. She thought she could hire a part-time employee who would work 5 months out of the year and be compensated $1,750 for the duration of the position.

United States

Kate was responsible for operations in the United States and overseeing production in Peru. From her home, she managed the website, online content, social media, marketing, and customer service aspects of Mayu and also attended sales events. She created an internship program and began employing students on an unpaid, 10 to 15 hour per week basis. Although it was time consuming, Kate felt that the use of interns could be a mutually beneficial experience and that "two heads were better than one." Once products arrived from Peru, Kate's mother was responsible for counting, ironing, and tagging inventory and outbound logistics such as shipping and handling. Kate knew that her mother would continue doing this forever so she planned to hire seasonal help for three months (November through January). The part-time help would be paid about $1,200 per month.

Team

Although Kate was receiving advice from a number of individuals, she did not have a formal advisory board. Her father provided her with legal advice, her uncle was a CPA, and her web designer guided her on all aspects of managing a website. Kate wanted to widen her support network and started thinking about contracting a product designer who excelled in knitwear, a professional photographer, and a clothing model as well as a team that could optimize her website. She knew that it was not in her budget to hire anyone on a full-time basis so she decided she could hire the necessary help on a per-project basis. Kate is a good networker and excels in finding high-quality help at minimum prices.

Mayu's Short-Term Plan

To take Mayu to the next level, Kate plans to hire a fashion designer and is already in contact with a woman who specializes in knitwear. The design fees per collection will be about $5,000 and include arrangements with a professional photographer, model, and hair and makeup team. The designer will take care of the creative vision behind Mayu. Kate will travel to Peru periodically to work with the artisans to create new collections. Each trip to Peru will cost about US$700 to $1,000.

Financials

The financial statements for the company include a 3-year pro forma income statement (Table 1); the first-year pro forma income statement by month (Table 2); and a 3-year pro forma cash flow statement (Table 3).

Table 1	Mayu's Projected 3-Year Income Statement (in Dollars)		
	Year 1	**Year 2**	**Year 3**
Net Sales	32,000	44,800	58,240
Cost of Goods Sold	6,400	8,960	11,648
Gross Income	**25,600**	**35,840**	**46,592**
Operating Expenses			
Advertising (*5 mo.)	2,500	2,500	2,500
Marketing & Promotion (AdWords *5 mo. & PR)	6,750	6,750	6,750
Social Media Platform	1,000	1,000	1,000
Dues & Subscription (FTF, etc)	300	300	300
Payroll Expenses			
Part-Time Employee Peru	1,750	1,750	1,750
Part-Time Employee USA	3,600	3,600	3,600
Product Design Fees	5,000	5,000	5,000
Administrative Expenses			
Website Logistics & Design	600	700	800
Travel to Peru	1,000	1,000	1,000
Office Expenses	500	700	900
Total Operating Expenses	**23,000**	**23,300**	**23,600**
Operating Income	**2,600**	**12,540**	**22,992**
Income Before Taxes	**2,600**	**12,540**	**22,992**
Net Income	**2,600**	**12,540**	**22,992**

Table 2 Mayu's First-Year Income Statement by Month (in Dollars)

	Q1			Q2			Q3			Q4			Year 1
	January	February	March	April	May	June	July	August	September	October	November	December	
Net Sales	3,500	3,000	2,000	500	500	0	0	500	1,000	3,000	10,000	8,000	32,000
Cost of Goods Sold	700	600	400	100	100	0	0	101	200	600	2,000	1,600	6,400
Gross Income	2,800	2,400	1,600	400	400	0	0	400	800	2,400	8,000	6,400	25,600
Operating Expenses													
Advertising (*5 mo.)	500	500	0	0	0	0	0	0	0	500	500	500	2,500
Marketing & Promotion (AdWords *5 mo. & PR)	1,350	1,350	0	0	0	0	0	0	0	1,350	1,350	1,350	6,750
Social Media Platform	1,000	0	0	0	0	0	0	0	0	0	0	0	1,000
Dues & Subscription (FTF etc)	300	0	0	0	0	0	0	0	0	0	0	0	300
Payroll Expenses													
Part-Time Employee Peru	583	0	0	0	0	0	0	0	0	0	583	583	1,750
Part-Time Employee USA	1,200	0	0	0	0	0	0	0	0	0	1,200	1,200	3,600
Product Design Fees	0	0	0	0	0	0	2,500	2,500	0	0	0	0	5,000
Administrative Expenses													
Website Logistics & Design	600	0	0	0	0	0	0	0	0	0	0	0	600
Travel to Peru	0	0	0	0	0	0	1,000	0	0	0	0	0	1,000
Office Expenses	500	0	0	0	0	0	0	0	0	0	0	0	500
Total Operating Expenses	6,033	1,850	0	0	0	0	3,500	2,500	0	1,350	3,133	3,133	23,000
Operating Income	(3,233)	550	1,600	400	400	0	(3,500)	(2,100)	800	1,050	4,867	3,267	2,600
Income Before Taxes	(3,233)	550	1,600	400	400	0	(3,500)	(2,100)	800	1,050	4,867	3,267	2,600
Net Income	(3,233)	550	1,600	400	400	0	(3,500)	(2,100)	800	1,050	4,867	3,267	2,600

Table 3	Mayu's Projected 3-Year Cash Flows (in Dollars)		
	Year 1	**Year 2**	**Year 3**
Cash In			
Cash Sales	32,000	44,800	58,240
Total Cash In	32,000	44,800	58,240
Total Cash Available	32,000	44,800	58,240
Cash Out			
Inventory	6,400	8,960	11,648
Operating Expenses			
Advertising (*5 mo.)	2,500	2,500	2,500
Marketing & Promotion (AdWords *5 mo. & PR)	6,750	6,750	6,750
Social Media Platform	1,000	1,000	1,000
Dues & Subscription (FTF, etc)	300	300	300
Payroll Expenses			
Part-Time Employee Peru	1,750	1,750	1,750
Part-Time Employee USA	3,600	3,600	3,600
Product Design Fees	5,000	5,000	5,000
Administrative Expenses			
Website Logistics	600	700	800
Travel to Peru	1,000	1,000	1,000
Office Expenses (tag, etc)	500	700	900
Estimated Income Tax Payment	0	0	0
Total Cash Out	29,400	32,260	35,248
Beginning Cash Balance	500	3,100	15,640
Ending Cash Balance	3,100	15,640	38,632

CASE QUESTIONS

1. Assuming demand continued to grow, how would Kate scale operations in Peru? She had already accepted a full-time job in Chicago and would be working on Mayu on a part-time basis.

2. How would Kate take Mayu from an in-person, event-based company to a successful online store if people could not see and feel the Alpaca fiber? She needed an online marketing strategy.

3. Admitting that finance was not her strong suit, Kate worried that the pro forma financial data she had calculated were missing something. She was looking for feedback on what she had done.

4. What fraction of equity would Kate give up assuming she would soon be seeking capital to expand operations?

5. How would Kate be able to partner with the many Americans who had asked her to help them also import knitwear from Peru? She did not want to give away her "trade secret" of the artisans whom she had worked hard to train.

Fitz-Ritter Wine Estate

Sean Patrick Sassmannshausen, OTH Regensburg, Bavaria, Germany Marco Biele, 4CGroup, Munich, Bavaria, Germany

Lambert T. Koch, Institute for Entrepreneurship and Innovation Research, University of Wuppertal, Germany

Abstract

The Fitz-Ritter Wine Estate was founded in 1785. In 1837, the estate broadened to include champagne production facilities. Today, the young owner, Johann Fitz, is the managing director of both companies, the ninth generation of his family to lead the business. German wine producers have been facing global challenges for several years. This case shows how an entrepreneurial spirit through generations of leadership has contributed to the survival of the vineyard. It also shows how a medium-sized business can cope with global challenges if it commits itself to take advantage of international opportunities. In this complex environment, Johann Fitz has to make irrevocable decisions concerning strategic positioning, customer relations, distribution channels, new business segments, investments, and the international business.

Introduction

Johann Fitz opens the door to his office on a Monday morning in August 2007, holding the first bottle of a brand-new product in his hands. The combination of premium sparkling wine and passion fruit will be the new FitzSecco passion fruit, a variant for the younger generation of wine drinkers. Johann is excited and rushes to the phone to call Alice, his mother, who has been responsible for the estate's marketing and exports for the last two decades. Impatiently, he dials her number. While he is waiting, he looks at his watch. It is a quarter past eleven, and the monument protection people seemed to be late. "They should be here by now." Refocusing on his phone call, he wonders why his mother does not answer the phone; he only get her voicemail. Johann opens his e-mail, searching for a correspondence from his mother, "August, 25—New York wine exhibition; August 27—Chicago; August 29—Detroit." New York City is seven hours behind; no wonder she is not answering the phone. He peruses the attached spreadsheet with the latest figures of Fitz-Ritter's exports. Johann calculates some key figures, unsure how to continue with the export business. Should he, as the new head of the company, expand foreign businesses or should he concentrate on domestic projects? Things are changing more rapidly on the domestic market, while the export activities require great attention and expenses but achieve relatively smaller sales volumes. The secretary interrupts Johann's thoughts: The monument protection group have finally arrived. Johann switches off his laptop. With a number of construction plans stacked under his arm, he welcomes two men from the local monument protection office, guiding them into the historical cross-vault cow barn located on the estate side. "I will call her later," he thinks. "Now, it is time for my next project."

Johann Fitz is part of the ninth generation of his family at Fitz-Ritter Wine Estates, succeeding his father, Konrad Fitz, who ran the family business for 37 years. In 2010, the business would be owned by the family for 225 years, but from artifacts found on the ground of the estate, it was known that the Roman invaders grew wine on that side, roughly 2,000 years ago. The young vintner inherited his passion for wine from his parents. At first, this passion remained unknown to him; his interests lay in other areas. Only weeks ago, however, he took over the lead of the Fitz-Ritter Wine Estate, right after the completion of his studies in economics at the University of California, Berkeley. The wine estate, founded in 1785, is located on the fringes of Bad Dürkheim, a wine-growing spa town at the edge of the Rhine Plain in southwestern Germany (Figure 1). Famous for its high-quality white wine, it is one of the largest wine estates in the area. Its 22 hectares (approximately 52 acres) are situated in the largest German wine-growing region, the "Pfalz" (Palatinate).

Johann represents a new type of vintner, one who combines respect for the traditional family business and entrepreneurial spirit. In the last 20 years, the German wine market has changed immensely. Globalization has had a tremendous impact on the European wine industry. Conservative strategies and antiquated structures had prevented German wine estates from achieving globally competitive positions. A few years ago, however, a young generation of vintners entered leading positions at an increasing number of wine estates, determined not to be smothered with so-called protective state intervention but

Figure 1 Antique Engraving of the Fitz-Ritter Estate

SOURCE: Johann Fitz

to face competition and to react successfully to the market forces. "Being a young German vintner is not just an occupation, it is a movement. These days, it is not just about age; it needs a certain entrepreneurial mind-set to be a young German vintner," claims Johann Fitz.

In the summer of 2006, Johann inherited the renowned family business, well-known for producing more than just wine. Growing the first Chardonnay ever in Germany (this happened in 1992) and launching a small museum and a boutique wine store, Alice and Konrad Fitz were always ahead of their local competitors in terms of innovative thinking and entrepreneurial spirit. "The production of premium wine and champagne needs passion," says Konrad Fitz. "Unfortunately, some German vintners lost track some decades ago, trying to compete with New World wine estates in mass production. The decreasing quality of some German wines, combined with high production costs, almost ruined the international standing of German wine and many wine estates."

The Fitz-Ritter Company: A Family Business Since 1785

The Fitz-Ritter Estate was founded in 1785. The founder, "old Mr. Fitz," was a merchant who decided to make a change and start something new. Family legend has it that the family would be of Scottish origin, explaining the—to German standards—uncommon family name. The vineyard is located at the famous *Deutsche Weinstraße* (German Wine Street) that, for a distance of 53 miles, crosses an area well-known for its warm, sunny climate and ideal grape-growing conditions. In addition, a champagne production was started in 1837. The origins of the Champagne Company, the family's sparkling wine production facility, in some way reflect the entrepreneurial spirit that would continue throughout the family and its winery. In 1832, Johann Fitz (the "Red Fitz") spearheaded the German vintners' protestations for the elimination of customs duties on wine exports (Figure 2), promoting a mutual trade area. Because of his involvement at the Hambacher Fest (a peaceful demonstration that had also taken place in 1832, calling for more liberty), he was persecuted by the police of the Bavarian King. The Red Fitz took refuge in France, hiding in the Champagne region, where he studied the production of champagne. Later, he returned home, accompanied by a French cellar master; together with some members of his family, he cofounded one of the very first German champagne productions, the Dürkheim Champagne Factory. It is now the oldest sparkling wine producer in the area and the third oldest in Germany.

Figure 2	An antique photo of the Red Fitz, combined with a coeval drawing of protestors at the Hambacher Castle, today is used as a label for a Fitz-Ritter cuvee red wine called Revoluzzer (*revolutionist*).

SOURCE: Johann Fitz

In 1842, despite the fact the Red Fitz was still wanted by the political police, the Dürkheim Champagne Factory became the supplier to the royal Bavarian court. As time and tastes changed, it became clear that the king would rather maintain his supply of great champagne than imprison a political antagonist, a sign that the Red Fitz was making quality wine and champagne. Thus traditional wine and champagne production roots go back more than 225 years. Now, Johann Fitz, several generations removed from the Red Fitz, has taken over from his father, Konrad Fitz, and is attempting to lead the company into a new and different age.

The family's entrepreneurial spirit is shown today in its vision and willingness to explore new opportunities to expand its business. On the ground floor of the Fitz-Ritter Wine Estate, the family business operates the museum and the attached Bacchus Boutique, a gift shop founded by Alice Fitz, who has been responsible for marketing and export for many years. After Alice married Konrad Fitz, she became familiar with the wine business (Figure 3). "First I fell in love with Konrad, but soon, I fell in love with the wine business too," she said. Her attempts at contributing something to the business were supported by her earlier studies in business and economics. One of the first actions she took was to launch the Bacchus Boutique, which at the time was a new idea among traditional winemakers and disregarded as foolish by many of them. But later, when it proved to be a success, it was imitated by almost all of them. In line with the boutique gift shop, Alice organizes charity events and classical concerts on the estate site. The company sponsors art galleries and wine festivals. Alice recalls, "Even Johann cannot imagine the shape this estate was in when we took it over. In 1970, no one here had ever heard the word *marketing*. To German vintners, it was absolutely unknown to build a brand by cultural or social endorsement and event marketing. Now this concept is broadly accepted, but most wine estates are too small to follow our strategy. Nevertheless, most of the bigger estates and cooperatives created their own brand strategy nowadays, but we still have some first mover advantages because our events have been well established at the time competitors entered."

Along with the boutique and the Fitz-Ritter branding, international expansion was an area in which the winery was leading its German counterparts. Alice began the effort with a focus on the U.S. markets because she was American and more familiar with them. According to the VDP (*Verband Deutscher Präedikat s-und Qualitaetsweingüter*, the Association of German Prädicate

Figure 3 The Fitz Family

SOURCE: Johann Fitz

Wine Estates), today's export average is about 20% of the total wine production, with a trend toward increasing growth (VDP, n.d.).

The Fitz-Ritter Estate started the export business in the late 1970s. It all happened more or less coincidentally. While Alice's mother was on vacation in Germany, they began thinking about how to deliver wine into the United States, not for business but simply for their own needs. From exploring various possibilities to ship wine to the United States for their private use, private purpose, the export business into the United States was born. A few years later, when Konrad and Alice went to wine exhibitions professionally to expose their products to the industry, importers from Japan, Great Britain, and the Netherlands became interested in Fitz-Ritter wines and started to order. "But everything started more or less with the export into the United States," Alice emphasizes.

The wine is shipped to the United States and unloaded and cleared by an importer, who needs an alcohol license. Moreover, the importer is also responsible for the distribution of the wine. Although Alice travels across the United States to promote the wine at trade fairs, often meeting and dealing directly with customers, she is not allowed to sell directly to them but rather sells only to the distributors through the importer due to restrictive import laws in the United States. She often experiences that customers place orders with her and she hands the order on to the distributor, but some distributors never hand the orders on to the importer. This is especially the case for smaller orders. The distributors feel that the margin from small orders is not worth the effort of the necessary paperwork with customs. If this happens to a larger number of small orders at the same time, the accumulated losses in potential orders are immense and so are the fruitless investments in sales promotion by Fitz-Ritter. The restrictive customs policies of the United States clearly do not favor the interests of smaller U.S. customers and of small estates producing small amounts of high-quality wine, such as Fitz-Ritter. Instead, they favor mass importers that export large quantities to only one retailer, and therefore, customs only has to do the paperwork of one large deal instead of many papers for several small deals.

The importers' and distributors' intermediate positions are very important for the export business as a whole. "You rely on the effort and contacts of your importer and your distributors," Konrad Fitz says. Alice adds,

> It has a lot to do with trust, and loyalty is hard to find. It took us years to identify trustworthy importers and distributors in the United States and other markets. It is a time- and money-consuming trial-and-error process. Trust is an emotion in the beginning, and proof only occurs when time passes by. Even if you have found a trustworthy, talented, and ambitious distributor, you still need to do a lot of sales promotion all by yourself. And if you are not present to offer the new vintage, the importer and distributors will forget you very soon. While Fitz-Ritter was obliged to give exclusive rights to one importer, this importer has many German wines in his portfolio. Exclusiveness is part of an adhesion contract: None of the licensed importers will negotiate exclusive contracts, so a family business like Fitz-Ritter only makes up a small portion of the importer's portfolio and thus, only relatively small efforts will be spent on sales promotion. Moreover, in a family business selling products made by good craftsmanship, customers want to know the entrepreneurial family behind the product so they can judge the product and the reliability of delivery by the people representing the company. Furthermore, the financial stability of the importer you choose is, of course, vital. In the United Kingdom, we trusted one import agent and were absolutely gutted. For this reason, we are not present in the UK market anymore, and we are still looking for a trustworthy importer to take on this market.

Alice has traveled all across the United States to promote her German wines, and she has also been present at national and international exhibitions. The Fitz-Ritter Gewurztraminer was especially embraced by the Americans because of its semiarid or smooth taste full of herbs and flavor with a low amount of alcohol. "While most German exporters focused on the Riesling, soon, the Gewurztraminer became our hot seller within the United States, where we positioned ourselves within a niche market," explains Alice. "But our Riesling is demanded, too," Konrad adds. Business in the United States is getting harder and harder. During the first phase of the financial crisis, there was a strengthening of the euro as compared to the U.S. dollar, making European wines more expensive for U.S. customers. Wine estates were tempted to lower the prices for their products in order not to lose market shares in the United States. Then, in the second phase of the financial crisis, the euro lost heavily against the dollar, so the margins for German wine estates on accounts receivable in U.S. dollars dropped while U.S. distributors and customers had gotten used to lower prices established in the first phase of the crisis.

The management of the Fitz-Ritter Estate also noticed that wineries active in the export scene are more competitive than their domestic rivals on the German market. Especially in the premium segment of the market, relationships with intermediaries are difficult, as sales volumes and accumulated margins are much smaller than in the mass market. Fitz-Ritter is present in many states, but turnovers concentrate on some New England states, New York City, Michigan, and California. Massachusetts has proven to be one of the toughest U.S. markets to enter. Penetrating all states with personal sales promotion is costly; one promotional tour caused estimated costs of an average of 5,000 euro, and up to five tours are necessary each year. Thus, Alice tries to build personal relationship and loyalty with distributors, who consequently care about pushing sales volume of Fitz-Ritter wines among all the different brands in their portfolio. This approach is not only driven by favorable deal structures but also partly depends on an emotional component of mutual sympathy and was, by chance, successfully established with two distributors in Michigan and California.

"The business has changed a lot," says Konrad Fitz. "Today, the winery has to sell its wine at exhibitions and through more innovative distribution channels. Several decades ago, the winery sold exclusively to commission agents without any direct sales. Commission agents actually traveled from door to door, offering their product portfolio. To their potential customers, usually stay-at-home mothers and wives, they offered the opportunity to taste the wine and learn more about each single product before buying any bottles. Thus, the wine distribution business was slow, but it was reliable, and good traders knew their business very well; knowing the high-purchasing customers in their area and their customers' tastes and price range resulted in reasonable sales levels."

Today, the door-to-door business model is antiquated. As the population became more urban and mobile and higher crime rates introduced hesitation to opening doors to strangers, door-to-door salesmen were increasingly treated with mistrust. Furthermore, fewer young people entered this business, causing a shortage of salesmen. Today, it seems that traveling salesmen in the wine retail business have reached an average age above 65 years. A new distribution model was needed, and Johann Fitz saw this early on: "When I entered the business, I instinctively knew [that] we desperately needed new distribution channels. This is why I started an online shop. There was the risk that a retailer would ban us, due to the fact that we decided to introduce direct customer services via the Internet, but thus far all is fine. We notice that online trade is an additional business with a certain set of customers and thus does not harm other distribution channels."

The English version of the online shop (http://www.fitz-ritter.de/en/shop/) is available for readers to find additional information on the wine estate.

It took some time and energy to convince our stakeholders, but we have to face market forces—and therefore we have to deal with changing consumer behavior and with demographics. Our wine has its quality; traveling salesmen were able to convince consumers that Fitz-Ritter is something special. Today, we need to renew our communication. The production of high-quality wine is much more cost intensive than mass production. We will only be able to continue with our business if we communicate our advantages in product quality.

The local climate, the geography of our landscape, and the nature of our soils provide the opportunity to produce high-quality wines in our vineyards. However, we need some ideas to sell those more expensive products in a highly competitive surrounding. In wine production, I basically focus on two areas: product quality and product portfolio. In the wine business, decisions on product portfolio—i.e., the variety of grapes you plant—are not to be changed easily. Therefore, they are regarded as strategic decisions. If we decided to produce different types of grapes on some acres (Figure 4), this would mean that on these acres over a period of at least three years, no grapes will be harvested at all. That's just due to the nature of vine, and there is nothing one can do about it. Planting vines is a long-range strategic decision; change needs three years at least and bears some risks, and the amortization of the plants takes many years. If your decision is led by trend and fashion, you better make sure that the kind of grape won´t be out of fashion again soon.

Figure 4 Wine acreage in Bad Dürkheim and the vineyards owned by Fitz-Ritter.

SOURCE: Johann Fitz

Vines have a productive life of 60 to 70 years. It takes them three to four years after planting for them to produce their first harvest, five to seven years to achieve full productive capacity, and up to 35 years to produce the quality needed for best wines. There is a correlation between age of vines and quality. In addition, the vintner can take a lot of actions to increase quality. Most activities are labor intensive and therefore costly. For Fitz-Ritter premium wines, for instance, workers cut off 50% of each bunch of grapes in spring, allowing the energy and sugar of the vine to concentrate in the remaining grapes, resulting in a much more intense flavor.

Two thirds of Fitz-Ritter's acreage is planted with Riesling vines. The best spots are the rolling hillsides named Herrenberg, Spielberg, Abtsfronhof, and Michelsberg. Due to their geographic situation and special soil, these hills offer the foundation for premium wine, especially the number-one premium class, Grosse Gewaechse (Great Growth), the label for the highest premium wines of the Association of German Prädikat Wine Estates (VDP-entitled estates). Each vine (i.e., each single plant!) was officially documented by the VDP with the aim to guarantee the highest quality. Quantities are limited (in 2006, the average outcome of a VDP wine estate was only 65hl per hectare or 2.471 acre) and growing, cultivating, and harvesting of grapes, as well as wine production, has to be carried out traditionally by hand, combined with the most modern innovations in sustainable enology for a gentle treatment of grapes and wine during the production process. Thus production remained a craft, not an industrial process and, as a result, is more expensive. For instance, hand picking and selecting of grapes is mandatory for VDP-classified premium wines, and 400 hours of work are needed for harvesting one hectare, which leads to a cost comparison of 500 euros per hectare (for non-premium wine harvested by machines) versus 2,500 euros per hectare (for handpicking of VDP-classified premium wines). The cost in wine production is also higher, for instance, because of a more gentle process of pressing the grapes. From such investments, a wine with its own personal character representing richness and complexity in taste is the reward for vintners, cellar masters, and consumers. Table 1 shows an excerpt of the comprehensive product portfolio of wines that the Fitz-Ritter Wine Estate was producing under Johann Fitz's leadership.

The German Wine Industry and the Development of a Global Wine Market

"The Riesling Renaissance" (Lynam, 2001) and "Following Hard Times, German Rieslings Rise Again" (Wolkoff, 2006) were headlines German winemakers were pleased to read. Such headlines restored their pride. After years of difficulty, the German wine industry was hoping that its fortunes were in fact changing, though it had to continue to adapt to a shifting competitive environment. The purchasing power of the German population had increased again, and foreign wines were well-known for a good cost-to-quality ratio. These two factors combined to keep Germany as the number one importer of wine in the world. And though a growing domestic demand for quality wines should have boded well for German wine estates, many things had occurred that made it less than certain that they would be able to capitalize on the opportunity.

German wines—Riesling, for example—still had a reputation of excellence, but the last 50 years put a "variety of demons" on them (Wolkoff, 2006). In the first two decades after World War II, Germans were drinking German wines, except for a small market segment at the higher end of the price scale that was occupied by famous French red wines. The giant overseas wine estates were not yet founded or at least not yet recognized. Transportation costs were high, creating a natural barrier to market entry, at least for non-European producers. But over the years, the situation changed. Wine consumption increased, and foreign wine became more and more fashionable—first Italian wines, then wines from Spain and other European origins. During this time, the so-called New World wine producers (e.g., Australia, Chile, New Zealand, South Africa, and the United States) began to learn the skills and grow the grapes necessary to compete in the global market. Decreasing transportation and production costs, combined with an increase in quality, made it possible to enter and aggressively compete with high volumes in the European market. The market entry coincided with fierce price competition among German discounters and supermarket chains, such as Aldi, Lidl, Metro Group, and Tengelmann Group.

To succeed, discounters searched for a cheap supply of wine of a good and stable quality. Therefore the ideal wine for these retailers was a generic, medium-quality cuvée that could be produced in a quantity high enough to satisfy the demand of millions of customers frequenting the discount outlets. New World wine producers had been able to meet these criteria. Moreover, they were able to differentiate themselves by marketing exotic origins such as South Australia, Napa Valley, Chile, New Zealand, and South Africa.

For a long time, the European producers and particularly the French, Spanish, and German vintners held to their traditions and downplayed overseas producers and their products. Consequently, the Old World winemakers were shocked when they finally realized the changing demand of retailers and wine consumers as well as the increasing quality of their competitors' products. This realization came as they witnessed the rising market shares of the New World producers (for more details, see, e.g., Bartlett, 2003). New methods of winegrowing, new production systems, and technical innovations combined with fewer regulations to result in competitive advantages for the New World vintners. They

Table 1 Product Portfolio 2007*

Nr.	Wine	Price € B to B	Price € E to C	Nr.	Wine	Price € B to B	Price € E to C
619	2005 Durkheimer Rittergarten Riesling	2.80	5.60	613	2006 Durkheimer Blanc de Noir	3.95	7.10
621	2006 Durkheimer Abtsfronhof Riesling	3.20	6.40	616	2006 Durkheimer Spielberg Chardonnay	5.15	9.30
624	2006 Riesling CLASSIC	3.20	6.40	425	2004 Durkheimer Abtsfronhof Gewurztram.	6.20	10.90
335	2003 Ungsteiner Herrenberg Riesling	7.70	13.50	627	2006 Durkheimer Abtsfronhof Gewurztram.	4.60	8.40
536	2005 Michelsberg Durkheim Ries. GG**	11.45	19.00	339	2003 Durkheimer Hochbenn Ries. "Ice wine"	62.00	93.00
533	2005 Kanzel Ungstein Ries. GG**	12.05	20.00	938	1999 Durkheimer Abtsfronhof Ries. Selection	46.00	70.00
511	2005 Durkheimer Dornfelder red wine	3.30	6.60	645	2006 Cuvée "Red Fitz"	4.10	7.40
612	2006 Pinot Noir	4.30	7.90	415	2004 Cuvée "Revoluzzer"	8.10	14.20
218	2004 Durkheimer Cabernet Dorsa	9.00	14.90	314	2003 Durkheimer Pinot Noir	9.90	16.50
416	2004 Durkheimer Spielberg Chardonay	9.95	16.50	001	Rittergold "dry" (0.75 litres) sparkling wine	2.85	5.70
A	FitzSecco Blanc	2.60	5.20	002	Rittergold "dry" (0.2 litres) sparkling wine	0.90	1.85
B	FitzSecco Rosé	2.60	5.20	003	Riesling Extra Brut (0.75 litres) spar. Wine	4.50	8.10
c	FitzSecco Passion Fruit (0.75 litres)	2.85	5.70	E4	2006 Fitz-Ritter Riesling (11.)	2.45	4.90
D	FitzSecco Passion Fruit (0.2 litres)	0.90	1.80	F3	2006 Fitz-Ritter Red Wine (11.)	1.85	4.70

'Figures taken from Fitz-Ritter price list (modified), business to business prices (B to B) modified for classroom calculations only.

** GG = "Grosse Gewaechse" (Great Growth)

E to C: Prices for direct sale from the Estate to private customers.

were able to produce comparable wine at lower costs and higher quantities and were able to flood Europe with it. The turning point in favor of the overseas producers clearly was the 1976 "Judgment of Paris," a blind test in which, for the first time, Californian wines were rated to be superior to French wines—as judged by a panel of 15 leading French wine critics (see Bartlett, 2003).

The first response of European vintners was twofold: There was a call for state intervention and protection on the one hand and an attempt to compete in mass production on the other hand. Soon, numerous regulations were issued concerning, for instance, grape varieties, acreage of cultivated land, and sugar content of wine. Price guarantees were given by the European Union (EU) and national agricultural subsidies in France and Spain that were meant to support vintners by converting the overproduction of low-quality wines into cash. Prices were stabilized by state intervention, as wine that could not be sold on the market was simply purchased by the EU via national state authorities.

Such attempts to respond to the entrance of the New World wine producers resulted in a disaster for the German winemakers. Germans tried to copy the successful strategy from overseas producers by mass producing white wines, without regard to differences in outer conditions. The production was increased at the expense of quality. One major obstacle, besides the less favorable climate, was the ability of New World producers to increase cultivable land by buying additional unimproved land very cheap, whereas in Europe, this strategy was impossible. The German wine producers faced geographical and regulatory limits that prevented them from increasing their cultivable land because all areas suitable for viniculture were already allocated (see Table 2). Therefore, increasing the production meant increasing the output of a given vineyard. This in turn lowered the quality significantly. Decreasing quality resulted in decreasing reputation. In addition, productivity increased slowly in comparison with the overseas wine industry because the landscape of many German vineyards did not allow for the use of heavy machinery and robots. Vineyards were typically located on very steep hillsides alongside river valleys such as Rhine, Moselle, and Main. Another setback for German vintners was suffered due to changes in international consumer demand in the 1990s, when there was a dramatic shift in consumption from light white wines toward red wines. Unfortunately, in the 1990s, the climate in

Table 2 Viniculture Companies in Germany*

company size from... to... EGE	Number of companies		
	1999	**2003**	**+ /−**
<8	12,233	10,688	−12.6
8 – <16	4,123	3,696	−10.4
16 – <40	4,716	4,21	−10.7
40 – <100	3,656	3,561	−2.6
100 – <250	648	1,193	84.1
>250	55	97	76.4
	25,431	23,445	−7.8

EGE (European unit), 1 EGE = 1,200 € contribution margin

SOURCE: Adapted; taken from Bundesministerium für Ernährung, Landwirtschaft und Verbraucherschutz "Ertragslage Garten- und Weinbau 2007: Daten-Analysen"; p.120

*Only companies with a contribution margin from above 75% from wine production

Germany was not very conducive to red wine production. The more unstable climate was another obstacle that—combined with strict regulations in wine making—caused inconsistent qualities and quantities, including the risk of crop failure. The conclusion after one generation of investment in mass production was that due to the small size of many estates, the limited acreage, and the steep hillsides of many vineyards (not allowing the use of machinery), domestic production could not ever be expected to cover domestic demand. For importers, this gap made it much easier to enter the German market.

German Import and Export
in a Changing Global Wine Market

Germany was the largest importer market for wine in the world, eventually to be replaced only by China (Robinson & Romei, 2013, p. 8). Unfortunately for German producers, the domestic demand was mostly being satisfied by imports. There were various reasons for this development. The wine drinking habits had changed in the last few decades; in many parts of society, drinking wine was subject to changes in fashion and lifestyle. This was not only true for the upper classes but also for students, skilled laborers, middle classes, and pensioners. These changing habits in the consumption and perception of wine were first surveyed in the world's largest nonproducing wine market, England. The marketing departments (an organizational element that for a long time was frowned upon or at least unknown to the traditional German and European "wine artisans") of New World winemakers identified Great Britain as an ideal target market because its then-growing demand offered opportunities for new entrants, winning the "Battle of Britain" (Bartlett, 2003, p. 8) in the wine industry. Success in the English market was regarded as an indicator for international competitiveness: "If you make it there, you'll make it everywhere," wine marketing managers said.

Since advertisements presented drinking wine as part of the common upper-class lifestyle, copying this style made members of the middle class feel like part of the upper class. This opened new and growing market segments around the world. The largest market for German wine outside Europe was located in the United States. As shown in Figure 5, German wine exports were still increasing to the United States. Since the late 1990s, the demand for German wine was rising consistently. The growth coincided with the first movers of the new generation of young German vintners who successfully started to reconsider their abilities to produce first-class white wines, especially the famous Riesling. Accordingly, the German wine exports were increasing, particularly outside the European market (see Table 3).

The most important export markets for German wine, especially white wine, were the United States, Japan, Canada, Russia, and China, whereas in Europe, the largest export markets for German wines were Great Britain, the Netherlands, Sweden, Norway, France, and Belgium. Table 3 underlines the changing export trend among German wine estates, which seemed to withdraw from highly competitive markets such as Great Britain and France. Instead, they focused more on newly growing markets such as the United States, the Scandinavian countries, and especially Russia. The activities in Asia (e.g., India and China) should not be underestimated in their future potential volume.

By the year 2002, EU Agriculture Commissioner Franz Fischler and EU officials found that protective policies found support from the wine producers' interest groups only in the short run. In the long run, protectionism resulted in an ongoing increase of rent-seeking phenomena, especially among French vintners. Additionally, intervention harmed consumer interests, since it resulted in less variety of choice and higher prices. For officials, explaining the benefits of EU intervention was getting harder each year. Furthermore, EU intervention once was meant to protect producers in order to give them time for change and improvement to regain competitiveness. Instead, uncompetitive structures were preserved, whereas New World producers continued improvements in productiveness and size.

Figure 5 German exports into the United States.

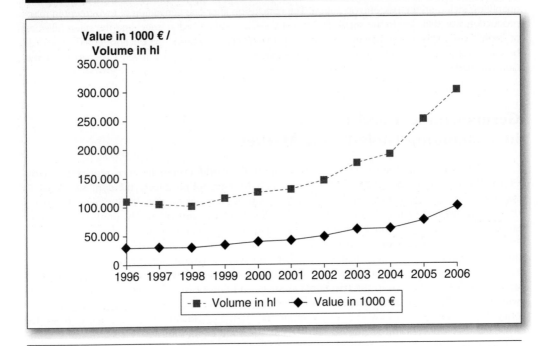

SOURCE: Verband Deutscher Weinexporteure e.V. (http://www.vdw-weinexport.de/) (after publishing of Statistisches Bundesamt der Bundesrepublik Deutschland)

Table 3 The global wine market at the time Johann Fitz took over from his father.

| Rank | Countries | 2006 | | | Annual percentage change (05/05) | | Percentage Share 2006 | |
| | | Value | Volume | | Value | Vol. | Value | Vol. |
		1.000 Eur	hl	Eur/hl				
1	EEC 25	354,661	2,185,513	162	9.7	2.5	63.2	75.2
2	Others	206,573	720,822	287	36.6	40.6	36.8	24.8
3	Great Britain	128,342	825,122	156	1.2	−8.1	22.9	28.4
4	USA	100,350	301,649	333	29	21.2	17.9	10.4
5	Netherlands	69,104	476,526	145	17.7	17	12.3	16.4
6	Norway	25,602	85,529	299	53.1	17.2	4.6	2.9

Rank	Countries	2006			Annual percentage change (05/05)		Percentage Share 2006	
		Value	Volume					
		1.000 Eur	hl	Eur/hl	Value	Vol.	Value	Vol.
7	Sweden	23,687	176,100	135	5.8	-2.1	4.2	6.1
8	Russia	22,765	169,132	135	113.9	172.6	4.1	5.8
9	Japan	22,759	62,394	365	1.6	0.9	4.1	2.1
10	France	18,542	104,334	178	−3.9	−4.4	3.3	3.6
11	Canada	15,308	57,211	268	49.4	40.7	2.7	2
12	Swiss	13,804	24,569	640	68,6	22.9	2.5	0.7
13	**SUMMARY**	**561,234**	**2,906,335**	**193**	**18.2**	**9.9**	**100**	**100**

SOURCE: VDW (Verband Deutscher Weinexporteure e.V.) http://www.vdwweinexport.de

Consequently, the 2006 bilateral trade agreement between the EU and the United States marked a turning point in the liberalization of the global wine market. The achievement of the agreement was the mutual acceptance of wine-growing methods and the protection of "semi-generic names" (e.g., Burgunder, Bordeaux, Port, or Champagne). The agreement's goal to open and deregulate the market was in contrast to previous Old World attempts to shield itself from the pressure of the New World winemakers (Table 4).

But the market was far from being truly deregulated. The EU was still paying huge amounts of state subsidies supporting domestic producers. Old-fashioned thinking relied on the faith that state subsidies and import quotas could control an increasing demand for foreign wine—a notion that was proving to be far from accurate. Protection resulted in strategic and technological inflexibility and a loss of entrepreneurial spirit.

In contrast, a new generation of German winemakers was willing to face the global challenge. Their strategic focus shifted from mass production to high-quality products combined with a mix of traditional and innovative but sustainable methods in viniculture and production. But the German wine was by far not the only one to improve. All around the globe, the overall quality of wine significantly improved over the last 50 years. "There is no doubt about the fact that the over-all quality of wine today is better than ever before," attested Konrad Fitz.

Johann Fitz and the New Entrepreneurial Spirit in the German Wine Industry

Johann Fitz was one of the young German vintners who realized that the business model of most German wine estates had to change. Even so, Fitz-Ritter had never been involved in mass production and had always been dedicated to producing top-quality wines; there still were a lot of things to do. Konrad was always open for improving the methods of production in the vineyards and cellars and Johann continued on this path by pursuing enological innovations most rigorously and conscientiously and without compromise. In addition to the online shop and the new product, FitzSecco passion fruit, one of his first projects as successor to Konrad Fitz was the refurbishment of the historical

| Table 4 | Development of the Institutional Setting in the Global and Domestic Wine Markets (from the Authors, Based on Interviews and Several Sources) |

Past	Present
Germany	Germany
German Wine Law 1971 WeinG 1994 Additional wine laws issued on state level Strict regulations of viticulture methods Rejection of non-European viticulture methods Strict rules for labeling wine Classification into four categories (quality wine with "Prädikat," quality wine of recognized regions, land wine, table wine)	German Wine Law 1971 WeinG 1994 Additional wine laws issued on state level Modification of Wine Law planned Criticism from top wine producers and their organizations (e.g., VDP; additional classifications introduced without legal protection) Regulations of viticulture somewhat eased at state-level legalization (e.g., rights for careful irrigation) Goal: better differentiation of quality vineyards, introduction of a system of categories in line with international standards
EEC	EU (previously EEC)
Each country has its own wine law Strong regulations rejection of non-European viticulture methods	Treaty between EU and United States (2006) Mutual acceptance of viticulture methods Unclear whether planned free trade agreement with United States will include a chapter on alcoholic beverages
United States	United States
Bureau of Alcohol, Tobacco, and Firearms (ATF) Approved Viticulture Areas (AVA) Percentage of grapes used from each AVA area is important for classification	Treaty between EU and United States guarantees protection of semi-generic brands, such as Champagne or Sonoma Valley Unclear whether United States will include a chapter on alcoholic beverages in the planned free trade agreement with EU, decreasing red tape trade barriers to wine imports
World	World
Conglomerate of bilateral treaties Old World versus New World viticulture methods State protection Protectionism against new viticulture methods, especially in EEC	Conglomerate of bilateral treaties Tendency toward more liberalization Downsizing protectionism New emerging markets with no or only limited local production (e.g., Russia, China, etc.)

cross-vault cow barn (Figure 6). Johann's idea was to convert this unutilized space into a ballroom and dining room with a winter garden, where dignified events can take place. Johann's idea of a modern wine estate is as simple as his mission statement: Deliver high-quality wine in combination with features to retain customers. The refurbishment of the cross-vault cow barn is just one means to that end: "If you celebrate your wedding here, you will receive a lifetime discount and a tailored label for your special day. This is the perfect way to win over customers and retain customer loyalty for our vineyard." One difficulty for vintners is customer retention; Johann sees the answer to that question in the combination of his products with events at the winery.

Figure 6	The refurbishment of the historical cross-vault cow barn, a part of the estate building that is assumed to date back to the Renaissance.

SOURCE: Johann Fitz

To Johann, the transformation of the historical cross-vault cow barn into a ballroom is a symbol of the new spirit he brought into the company. Even though he was unsure about taking over the company, he is now searching for opportunities and change. "It required a little convincing, but soon, I knew that I wanted to run the company and implement new ideas," emphasizes Johann.

My parents were leading the vineyard with an entrepreneurial mindset, and I want to continue this track. And continuation means change. Like, for every human being, my attention and power is limited. I need to concentrate on very few key projects at a time. Consequently, I have to develop the estate step by step. I need a priority list, showing which projects or opportunities are crucial for success and then concentrate investments on first things first.

This is why he is still unsure about expanding or ceasing the export business with all its inherent risks and all the expenditures it requires.

"Export is an affair of my mother's heart," Johann explains. "She put so much effort in it, but the weak dollar is wearing the profits down." A small company such as Fitz-Ritter has to pass through 100% of all currency changes.

Our Incoterms (International Commercial Terms) usually refer to CIF when ocean carriers are used (cost, insurance, and freight paid by the wine estate to the port of destination) and CIP in the case of airfreight (carriage and insurance paid to a named destination). In the international wine business, it is commercial custom that prices are negotiated in foreign currencies on the day of order. Payment is due after delivery. Hence, we carry the risk of exchange rates, and I can tell you, we have not been lucky with the euro-to-U.S.-dollar ratios during the past few years. Just to increase the price in U.S. dollars is not the answer, because we soon would bust market prices and our wine would become unsellable.

But Johann is optimistic: "I will find a solution and make a decision, one way or the other." He is someone who likes to tackle a problem, "I am a person who likes to put my hand on it." Recounting a story from his years of study at the University of California at Berkeley, he says,

During the summer, I took part in a management program and there was a competition where students had to run a small company. I was the manager of a painting company. It was exciting. I did all the planning and administrative processes by myself, and I even employed some people for operational work. I did very well and finally won the competition. It was a great experience. But then, after winning, I was supposed to explain and teach my strategies and ideas to other students, but there I failed badly,

he says with a smile on his face. "I am a person who just does things, but I am not one to talk about it. I am not a coach or a teacher."

Although the idea of refurbishing the cross-vault cow barn provided a promising opportunity to build a lasting connection between customers and the Fitz-Ritter brand, Johann had to be careful not to stray too far from the core business. Johann had to care for the investments and search for capital:

We have returns on investment from wine production, but the surplus reserve cannot cover the entire project. It can only contribute a little equity to the amount of cash needed. So I faced the task of financing the project. First, I limited the need for capital by having a clear focus on our core competence. The project is intended to foster our sales of wine during the event and for future delivery. It is not designed to run a restaurant. This would mean the need to employ an excellent chef, additional cooks, stagers, waiters, and so on. Therefore I decided to outsource the catering. Guests are free to choose any caterer they like, and thus all the diverse demands for cuisine that may occur can be easily fulfilled. The only product I put restrictions on is wine and champagne. It has to be purchased from the Fitz-Ritter Wine Estate or our Sektkellerei Fitz KG, respectively (i.e., the official name of the sparkling wine business). Aside from that, the outsourcing of catering is to our advantage because our fixed costs are much lower and total calculation is detached from variable costs. Consequently, the need for capital is equated with the costs of transformation of the site only. A positive cash flow and the breakeven point will be reached almost with the first bottle sold after the interests on the invested capital are paid.

Table 5 shows the investment costs and the source of funds.[1] In the financial plan, the KfW (Kreditanstalt für Wiederaufbau) Bank plays a decisive role. This public financial institution was originally created to help Germany recover from World War II and to distribute aid from George C. Marshall's European Recovery Program (ERP). Most European countries used the money from the program for direct state subsidization, but the German government chose a different model: They founded the KfW Bank as a grant holder. The KfW Bank did not spend the money on subventions but invested it by offering loans to innovative small and medium-sized enterprises (SMEs). Hence, the aid, once given by the United States, still accumulates interest and remains available to the

German economy. Furthermore, despite considerable progress, the market for informal equity is not well developed in Germany. For this reason, the KfW Bank offers not only investment loans but also mezzanine capital. On the condition that the entrepreneur will get involved with 15% equity, up to an additional 25% of the total investment can be financed by the mezzanine capital program. The remaining 60% of the investment can be covered by an investment loan.

The new cross-vault cow barn project looks promising. Although the project has just been started, 15 couples have already booked the room and the garden for their wedding parties at a rent of 2,100 euro per day. In addition to the rent, Johann plans to sell around 100 bottles per event at retail prices (see Table 1). At least 40 to 45 events per year could be scheduled, most of them throughout the season. For Johann, the economic considerations behind the project are clear: "Aside from the cash that we put into the project, we use our estate's garden and the ancient cross-vault next to it, both representing assets that have been idle for many years but soon will contribute to our business." Market analysts state that the average German couple spends 14,000 euro on their wedding. In addition, many companies, clubs, associations, and private persons are looking for unique locations to make their function a very special event. Thanks to word of mouth, Internet advertisements, and a Google strategy,[2] the business plan expects the bookings to increase to 60 or even 70 events yearly until the fourth year. Operation of the facility opened in May 2008.

Confident in his future plans, Johann is talking about his strategy and his mission to help Fitz-Ritter become one of the best German wine estates. "We work very hard on increasing the quality of our wines," he emphasizes. From the first seeding to the harvest, the vintner's family and its employees controlled almost all aspects of the value chain. Even filling the wine into bottles, labeling, marketing, and selling is done by the small group of people at the Fitz-Ritter winery. "Today, this is special," says Konrad Fitz. "We do everything on our own. It is demanding, but we believe that you can taste it. High-quality wine is our passion and we control the total process" (Figure 7).

Table 5 Entrepreneurial Finance for SME in Germany—An Example

Total Investment					500,000 €	
Sources of Capital						
Equity from surplus reserve:					75,000 €	
Mezzanine Capital from KfW Gründerkapital (Capital for Entrepreneurship Program):					125,000 €	
Investment loan from KfW Gründerkredit (Entrepreneurship Loan):					300,000 €	
Interest Rates and Amortizations (Year 1 starts on January 1, 2008)						
Mezzanine Capital from KfW						
Year	1	2	3	4–7	8–15	
Interest %**	0.65	0.65	0.65	2.65	2.65	
Amortization*	0.0	0.0	0.0	0.0	1/16 per half year	
Investment Loan from KfW						
Year	1	2	from year 3–10			
Interest %**	1.25–7.65 (depending on rating), Fitz-Ritter is rated A (1.25)					
Amortization*	0.0	0.0	1/16 per half year			
*if required by the entrepreneurial enterprise, amortization can be expedited						
**interest rates are subject to change; for actual rates, see http://www.kfw.de						

Johann's next plan is to further increase the quality of wine by investing in human resources and know-how: "You can always increase the quality of wine. We have achieved a lot but still have some space left to climb up the ladder to the top German vineyards." The shift in methods of achieving quality had been drastic during the last 15 years, along with the way that such achievements in quality are measured and communicated. The Internet and other types of easily accessible

Figure 7   The Fitz-Ritter wine cellar, where high-quality wines are matured traditionally in oak barrels.

SOURCE: Johann Fitz

mass media create more transparency; consumers are able to quickly share their wine experiences with others. Peer-to-peer recommendations, expert opinions, and ratings became more popular. Some of the so-called experts, especially those who published in the weekend issues of leading newspapers, and some bloggers have a lot of power; they influence consumer behavior and thus give incentives for higher quality. Today, markets reward quality more than years or decades ago.

For this and other reasons, Johann is monitoring the market for additional high-quality acreages he might be able to purchase, but this proved impossible. "Purchasing good wine from another vintner is alternative possibility, especially in the cuvée and sparkling wine production," the young vintner adds. This strategy is more feasible and can help to bypass bottlenecks in delivery, for instance, with his latest innovation, FitzSecco passion fruit. As Johann explains, "It is a product for young people who like to enjoy good quality wine with the flavor of passion fruit. It is a stylish product that is brand new and already the 'in' drink here in our region. Demand is higher than we thought, so for production, quality wine has to be bought in addition to our own volume. With this new, flavored sparkling wine, Fitz-Ritter is targeting young people, especially young women. It has a great potential to become the next hot seller of our vineyard."

In addition, FitzSecco passion fruit will soon be available in smaller "Piccolo" bottles (0.2 liters), with the latest trend in bottle caps applied, the "twist and pop" cap. Due to its low alcohol content and fruity, refreshing taste, it is a good alternative to the alco-pops sold at pubs and clubs, which have faced increasing criticism in public debate after some incidents related to their high alcohol percentage. "Changing our product portfolio, I can imagine dedicating our entire acreage to the production of premium wines of highest quality and rounding out the portfolio with quality wine bought from other vintners," Johann said. "The additional wine would be placed in the medium price range and [would be used] in the production of cuvées for champagne-style sparkling wines and trendy products like FitzSecco passion fruit" (Figure 8).

Perspectives and Discussions

The Fitz-Ritter company is facing a crucial period in its history where several decisions will have to be made that depend massively on the strategy Johann wishes to pursue. The wine industry has changed and continues to evolve. In Germany and elsewhere in Europe, smaller wine estates

Figure 8 | Wine Tasting in the Estate's Cellars

SOURCE: Johann Fitz

already had to react to the challenges of a global wine industry. In Germany, a consolidation process in the wine industry has started but has not reached its inflection point yet. Rumors persist that some of the largest German vineyards have received takeover offers from overseas. In this situation, would the succession process at the Fitz-Ritter company strengthen or weaken the company? The new, young head, Johann Fitz, started within a rough industry. But he enjoyed an excellent education in enology, economics, and entrepreneurship. His father, Konrad Fitz, has retired but is still on the estate to help with his rich experience. His mother, Alice, is willing to promote exports for several more years. The company is 100% family owned. Nevertheless, future plans have to be made—it is simply not enough to rest on what had been achieved so far.

The new projects Johann Fitz has executed so far are all in line with the overall strategy of the company: the development of a premium-quality wine estate that combines tradition and innovation. Projects included the following:

– The introduction of new products, such as the FitzSecco passion fruit sparkling wine
– A reorganization of product portfolio, stressing those products with the highest quality and prices
– The reorganization of distribution channels in the domestic market, including the establishment of an Internet shop
– The historical cross-vault cow barn project to increase direct sales on-site at the estate, which also has the potential to increase customer loyalty
– New labels and elegant designs for bottles containing the most expensive wines (Figure 9)
– Investments in human resources; for example, hiring a famous first-class enologist and employing a cellar master of excellent craftsmanship

Yet more decisions lay ahead for Johann. Because every project mentioned above bears the risk of failure, it is necessary to have alternative plans. At this point, many questions remained and many options were available.

Why not concentrate on the domestic market and leave the cost-intensive and often difficult export business to competitors? Even though she had decades of experience, Alice admits, "The

Figure 9 New Products and New Designs for Bottles and Labels

SOURCE: Johann Fitz

export business is a perplexing and troublesome job, with markets not easy to understand." Domestic demand is sufficient, especially if the historical cross-vault cow barn project turns out fine. So why should Johann Fitz continue with the export business? What are the possible rewards of international entrepreneurship in the case of the Fitz-Ritter wine estate? Should the 25% of the given production capacity that is used for international business be dedicated to the domestic market in the nearer future?

What about the distribution and product portfolio? Do changes in climate offer new opportunities for differentiation of the product portfolio? Are there any growth strategies Fitz-Ritter should take advantage of? In which areas of the Fitz-Ritter business can one recognize such opportunities for growth? Are exhibitions and Internet appearance enough to survive or would additional communication be needed? How can the company use its latest innovation, the FitzSecco passion fruit? What could the marketing plan for FitzSecco passion fruit look like? And how can Johann gain and retain more young customers?

These difficult questions are on Johann's mind when he returns from the cross-vault cow barn refurbishment site. The monument protection officials felt comfortable with the way the ancient renaissance character of the building has carefully been preserved. After taking leave from the officials, he enters his office. The phone is ringing. It is Alice calling, with excitement in her voice, "Johann, our premium wine is positively reviewed by today's *New York Times* and the *Wine Spectator* ranked the Michelsberg and the Kanzel Ungestein Riesling above 90 points. So to speak, we have just entered the international champions' league at a top rank."

"What news, and the day has just started," Johann says. "Our strategy seems to be turning out fine, and tonight, we shall definitely open one of the best bottles of champagne from our cellar." But before this, Johann makes good use of the day, considering the rewards of the challenging export business from a new perspective, rethinking his opportunities, and reweighing his options.

NOTES

1. To protect the company's interests, all financial data and sources of funds have been subject to modification. Nevertheless, the data given are realistic and the sources of finance are the most important for entrepreneurial start-ups and business successors in Germany. They were chosen to give the case a universal validity for entrepreneurial finance in Germany.

2. Searching for a wedding room at http://www.google.de from a place located within in a circle of 100 miles around Bad Durkheim, one would find the "historical cross-vault cow barn" among the first hits. The city of Frankfurt, financial capital of German economy, is located within this circle.

REFERENCES

Bartlett, C. A. (2003). *Global wine wars: New world challenges old.* Boston, MA: Harvard Business School Publishing.

Lynam, R. (2001, March). The Riesling renaissance. *Hong Kong Business, 18*(225), 98.

Robinson, J., & Romei, V. (2013, December 6). The new bunch: Wine—the world is drinking more than ever, despite its waning appeal in southern Europe. *Financial Times*, p. 8.

Verband Deutscher Präedikat s-und Qualitätsweingüter (VDP) [website]. (n.d.). Retrieved September 29, 2008, from http://www.vdp.de/verband/daten-zahlen-fakten/

Wolkoff, I. (2006, June, 2). Following hard times, German Rieslings rise again. *Medical Post, 42*(20), 39.

Intelligent Leisure Solutions

Robert Hisrich and Cristina Ricaurte

Introduction

Intelligent Leisure Solutions (ILS) is a group of five companies based in Brazil working to create, implement, and manage intelligent solutions. As a completely technology-based solutions company, ILS is unique in its approach to travel, real estate, technology, and sustainable tourism. With high growth in the tourism industry, Intelligent Leisure Solutions' founding entrepreneur, Robert Phillips, is working to find the most appropriate, innovative growth strategy for expansion and sustainability of the business.

Geographic Background

Brazil is located on the eastern, Atlantic Coast of South America with a slightly smaller geographic area than the United States (see Figure 1). With the fifth largest country population in the world, it is home to more than 200 million people. Brazil's economy is larger than that of all other South American countries, characterized by developed mining, manufacturing, agricultural and service sectors, and is increasing its presence in world markets. After the global recession in 2008, Brazil was one of the first emerging markets to begin recovering with about a 5% growth in 2010 (Central Intelligence Agency [CIA], 2010).

Brazil's economy is now the eighth largest in the world. It recently acquired a temporary seat on the United Nations Security Council until the end of 2011 and is seeking a growing international role and geopolitical influence (Economist Intelligence Unit, 2010a). Brazil's government, led by Dilma Rousseff of the Worker's Party, welcomes private sector concessions, although bureaucracy still impairs efficiency. Foreign direct investment is welcomed, although domestic investors receive priority in certain areas, especially in the oil and energy sectors. Development of the export industry continues to be a priority and trade barriers are expected to be lowered. Brazil's tax system is poorly structured and tax evasion is widespread while the tax breaks applied to lessen the burden of the financial crisis of 2008 are scheduled to be lifted; yet, the overall tax burden will continue to be high. Both foreign and national companies spend considerable resources toward managing their tax issues. Compliance with environmental law is a new crucial aspect of doing business in Brazil, and intellectual property rights must be respected (Economist Intelligence Unit, 2010b). The looming 2014 World Cup and 2016 Olympics are expected to bring an increase in public–private partnerships (Economist Intelligence Unit, 2010a).

SOURCE: Used by permission from Robert Hisrich and Cristina Ricaurte.

Figure 1 Map of Brazil

SOURCE: CIA (2010).

Brazil's middle class is expanding due to the prosperity brought about by sound macroeconomic policies since 2000 (Euromonitor International, 2010). For the first time in Brazil's history, 50% of its citizens, more than 94 million people, belong to the middle class. Many low-income Brazilians have benefitted from new opportunities for stable jobs in the past decade. Because more people are being hired in the formal economy, access to working benefits such as health care, transportation, and food has increased. The real average monthly income grew 2.3% between 2008 and 2009

(Euromonitor International, 2010); this new middle class has access to certain products and services for the first time in their lives and are demanding more products and higher quality of service.

Lower fertility rates are also contributing to higher disposable incomes. Brazil's fertility rate of 1.9 children per woman in 2009 has allowed parents to spend more on consumer goods and services (Euromonitor International, 2010). This has also resulted in a rise in demand for travel services, as families are increasingly able to afford vacations.

Brazil has a very young population, with 33.2% of its population in its twenties and thirties (see Table 1). This segment of the population is technology savvy with financial independence and the means to travel (Euromonitor International, 2010). They tend to travel to different regions of Brazil and to other countries over the holidays, and are looking for comfort and efficiency in their services. The annual disposable income will increase by 2020 (see Table 2). The number of families in the US$75,000 income bracket will more than double from 1.7 million households in 2010 to 3.6 million in 2020 (Euromonitor International, 2010).

The tourism industry in Brazil grew 22% from 2003 to 2007, almost 3% more than the overall Brazilian economy during that time (Euromonitor International, 2010). Leisure and recreation spending is expected to grow by 65% by 2020 (see Table 3) with more Brazilians traveling during Carnival, Christmas, and other vacation times. Many Brazilians are starting to buy vacation packages through travel agencies and airlines that can be paid for in installments; the amount spent in this area grew 27.5% from 2005 to $5 billion Brazilian reals in 2009 (see Table 4) (Euromonitor International, 2010). People in the upper and upper-middle classes are the primary customers for these packages.

Table 1 Brazil's Consumer Segmentation, 2010–2020 (in thousands)

	2010	2015	2020	Growth (%)
Babies/Infants (0–2 years)	9,084	8,070	7,656	−15.7
Kids (3–8 years)	20,236	17,859	16,005	−20.9
Tweenagers (9–12 years)	13,928	13,490	11,865	−14.8
Teens (13–19 years)	23,347	24,104	23,627	1.2
People in their twenties	35,258	33,749	33,335	−5.5
People in their thirties	29,875	33,207	34,611	15.9
Middle-aged adults (40–64 years)	50,359	56,508	62,662	24.4
Older population (65+ years)	13,335	15,877	19,290	44.6

SOURCE: Euromonitor International (2010).

History of the Entrepreneur and Company

Robert Phillips, founder and CEO of Intelligent Leisure Solutions, has a BS in electrical engineering and an MS in space power. He worked in space power and in oil exploration in the United States and received an MBA from Thunderbird School of Global Management in 1994. He is a U.S. citizen who spent most of his childhood living in South America, specifically in Brazil, Bolivia, and Colombia (Guthry, 2010).

Phillips began Intelligent Leisure Solutions in 1998 while working at Odebrecht, the largest engineering, construction, chemical, and petrochemical company in Latin America. As an internal consultant for tourism, tourism development, and real estate projects in Brazil, Phillips acted as a liaison between McKinsey and Ernst & Young, two large consulting firms in the United States, who were hired to evaluate tourism industry possibilities for Odebrecht. When Odebrecht decided not to invest in the tourism sector, Phillips saw a market opportunity and developed a Web-based travel company to sell Brazil to the world. Focused completely on Internet marketing, the company was unique among travel companies in Brazil in its innovative marketing strategy. In 2003, Phillips left Odebrecht to start DiscoverBrazil.com, a self-funded, Web-based travel company (now Intelligent Travel Solutions, or ITS), with the help of two partners, both colleagues from Odebrecht.

DiscoverBrazil.com began selling travel from Phillips's home office, and expanded to offer Central and South American luxury vacation packages, growing to 11 travel consultants, four websites, and monthly sales of US$300,000. The team acquired expert knowledge in Internet marketing and technology through their application of solely Internet marketing during their first few years

Table 2 Annual Disposable Income Per Household, 2010–2020

	2010	2015	2020	Growth (%)
Above US$500	55,224	60,306	65,374	18.4
Above US$1,000	54,662	59,873	65,026	19.0
Above US$5,000	45,673	52,420	58,709	28.5
Above US$10,000	32,705	40,290	47,466	45.1
Above US$25,000	11,969	16,801	22,052	84.3
Above US$45,000	4,535	6,696	9,238	103.7
Above US$75,000	1,790	2,654	3,697	106.6
Above US$150,000	569	798	1,069	87.9

SOURCE: Euromonitor International (2010).

NOTE: Constant value at 2009 prices.

Table 3 Consumer Expenditure by Broad Category (in billions of reals), 2010–2020

Product	2010	2015	2020	Growth (%)	CAGR[a] (%)
Food and nonalcoholic beverages	527	678	839	59.3	4.8
Alcoholic beverages and tobacco	40	50	61	51.2	4.2
Clothing and footwear	68	80	90	31.5	2.8
Housing	313	397	492	57.4	4.6
Household goods and services	107	135	163	52.8	4.3
Health goods and medical services	95	126	160	68.9	5.4
Transport	281	372	469	67.1	5.3
Communications	118	160	209	77.8	5.9
Leisure and recreation	72	95	119	65.1	5.1
Education	153	204	259	69.6	5.4
Hotels and catering	56	68	79	40.5	3.5
Miscellaneous goods and services	296	390	487	64.6	5.1
TOTAL	**2,126**	**2,755**	**3,427**	**61.3**	**4.9**

SOURCE: Euromonitor International (2010).

NOTE: Constant value at 2009 prices.

[a]CAGR = compound annual growth rate.

Table 4 Consumer Expenditure on Package Holidays (in millions of reals), 2005–2009

Product	2005	2006	2007	2008	2009	Growth (%)
Package holidays	3,976	4,301	4,635	4,941	5,071	27.5

SOURCE: Euromonitor International (2010).

NOTE: Constant value at 2009 prices.

Table 5	Awards and Honors Won by Intelligent Leisure Solutions Companies

- Winner – 2008 UN World Tourism Org Ulysses Award for Innovation in Tourism Enterprises
- Nominee – 2009 and 2010 World Travel Award as World's Leading Travel Agency
- Nominee – 2010 World Travel Award as World's Leading Travel Management Company
- Winner – 2009 and 2010 World Travel Award as S. America's Leading Travel Agency
- Winner – 2008, 2009, and 2010 World Travel Award as S. America's Leading Travel Management Company
- Winner – 2008 and 2010 World Travel Award as Central America's Leading Travel Agency
- Robert Phillips, managing partner, elected President of American Society of Travel Agents (ASTA), Brazil Chapter
- Selected as an Affiliate Member of the UN World Tourism Organization by Brazilian Ministry of Tourism

of operations, allowing them to attain first-place results in Google's and Yahoo's search engine results pages (SERPs) for their business keywords.

Phillips and the team began setting up websites for Brazilian companies using the Internet marketing techniques they had developed for the Discover Brazil sites. Within weeks, these sites attained first placements in SERPs, something that usually took at least 3 to 6 months to achieve in the travel sector in English. In 2007, Intelligent Web Solutions (IWS) was created out of these results, and soon after, Intelligent Content Solutions (ICS) was created when Phillips partnered with another entrepreneur with translation experience. The result was an award-winning, integrated service that included Web marketing, Web business services, Web content creation, and translation service (see Table 5).

Organizational Structure

Intelligent Leisure Solutions Consulting (ILSC) is an efficient outsourcing service, with a broad network of specialized partners for each outsourced service. Demand is identified, and innovative, intelligent solutions are created, turning this demand into business opportunities. ILSC started with two employees. In 2007, the company had 26 employees. The company was restructured because of the financial crisis of 2008 and foreign exchange debt to 12 employees, which then grew again to 16 employees in 2009 (Guthry, 2010).

Throughout the creation of IWS, ICS, ITS, and IRES (Intelligent Real Estate Solutions), Phillips continued his work with ILSC, which helped fund new projects. In 2009, Phillips brought three new partners into ILSC who helped Discover Brazil evolve into a group of five companies. Due to tax structure requirements in Brazil, companies need to be kept separate to qualify for certain tax incentives.

The group has incorporated Internet technology into the horizontally integrated leisure chain. The companies in the group offer a range of services from leisure development to the marketing and distribution of products. It is able to use shared knowledge between the five companies resulting in a strategic advantage. The group considers itself unique in that it has its own business laboratory (ITS) where it is able to test and develop its integrated services and Web techniques.

Intelligent Leisure Solutions is made up of five companies, each focusing on its own market niche:

Intelligent Leisure Solutions Consulting (ILSC) is a leisure, real estate, travel, tourism, and entertainment development consulting company with customers ranging from independent project owners, banks, investment funds, universities, and municipal, state, and federal governments. The company has a strong international and multicultural team located within Brazil. Its strategic advantage is its knowledge of the entire travel real estate market and its all-in-one solutions for tourism consulting, Web marketing, real estate brokerage, and travel consulting. With rapidly growing tourism and real estate industries in Brazil, ILSC hopes to capitalize on increased foreign investors in the next decade. Sample clients include the Ministry of Tourism of Brazil, the Secretariat of Tourism of Bahia, the World Bank, the Inter-American Development Bank, the CERT Foundation, Sapiens Park, and Zank Boutique Hotel. ILSC is also the exclusive representative for Odebrecht and Gehry Technology in Brazil and has recently won the bid to provide services for the Panama Metro and the Olympics and World Cup arenas in Brazil.

Intelligent Real Estate Solutions (IRES) offers complete real estate brokerage solutions in Brazil with clients such as international investors, banks, and funds investing in real estate and real estate projects in Brazil. This member company also has a cross-cultural and multilingual team that is able to provide foreign investors with services in their own languages. Because most ILSC clients need real estate consulting and brokerage services, IRES is able to offer these additional services as part of an integrated solution.

Intelligent Web Solutions (IWS) offers Internet marketing and business plan consulting and development, specializing in both search engine optimization and search engine marketing. Customers of IWS want a presence online and include small, medium, and large companies, artists, banks, universities, and governments. Since few companies in the tourism sector offer content creation solutions, IWS offers this combined with project management and global services knowledge.

IWS believes it will be able to grow efficiently because of the lower costs of Internet marketing compared to traditional marketing, offering cost savings up to 90%. Internet marketing can reach anyone around the world with access to the Internet. Since any company interested in using Internet marketing is a potential IWS client, the firm capitalized on this by holding its second Internet Marketing Road Show in 2010. Through this, Intelligent Leisure Solutions entered the European market in 2009 with two new large clients.

Sample clients include in Spain—Universitat Oberta de Catalunya (www.uoc.edu) and Costa Brava of Girona (www.costabrava.org); in Argentina—Festival de Verão and Pepsi (www.sociallize .com.br), and Finca don Otaviano (www.FincadonOtaviano.com.ar); in Brazil—Carlinhos Brown (www.CarlinhosBrown.com.br), Physio Pilates (www.PhysioPilates.com), and Odebrecht Real Estate and Tourism projects, including Reserva do Paiva (www.reservadopaiva.com), Hangar Business Park (www.hangarsalvador.com.br), Boulevard Side (www.boulevardside.com.br), Quintas Private (www.quintasprivate.com.br), Mitchell (www.mitchell.com.br), and The Planet Fashion Wear (www.theplanet.com.br).

Intelligent Content Solutions (ICS) provides full-service Web content creation and translation to both individuals and companies needing translations and Web copywriting services. The company offers website translation into any language through its international team working within Brazil and its consultants located around the world. Only techniques that have been tested in the business laboratory (ITS) are offered to clients. Since companies increasingly want to sell their products globally, ICS has many opportunities for growth.

Intelligent Travel Solutions (ITS) offers personalized luxury travel solutions in Central and South America to individual travelers, travel agencies, tour operators, schools, universities, churches, other institutions, companies from diverse sectors, and countries offering incentive trips. All ITS's employees are multicultural and multilingual consultants, not travel agents, who apply in-house Web marketing techniques to establish the image of Central and South America as luxury travel destinations.

ITS is the first Web-based tour operator in Brazil and it promotes local development of sustainable tourist activity through excellence in its services. Opportunities for growth can be seen in applying this low-cost model to smaller regional and specialty travel websites.

Obstacles Faced

- **2008 Economic Crisis**—This represented a significant challenge to Intelligent Leisure Solutions as the decrease in demand led to a loss in revenue for the business. This was addressed by restructuring the business to travel consultants working from home instead of from corporate office space. This allowed the company to cut costs and implement a differentiated commission structure (Guthry, 2010).
- **Human Resources**—In Phillips's words, "What I have found to be one of the primary obstacles is human resources and human resource selection. If I were hiring a lawyer or a finance guy, that's all pretty standard. But when you go to set up an Internet-based travel company, who do you use as your foundation?" Phillips identified capable staff and implemented quality training, procedures, and a business culture appropriate for each company.
- **Lack of Understanding of the Need for the Products**—Since IWS offers an integrated travel solution, something not currently seen on the market, many prospective clients need to be educated about the company's products. The sales strategy for Intelligent Leisure Solutions was designed to first educate consumers about the product, overcome skepticism of the Web-based approach, and effectively present the quality of its products. A network of past clients was then built to demonstrate credibility and generate new clients.
- **Project Management Standards**—These standards, not yet developed in the industry, were developed by the group through trial and error.

Financial Information

Intelligent Leisure Solutions was initially self-funded by Phillips until 2005, when it received investments from two individuals. It has been funded periodically by investments throughout the life of the business. The business is currently being funded by the group's operations (see Table 6).

Industry Overviews

Marketing Consulting Industry Overview

The management and marketing consultancy market in the United States had a value of $106.9 billion in 2009 (Table 7; Figure 2), with a compound annual growth rate (CAGR) of 4.4% between 2005 and 2009 (Datamonitor, 2010d). This market has experienced steady growth and is forecasted to reach $161.2 billion in 2014, an increase of 50.7% since 2009, representing a CAGR

Table 6	Intelligent Leisure Solutions' Estimated Net Operational Profit, 2005–2009 (in U.S. dollars)				
	2005	**2006**	**2007**	**2008**	**2009**
Estimated Operational Profit (net)	$120,000	$360,000	$480,000	$390,000	$640,000

SOURCE: Guthry (2010).

Table 7 U.S. Management and Marketing Consultancy Market Value, 2005–2009

Year	Dollars (in billions)	Euros (in billions)	Growth (%)
2005	90.0	64.7	—
2006	99.7	71.7	10.8
2007	108.4	78.0	8.8
2008	113.6	81.7	4.8
2009	106.9	76.9	5.9
CAGR 2005–2009			**4.4**

SOURCE: Datamonitor (2010d).

Figure 2 U.S. Management and Marketing Consultancy Market Value, 2005–2009

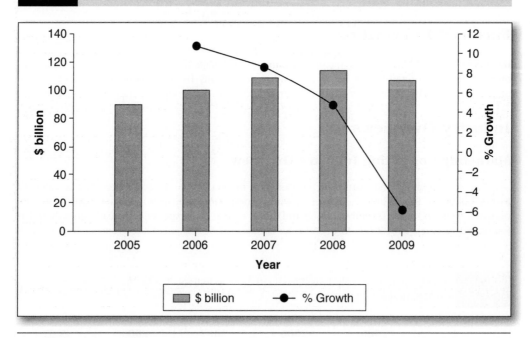

SOURCE: Datamonitor (2010d).

of 8.6% between 2009 and 2014 (Figure 3). The largest segment of the management and marketing consultancy market in the United States is corporate strategy with 27.8% of the total market, while the operations management segment accounts for 26.5% (Table 8). The United States represents 39.3% of the global market value (Datamonitor, 2010d).

Figure 3 U.S. Management and Marketing Consultancy Market Value Forecast, 2009–2014

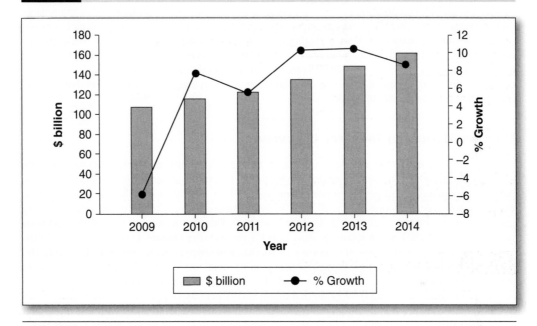

SOURCE: Datamonitor (2010d).

Table 8 U.S. Management and Marketing Consultancy Market Segmentation

Category	Share (%)
Corporate Strategy	27.8
Operations Management	26.5
Human Resources Management	10.6
Information Technology	8.8
Other	26.3
Total	**100**

SOURCE: Datamonitor (2010d).

The size of this market is the total revenues received from corporate strategy services, operations management services, information technology solutions, human resource management services, and outsourcing services. Since management and marketing consultancies provide objective external advice to improve business performance, this service involves specific professional knowledge, which can be costly.

Strong brand reputations are important in this industry, as evidenced by the success of large global organizations such as PriceWaterhouseCoopers and Deloitte. The time and experience required to build this reputation presents a strong barrier to entry in this industry. Also, many large organizations employ in-house analysts and marketing teams as a substitute for consultancy services.

The leading management and marketing consulting firms employ economies of scale and are multinational and multidisciplinary. Reputation for cost-effectiveness and an excellent track record are keys to success in this market. There is significant fragmentation within the market with smaller companies focusing on specific markets and industries and servicing particular buyers that they are more suited for (Datamonitor, 2010d).

Internet Marketing Industry Overview

The Internet marketing industry consists of the search engine marketing industry and the social media industry. The search engine marketing industry is segmented into money spent on paid search marketing and search engine optimization (SEO), as well as spending on search engine marketing technology (Econsultancy, 2010). The North American search engine marketing industry grew from $13.5 billion in 2008 to $14.6 billion in 2009. Due to the recession, market conditions were difficult and 2009 was a relatively slow year for the industry (Figure 4) (Econsultancy, 2010).

Of the four media forms—Internet/social media, newspaper, magazine, and TV—only the percentage of time spent using Internet/media is on the rise, while the percentage of time spent using the other forms is decreasing. This has led to an increase in companies shifting spending into search engine marketing from other marketing and IT activity (Figure 5) (Econsultancy, 2010). In 2009, there were 1.8 billion global Internet users, a 13% increase from 2008, with just under half (46%) from five countries: Brazil, China, India, Russia, and the United States. In the United States alone, there were 240 million users, a 4% increase from 2008, indicating a 76% penetration rate per 100 inhabitants. In Brazil, there were 76 million users, up 17% from 2008, indicating a 39% penetration rate (Meeker, Devitt, & Wu, 2010).

Figure 4   Value of North American Search Engine Marketing Industry, 2004–2010

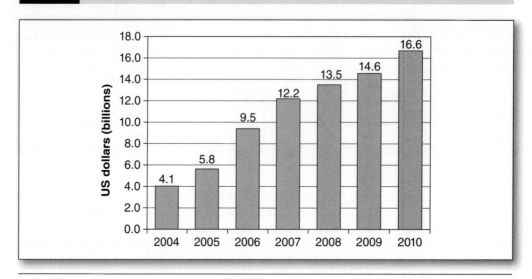

SOURCE: Econsultancy (2010).

Figure 5 Funds for Search Marketing Programs Being Shifted From Which Marketing/ IT Programs?

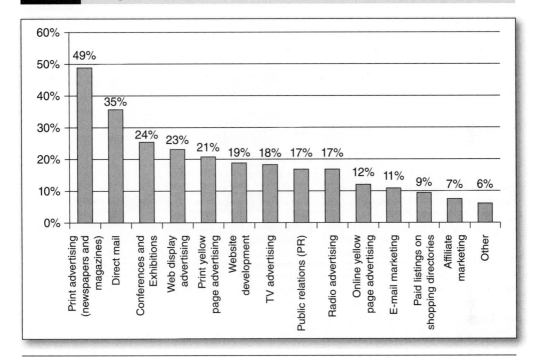

SOURCE: Econsultancy (2010).

According to a survey done by Econsultancy of 1,500 client-side advertisers and agency respondents, the number of companies using SEO has remained at 90% since 2007, while paid search marketing has increased from 78% in 2009 to 81% in 2010 (Figure 6). More than half of companies surveyed expected to spend more on paid search and SEO in 2010 than they did in 2009, anticipating an average increase in spending of 37% and 43%, respectively (Econsultancy, 2010).

One fifth of companies surveyed spent over $1 million on paid search in 2009, compared to a modest budget of less than $25,000 for social media marketing for 73% of companies (Figure 7). This includes 23% of companies reporting a budget of zero for social media marketing (Econsultancy, 2010). Yet the use of social marketing is on the rise. Fifty-nine percent of companies say their budgets for social media marketing will increase in 2010 (Econsultancy, 2010).

With 1.5 billion visits to social networks every day (Parker & Thomas, 2010), 74% and 73% of companies report using Facebook and Twitter, respectively, to promote their brand (Figure 8) (Econsultancy, 2010). Facebook is the largest social network in English-speaking countries with 620 million global visitors in 2009, while Twitter boasts 102 million users (Meeker et al., 2010).

Google's dominance as a search engine is clear. Ninety-seven percent of companies are paying to advertise on Google AdWords, and 71% are paying to advertise on Google search network, with 56% using the Google content network (Figure 9). Only 50% of respondents used Yahoo! Search in 2010, a drop from 68% in 2009 and 86% in 2008 (Econsultancy, 2010).

For many marketers, the measurement of return on investment (ROI) for paid search, social media marketing and SEO is a particular challenge. Forty-three percent of respondents report ROI

Figure 6 Type of Organizational Internet Marketing Activity

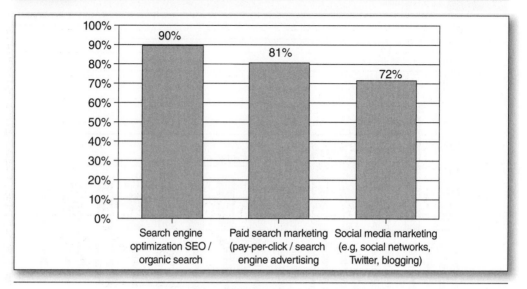

SOURCE: Econsultancy, "State of Search Engine Marketing Report 2010," in association with SEMPRO (2010).

Figure 7 Company Social Media Marketing Budgets, 2009

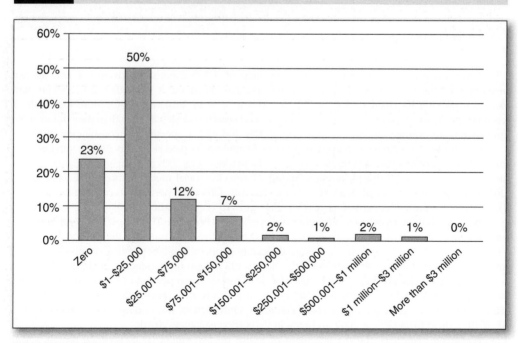

SOURCE: Econsultancy (2010).

Figure 8 Social Media Sites Used to Promote Brand/Company by Company Usage Rate, 2010

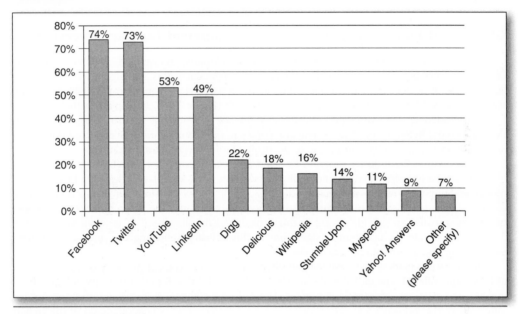

SOURCE: Econsultancy (2010).

Figure 9 Percentage of Companies Paying to Advertise on Each Search Engine

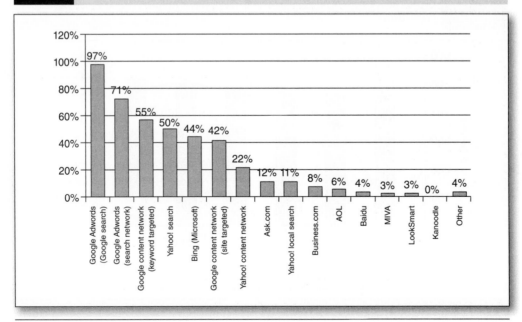

SOURCE: Econsultancy (2010).

measurement for paid search as one of their top three challenges, while 42% say the same for both social media marketing and SEO (Econsultancy, 2010).

Global Real Estate Management and Development Industry Overview

The size of the global real estate management and development industry is $461 billion, a decrease of 8% since 2009. It had a compound rate of change of –0.3% since 2005. No growth was expected in 2010, but steady growth was expected in 2011 and was forecasted to increase to $511 billion by 2014, with an expected CAGR of 2.1% for the period 2009–2014 (Figure 10) (Datamonitor, 2010c).

The residential segment of the industry accounts for 56.7% of the industry with the nonresidential segment being 43.3%. The leading companies in the industry are in Europe and the United States, accounting for 36.3% and 33.7%, respectively (Table 9) (Datamonitor, 2010c).

Buyers within the industry range in size and financial strength so large buyer power is mitigated by strong financial strength and ability to negotiate with key players, keeping buyer power moderate. Supplier power is moderate, with a large number of construction contractors offering essential key services. Substantial capital is required for entry into the market, although business or mortgage loans can provide access to this capital, and the likelihood of new entrants into the market is moderate. Competition is significant in the industry, reflecting the uncertain business environment and an unstable financial situation.

Players in the market try to differentiate themselves by the types of property or services, such as brokerage, offered. The global real estate management and development industry is highly fragmented, and name recognition is important. The top four companies in the industry account for only 3.9% of the industry's size. Of these top four companies, one is headquartered in the United States and the remaining three in Japan (Datamonitor, 2010c).

Figure 10	Global Real Estate Management and Development Industry Value Forecast, 2009–2014.

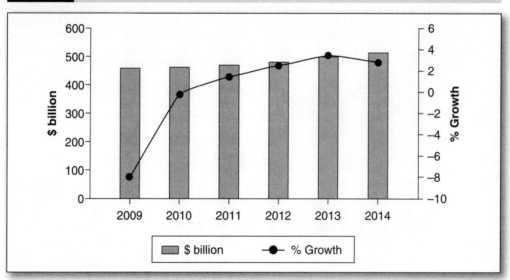

SOURCE: Datamonitor (2010c).

Table 9	Global Real Estate Management and Development Industry Segmentation, 2009

Region	Share (%)
Europe	36.3
United States	33.7
Asia-Pacific	20.9
Rest of the world	9.1
Total	**100**

SOURCE: Datamonitor (2010c).

Global IT Consulting Industry Overview

In 2009, the size of the global information technology (IT) consulting and other services market was $498.2 billion, with a CAGR of 5.1% from 2005 to 2009. The market declined by 0.6% in 2009, but is expected to increase in the years ahead. The industry is forecasted to grow to $561.5 billion by 2014 (Figure 11) (Datamonitor, 2010b).

The sales of integration and development services was the most significant segment of the industry, with revenues of $246.7 billion, a total of 49.5% of the market's value. The top markets were the Americas (51.9%) and Europe (27.8%).

The industry is highly fragmented, with large, multinational players operating with numerous small firms. Key customers are businesses and government agencies, which range in size and financial strength. Brand recognition is crucial to the industry because quality IT service is a key factor in the success of the customer's businesses. Suppliers have highly skilled employees and provide both hardware and software. Because customers are dependent on being provided dependable service from their suppliers and switching costs are high, supplier power is strong overall. While small companies can differentiate themselves by specializing in certain industries such as health care or financial services, the overall likelihood of new entrants is moderate.

The top four companies in the industry account for 13.8% of industry sales (Datamonitor, 2010b). Competition is intense as the key companies continue to grow and have focused on diversification to lessen the degree of competition.

Global Internet Software and Services Industry Overview

This industry is composed of companies developing and marketing Internet software and/or providing Internet services, including online databases and interactive services, Web address registration services, database construction, and Internet design services (Datamonitor, 2010a). The size of this industry is $893.7 billion (Figure 12), an increase of 9.1% in 2009 representing a CAGR of 14.7% (Datamonitor, 2010a). It is forecast to increase 75.4% to $1,567.7 billion by 2014 (Figure 13).

The industry is split into two segments—the broadband segment, by far the largest (74.4% of the industry's overall size), and the narrowband segment (25.6%). Asia-Pacific is the largest regional segment of the global Internet software and services industry, accounting for 41.2% of the market's volume, followed by the Americas region with 33.2% of the global industry. The industry is

Figure 11 Global IT consulting and other services market value forecast, 2009–2014.

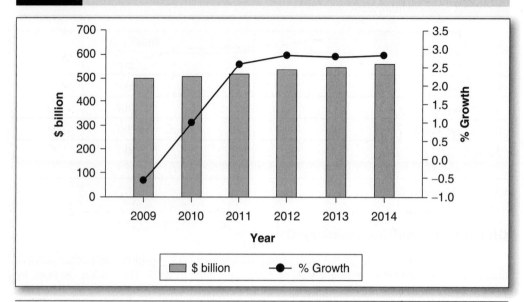

Figure 12 Global Internet software and services industry value, 2005–2009.

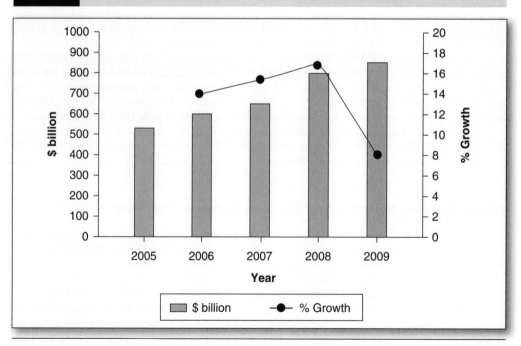

Figure 13 Global Internet software and services industry forecast, 2009–2014.

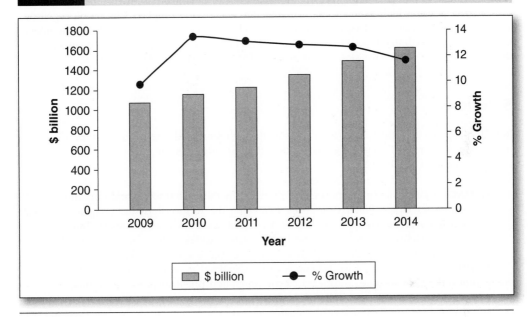

SOURCE: Datamonitor (2010a).

Table 10 Global Internet Software and Services Industry Forecast, 2009–2014

Year	Subscribers (billions)	Growth (%)
2009	1.3	11.6
2010	1.4	11.0
2011	1.6	9.7
2012	1.7	9.1
2013	1.9	8.5
2014	2.0	7.9
CAGR: 2009–2014		**9.2**

SOURCE: Datamonitor (2010a).

forecasted to increase its subscribers up to 2 billion by 2014, a 55% increase since 2009 (Table 10) (Datamonitor, 2010a).

The industry is highly fragmented with large multinational companies accounting for only 8% of the global market. Because brand recognition is so important in the industry, companies such as Google and Yahoo! have global recognition and buyers such as individual consumers tend to frequent the brand. Commercial buyers do not consider brand recognition a significant factor in purchasing. Buyer power is moderated by the large pool of potential customers.

Supplier power is high, as many companies tend to rely on sole suppliers with strong negotiating skills. Entry in the industry is dependent upon high levels of technical expertise and R&D investments. While a strong growth trend has attracted new entrants, intellectual property is a strong barrier, as are the costs to comply with regulations such as the Digital Millennium Copyright Act (Datamonitor, 2010a).

Solutions

Robert Phillips feels that the company can grow through increased operations, new projects, new investors, and increased consulting. To do this, Phillips proposes the following for each of the group's companies (Guthry, 2010).

- **ILSC**—To capitalize on opportunities provided by the 2014 Brazil World Cup and the 2016 Summer Olympics, Phillips proposes solidifying the relationships the company has with other international companies, such as Advanced Leisure Services of Spain, Target Euro of Italy, and Gehry Technology of the United States. Additionally, a new website should be created for ILSC using the company's innovative Web marketing techniques.
- **IRES**—In this group, a leader needs to be identified to step in and grow the business, finish the IRES website, and begin offering high-end Brazilian properties online.
- **IWS**—In this group, a portfolio of success stories needs to be created and a strategy implemented to achieve international recognition and awards, update the website and translate this website into multiple languages to reach new clients, and partner with value-added providers. Additionally, IWS will work to strengthen the Internet Marketing Roadshow, which was put together by IWS to help companies understand what ILS does and why it is needed.
- **ITS**—In this group, a complete revision of ITS's existing websites must be done, as well as the creation of a new website structure applying new technologies and trends that have developed since the site was launched and allowing for rapid expansion into new destination areas and markets by replication. Also, opportunities in the Brazilian tourism industry offered by the 2014 Brazil World Cup and the 2016 Summer Olympics must be capitalized on.
- **ICS**—In this group, film, documentary, and training video dubbing and subtitling needs to be developed and offered as part of its service portfolio.
- **Overall**—Phillips proposes to continue to maintain the spillover effect between the companies to capitalize on shared knowledge, be up-to-date on trends and developments in tourism and Internet technology through continuous research, maintain the group's financial sustainability, and replicate the group's success stories by applying its successful website business model and operational system to new websites. Also, many of the companies' websites, some more than 8 years old, have not been redone since their initial creation and will be updated shortly.

CASE QUESTIONS

1. How should Phillips go about solidifying the relationships Intelligent Leisure Solutions has with other international companies? How can these relationships benefit ILS?

2. How should Phillips identify a leader to grow the real estate solutions business? Because finding qualified employees for such a niche business was one of Phillips's biggest obstacles when starting the business, what are the pros and cons of hiring from within? From outside?

3. Is documentary and film dubbing too far outside Intelligent Leisure Solutions' core line of products? How could this affect the group's focus?

4. Does Intelligent Leisure Solutions need to develop a presence offline? Will its online presence be enough to capitalize on the 2014 World Cup and 2016 Summer Olympics?

5. Does Phillips demonstrate a clear vision for Intelligent Leisure Solutions? How does this impact the group's ability to grow sustainably?

6. Which of the following traits of a fast-growing firm (clear vision, retention of small company traits, market-driven behaviors, belief in customer service, shared focus, and increasing flexibility) does Intelligent Leisure Solutions exhibit that may lead it to quick growth?

7. Phillips seems to be focusing on all four growth strategies: penetration strategies (existing market, existing product), product development strategies (existing market, new product), market development strategies (new market, existing product), and diversification strategies (new market, new product). Is there one that he should focus on first?

REFERENCES

Central Intelligence Agency. (2010). *The world factbook.* Retrieved from https://www.cia.gov/library/publications/the-world-factbook/index.html

Datamonitor. (2010a). *Global Internet software & services: Industry profile.* Retrieved from http://www.marketresearch.com/Datamonitor-v72/Global-Internet-Software-Services-6445589/

Datamonitor. (2010b). *Global IT consulting & other services.* Retrieved from http://www.datamonitor.com/store/Product/global_it_consulting_other_services?productid=D3F44101-8292-4FBE-9614-1C6ED508C2CA

Datamonitor. (2010c). *Global real estate management & development.* Retrieved from http://www.companiesandmarkets.com/Market-Report/global-real-estate-management-development-market-report-624768.asp

Datamonitor. (2010d). *Management & marketing consultancy in the United States: Industry profile.* Retrieved from http://www.amazon.com/Management-Marketing-Consultancy-United-States/dp/B004FFWN4W

Economist Intelligence Unit. (2010a). *Country forecast Brazil.* Retrieved from http://www.eiu.com/index.asp?layout=displayIssue&publication_id=490003649

Economist Intelligence Unit. (2010b). *Country report Brazil.* Retrieved from http://www.eiu.com/index.asp?layout=displayIssue&publication_id=1720000972

Econsultancy. (2010). *State of search engine marketing report 2010.* Retrieved from http://econsultancy.com/us/reports/sempo-state-of-search-2010

Euromonitor International. (2010). *Consumer lifestyles in Brazil.* Retrieved from http://www.euromonitor.com/consumer-lifestyles-in-brazil/report

Guthry, D. (2010). *Thunderbird 2010 Alumni Entrepreneur of the Year nomination: Robert Phillips.* Glendale, AZ: Walker Center for Global Entrepreneurship.

Meeker, M., Devitt, S., & Wu, L. (2010, November 16). *Ten questions Internet execs should ask & answer.* San Francisco, CA: Morgan Stanley. Retrieved from http://www.morganstanley.com/institutional/techresearch/pdfs/tenquestions_web2.pdf

Parker, G., & Thomas, L. (2010). *The socialisation of brands: Wave 5.* New York, NY: Universal McCann. Retrieved from http://www.umww.com/global/knowledge/download?id=1791&hash=F1C9F17E9E5CB4A2681D744A9AD018B3413C00BFad20708460e44685b4e8a7cb5612c496&fileName=Wave%205%20-%20The%20Socialisation%20Of%20Brands.pdf

Logisys

A Small Company
With an International Potential
Problem to Analyze:
Managing Company Development

Dominika Salwa[1]

Introduction

Logisys is a small company established by young engineers from Krakow, Poland. Due to the qualifications and abilities of the founding partners, the company is thriving and making a mark in its industry. After receiving the prestigious European Auto-ID Award and the gold medal at the International Fair in Poznan, Poland, within its first year and a half of existence, the future of Logisys seems very bright. But one question remains: As the company enters the international scene, will it use its carefully gained competitive advantages to help unlock the potential that still lies within?

First, we will take a look at how the idea for the product was born, and then we will see how a plan of action was slowly, but successfully carried out.

Before the Beginning: An Idea Is Born

The Logisys founders met while working at another company, Incam. During the year and a half that they were there, the company went through a period of growth that impressed both its workers and potential customers. This initial success, however, was shadowed by internal issues, including a stormy relationship between Incam's founders that generated a multitude of problems and lowered the morale of the employees. These problems spurred some employees and shareholders to discuss purchasing Incam and creating a new company. These employees were Martin Rosiek, a shareholder who was also responsible for Incam's finances and proprietary matters; Bart Jacyna, a hired manager who helped develop and restructure Incam; and Luke Musialski, an engineer and project manager.

AUTHOR'S NOTE: The author would like to thank the entrepreneurs from Logisys, Bartosz Jacyna, and Lukasz Musialski, for their help in developing this case.

SOURCE: Used by permission from Dominika Salwa.

Jacyna, a graduate of the Academy of Economics in Krakow, suddenly left Incam to pursue a career opportunity in Germany that did not materialize. Unemployed, but reluctant to go back to Incam, Jacyna stayed in contact with his former colleagues while he searched for a career or company that he could be passionate about. Jacyna had excelled as manager at Incam, where he created a flatter organizational structure with better management and administrative practices. He had also served as a mediator for Incam's quarrelsome founders. His sudden departure made the atmosphere even more unpleasant, since there was no one else to fulfill the main managerial functions.

The idea of purchasing Incam was raised again as Jacyna and his former coworkers pondered their options during casual conversations at social gatherings. This idea was rejected, since the likelihood of all of the shareholders selling out was not guaranteed. An alternative option was needed.

One day, Musialski announced, "I've got an idea for a product." After a promising preliminary test, Jacyna, Rosiek, and Musialski began the process of establishing a new company built around the new product. The creation of Logisys gave the trio confidence that their personal dreams (ambitions) would be protected and realized. Also, they were able to attract three crucial engineers and IT (information technology) specialists from Incam to their new venture, which augured a bright future for Logisys. Rosiek began to sever his ties with Incam by selling off his shares. With the new company established and staffed, Jacyna and Musialski turned to working on product concepts and strategy.

Difficult Beginnings: New Place, New Company, New Challenges

Gentlemen, we are people who actually don't know anything about business. We know something about technology. We know already something about carrying out an information technology project. But, we know nothing about sales, zero about the market, and just a bit about running our own company. The main condition for our success is not what we know already, but how fast we learn what we don't.

This was Jacyna describing, in a circle of his new partners, the situation they were in when they established Logisys in May 2005. His sincerity and straightforwardness came from the strong relationships the partners had formed while working at Incam, as well as their knowledge of the basic business and strategic challenges that the new company faced.

The founding of Logisys provided Jacyna with the chance to find a career that he could be passionate about. Musialski, the creator of Logisys's hallmark product, had more reservations since he had not planned on leaving Incam so soon. However, he was drawn to the idea of a new company built around his product idea and with the right people leading it. Rosiek saw Logisys as a place where as a co-owner he could work at a decisive level with people he could trust. The three computer specialists hired from Incam saw their move to Logisys as a stepping-stone in the development of their careers in Poland. The market for computer specialists was flourishing, offering opportunities for high earnings and attractive work environments. Jacyna, Musialski, and Rosiek could not guarantee that the engineers would stay at Logisys for long. What Logisys could offer them, however, was creative freedom, full independence, and the necessity of using their intellects.

The company's first headquarters was a couch in Musialski's house, which was moved after a few weeks to a small flat. At first, Jacyna primarily took care of the basic administrative, legal, infrastructure, and strategic planning tasks related to establishing Logisys. He registered the company in a court and handled other regulatory issues, created the first financial plans, and hired an accounting firm. He also purchased basic office equipment (desks, phones, computers, stamps, etc.), worked on the website concept, looked for the best name for the new product, and handled design of the logo and other visual identifications for Logisys. Musialski and the rest of the team focused on the concept for the new product, which was a huge innovation in logistical processes operations. Rosiek was still working on leaving Incam.

The Conception of a New Product: Thoughts on Agilero

One of the major projects at Incam was the integration of automatic identification devices. Musialski's new product idea focused on the same area.

His solution that became pivotal to Logisys was connectivity software, or middleware, that provided a linking component for the integration of automatic identification devices. Why? Quite simply, a tool was needed to bridge the gap between the "eyes and ears" of sophisticated systems—auto-ID equipment or industry automation (automatics)—and the devices and technology that already existed in highly sophisticated systems. Automatic identification technologies (which are mainly represented by radio terminals, bar code scanners, RFID [radio frequency identification] printers and readers, automatic scales, and measurement systems) complicate the integration of projects. Not all companies are ready for this. Also, systems providers often get lost in this jumble of new devices and their applications. A market existed for a tool that could integrate all of the devices and applications with the main system in a cohesive, fluid manner. This was exactly the gap that Logisys filled, thanks to its new integration platform, Agilero (see Figure 1). The system had a different approach to solving the linkage problem than any other on the market.

From defining the idea to the actual implementation of the product took a long time. Agilero's architecture had to be thoroughly thought out to meet both present and future market requirements. In order to accurately assess the market requirements, the creators analyzed approximately 160 implementation requirements and then defined functional features of the integration platform:

Reliability—guaranteed minimal risk of system going down. The system works online, offline, or in batch mode. The batch system allows for the possibility of data transmission after putting it into the communication dock.

Integration ability—certainty that the new solution is easy to match to existing and future systems, regardless of the type or brand of the device, the medium of transmission, and the standard of communication with the main system.

Flexibility—guarantee that the system will be able to develop with increasing and changing user needs.

Efficiency—certainty that system will be a strong link in the enterprise development chain.

Security—guarantee that system and data are always in trustworthy hands. Only designated individuals can access them.

The close focus on the conception of the product was a good investment, since it allowed for the prediction of potential problems and reduced the number of corrections needed at the beginning of implementation. Agilero is an integration platform based on SOA (service-oriented architecture). It is the only all-in-one integration platform in Poland (maybe even in Europe), without any competitors using the same approach.

"We're Still Novices, But We're Heading in the Right Direction"

At the end of June, Rosiek, exhausted from the final formalities of divesting himself of his partnership at Incam, finally officially joined the Logisys team. The Logisys founder had given up trying

Figure 1 Schema of Logistic Processes Operation Before and After Applying Agilero

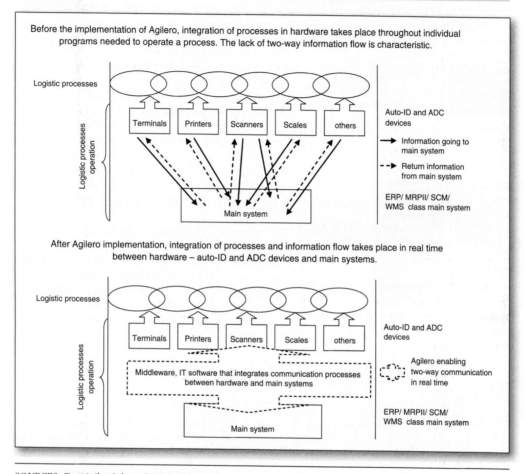

SOURCES: Dominika Salwa, Bartosz Jacyna.

to purchase Incam, since the co-owners had demanded double or triple its estimated worth. Rosiek had to take a deep breath. As Incam's founder, he was emotionally attached to the company. Shortly after joining Logisys, he went on a previously reserved 3-week holiday.

Meanwhile, the premise of the product needed verification. During the summer holiday period, the Logisys entrepreneurs spent the time arranging their first business meetings with potential partners and essentially visiting half of Poland, including Warsaw, Poznan, and Gorny Slask. On their first "tour list" were 12 companies, where they presented the Agilero product idea, collected opinions, made potential contacts, and first and foremost, learned. Each meeting was thoroughly discussed and analyzed according to Musialski's thesis that "unaware knowledge is useless." July and August proved to be a good time for these meetings, since most companies had free schedules and agreed to see them without the typical long wait for a meeting. In spite of having taken first steps into the market, the results were rather poor. At that time, however, the germs of a future partnership started coming together.

At the end of 2005, Logisys signed a partnership agreement with Softex Data, a company with RFID device competence, where different RFID applications have been tested since 2004. Softex treated RFID as its future market, as its current markets were already mature and stagnant.

Logisys made preliminary contacts with several companies, including Anixandra (the largest distributor of LXE brand handheld computers in Poland) as well as Unitech, and the Cisco net Koncept-L (supplier of Symbol, PSC, Unitech, and Psion brand devices); and Talex (integrator, SAP, and Axapty main systems, logistics, transport, and telecommunications solutions supplier). Future plans centered around dealing with companies specializing in: the implementation of ERP/MRP II class main systems, logistic consultancy, supplying IT solutions to the logistic processes operation, and suppliers of auto-ID and ADC (automatic data capture) devices.

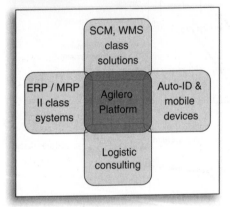

Figure 2 The Place of Logisys Products and Services in Logistic Processes

SOURCE: Logisys.

The Market: "We Create It"

To understand the criterion for choosing potential business partners, one should pay attention to the specificity of the Logisys product's location in the market of products and services connected to the management system of logistic processes (see Figure 2). An important market discovery was the identification of who most often decides to implement middleware or to use another platform of terminal management. Typically customers—final users—follow the suggestions of the system integrators and device suppliers, since the customers often do not know how necessary or useful the middleware class software application is.

The lack of customer knowledge of the role of the Agilero platform influenced the way Logisys perceived the market and took action. As Jacyna said, "We do something that the average customer doesn't understand at all. He doesn't know that what we do is very useful. We built awareness of the market, thereby creating it." Musialski added,

> This "component" [middleware] is often skipped. Everybody thinks around this "component" that somehow it'll go in, someone will cover it. . . . With the passing of time it turns out that no one covers it and no one even feels like doing it, because there's a cost. . . . And precisely in the middle there is a gap, exactly in that juncture.

Although the missing component in the integration between devices and systems—middleware—is logical, Musialski noted, "Logic isn't an argument good enough to make a thing exist [in the awareness of the customer—the final user]."

Potential Logisys partners (that means companies whose decisions make the shape and architecture of solutions for logistic processes management) are aware of the necessity of middleware, but usually in Poland they use makeshift and single solutions. These solutions enable integration, but are potentially costly in the long term.

Musialski concludes the market analysis by noting,

We do realize that the market we act in is uneducated. To survive we have to educate it! Our great mission is to teach the market what it should look like in normal life. Maybe we differ from other companies which might or might not intentionally practice the "red ocean strategy" in the Polish market. We claim that enlarging the cake (blue ocean strategy) is worth more. Customers should be convinced that they may make a profit by using such solution.

Teaching customers this way foretells Logisys's chances for the future. Companies with an awareness of the significance of quality systems and devices in the functioning of their own logistic processes will appreciate the middleware Agilero.

Outside—Making a Move, Inside—Solving Problems

In January, 2006, Logisys's product was almost ready to introduce into the market. The first order came from Rosiek in mobile technologies; it was the first sale. The Wincor Nixdorf company needed an updated version of a solution that Rosiek had previously developed. Logisys took on the task of making new versions of his previous solution. As the first order and the first sale, it was a coincidental rather than intentional move by Logisys. They were trying to obtain their first customers.

Meanwhile, attention to the company's internal matters was needed. Jacyna was responsible for management and administration. He continued to work on the website and first marketing materials. Musialski remained the product manager of Agilero, controlling the design and preparation of the first prototype by the former Incam engineers. Musialski was responsible for all the decisions connected with technology.

Despite everyone's commitment, something was wrong. Each partner felt work discomfort and growing tension. Rosiek felt left out; Jacyna and Musialski thought he had only himself to blame. Since the situation involved friendship, it was particularly delicate. The problem primarily arose from differences in the role that Logisys played in the lives of the shareholders involved in building the company.

Further complicating the situation, the partners were providing the funding to run the company in its start-up phase and these funds were running out. At the beginning of January 2006, Musialski, Jacyna, and Doris, Jacyna's wife, made a most difficult and emotional business decision: They would part with Rosiek and buy out his share of the company.

Musialski bought the full 5% of Rosiek's shares. Soon after, Jacyna decided to sell 3% of his shares to Musialski. He thought that this would better reflect Musialski's noncapital contribution when creating the company. So, at that point, Musialski owned one third of the company's shares and Jacyna and Doris owned the rest.

Rosiek's leaving was a turning point for the company. Musialski and Jacyna now fully realized their huge responsibility, but that only amplified their determination to accomplish the aims and tasks of the company.

Becoming conscious of their weakness was also a landmark. As Jacyna recollected,

We thought we were wonderful, that we had a technology, but no one wanted to listen to us. It doesn't matter how it works, but what it gives. We could talk for hours how it works, but when we needed to tell what advantage it provided, we faltered.

The company also needed funds. To address that problem, Logisys signed an investment contract with Doris without changing the structure of company's ownership. Doris raised capital from her parents to provide development with funds from an outside source for 1 year.

From a Name to a Marketing Strategy

Jacyna began to consider company and product names, considering both Mobisys and Logisys. As combinations of prefixes of the words *mobile* or *logistics* and *systems*, they both addressed directly the company's need to explain its function. Logisys was chosen as the company name. Yet, opinion was divided when it came to Agilero—the name of the product. This name comes from the word *agile*, which describes largely the benefits of the product. The ending—*ro*—was to signal the harmonious spirit of the southern European countries. In the name selection for Agilero, Logisys worked with the company Media United and directly with a patent office. There were a few guidelines for the name: unregistered, explicitly readable in a few main languages, and with a free Internet domain.

Musialski did not initially like the Agilero name much, but the time pressure and Jacyna's imploring requests to trust him took precedence. After a few months, Musialski admitted that the name was good: "It's not globally optimal, but at least local." In spite of the irritating confusion between the product name and the singer Christina Aguilera, the memorable name became a definite plus.

Jacyna and Musialski also arranged the company's brand. Media United came up with the gray and orange Logisys logo. Quite by accident, the Agilero logo emerged from the Logisys logo. While working on the Logisys logo, a Media United employee cropped it down to the *og* part of the name. The effect was sensational. The fragment was immediately adopted as Agilero's logo (see Figure 3). "We were at once united in that issue," recollected one outside partner.

Figure 3	The LOGOS of Logisys and Agilero

SOURCE: Logisys.

During the development stage, the partners had decided that the Agilero platform should not be dependent on Logisys to exist. Therefore, uniting the company and product by the logos and not the names was an intentional move. They wanted to keep the company and product brands separate.

The founders also decided not to use traditional titles for the various positions in the company. Using manager or president of the board seemed very exaggerated and a bit pompous considering the company's size and the age of those involved. Instead, the founders decided to use the name "partner" for the various employees. As a marketing strategy, this title implies that the "partner" has the ability to make decisions and has greater management and knowledge of the supplied services. Jacyna led the process of naming the positions by copying consulting companies.

The company finally decided to hire LAP Development, a consulting company, to design the marketing strategy. This inspired Logisys's employees, as the company evolved from an unfocused and unimaginative position to having well-organized, self-contained information making Logisys more understandable to potential partners and customers. New, good-looking promotional brochures that illustrated Logisys's work were developed in Polish, English, and German.

In late 2005, almost a year after Logisys began to cooperate with LAP Development, another critical problem came to light. The company's tagline, "Mobile solutions for demanding people," was wrong. Many potential customers were misinterpreting its meaning. This misunderstanding should have been resolved much earlier, when LAP Development first suggested that the motto be changed from "Mobile solutions for demanding people" to "Mobile solutions for logistics."

Developing the Company's Operational Capacity

A thorough marketing strategy required both discipline and time. New development opportunities began to appear on the market in 2006, and Jacyna needed to give some tasks away to focus on business development. Therefore, Logisys decided to add an office manager who would manage the office, its administration, and the company.

The company used Searchlight, a personnel consultancy company, to recruit its employees. Jacyna approached the employee selection process very carefully, because each new employee became a crucial company asset. Jacyna also thought that as the firm developed, each employee should specialize in some particular company function.

Searchlight offered five candidates. From the interviews, Jacyna narrowed the choice to two people. At first, Agnes seemed to be a good choice, but Jacyna believed her specific style of work organization would not be accepted at Logisys. Despite the stress of competition, the other candidate, Dominic, remained calm and reasonable, which influenced Logisys's decision to hire her.

At about the same time, Logisys landed a new business partner for the venture. The Hogart Company, noticing customer interest in the Agilero platform, decided to sign a partnership contract with Logisys. Hogart valued the concept of Agilero: "On the one hand it corresponds best to logistic processes requirements. On the other hand it has open architecture that increases the field of application and integration," commented one Hogart manager. Hogart is a leader in the implementation of Oracle systems in Poland and a recognized IT consultant in the implementation of management operating systems and the service of integration applications. In 2006, Hogart was named best provider of ERP (enterprise resource planning) systems for industry.

Another opportunity appeared on the horizon—participation in the Euro-ID Messe, or fair, in Köln, Germany. Logisys decided to take part in the messe.

A Prize Brings New Opportunities

Surfing the Internet, Jacyna happened on the Euro-ID Messe, organized in Germany, and he sent in an application. He purchased a special software kit called Demopoint, which was tailored to small, start-up companies, so that the team could prepare a demo of the Agilero platform. In addition, Jacyna applied for the prize awarded at the fair.

Jacyna's effort was rewarded with a great surprise. Musialski and Jacyna received a message that they had won the Euro-ID Award 2006, in the bar code category (it was emphasized that the Agilero solution also integrates devices based on RFID technology). What a joy, what a success, what a chance for the only Polish company attending the fair! This award provided the way for Logisys to become known abroad.

One of the first results of the new recognition was a partnership offer from the RFID Konsortium. The RFID Konsortium consisted of about 10 small German companies that came together to provide a joint solution for the implementation of RFID tagging in supply chains of German retail giants, METRO and REWE. The companies modernized the tagging of goods by changing the bar code to a radio tag, which became the new standard. Until then, tagging was mainly on a level of palettes. RFID implementation enables tracking at the level of the carton on the palette. The change to RFID tagging transfers the responsibility of logistic processes to the supplier. This new situation means that suppliers track batches of their goods and care for the stock of customers. RFID tagging enables carrying out this strategy.

The creator of RFID Konsortium had started out providing consulting services for fresh food producers (fruits, vegetables, meat, salads, flowers, etc.). He noticed that these mainly small and medium-sized companies were not ready for such new tracking technology. About 3,000 out of 10,000 of METRO's and REWE's suppliers are fresh food suppliers (so-called *Frischbereich*) and only 300 of them are big companies that understand RFID tagging and can afford to implement the required changes.

RFID Konsortium was created as a way for these small and medium-sized enterprises to be able to use the RFID technology. It gathers companies (see Table 1) that each have a certain slice of knowledge of the market in IT and RFID. Thus, the Konsortium provides very comprehensive service for companies that deal with the *Frischbereich* business.

Offering the middleware Agilero, Logisys holds an important position in the consortium. First, as the producer of Agilero, it influences the entirety of the offered product. It lets consortium

Table 1 Companies Belonging to RFID Konsortium and Their Fields of Specialization

Company	Description
Schmitt	EDI solutions based on EDI EUREXc products
BWT	Weigh systems
Sato	Printers, bar code labels, and RFID producer
Michael Letterer	Consultancy in the area of technical processes, map project management
DeMann	Logistic automatics, RFID device assembly
PS4B	Programming company
Sys-Pro	ERP supplier for food trade
UBCS	Consultancy in processes, changes management, and business cooperation
VDEB	Small and average-sized consultancy and IT companies' union in Germany
Logisys	Middleware to the integration between devices and superior systems

SOURCE: RFID Konsortium (www.rfid-konsortium.de).

members omit license granting by a third party. Second, Agilero integrates devices independently of the type, brand, or role in the whole process. When it comes to *Frischbereich* suppliers' diverse logistic processes, it does not increase costs.

Together member companies of the RFID Konsortium can serve a large number of customers. Separately, each company could only serve just a small portion of the market.

Important Staff Rotations

Despite the success at Euro-ID Messe fair, two crucial engineering employees gave notice. The job market in Poland in the IT trade had become an employee's market with numerous opportunities for finding interesting, well-paying jobs. Logisys was still in the initial development stage and could not afford those financial demands.

After a short period of crisis, the partners reached the conclusion that the situation was not as bad as they had supposed. One of the former Incam engineers stayed with the company and Agilero was by and large ready. This engineer, named Tom, was aware of the opportunities that Logisys held for him and the job suited him very well. In spite of his young age, he was a mature worker. Tom also got a raise—more than he had expected. In return, he signed a contract for a 6-month period, which protected the interests of the company. Tom took over responsibility for research and development, especially for Agilero.

Meanwhile, more potential partners and customers started to implement Logisys's solutions. Wix Filtron company, a customer of Hogart, decided to implement Agilero, which was very important and time-consuming.

The next customer was Merlin.pl, the biggest online bookstore in Poland. With Logisys's service, the company became twice as efficient in packing and sending its products without increasing costs. This was a huge success and another good reference for Logisys.

A can-packaging company (a leading producer of aluminum drink containers in Central Europe) and Dako (a wrapping-paper print house) were next to use Logisys's product to increase the efficiency of their processes. The Agilero platform was also implemented in a laboratory of the High School of Logistics at the Logistics and Storing Institute (the largest institution of logistic education in Poland).

At this point, the company needed to turn its attention to the organization of many areas of management and structuring information in- and outflow.

Introducing a New Organizational Order

The organizational structure of all small enterprises develops very dynamically. One person handles many different tasks and positions. Then as the company continues to develop and grow, it must sort out and name these different positions and the duties connected with them.

In the case of Logisys, there were three partners, but only two of them functioned as managers, determining what was going on in the company. They shared tasks according to their abilities and competencies. Since Musialski was the designer of Agilero and developed the product concept with the former Incam engineers, he naturally became the project manager, consultant, and seller.

Initially, Jacyna took care of office administration and business development and added marketing a year later. Hiring Dominic to take over the time-consuming business support functions and general office administration freed Jacyna to focus on project development.

With the departure of the two computer specialists Logisys had to find new employees. Luckily, two more former Incam workers, Peter and Luke, joined the team. Additionally, two more trainees,

Jack and William, were employed to handle extra work. The whole IT team focused on improving Agilero and completing other projects ordered by customers.

During the second half of 2006, the rest of the positions at Logisys crystallized. Tom, who had been part of Agilero's design team from the beginning, became a project manager and Agilero's product manager. Peter was placed in customer service and support. Luke and Tom in cooperation with Peter ran the entire research and development department.

By the end of 2006, Logisys urgently needed to complete numerous marketing tasks. So, the company hired Ann, a student, for a marketing internship, during which she slowly took on many of Jacyna's marketing tasks.

A breakdown of employee roles in each department is presented in Table 2. Arranging the organizational structure required the placement of each person within the correct section and with the proper tasks. Moreover, an internal document, "My Logisys," was created for each worker. This document served as an operations manual for each employee, explaining the company's identity, vision and mission, goals, strategies, and the values it represents. The document also brought the structure of the organization and career development paths closer. The final section, "Help," contains everything from a dictionary of useful Logisys terms, and advice for getting along with irritating coworkers, to answers to simple but vital questions like "Who will clean up my desk?" and "Where is the coffee?"

Table 2 Departments, Their Functions, and Individual Positions in Logisys

Department	Function	Personnel Positions
Research and Development	• Agilero's development • Device testing • Device certification	manager, analyst, designer, device tester, developer, documenter, instructor, application tester, servicer
Service and Support	• Coordination of contact (applications) with the customer in service and diagnostic issues • Commission and collection of service activities realization • The completion of service proceedings according to service contracts	manager, diagnostic tester, supporter, customer service, coordinator
Development	• Technical support of Agilero's implementation • The completion of service repairs	manager, system analyst, designer, tester, developer, documenter, instructor, implementer, servicer
Consulting	• Developing substantive competencies of Logisys • Sales/providing customers with knowledge and analytics • Generating advisory IT projects through sales support	manager, consultant, analyst, sales support, knowledge manager

Department	Function	Personnel Positions
Marketing	• Developing and making the knowledge about the market available • Managing partner relationships • Coordinating the production of advertising tools and coordinating promotional activities	manager, marketing analyst (information manager, researcher), PR specialist and manager, event-, creative-, site-manager and specialist, graphic designer, copywriter
Sales	• Coordinating sales and trade activities (especially during the early contact stage with a customer) • Global management of relations with customer • Sales plans accomplishment	manager, sales specialist, partner relations specialist
Project Management	• Range, time allocation, risk and project budget management • Project realization management and coordination • Generating additional orders and projects for current customers	manager, sales support, project preparation, project accomplishment, customer service (at designing and after implementation)
Administration (Business Support)	• Providing Logisys employees with a good work environment • Managing the company's legal and financial safety • Providing reserves and competence of the company	marketing manager, business developer, finance manager, area manager

SOURCE: Logisys.

The Identity of Logisys and Crucial Issues

After discussing it with their lawyer, the Logisys partners chose to become a limited liability company, which is typical for small enterprises. This type of legal incorporation status gave the company more flexibility to revise its status and organization in the future.

Specific traits of the founders were directly translated into Logisys's identity, culture, and style of task completion. Jacyna—determined, with great business sense, unassuming, attentive observer— is up-to-date on matters that concern him. As he admits, he likes attaining the few visions that he has on his scorecard. He judges his own abilities as low, however, seeing a serious gap between what he knows and what he thinks he should know. While a lack of knowledge sometimes translates into avoiding tasks, Jacyna instead is adept at involving and encouraging other people to find the right person to take on those tasks. He knows how important knowledge is for organizing and he works to acquire it at the right time. He values coworkers. He says when something appeals to him, but he can also bluntly say when something is wrong. He treats many things seriously. He keeps a short distance between himself and business matters.

Musialski, always smiling, has a more distant relationship with business matters. As a great theorist, he can win over the person he is talking to, even if he does not have it right. He has a typical scientific mind, demanding that everything be presented to him "in black and white," including the justification. Otherwise, he will not believe. For example, with the name Agilero, Musialski did not want to believe the mind-boggling marketing truths that Jacyna explained to him. Although he usually gets to the bottom of the matter, he became resigned to the name and let it go through without fully believing. Now he appreciates this part of marketing, saying, "Most people take decisions, let's say, irrationally. They don't have any objective reasons that would let them take this one, not the other decision. All these reasons are subjective." He calls marketing building these subjective reasons. Musialski can accumulate and process information in amazing ways. He sees details that Jacyna arranges generally, fulfilling his role as a partner.

Together, the two managing partners seem to have achieved a synergy that neither of them could on their own. They both like doing things properly, which is reflected in the company. This probably explains why Logisys won not only the European Auto-ID Award 2006, but also the gold medal at the International Fair in Poland in August 2006. These awards and a growing reputation for quality, helped to create and sustain perceptions of Logisys as a solid partner in the market.

Once again, it is the managing partners' features that underlie the value of the company. Logisys is characterized by professionalism, quality, knowledge, communication, continuous improvement, independence, responsibility, focus on outcomes, and care for the good name of the company. The partners aspire to having the company be recognized as a substantive leader. They do not consider reducing price at the cost of quality at all. In the long-term perspective, they can achieve satisfying success only by maintaining high product quality and service at an appropriate price. "Logisys competes through quality and range," repeat the partners.

The partners began to create Logisys's image through substantive, informative articles in the trade press. This marketing effort made them recognizable as specialists in their field.

In spite of the high quality of management for such a small enterprise, the company still contends with problems characteristic of small enterprises at this developmental stage. The market is not precisely described, well identified, or characterized. The company's reserves "are developing," but they are not ready for many large implementation projects. Since the company lacks trade experience, it needs a good sales specialist who can develop contacts. Everything is a process. Nothing can be fulfilled immediately and that is why proper planning and care of the company's development are so important.

Finances

Logisys is a typical "start-up" company, established with a plan to specialize in one area: advisory IT services. As with every small company, it had to invest money first, and only after a time expect a return on the invested capital.

Money to run the business came from three sources: the contribution of the co-owners, extra money from shareholders, and the investment contract signed with Doris. The company's first revenues from sales in 2005 and 2006 did not cover the operational costs (see Table 3). The company planned to reach a cost-revenue balance by the first half of 2007.

Plans for the Future

Logisys developed in a way characteristic of small enterprises. Based on intellectual capital, without a clearly defined market, people wanted to make the idea a reality. Logisys has a chance to join the

Table 3 Logisys's Balance Sheet in 2005

Assets

+/−	Pos.	Position name			Year's beginning 2005-01-01	Year's ending 2005-12-31/ Year's beginning 2006-01-01	Year's ending 2006-12-31
−	A	Fixed assets			0,00	5,419,68	17,855,74
	−	I	Intangible assets		0,00	0,00	0,00
			1	Costs of finished development works	0,00	0,00	0,00
			2	Company's value	0,00	0,00	0,00
			3	Other intangible assets	0,00	0,00	0,00
	−	II	Tangible fixed assets		0,00	3,319,68	15,755,74
		−	1	Property, plant and equipment	0,00	3,319,68	15,755,74
			2	Engaged fixed assets	0,00	0,00	0,00
			3	Down payments for fixed assets	0,00	0,00	0,00
	−	III	Long-term debtors		0,00	0,00	0,00
			1	From subsidiary and associated companies	0,00	0,00	0,00
			2	From other companies	0,00	0,00	0,00
	−	IV	Long-term investments		0,00	2,100,00	2,100,00
			1	Properties	0,00	0,00	0,00
			2	Intangible assets	0,00	2,100,00	2,100,00
		−	3	Long-term financial assets	0,00	0,00	0,00
			4	Other long-term investments	0,00	0,00	0,00
	-	V	Long-term deferred expenses		0,00	0,00	0,00
			1	Deferred income tax	0,00	0,00	0,00
			2	Other deferred expenses	0,00	0,00	0,00
−	B	Current assets			50,000,00	53,632,77	164,664,57
	−	I	Stocks		0,00	0,00	0,00

(Continued)

Table 3 (Continued)

+/-	Pos.		Position name		Year's beginning 2005-01-01	Year's ending 2005-12-31/ Year's beginning 2006-01-01	Year's ending 2006-12-31
		1	Materials		0,00	0,00	0,00
		2	Half-finished and under way products		0,00	0,00	0,00
		3	Ready products		0,00	0,00	0,00
		4	Goods		0,00	0,00	0,00
		5	Advance payment for supply		0,00	0,00	0,00
−	II		Current receivables		0,00	12,515,20	151,162,15
−		1	From subsidiary and associated companies		0,00	0,00	0,00
−		2	From other companies		0,00	12,515,20	151,162,15
−	III		Short-term investments		50,000,00	40,699,08	12,270,29
−		1	Short-term financial assets		50,000,00	40,699,08	12,270,29
		2	Other short-term investments		0,00	0,00	0,00
	IV		Short-term deferred expenses		0,00	418,49	1,232,13
			TOTAL ASSETS		50,000,00	59,052,45	182,520,31

Liabilities

+/-	Pos.		Position name	Year's beginning 2005-01-01	Year's ending 2005-12-31/ Year's beginning 2006-01-01	Year's ending 2006-12-31
−	A		Shareholders' equity	50,000,00	50,295,10	−249,037,59
		I	Share capital	0,00	50,000,00	50,000,00
		II	Due payments on share capital (negative quantity)	0,00	0,00	0,00
		III	Own shares (negative quantity)	0,00	0,00	0,00
		IV	Reserve capital	0,00	150,000,00	150,000,00

+/−	Pos.	Position name		Year's beginning 2005-01-01	Year's ending 2005-12-31/ Year's beginning 2006-01-01	Year's ending 2006-12-31
		V	Revaluation capital	0,00	0,00	0,00
		VI	Other reserve capitals	0,00	0,00	0,00
		VII	Prior years' profit (loss)	0,00	0,00	−149,704,90
		VIII	Net profit (loss)	0,00	−149,704,90	−299,332,69
		IX	The deduction from net profit in working year (negative quantity)	0,00	0,00	0,00
−	B	Liabilities and reserves for liabilities		0,00	8,757,35	431,557,90
	−	I	Reserves for liabilities	0,00	0,00	0,00
			1 Reserve for deferred income tax	0,00	0,00	0,00
			2 Provisions for pension and similar benefits	0,00	0,00	0,00
			3 Other provisions	0,00	0,00	0,00
	−	II	Long-term liabilities	0,00	0,00	384,546,40
	−	1	To subsidiary and associated companies	0,00	0,00	384,546,40
	−	2	To other companies	0,00	0,00	0,00
	−	III	Current liabilities	0,00	8,757,35	47,011,50
	−	1	To subsidiary and associated companies	0,00	0,00	0,00
	−	2	To other companies	0,00	8,757,35	47,011,50
		3	Special funds	0,00	0,00	0,00
	−	IV	Accrued expenses and deferred income	0,00	0,00	0,00
			1 Negative company's value	0,00	0,00	0,00
	−	2	Other accrued expenses and deferred income	0,00	0,00	0,00
		TOTAL SHAREHOLDERS' EQUITY AND LIABILITIES		50,000,00	59,052,45	182,520,31

SOURCE: Logisys.

circle of typical pioneering enterprises that make it. These successful enterprises stand out from others because their founders clearly described a vision of the company's development. Logisys seems to prove this general rule.

Further company development will depend on the ability to learn quickly, as Jacyna often emphasizes, as well as on the ability to predict and acquire needed human, financial, and material resources. Human resources seem to be especially crucial for well-balanced company development in the long run. The managing partners often emphasize human resources, because each worker that comes to the company has a chance to be promoted. Promotion stages include the following levels: junior, specialist, self-reliant, operational-tactical management, and strategic management. Not every employee, however, goes through every stage. The company might employ an experienced specialist in a specific field. Then, he or she may move from the specialist level to project manager. Such plans might apply, for instance, to workers sought after to develop the sales department. Plans for human resources include employing an intern in the development department, a person to coordinate the RFID Konsortium project in Berlin, and a production manager.

Logisys has a clearly charted strategy for activities and strategic plans for the next few years. The company is going to implement standards for the completion of projects and design documents and evaluations of projects and production range. Contracts will be implemented on the projects to allow the company to reach income-costs balance.

Activities connected to marketing will include achieving the status of an expert in integration of mobile devices and auto-ID in Poland. Publications in the press and marketing through partners and equipment suppliers will be useful to achieve this aim. Pricing policies will be revised.

In the finance field, priority will be given to the full balance of current income and costs.

Organizational change is needed in the structure of the company to improve employees' efficiency. The ultimate effect will be increased salaries for the employees.

Logisys has a chance for international sales, especially through the Agilero platform

Participation in the RFID Konsortium is the mainspring of Logisys's international development, allowing for quicker entry into the German market. Austria should easily be the next market, since it has a similar mentality and organizational style as Germany. The first prize at the Euro-ID Messe 2006 and the gold medal at the International Fair in Poland are confirmation of Logisys's and the Agilero platform's quality. The company left the Polish market's borders and is recognized by other nations. Information of Swedes' interest in suggested solutions have come to the company. The British market also shows potential opportunities. There may be many digressions in the development of potential foreign markets, since 2007 was concentrated on Poland and the RFID Konsortium.

If growth and development of the company maintain their current rate as planned, 2008 may be a landmark year in terms of achievement, company size, supplied markets, partnerships, and so on. The year 2008 could also see a change in the company's business model. Assuming that Agilero evolves into a separate, easy-to-sell product, the company will face the decision concerning implementation of two business models—Agilero (a product) and Logisys (a consultancy)—as separate entities.

Glossary of Terms

ADC (automatic data capture) is a key to success in a range of enterprises' information strategies. Accurate, reliable data download allows the optimization of company processes. The growing importance of ADC is visible in every trade, especially in logistics and transport.

Automatic identification is a technology that identifies the units of a logistic process. Bar code and radio tag technology are most often used in automatic identification. Image recognition technology also exists, but is less popular and used in very specific conditions. Auto-ID devices identify logistic units, such as bar code readers (also called scanners), mobile terminals, and bar code printers.

EDI (electronic data interchange) is a set of standards for streamlining electronic information interchange outside and inside the enterprise.

Main systems of enterprises are IT systems used to streamline enterprise management. These systems enable optimization of resources. These include:

- **ERP** (enterprise resource planning)
- **MRP II** (manufacturing resource planning)
- **SCM** (supply chain management)

Among types of main systems found are SAP, Axapta, JDEdwards, Navision, and others.

RFID (radio frequency identification) is identification technology that uses properly modulated radio waves to carry the data. RFID tagging technology introduces a new quality of optimization of logistic processes. An RFID tagging label contains a chip with an antenna that enables data gathering and transmission by radio. Appropriate logistic information is not placed on documents (it is natural that they are unreliable) but on logical units themselves, thanks to RFID labels.

CASE QUESTIONS

1. Try to identify Logisys's development stage. Justify your opinion in detail. Compare your answer with company development stages according to L. Greiner. What are the similarities and differences?

2. Create vision and strategic goals for Logisys.

3. Present an analysis of strong and weak features of Logisys and chances and threats that the environment makes.

4. Plan the recruitment process for a position of office manager in Logisys. Consider three stages of recruitment procedure.

5. What activities are hidden in the role of "project preparation" for a project manager?

6. Show changes in the organizational chart considering the number of workers and their positions. Try to create an organizational chart of Logisys considering co-owners' plans that concern the company's development in the first half of 2007.

7. Perform elements of implementation of the marketing function and its importance for Logisys.

8. Where might have the personal problems between three partners originated?

9. What was the key to the selection of business partners? Why did the Hogart Company decide on a partnership contract with Logisys?

10. Assess the financial standing of Logisys in 2006.

11. Try to show on a graph how the financial situation of the company would look in relation to its development phase (use the schema of the phases of life cycle).

12. Concept questions: Try to perform further development of Logisys and Agilero, taking into account opportunities and threats that national and international markets pose.

NOTE

1. Dominika Salwa is an assistant professor in the Department of International Management at Krakow University of Economics, Krakow, Poland.

Infobip

Violeta Šugar, Roberta Kontošić

Introduction

Infobip is a global provider of mobile solutions, connecting mobile network operators and enterprises by an in-house developed and operated mobile services cloud. The company started through the enthusiasm of a young engineer, Silvio Kutić. From only a few people who worked tirelessly on the realization of the idea to 600 employees today to meet the needs of 140,000 clients worldwide—including WhatsApp, Twitter, and Uber—Silvio Kutić led with perseverance, courage, and faith in his idea. Doing what he really liked was truly motivating.

History

Silvio Kutić, founder and CEO of the Croatian information technology (IT) giant, at the end of his study at the Faculty of Electrical Engineering and Computer Science in Zagreb, found himself contemplating his future as well as the purpose of his life. It was in the summer of 2001 when he found the inspiration and strength he needed in the books of Joseph Murphy; these helped him to recall his neglected passion—IT. Solving real problems with IT was something that always fascinated Silvio Kutić.

It did not take long for one of his bigger assignments to occur. At the end of 2001, Silvio designed a project—Virtual Municipality—for his hometown, Vodnjan. The idea was to make a software solution for communication between the town officials and the residents of Vodnjan. The platform needed to facilitate the communication channels within the community as well as serve as a promotion of the local products and events. The online Content Management System (CMS)[1] allowed the local companies, associations, and small and medium-sized enterprises (SMEs) to create virtual work areas and to send all information through the web. It was a kind of social network. In the summer of 2002, after the implementation of the project that joined together modern technology (such as the Internet and mobile phones), allowing fast, efficient, and prompt exchange of information, Silvio Kutić and his associates recognized short message services (SMS) as the most accepted method of communication. They had recognized the problem of combining a large and complicated system that included Internet, CMS, mail groups, and SMS and came up with the solution, a new project called mojnet.hr, made of CMS and SMS. Even though the project failed, Silvio and his companions were not discouraged.

In May 2003, the company launched a new web application and named it Infobip. With no business management experience, they struggled to find the right market niche. They were looking for clients in bars, restaurants, discotheques, shops, and educational institutions. One of their first big clients was the *Big Brother* television show, followed by the biggest Croatian supermarket chain, Konzum. But this was far from enough clients for the survival of this small firm from Vodnjan. The team broke up. Only Silvio Kutić and Izabel Jelenić stayed, determined to succeed.

Although the situation was hard, the two were happy doing what they loved and this was the inspiration for moving forward. At one point, they realized that it was impossible for them to do the programming and run a business at the same time. Hence, Silvio and Izabel decided to give their business one last chance. While looking for information about various companies, Silvio determined that instead of looking for a direct contact with each company, they could position their services as a system, an aggregator between other applications and operators. That was the innovation! They connected with operators in South Africa, then with those from Russia, and started to sell their services in Europe. Finally, the company started earning a profit. What they previously earned in a month become their daily income. In April 2006, Silvio and Izabel founded Infobip LLC and started operating throughout Europe.

Silvio's brother Roberto Kutić joined Infobip full time in 2009, although he was a member of the team from the beginning. He contributed his valuable experience from a big company, the Uljanik Shipyard in Pula, where he previously worked. Infobip was ready for expansion. A new office in the Croatian capital, Zagreb, was opened and Silvio started a promotional campaign worldwide. He visited more than 60 countries. In 2006, Infobip founded offices in Moscow and Munich and grew rapidly. Infobip had 10 employees in 2006, 30 in 2007, and more than 600 in 2014.

It is interesting that Infobip grew so large after being started in the entrepreneurial incubator "Izazov"[2] in Pula, where start-up entrepreneurs can use subsidized facilities, such as business office space, technical support, mentoring, and training courses.

Infobip in 2014

Today, Infobip has more than 600 employees (see Figure 1) and 140,000 clients, including Twitter, WhatsApp, and Uber. Since 2012, they have worked with big banks, and their growth rate is 80% on a global basis. The company reinvests all their profits, and of course, there is no crisis now. During the first five months of 2014, over five billion people used their services. They implemented the infrastructure in 100 telecoms worldwide. The major markets, listed in order of importance in terms of market volume, are Asia, the former U.S.S.R., Latin America, Africa, Europe, and the United States.

Today, Infobip is an international company managed from several locations: London, Vancouver, Curitiba, Moscow, Istanbul, and Kuala Lumpur (see Figure 2). Global offices mostly employ local people; people from Croatia are essential in the early stages—getting the office set up as well as legal and financial matters settled—so that the business unit can start operating. In time, local people are hired and they constitute the majority of the workforce. This is the case not only in Turkey and South Africa but also in Latin America, Malaysia, India, Canada, Nigeria, the United States, and so on.

While the organization of any big international company is complex, Infobip has a well-developed structure. Product and development managers are organized in Scrum teams of 8–10 members, enabling effective team collaboration on complex projects.

Infobip has several annual brainstorming meetings of all team leaders and Dev Days (meetings of all developers regarding different themes as well as some smaller meetings of developers regarding a specific theme). Infobip's organizational culture is also familiar with team building and "fun days," where all teams play all day with some new stuff that could potentially be mainstream in the future.

The Infobip Academy

In Infobip, there is a strong belief that companies are people; the company invests in their future employees through education and has founded the Infobip Academy in Vodnjan, Croatia. The Academy is a combination of training and selection process. The Academy is not only a selection

| Figure 1 | The Growth of Employees in Infobip over the Years |

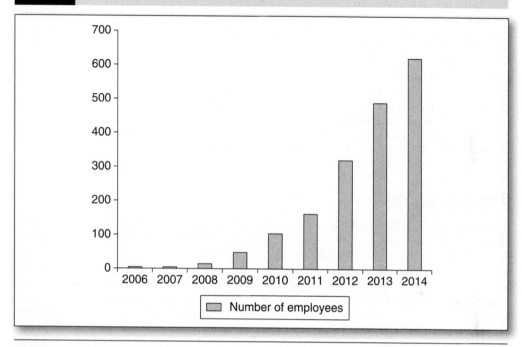

SOURCE: Figure courtesy of Infobip.

| Figure 2 | Infobip Offices Worldwide |

SOURCE: Figure courtesy of Infobip.

media but also a tool that enables both learning and introducing potential employees to their new responsibilities. Launching a new venture in an environment lacking IT experts forces Infobip to train and create their own professional workforce. The Infobip doors are open to everyone. The most important feature of potential employees, according to Silvio Kutić, is their attitude, since all the skills needed can be learned.

The Infobip International Academy offers different programs suitable for an international environment and a specific market niche. The official language, both in the Academy and organization, is English. Until now, about 400 candidates have studied at the Academy; 270 of them have been employed. Infobip is constantly looking for new employees and does head-hunting within student organizations. Infobip employees have both the opportunity and responsibility to improve their skills; they are encouraged to attend various professional conferences, where they can learn and network.

The Infobip Business Model

The Infobip market position is between the mobile operators and the enterprise sector. Enterprises on the one side of this two-sided business model get a reliable and simple approach to mobile services, usually professional SMS notifications or mobile payments. Integration is done in a very short period of time and without capital investment. Partner enterprises have the possibility to connect with almost every global operator through one access point or via specialized applications. For large companies, Infobip experts have developed more complex enterprise stand-alone solutions, including mGate. This is something developed beside the application in the cloud. With Infobip's services also comes a 24-hour technical support in 10 languages that quickly receives and responds to inquiries. Support is closely linked to development, making the strengths of Infobip its platform and support.

Mobile operators are on the other side of the business model and they, in collaboration with Infobip, have the possibility to monetize their resources. Operators are the key component in Infobip's niche. Numerous Infobip solutions are related to mobile operators; there are 300 signed contracts with operators worldwide. Innovativeness in Infobip is not only connected with technical solutions but also with new business models.

Today, in a globalized dynamic world where everything changes quickly, Infobip is constantly improving their business model and creating new solutions in order to meet the market needs. This is extremely important because mobile operators are looking for new ways to monetize their investments. Thanks to long-term work with mobile operators' technology, Infobip has gained experience that allows the company to develop specialized solutions for mobile operators such as the sGate system for filtering (variation of firewall in IP protocol), the cGate solution for direct payment among mobile operator systems, or USSD gateway.

Infobip's strength lies in the ability to bring value to all the stakeholders in the value chain. As they develop their own solutions for operators, Infobip has a unique benefit of implementing these solutions at the operator's premises free of charge. In this way, Infobip is bringing turnover to operators that enter into revenue sharing with them.

At the moment, Infobip is managing their business from 30 offices, with the biggest ones in Pula, Zagreb, Kuala Lumpur, Moscow, Buenos Aires, and Johannesburg. Monitoring systems are fully automated, architecture is distributed through six georedundant data centers, and more than 250 services are supported in production. Infobip needs to ensure load balancing, a high availability of systems, and high volume traffic because SMS are time sensitive and clients ask for real-time delivery. Furthermore, Infobip currently has various quality certificates, such as PCI DSS, ISO 9001, and ISO 27001, which vouch for their reliability, innovativeness, security, and flexibility.

Infobip Services

Infobip's mobile technology in the cloud is a complex global system, developed and constantly maintained. It is a mix of the Internet and telecommunication technologies, from SS7 protocol to the most challenging IP architecture. The whole system is built in-house and enables Infobip to deliver messages to more than a billion different mobile phone numbers.

By connecting to the Infobip mobile services cloud, any enterprise, financial institution, developer, retailer, and marketer can easily reach its customers, no matter where they are from or which mobile network they use. Infobip's convergent offering of SMS messaging, mobile payments, and push notifications helps reach, engage, and monetize clients' mobile users (see Figure 3).

Today, the Infobip cloud is connected with 300 mobile operators worldwide and has implemented innovative solutions for more than 100 mobile operators. Infobip's most important data centers are in Frankfurt, Washington, Moscow, Johannesburg, and Mumbai on more than 250 servers with more than 100 services that provide real-time delivery of SMS messages and other provided services. Besides its global presence, Infobip keeps development offices in southeastern Europe—Pula, Zagreb, Sarajevo, and Belgrade.

The Industry

Infobip is a part of an application to person (A2P) niche, which is somewhat different from the person to person (P2P) where one person sends a message to another person.

According to Juniper Research, the revenues from A2P SMS will be valued at almost $60 billion by 2018, which is up from $55 billion in 2013. The SMS remain a far greater form of communication in all kinds of business organizations, especially for those that are financial services or ticketing providers, because of the SMS security and reliability of A2P communications. A2P SMS should see growth both in terms of traffic and revenues over the forecast period.

Figure 3 Infobip's Services—The Mobile Services Cloud

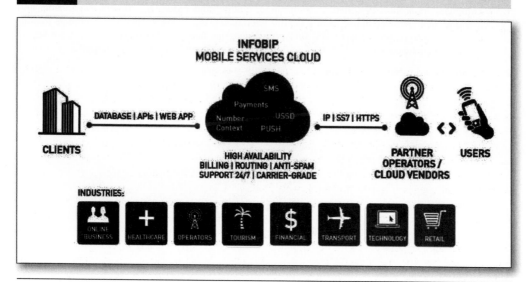

SOURCE: Figure courtesy of Infobip

The growth in A2P SMS revenues comes at the same time as P2P SMS revenues are in decline. Mobile operators are losing out as their customers switch to over the top (OTT) messaging platforms, which have the allure of being "free" because these services are used over the network service of your service provider. Moreover, by 2018, the instant messaging (IM) traffic will be around 63 trillion messages, but these only account for just over $3 billion in revenues; also during the forecasted period, China and the Far East will generate the most traffic across all mobile messaging formats.

The Future

Infobip continues to develop their own products and services according to their initial mission: "We create a seamless interaction of business and people through mobile." They are working on improving existing services, but they are also preparing for a new launch: a new mobile platform that will change the way communication occurs between people and enterprises. They have no doubt that there will be some failures at the beginning, but most importantly, the company will be able to learn from these failures and mistakes, and further product results will be closer to the solution and clients' needs.

Recognized worldwide, Infobip often gets invitations for relocation from various countries, away from Pula and Croatia, but Silvio Kutić does not consider any of them, even though the incentives and conditions would be much better compared to Croatia. He is determined to stay in Istria and open new working possibilities for young people in search of their future. In the end, companies are people—extremely good people—and team players pursuing the same goals with a strong motivation to succeed.

NOTES

1. A computer application designed for publishing, editing, and modifying content; organizing; and deleting as well as maintenance from a central interface (Boag, P. [2009, March 5]. 10 things to consider when choosing the perfect CMS. *Smashing Magazine*. Retrieved February 5, 2015, from http://www.smashingmagazine.com/2009/03/05/10-things-to-consider-when-choosing-the-perfect-cms/)

2. A Croatian word meaning *challenge*

Mojitos Night Club

Gregory Stoller and Jeremy Bass[1]

Introduction

In the summer of 2005, Jody Mendoza Pekala and her partner, Eric Liriano, opened Mojitos, a Latin lounge and nightclub in downtown Boston (http://www.mojitosboston.com), strategically located near Quincy Market, the Boston Common, Public Garden, and historic Opera House. Mojitos caters to the Hispanic community as well as anyone who loves Latin music and culture. In 2007, Mojitos had been open for 1½ years, half of the time Jody and Eric were contractually obligated to work together.

While Mojitos had met or exceeded all expectations, now it is time for Jody to plan her next move. Sitting at her desk, Jody considers her options: (1) selling Mojitos and buying a new location or (2) expanding from the nightclub into other areas within the entertainment field. Coupled with either option is the prospect of continuing to work together as partners, seeking an early buy-out of the remaining contract term, or Jody going off on her own once the contract period has expired.

History

While an MBA student at Boston College's Carroll School of Management in 2004, Jody was approached by Eric Liriano to partner up and create a nightclub. Eric had realized that with the closing of Sophia's that same year, there was an unmet demand for an upscale Latin venue in Boston. Initially, both Jody and Eric were cautious and wanted to be sure that their vision was aligned and that this partnership was going to work.

Eric was a financial planner at Robert Fine and Associates, an investment brokerage house. He was a successful partner in the firm and was involved in real estate. Eric was looking for an additional means of diversifying his revenue stream and holdings, and he viewed Mojitos as primarily an investment opportunity but also as the realization of a dream. More importantly, Eric was prominent in the Latino professional and social community and believed Mojitos would complement his previous achievements. He was interested in finding the right partner to drive the business and oversee the management of the day-to-day operations, as he wanted to focus on his business as a financial planner and had no prior experience in the entertainment field.

Jody had been in the entertainment field for ten years. She had been the general manager and a driving force behind Sophia's for four years in its heyday. She also owned a Latin promotions and marketing company called Avivé Productions (http://www.aviveproductions.com), which was responsible for producing many of the area's most successful Latin entertainment events, including nightclub nights, concerts, cruises, and other special events. Avivé Productions had established a core clientele of upscale Latinos who supported all of their events.

Eric had met Jody at Sophia's many years before and had followed the success of Avivé Productions. His faith in Jody was a motivating point behind her decision to partner with him.

During the first few months of working together, getting to know the other's personalities, goals, and responses to various situations was going to be a priority. Eric recognized this and early on in their relationship made an appointment with a business coach to ensure that all underlying issues could be addressed and resolved in an amicable manner. This set the groundwork for the open and honest communication that has continued to play a significant role in the success of the operation. In terms of personality, Eric and Jody are very different, but this fact, along with their different skill sets, has ultimately been good for the business.

In the planning stages of the partnership, the main issues they discussed were their respective visions for the club, whom they were going to target, and the type of employee culture they believed would be best for the nightclub. Both Eric and Jody believed in providing a safe, upscale yet energetic environment where people could enjoy Latin culture and entertainment. They agreed that different subsections within whatever demographic they would be targeting would have to be catered to on different nights.

As it related to corporate culture, Jody advocated the development of a sense of ownership within all employees as the key to driving word of mouth and achieving success in this type of industry. "Every employee is a promoter," she believed. Although their visions for the venue were not exactly the same, they were generally compatible. Eric believed in Jody's ability to perform as promised, and Jody believed in Eric's ability to provide her with the necessary flexibility to achieve their goals. Because of this, they decided to take the leap of faith and quickly began discussing the practical aspects of launching the business, such as financing, projected revenue, and executing the business plan.

The timeline was short; the tentative decision to go ahead was made right before MBA finals week in May 2005, with a projected opening date of August 2005. Jody began writing the business plan while studying and taking her final exams, and the plan was subsequently presented to the bank within two weeks thereafter. Eric selected Benjamin Franklin Bank, a small local bank. As Eric explained his decision:

> "Small banks are more likely to take on a risky venture than established banks. Larger banks are less frequently approached by hopeful entrepreneurs and may have certain SBA [small business administration] quotas. But, SBA loans are not that desirable to banks because they generate less than conventional loans."[2]

Benjamin Franklin Bank accepted the business plan and authorized the loan within two weeks, given certain conditions Eric was confident they could meet. Eric invested two thirds of the purchase price on his own, and the SBA loan covered the remaining third, with his Porsche SUV as collateral. Jody did not invest money. Her contribution in exchange for ownership was the business plan and contract to manage for a period of three years.

A location in downtown Boston was found at 48 Winter Street and the concept was approved in theory by the building's landlord. The location had two floors and a middle lobby area for a total of about 5,500 square feet. A five-year lease was negotiated, with the starting rate of $24 per square foot with annual increases of 5%.

Even with a location so close to Tremont Street, one of Boston's main thoroughfares, and easy access from the Park Street MBTA station and the Public Garden, there were a number of challenges they faced. The target Latino clientele was not familiar with the area, downtown parking was expensive, and the City of Boston would not permit valet service in this area. While the venue was licensed to serve food, it had no facilities in which to prepare it. Finally, with two floors, the entertainment required twice the planning and logistical management, and each individual floor would have to be unique yet complementary to the overall concept.

Despite the challenges, Jody positively reflected on beginning to conquer these early challenges:

"We were optimistic that these challenges could be overcome. The first issue was somewhat easier to solve, as we could familiarize the clientele with that area of downtown Boston through advertising. A map was made that included familiar landmarks and was put on all marketing collateral. The closest garage was contacted and a special rate for Mojitos customers of $7 for the night was agreed upon. The location of this parking garage and the $7 price was also included on the map.

I believed that because of the lack of preparation facilities, the issue of food would have to be addressed at a later date. This would reduce our expected revenue by about 10% to 12% (see Exhibit 1). Without food, patrons would arrive later at the venue, further reducing the revenue. However, building a kitchen was cost prohibitive at that time and getting the necessary permits to do so would have delayed opening."

Exhibit 1   Projected vs. Actual Revenues

Projected Revenue by Department

Department	Revenue	% of Sales
Bar	$ 11,011.58	0.89
Food	$ 1,383.75	0.11
Total	$ 12,395.33	1.00

Department	Revenue	% of Sales
Bar	$ 572,601.90	0.78
Food	$ 71,955.00	0.10
Total	$ 644,556.90	1.00

Actual Revenue by Department

Department	Revenue	% of Sales
Bar	$ 12,456.31	1.00
Food	0	0.00
Total	$ 12,456.31	1.00

Department	Revenue	% of Sales
Bar	$ 647,727.99	1.00
Food	0	0.00
Total	$ 647,727.99	1.00

However, the lack of food service combined with the limited physical capacity on each floor meant that there was no room for error in terms of the entertainment lineup and promotional tactics. "I knew that once we began to execute our entertainment strategy and undertake the promotions," Jody said, "I would have to utilize all of the previous lessons I had learned over the past 10 years and call in favors from all of my contacts."

The next step in the process was negotiations with the city regarding its liquor licenses. In theory, opening a nightclub is easy, but obtaining a liquor license is the difficult part. Boston does not grant new licenses, so an existing one must be located, negotiated for, and purchased. In addition, the previous owner's track record is held against the new owner in licensing courts.

Because the safety of the public is at stake and alcohol is being served, the city prefers to err on the side of caution in nightclub hearings. In short, a license holder is guilty until proven innocent. If the previous occupants were caught overcrowding, it is assumed that future occupants will also overcrowd, even if the two owners never knew one another or had any prior dealings, until the current license holder has proven that this will not happen for an extended period of time.

Furthermore, if the previous owner has outstanding debts, these become the responsibility of the current owner once the license is purchased and transferred. For many of these same reasons, liquor licenses at locations that were properly managed are very expensive and are typically bought by large corporations or chains. The location at 48 Winter Street had been poorly run and had considerable debt attached to it. The nightclub occupying the space before Mojitos had been a nightclub with what Jody describes as an "identity crisis." Each night had a different theme ranging from trance to hip-hop to alternative lifestyle nights, none of which generated revenue. Given the poor financial shape the prior club was in due to their lack of revenue, it was relatively easy to secure the space because the owners seemed desperate to sell and the landlord wanted a more responsible replacement tenant.

However, even with the landlord's endorsement, the liquor license challenges would lie in convincing the Liquor License Board that the new tenants at 48 Winter Street were better business operators and interested in cooperating. The Board is always skeptical of promises, and time would be necessary for Mojitos to prove it was sincere in living up to them.

Description of Mojitos' Interior

Across its two floors, the approximately 5,500 square feet of space has a capacity of 300 people. There is also a middle floor that is used for accepting a cover charge, checking coats, stamping parking validations, and providing information to patrons. The upstairs "Lounge Level" (floor #2) is used as a cocktail area in the earlier hours and develops into a dance scene later at night. The décor features exposed brick walls, hardwood floors, antique style accents, and reddish burgundy walls. The downstairs "Club Level" (floor #1) is characterized by a unique artistic wall mural that features various legendary Latin musicians such as Celia Cruz and Tito Puente and is visible as patrons enter. According to Jody, "This mural is always commented upon and frequently photographed by patrons." A VIP room featuring Caribbean art and blue velvet chairs is off to the left. Ahead of this, a long bar serves the patrons and the dance floor is powered by a strong sound system. (Pictures of the club itself are available at http://www.mojitoslounge.com, and a Citysearch review is available in Exhibit 3.)

The overarching theme of the club is high-energy Latin entertainment in a comfortable, welcoming setting. The target market includes professional Latinos, the trendy young Latin crowd, mainstream Bostonians, and Boston's diverse student population. Live entertainment is available on selected evenings, and DJs spin the crowd favorites and trendsetting hits on the nights Mojitos is open. Because of the two levels, Mojitos can offer two diverse yet physically connected experiences and entertainment styles under the same roof.

Business at Mojitos

In order to meet the financial objectives, and with only a 300-patron capacity, Mojitos has to be full on Fridays and Saturdays and use the cumulative total of the "off" nights to generate the equivalent of one weekend night. Enticing patrons to go out on an "off" night is difficult in a downtown Boston location, and the expenses of staff and utilities may be greater than the profit realized. For many of these reasons, Mojitos was scheduled to be open only from Thursday through Sunday.

The revenue at Mojitos would have to be immediate and also sustainable in order to consistently meet the targets. As Jody explains, these two objectives are difficult to achieve concurrently:

"Typically, when nightclubs open, there are two main cycles of business, and successful venues go through one or the other. The first is a soft opening with a slow and steady build. These clubs, if run well, slowly become part of the nightlife landscape. They are not trendy or packed; they just enjoy a steady business.

The other type of successful nightclub is typically brought to the market with glitz and hype. They are home to the trendy international students and club types for about a year. After that, the general market catches on to the venue and the trendy types move on to the latest and greatest venue fad. Mojitos could not afford to be either, frankly. Rather, Mojitos had to be a hybrid that would open with a bang, yet become a nightlife institution. In order to achieve this, the elements that contribute to these two nightlife phenomenon were carefully analyzed. Mojitos needed immediate revenue but needed to sustain this revenue in order to meet the objectives."

Mojitos opened amid rave reviews from the Latino community on August 12, 2005. Eric and Jody had hit on the right combination that filled the unmet need in the market. (See Exhibits 2, 4, 5, and 6 for Mojitos financials, a review by the *Boston Globe*, a description of the owners and key employees, and a "Day in the Life of a Nightclub Owner," respectively.)

Industry Analysis

In 2004, the bar/lounge and club industry, which are known in the U.S. Economic Census Reports as "Drinking Places,"[3] brought in over $1.5 billion dollars in the United States.[4] The average person

Exhibit 2	Proforma Yearly Income Statement (**)			

	Year 1		Year 2	
Revenues				
Bar	$	695,597.76	$	784,290.00
Other	$	109,200.00	$	143,000.00
Total Revenues	$	804,797.76	$	927,290.00
Expenses				
Beverage Costs	$	128,719.55	$	139,119.55
General Expenses	$	543,814.41	$	623,031.57
Total Expenses	$	672,533.96	$	762,151.12
Operating Income	$	132,263.80	$	165,138.88
SBA Loan Payment	$	25,866.08	$	25,866.08
Earnings before Taxes	$	**106,397.72**	$	**139,272.80**

**These numbers are not actual financials; they are used to represent relative proportions for this case study.

Exhibit 3 Citysearch Review of Mojitos (http://www.citysearch.com)

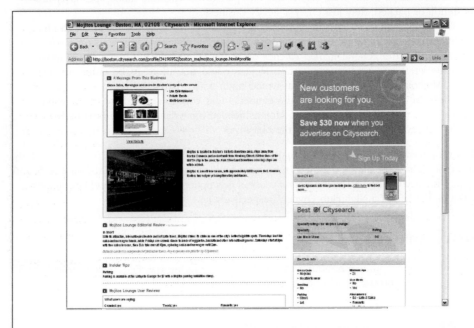

Mojitos Lounge Editorial Review by Citysearch Staff

In Short

With its attractive, international clientele and hot Latin tunes, Mojitos stakes its claim as one of the city's hottest nighttime spots. Thursdays host live salsa and merengue bands, while Fridays see crowds dance to a mix of *reggaeton, bachata,* and other international genres. Saturdays start at 9:00pm with free salsa lessons, then DJs take over at 10:00pm, spinning salsa and merengue until 2:00am.

Editorial content is independent of paid advertisers. Any expenses are paid for by Citysearch.[1]

[1]Mojitos Lounge. (n.d.). Retrieved February 7, 2015, from http://boston.citysearch.com/profile/34196952/boston_ma/mojitos_lounge.html

spent $1,294 on food and beverage in a licensed establishment in 2004,[5] and the alcoholic beverage industry was on the increase financially for a fifth consecutive year.[6]

According to *Nightclub and Bar Magazine*, there are between 59,000 and 63,000 nightclubs, bars, pubs, and taverns in the United States. Specifically, at any particular point in time, there are an estimated 20,000 nightclubs in America. Based on results of the Mintel research, conducted for their 2002 report, approximately one third of the U.S. adult population over the age of 18 attends nightclubs at least once a year; the highest attendance rate is between the ages of 18 and 29 (some clubs host underage events for adults aged 17–20), where 55% of the population report visiting a nightclub. Further, Hispanics are the most active patrons of nightclubs.[7]

Exhibit 4 "Loco for Latin," *Boston Globe*, Sarah Tomlinson, Globe Correspondent

August 31, 2005

One of the most significant developments in the local Latin scene was the opening last month of Mojitos, a nightclub with plans to offer two floors of Latin dancing five nights a week in its swanky Downtown Crossing digs.

The owners of Mojitos say they hope to fill a void created by the closing last year of Sophia's, the popular Fenway-area salsa destination, according to Jody Mendoza Pekala, a former manager at Sophia's who is now a managing partner of Avivé Productions, which runs Mojitos, along with a summertime Sunday night salsa cruise. Pekala says she and her partners heard Latin-dance enthusiasts clamoring for a particular type of dance destination. "An upscale Latin venue," she says, "a venue they can go to and hear salsa and merengue and be surrounded by a good looking, well dressed crowd that's out to have a good time."

Throngs of exuberant dancers are indeed enjoying themselves on a recent Saturday night at Mojitos. People representing a wide range of ages and ethnicities jam both dance floors. The club's basement room boasts a sweaty, sexed-up dance party, as the heavier sounds of merengue and reggaeton blare amid vivid murals of famous Latin entertainers. In the more elegant upstairs bar, a serious salsa crowd spins and claps and spins some more. Couples show off synchronized dance moves, and groups of friends dance together.[2]

---

[2]Tomlinson, S. (2005, August 31). Loco for Latin. Retrieved February 12, 2015, from http://www.boston.com/ae/events/articles/2005/09/01/loco_for_latin/

Exhibit 5 Description of Owners and Key Employees

Eric Liriano: Owner/Investor

Eric Liriano was a financial planner with Robert Fine & Associates. About a year after Mojitos opened, Eric opened his own investment brokerage house, Liriano Wealth Advisory Group, LLC. Mr. Liriano manages over 200 million dollars of investment assets and has implemented a life insurance portfolio worth over 800 million dollars. He is also the president of the Latino Professional Network, a Boston-based nonprofit organization with 1,500 members.

Mr. Liriano has resided in the Boston area since 1972. He attended and received his undergraduate degree in Communications and Business Marketing from Boston College in 1988. Mr. Liriano is originally from the Dominican Republic.

Jody Mendoza Pekala: Managing Partner

Jody Mendoza Pekala is a Puerto Rican raised in the United States with an extensive background in the Latin nightclub and entertainment industry. After finishing her undergraduate degree in psychology, she accepted the position as general manager at Sophia's. Under her guidance, Sophia's became the premier destination for Latinos in the area and brought in over 2 million dollars in annual sales. She recognized the need for an organized effort to cater to the Latin

(Continued)

Exhibit 5 (Continued)

community's entertainment needs. Therefore, she founded Avivé Productions, a Latin Entertainment marketing and promotions business in 1999.

Avivé Productions was formed and the nights became legendary in Boston and surrounding areas at Sophia's and, later, the Roxy and other Latin hotspots. Avivé Productions also organized concerts, special events, and the Boston Harbor Latin Cruises. The customer base and reputation built through Avivé Productions was leveraged to create a base crowd at Mojitos. This played a critical role in the early success of Mojitos. As the managing partner of Mojitos, she was contracted for three years in exchange for salary, a percentage of ownership outright, and the option to buy a designated percentage.

David Mendoza Pekala: Manager

When David Mendoza Pekala was appointed as the manager of Mojitos, he had his work cut out for him. He had just enrolled as a full-time student at Brandeis University and had little experience in the nightlife industry. He had just returned from Iraq, where he was given a Purple Heart. With a limited budget for management, Jody needed someone who would accept a comparatively low salary but who had complete dedication, was trustworthy, could work very long hours, and thrived under pressure. Jody turned to her brother David, and her faith in his ability to be a successful manager paid off. He was able to learn the business quickly and he comfortably assumed a leadership role at Mojitos.

Exhibit 6 A "Day in the Life of a Nightclub Owner"

Interview with Jody Mendoza Pekala, managing partner of Avive Productions, February 2007

Before explaining what a day in my life is like, it is necessary to explain what the roles are of the critical players in our organization. What you see at nighttime is the product of all of the work that has been done in preparation leading up to an event. It is like the theatre; people have already rehearsed and now they are just acting their parts out. There are many elements that people don't see or even imagine that are part of the night. Most people imagine that we just open our doors and people come. That is very far from the reality.

There are three main departments that I oversee, and I work closely with the key employees of each department. The first is Back of House Operations, the next is Entertainment and Event Planning, and the last is Front of House Operations.

Back of House Operations include both the physical upkeep of the venue and product ordering and record keeping. This work is performed during the day and there are three departments. The operations manager is in charge of keeping the physical location in working order. This includes changing filters, repairing plumbing issues, sanding floors, and much more. The bar manager is in charge of maintaining inventory records and ordering products, including dry goods. The human resources manager maintains payroll and employee records.

Entertainment and Event Planning are the creative end of the business. It can be very exciting but also challenging. This is what people talk about and what drives the entertainment experience that people take away from the venue. The strategizing and planning for this all happens during the day.

Planning for a typical Saturday night will happen a month to two months prior to the actual night. We start our planning session with "What are we going to do to make this particular Saturday special?" We look at the previous year's sales and at recent trends in sales by night, review upcoming holidays, recall successful promotions run the year before, and just brainstorm. We envision a party including performers, DJs, hosts/MCs, dancers, photographers, decorations, costumes, and interactive games to keep the crowd involved. The ideas we come up with are then matched with a target clientele and sponsors. An advertising and/or promotions campaign is created against the budget, which is based off of the projected revenue.

In our budgets, we have a best-case scenario, wherein sponsors augment our budgets, and the worst-case scenario where we have to pay for everything ourselves. We then write proposals and meet with potential sponsors. When we have their commitment and input, we move on to media buying. Bigger campaigns may include television, radio, and newspaper ads as well as flyers/posters and Internet advertising. Performers and other key personnel such as celebrities are confirmed at this time in order to include their images on the advertising and promotional materials.

The final department is Front of House Operations. The face that everyone sees as the manager of the establishment is the night manager. He makes sure that during our hours of operation, the staff and entertainers are present and performing as expected. He is also entrusted with ensuring that Mojitos operates according to all local and state laws regarding capacity laws, fire prevention laws, minimum drinking age laws, and general safety laws. He works closely with the head of security to ensure this. The only two managerial positions that patrons are really aware of are the night manager and the head of security. The rest is performed behind the scenes.

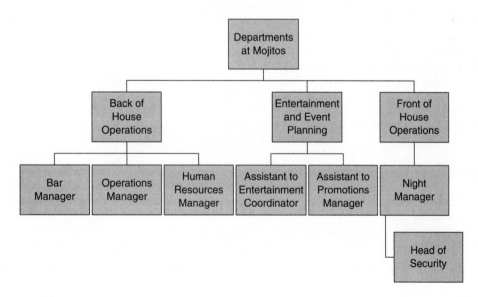

Most of my work is done during the day. A typical day will start at about 10 or 11 in the morning. I arrive at the office. One of my assistants will give me the opened and sorted mail— mostly bills, of course. I start by returning phone calls and planning the day. I have meetings

Exhibit 6	(Continued)

scheduled two days a week. The meetings are with representatives from liquor companies, potential promoters, entertainers, and repair personnel. Most of the time is spent on the phone or in meetings and communicating my plans to the key personnel so that they can execute the plans. The rest of the time, I review the reports given to me by each department and evaluate how we are doing and what we need to improve.

At night at the club, I just watch everyone do their job. I only interfere if someone isn't doing their job correctly, and then I pull them aside. I interact with patrons almost the whole night. The main goal that I have each night is to listen to the people and find ways to improve what we are offering. I talk to people, overhear conversations, handle complaints, diffuse potential situations, and introduce people to one another. At night, I am essentially a hostess; it is like having a party at your home. Sometimes I get to meet baseball players and drink champagne, other times I am rushing to stop a bathroom from overflowing. All of the long hours and lack of sleep are worth it when you see people having the time of their lives celebrating a birthday or anniversary or simply dancing to forget their daily problems. Every once in a while, they notice that it was you and your team who made it possible, and they say "thank you."

Cathy E. Minehan, president and CEO of the Federal Reserve Bank of Boston, said in the spring of 2006 that the "economy has become solidly self-sustaining, with annual GDP [gross domestic product] growth for the last half of 2004 better than 4 percent."[8] Based on these positive trends, it appeared that the upturn in the economy could finally begin translating into increased spending among consumers.

Locally, the harvesting of these economic predictions and the observed drinking patterns in the Boston area are supported by a recent Gallup Poll. This bodes well for nightclubs who obtain their highest financial margins from alcohol sales. Among those who drink, the percentage saying they have had at least one drink in the past week has risen from 48% in 1992 to 68% today. The sharpest increase in reported drinking has come in the past three years.[9] Of people who consume alcohol, 55% of people reported that they had between one and seven drinks in the last week.[10]

Factoid About Disposable Income in Boston

According to data from 2002, there were 650 full-service restaurants and 197 drinking places within the Boston city limits. These venues employed over 19,000 people with payroll expenses nearing $300 million and generated close to a billion dollars in sales.[11] With over 75% of the Boston population (according to the 2000 census, 589,141) over the age of 20, the 847 venues that could serve alcohol are perpetually busy.[12]

Background Information and Industry Trends

The name *Mojitos* is derived from a Latin American drink of the same name that contains rum, fresh lime, and mint leaves. The combination is currently enjoying increasing popularity across the globe in trendy venues and is the third-most-ordered drink in the New York metropolitan area.[13] The rum industry has also experienced dynamic growth driven by the popularity of the Mojitos drink.[14] In terms of timing, the nightclub has been able to capitalize on the drink's increasing popularity through seemingly instant name recognition.

Minorities are now the majority diverse ethic grouping in Boston, and Hispanics represent one of the fastest growing cross sections, according to the Boston Redevelopment Authority. In addition to the increase of Hispanics, there is also a demand in mainstream America for Latin entertainment and cuisine. *Nightclub and Bar Magazine* asserts, "The demand for all things Latino is not just a flash in the pan. Research shows the popularity will last at least 14 to 28 years and maybe much longer. It will eventually become a wave (56 years or longer) and will become a part of the American lifestyle for years to come."[15]

Latino Culture/Market Research

The general public became aware of the phenomenal growth rate of Hispanics in America after the 2000 census. As of 2000, approximately one in eight people in the United States is of Hispanic origin.[16] By 2007, it is estimated that one in five will be of Hispanic descent.[17]

As of 2003, the population of Hispanics in the United States reached 39.9 million, with a growth rate of almost four times that of the total population.[18] The U.S. Census Bureau projects that the U.S. Hispanic population will reach 50 million by 2007. According to HispanTelligence, the U.S. Hispanic purchasing power grew 8% to almost $540 billion and is expected to reach $638 billion by 2010.[19] Younger Hispanics control a greater share of their ethnic group's total purchasing power than their non-Hispanic counterparts. Hispanics aged 15 to 34 earn 37% of total Hispanic income versus 21% for non-Hispanic whites.[20] More than 86% of those have been born in the United States and are English dominant.[21]

Additionally, we have now entered the Hispanic Baby Boom, with a 3.51% birth rate in Hispanic households—twice the national average.[22] The median age for Hispanics is 26.7 years old, compared to the median age for Whites of 39.6, Blacks of 31 years, and Asians of 34.

According to other Census Bureau figures, there were 430,000 Hispanics in Massachusetts in 2000, representing a 50% growth rate in the 1990s.[23] In Boston neighborhoods and Chelsea alone, there are approximately 100,000 Hispanics, based on figures from the Boston Redevelopment Authority. The majority of the Latino population in Massachusetts lives in five key places.[24] Boston, which has a Latino population of 85,089 that accounts for 20% of the total Massachusetts Latino population; Lawrence, 43,019 (10%); Springfield, 41,343 (9.6%); Worcester, 26,155 (6.1%); and Chelsea, 16,984 (4%).

As of 2000, 14.4% of Bostonians were of Hispanic or Latino origin, which is higher than the national average of 13%.[25] The Boston area, according to the Boston Neighborhood Profile produced by the census, includes the neighborhoods of Allston/Brighton, Dorchester, East Boston, Hyde Park, Jamaica Plain, Mattapan, Roslindale, Roxbury, and South Boston. (See Exhibit 7 for the number of Latinos in the Boston area by country of origin.) There have also been very significant increases in the Hispanic population in East Boston, Hyde Park, and Mattapan.[26] East Boston is now home to the largest Hispanic community in the Boston area, with 14,990 Hispanics comprising 39% of the total population as of 2000.[27]

In 2000, Jamaica Plain had 8,958 Hispanics comprising 23.5% of the total population, experiencing a decline of 1,613 people or 15.3%. Although geographically near Boston and surrounding areas, Chelsea is considered a separate area by the census. Chelsea has a large Hispanic community, with 16,984 people, and has experienced a growth rate of 98.1% in the last decade. Hispanics now represent 48.8% of that population and Chelsea now has the fifth largest population of Hispanics. The largest group in Chelsea is Puerto Ricans at 31.6%.[28] Overall, minorities are now the majority in Boston. Hispanics and Asians are the fastest-growing groups in Boston.[29]

| Exhibit 7 | Number of Latinos in the Boston Area by Country of Origin |

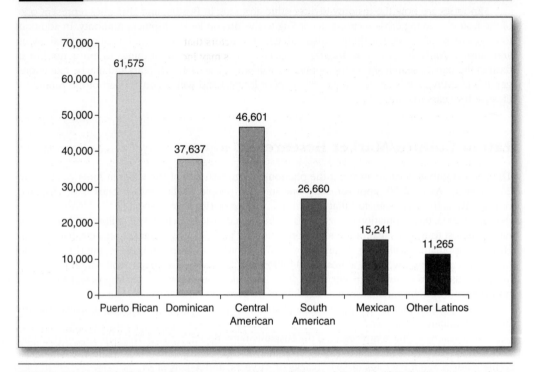

SOURCE: Lewis Mumford Center for Comparative Urban and Regional Research. (2000). Hispanic population and residential segregation. Retrieved February 6, 2015, from http://mumford.albany.edu/census/HispanicPop/HspPopData.htm

Nexus of Local Industry Trends and Mojitos' Marketing Strategy

The Mojitos target market can be broken down into two categories: Latinos and those that love Latin entertainment. The key to the success at a nightclub is to keep the venue busy on all days that it is open. Jody felt very strongly that Mojitos should only offer Latin entertainment in order to avoid the perceived "identity crisis" that its predecessor faced as well as those of other venues. She explains:

> "The challenge was to keep the lineup under the umbrella of Latin entertainment, while keeping the performers varied and the venue full. A unique and distinct experience had to be created that featured the preferred music, drinks options, and entertainment preferences of a targeted group. The advertising had to reflect the entertainment featured and had to be directed at different segments or subsets of the target market for different floors on different nights. This meant that the nuances of the Latin market in Boston had to be understood and promotions had to resonate with the desired audience.

We knew we would be bucking the trend by not remaining open more days per week, but we thought this was a risk we could and should take. I guess the future will determine whether it was a sound decision."

There are unique sociological and psychological factors that characterize and differentiate the Hispanic community in New England. Because Hispanics may include people from many countries in addition to those from various cultural and socioeconomic backgrounds, it is necessary to understand the multitude of complex factors at work. Latinos are a very diverse ethnic group and there is no easy way to segment the population.

Segmentation for the marketing for Mojitos was performed on two levels: country of origin and general level of acculturation, including language preference. Segmentation by country is necessary because there are certain preferences in terms of entertainment, food, and products that are observed within groups of people who share a country or region of origin. The following countries or regions were identified as optimal target groups:

- Puerto Ricans
- Dominicans
- South Americans, primarily Colombians and Venezuelans (also includes Peruvians, Bolivians, Argentines, and Ecuadorians)
- Central Americans, including Salvadorians, Guatemalans, Panamanians, Hondurans, and Nicaraguans

However, segmenting by country of origin alone is not sufficient. The second level includes language of choice that reflects the degree of acculturation within American society. Socioeconomic status is often tied to a person's ability to communicate. This was kept in mind when preparing advertising materials for certain neighborhoods. (See Exhibits 8, 9, and 10 for demographic information on the Hispanic population, and Exhibit 11 for Mojitos' target market segment.)

Challenges During the First Year of Business

After a very successful opening and outstanding first few months, Mojitos was facing the deep winter months that meant decreased sales. Traditionally, nightclubs experience a drop in sales beginning in December that lasts into February. This drop in business is due to office holiday parties, a partial evacuation of students for winter break, and a shift in disposable income toward holiday shopping. Because Mojitos is a Latino club, there was the added difficulty of reduced attendance due to seasonal travel. Many of the patrons visit family in their respective countries of origin during these months. Finally, the initial buzz had worn off and Mojitos faced its first test.

However, this challenge had been anticipated and promotional strategies were put into place to minimize the impact typical during this season. One of the ways this was done was through rewarding regular customers and encouraging their repeat business. Jody explains:

"As you learn in business school, it is easier to retain customers than it is to acquire new ones. Therefore, VIP cards were printed and distributed to the regular clientele. This not only cultivated the core group of regulars, but also rewarded them during the holiday season when budgets are tight. By using various promotional techniques such as the VIP cards, the team at Mojitos was able to exceed expected sales in the early part of 2006."

Exhibit 8	Hispanics in Boston

Puerto Ricans

There are 3.4 million Puerto Ricans in the United States, according to U.S. Census figures from 2000, which is 9.6% of the total Hispanic population.[1] However, in Boston, Puerto Ricans account for 32.3% of the total Hispanic population.[2] In Boston, as with other parts of the country such as New York, Puerto Ricans are typically part of an earlier immigration wave. In the United States as a whole, only 26.7% are recent arrivals. The term *recent arrival* refers to anyone who has arrived here in the last 10 years.[3] The Puerto Ricans living in Boston are often quite acculturated and many are second or even third generation. Puerto Ricans are slowly starting to leave the city's traditional Hispanic neighborhoods such as Jamaica Plain and move outwards toward the suburbs as they experience an increase in economic status.

Dominicans

In the United States as of the 2000 census figures, there were 765, 000 Dominicans, which was 2.2% of the total Hispanic population.[4] According to estimates based off of the supplement to the census, the number may be as high as 913,000.[5] Of these, 62.7% are foreign born and 45.3% are recent arrivals.[6] In Boston, Dominicans account for 15.3% of the total Hispanic population.[7] From 1990 to 2000, the change in percentage for Dominicans was 63.5%, indicating that this group is increasingly important when considering the city's Hispanic population. The change in percentage also indicates that a number of these Dominicans are comparatively recent immigrants. There is also a significant number of second generation Dominicans in the area. Because there has been less time to acculturate, the Dominican community is quite visible, more so than the Puerto Rican community. They live primarily in Jamaica Plain, Roxbury, Lynn, and Lawrence. Dominicans have taken over the bodegas (corner stores) that Puerto Ricans previously dominated.

Colombians

In the United States overall, there are 471,000 Colombians, which account for 1.3% of the total Hispanic population.[8] The majority of these (71.7%) are foreign born and 38.4% are recent arrivals.[9] In Boston, there are 14,109 Colombians, which is roughly 7% of the Latinos in the area.[10] The change in percentage for Colombians was 71.2%, much of which is concentrated in East Boston. The Colombian community includes many recent immigrants, as the change in percentage confirms.

Salvadorians

In Boston, Salvadorians are comparatively prominent and they represent the largest community from any Central American country. In the United States as a whole, there are 655, 000—1.9% of Hispanic population.[11] Most (69.6%) are foreign born and 45.9% are recent arrivals.[12] Many immigrated in the 1980s to escape the genocide occurring in El Salvador. Many of these refugees obtained visas for political asylum, of which a large number are still pending. In Boston, Salvadorians account for 6.3% of the Hispanic population.[13] The change in percentage for Salvadorians from the 1990s to 2000 was 67.8%; most of this increase was seen in East Boston and Somerville.

Mexicans

Mexicans constitute 58% of the total Hispanic population in the United States.[14] However, in Boston, only 4.8% of the Hispanic population is Mexican.[15] The difference in Boston's Hispanic population compared to the rest of the country is very significant. The number of Mexicans is rising in Boston, however, with an increase in the percentage of 89.4% between 1990 and 2000. Proportionately, the Mexican community is not what it is in other parts of the country. In other parts of the country, there are established Mexican communities, in some cases, for several generations. In the Boston area, the Mexican community, while growing rapidly in terms of proportion, is not yet the force it is in the rest of the country.

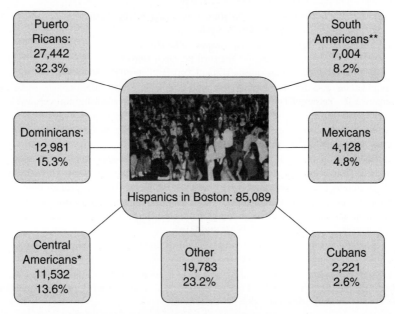

Puerto Ricans: 27,442 32.3%

South Americans** 7,004 8.2%

Dominicans: 12,981 15.3%

Mexicans 4,128 4.8%

Hispanics in Boston: 85,089

Central Americans* 11,532 13.6%

Other 19,783 23.2%

Cubans 2,221 2.6%

*This includes Salvadorans (5,333), Guatemalans (2,554), Hondurans (1,822), Panamanians (527), Nicaraguans (247) and Other Central Americans (1,049).
**Colombians (4,065), Peruvians (759), Venezuelans (638), Argentineans (421), Ecuadorians (385), Chileans (315), and Other South Americans (306).

---

[1]Guzman, B. (2001, May). The Hispanic population: Census 2000 brief. Retrieved February 6, 2015, from http://www.census.gov/prod/2001pubs/c2kbr01-3.pdf

[2]Melnik, M. (2011, November 29). Demographic and socio-economic trends in Boston: What we've learned from the latest Census data. Retrieved February 6, 2015, from http://www.bostonredevelopmentauthority.org/getattachment/83972a7a-c454-4aac-b3eb-02e1fddd71e3/

[3]Gonzalez, A. (2002, January 24). The impact of the 2001/2002 economic recession on Hispanic workers. Retrieved February 6, 2015, from http://pewhispanic.org/reports/report.php?ReportID=8

[4]Guzman, B. (2001, May). The Hispanic population: Census 2000 brief. Retrieved February 6, 2015, from http://www.census.gov/prod/2001pubs/c2kbr01-3.pdf

(Continued)

Exhibit 8 (Continued)

[5]Gonzalez, A. (2002, January 24). The impact of the 2001/2002 economic recession on Hispanic workers. Retrieved February 6, 2015, from http://pewhispanic.org/reports/report.php?ReportID=8

[6]Logan, J. R. (2001, September 10). *The new Latinos: Why they are, where they are*. Albany, NY: Lewis Mumford Center for Comparative Urban and Regional Research University at Albany. Retrieved February 6, 2015, from http://mumford.albany.edu/census/HispanicPop/HspReport/HspReportPage1.html

[7]Melnik, M. (2011, November 29). Demographic and socio-economic trends in Boston: What we've learned from the latest Census data. Retrieved February 6, 2015, from http://www.bostonredevelopmentauthority .org/getattachment/83972a7a-c454-4aac-b3eb-02e1fddd71e3/

[8]Guzman, B. (2001, May). *The Hispanic population: Census 2000 brief*. Retrieved February 6, 2015, from http://www.census.gov/prod/2001pubs/c2kbr01-3.pdf

[9]Logan, J. R. (2001, September 10). *The new Latinos: Why they are, where they are*. Albany, NY: Lewis Mumford Center for Comparative Urban and Regional Research University at Albany. Retrieved February 6, 2015, from http://mumford.albany.edu/census/HispanicPop/HspReport/HspReportPage1.html

[10]Hispanic populations data for the metropolitan statistical area. (2000). Metropolitan racial and ethnic change—Census 2000. Retrieved February 6, 2015, from http://mumford.albany.edu/census/HispanicPop/ HspPopData/4160msa.htm

[11]Guzman, B. (2001, May*). The Hispanic population: Census 2000 brief*. Retrieved February 6, 2015, from http://www.census.gov/prod/2001pubs/c2kbr01-3.pdf

[12]Logan, J. R. (2001, September 10). *The new Latinos: Why they are, where they are*. Albany, NY: Lewis Mumford Center for Comparative Urban and Regional Research University at Albany. Retrieved February 6, 2015, from http://mumford.albany.edu/census/HispanicPop/HspReport/HspReportPage1.html

[13]Melnik, M. (2011, November 29). Demographic and socio-economic trends in Boston: What we've learned from the latest Census data. Retrieved February 6, 2015, from http://www.bostonredevelopmentauthority .org/getattachment/83972a7a-c454-4aac-b3eb-02e1fddd71e3/

[14]Guzman, B. (2001, May). The Hispanic population: Census 2000 brief. Retrieved February 6, 2015, from http://www.census.gov/prod/2001pubs/c2kbr01-3.pdf

[15]Melnik, M. (2011, November 29). Demographic and socio-economic trends in Boston: What we've learned from the latest Census data. Retrieved February 6, 2015, from http://www.bostonredevelopmentauthority .org/getattachment/83972a7a-c454-4aac-b3eb-02e1fddd71e3/

Unfortunately, with the spring months came a new set of challenges, and these were unexpected. Boston experienced record-breaking rain fall for the months of May and June, logging 22.57 inches, the most since record keeping began in 1872.[30] These two months are typically two of the busiest months for nightclubs. Jody recalls,

> "Mojitos experienced property damage and a sharp decline in sales. The staff and patrons alike were not interested in going out—they were depressed due to the weather. Three employees moved to Miami to get away from the rain, and many patrons left the city as well. Those that remained complained of a depressed local economy and many experienced flood damage to their homes. Promotions were difficult because flyers and posters dissolve in the rain and are of no value. With the additional expenses and decline in revenue, advertising was not a viable option. All efforts were geared toward surviving the first year of business. In addition, I was still a full-time student at Boston College, so I was always torn between Mojitos and school."

Exhibit 9   Hispanic Ancestries of Bostonians, 2000[1]

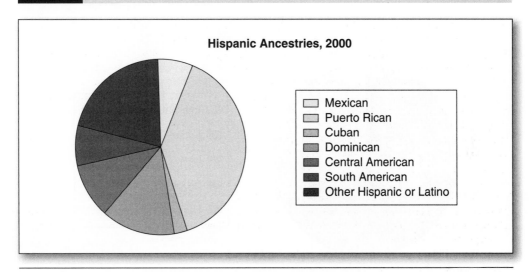

[1]CensusScope. (2000). Massachusetts ethnic and racial heritage. Retrieved February 6, 2015, from http://www.censusscope.org/us/s25/chart_ancestry.html

Exhibit 10   Hispanic Ancestries in United States, 2000[2]

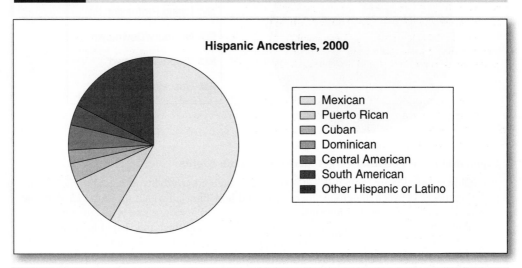

[1]CensusScope. (2000). United States ethnic and racial heritage. Retrieved February 6, 2015, from http://www.censusscope.org/us/chart_ancestry.html

Exhibit 11 Mojitos' Target Market Segment

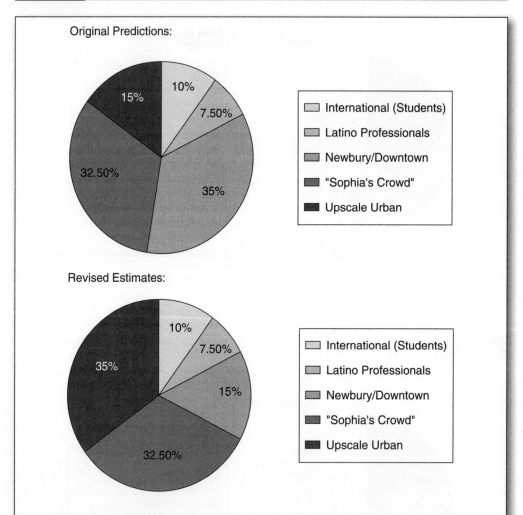

Original Predictions:

10%
15%
7.50%
32.50%
35%

International (Students)
Latino Professionals
Newbury/Downtown
"Sophia's Crowd"
Upscale Urban

Revised Estimates:

10%
35%
7.50%
15%
32.50%

International (Students)
Latino Professionals
Newbury/Downtown
"Sophia's Crowd"
Upscale Urban

Segmentation of Potential Target Markets for Club Nights

The following groups are broken down according to their compatibility in regard to the following two aspects: between the groups themselves and how they fall within the club's ideal, music preference, and their expected response rate. The expected response rate is assigned a numerical value, which is based on their historical response rate and their anticipated interest level.

Each group is also assigned a numerical value that indicates their relative value to the venue in terms of bar sales. This is all proprietary information that is based on firsthand experience and interviews with numerous club owners and promoters who have shared bar receipt totals.

International Students

The international students are an attractive demographic because they typically have the funds to go out frequently and are not concerned with what they spend when they are out. They are unattractive in the sense that there is intense competition to attract them. They are also very fickle and are always looking for the next club opening. They fit well with the club's ideal demographic. Their music preference is Latin, international, reggaeton and hip hop.

Their response rate is unpredictable. It was predicted that there would be considerable interest in Mojitos in the first year and sporadic interest later. It is possible that a loyal following can be cultivated, but they are not the ideal target because of the short-term nature of their interest and seasonal presence in the city. Before Mojitos opened, we anticipated that they would make up about 10% of the patrons and spend approximately $20 per visit. This has proven to be an accurate prediction.

Latino Professionals

This group consists of well-educated professionals who are striving for success. They like to know what is hot and will go out occasionally. When they do go out, they want to project a good image and will spend accordingly. They are attractive in the sense that they blend well with most crowds. The downside of this group is that they do not go out frequently and there are a limited number of them. When they do go out, they do not appreciate paying a cover charge. Rather than count on this group for weekly attendance, we have focused on creating special events that are of interest, perhaps after-work events, which are held approximately once a month. This segment is expected to be 5%–10% (7.5% used in the analysis) of the patrons and spend an average of $15 per person. In reviewing this a year and a half after Mojitos opened, this prediction has proved accurate.

The Newbury/Downtown Crowd

This group consists of professionals who are open-minded and enjoy cultural exploration. They spend freely and appreciate anything novel. They are not likely to go to the venue every weekend, but they will visit a few times a month. Because of the sheer numbers in this demographic, they are very attractive to the club. They have sophisticated tastes in terms of food and beverage and are accustomed to good service. This group will be targeted very heavily for the holiday season for corporate parties. We expected that this group would account for approximately 35% of our business and spend $12 per visit on beverages. Upon reviewing this prediction a year and half later, this amount should be adjusted to 15%.

The "Sophia's Crowd"

This group is not literally the people who used to go to Sophia's, although Avivé does own a complete database of all of those people and they regularly attend our events. It is a term used to describe people who fall between the international crowd and the upscale urban crowd. They are people who enjoy to party and actively plan this aspect of their lives out. They identify with the scene they adopt and bring groups of friends. They will spend a moderate amount ($10) per night, but the total amount per week is considerable. We anticipated that this crowd would make up about 30%–35% of our patrons and this prediction is more or less accurate upon review.

The Upscale Urban Crowd

This crowd consists of primarily Puerto Ricans and Dominicans who are somewhat acculturated. They are image conscious and they love their culture and music, mostly merengue and reggaeton but also salsa and bachata. This crowd wants to go to a venue that is upscale. We expected that there would be a good response rate and that Mojitos would appeal to them. They are comfortable spending money but not extravagantly, perhaps $10 per person on average. We expected about 15% of our total crowd to be representatives of this group. The reality has been closer to 35% and they spend closer to $15 per person.

(continued)

Exhibit 11 (Continued)

Predicted Sales by Targeted Groups*

Average per Person/Percentage of Crowd	International (Students)	Latino Professionals	Newbury/Downtown	"Sophia's Crowd"	Upscale Urban	Total Sales
	$20.00	$15.00	$12.00	$10.00	$10.00	
	10%	7.50%	35%	32.50%	15%	
75 Patrons	$ 150.00	$ 84.38	$ 315.00	$ 243.75	$ 112.50	$ 905.63
100 Patrons	$ 200.00	$ 112.50	$ 420.00	$ 325.00	$ 150.00	$ 1,207.50
150 Patrons	$ 300.00	$ 168.75	$ 630.00	$ 487.50	$ 225.00	$ 1,811.25
200 Patrons	$ 400.00	$ 225.00	$ 840.00	$ 650.00	$ 300.00	$ 2,415.00
250 Patrons	$ 500.00	$ 281.25	$ 1,050.00	$ 812.50	$ 375.00	$ 3,018.75
300 Patrons	$ 600.00	$ 337.50	$ 1,260.00	$ 975.00	$ 450.00	$ 3,622.50
350 Patron	$ 700.00	$ 393.75	$ 1,470.00	$ 1,137.50	$ 525.00	$ 4,226.25
400 Patrons	$ 800.00	$ 450.00	$ 1,680.00	$ 1,300.00	$ 600.00	$ 4,830.00
450 Patrons	$ 900.00	$ 506.25	$ 1,890.00	$ 1,462.50	$ 675.00	$ 5,433.75

Revised Sales Estimates by Targeted Groups*

Average per Person Percentage of Crowd	International (Students) $20.00 10%	Latino Professionals $15.00 7.50%	Newbury/ Downtown $12.00 15%	"Sophia's Crowd" $15.00 32.50%	Upscale Urban $15.00 35%
75 Patrons	$ 150.00	$ 84.38	$ 135.00	$ 393.75	$ 1,128.75
100 Patrons	$ 200.00	$ 112.50	$ 180.00	$ 525.00	$ 1,505.00
150 Patrons	$ 300.00	$ 168.75	$ 270.00	$ 787.50	$ 2,257.50
200 Patrons	$ 400.00	$ 225.00	$ 360.00	$ 1,050.00	$ 3,010.00
250 Patrons	$ 500.00	$ 281.25	$ 450.00	$ 1,312.50	$ 3,762.50
300 Patrons	$ 600.00	$ 337.50	$ 540.00	$ 1,575.00	$ 4,515.00
350 Patron	$ 700.00	$ 393.75	$ 630.00	$ 1,837.50	$ 5,267.50
400 Patrons	$ 800.00	$ 450.00	$ 720.00	$ 2,100.00	$ 6,020.00
450 Patrons	$ 900.00	$ 506.25	$ 810.00	$ 2,362.50	$ 6,772.50

Total Sales

*These numbers are not actual; they are used to represent relative proportions for this case study.

When the rains ended and the summer of 2006 finally arrived, Mojitos, along with all of the local businesses, began to rebound. Mojitos introduced a number of original and successful campaigns, such as the "Face of Mojitos" (a ladies model search) and the "Saturday Showcase Series" (a biweekly performance of dances from around the world). These promotions helped to put Mojitos on top of the nightlife scene and the finances of the business were again stable. The first year of business ended on a record-breaking month of sales.

The Future of Mojitos

Jody is sipping on her morning coffee, reviewing the first year's numbers, and while satisfied with Mojitos' performance to date, she is still struggling with her short-term and long-term business-planning strategy. The fit with the projected numbers in the business plan to date was nearly perfect. But how could this be sustained and improved? How could business be transformed from the trendy place to go to a nightlife institution? Promotions have been the driving force behind business development, but are they enough? Has Mojitos reached a point where advertising is a viable option? Are any groups that could be targeted that are being neglected?

Sustainability

There doesn't seem to be an easy answer for how to both sustain and improve Mojitos in the next year. Jody and Eric covet the opportunity to move from trendy hot spot to nightlife institution, but it's unclear how to exactly get there. The market has changed and the competition has increased. The concept for Mojitos and the marketing has evolved accordingly so far, but it must continue to do so in order to capitalize on the explosive local and national Hispanic trends.

Partnership as Marriage

Ever present in Jody's mind is also the issue of succession planning not only for the overall business but also vis-à-vis her relationship with Eric. The decision is anything but binary in the sense that any number of options is possible either with or without Jody and Eric working as a pair.

NOTES

1. This case was prepared by Jody Mendoza, with assistance from Jeremy Bass, under the supervision of Boston College professor Gregory L. Stoller as the basis for class discussion rather than to illustrate either effective or ineffective handling of an administrative situation. Much of the demographic research in this case has been prepared using publicly available sources and cited as used.

   Copyright © 2007, Gregory L. Stoller. No part of this publication may be reproduced, stored in a retrieval system, used in a spreadsheet, or transmitted in any form or by any means—electronic, mechanical, photocopying, recording, or otherwise—without the permission of the author.

2. In the event of default by the debtor, the SBA guarantees repayment of the loan to the lender.

3. Defined by North American Industry Classification System (NAICS) code 7724.

4. Bucchioni, P., & Allen, K. (2015, January 14). *U.S. Census Bureau News*. Washington, DC: U.S. Department of Commerce. Retrieved February 6, 2015, from http://www.census.gov/retail/marts/www/marts_current.pdf

5. Ibid.

6. The Beverage Information Group [website]. (2015). Retrieved February 6, 2015, from http://albevre search.com/search/press+release+9/page/1/?s=press+release+9

7. Mintel Reports. (n.d.). Nightclubs — US — 2002. Retrieved February 12, 2015, from http://reports .mintel.com/display/1101/?__cc=1

8. Minehan, C. E. (2005, April 1). *The U.S. Economy: 2005 and beyond.* Boston, MA: Federal Reserve Bank of Boston. Retrieved February 11, 2015, from http://www.bos.frb.org/news/speeches/ cem/2005/040105.htm

9. Alcohol and drinking. (2015). Retrieved February 6, 2015, from http://www.gallup.com/poll/1582/ alcohol-drinking.aspx

10. Ibid.

11. City-Data.com. (2015). Boston, Massachusetts (MA): Accommodation, waste management, arts, entertainment & recreation, etc. Retrieved February 6, 2015, from http://www.city-data.com/business/ econ-Boston-Massachusetts.html

12. Schorow, S. (2012). *Drinking Boston: A history of the city and its spirits.* Gilsum, NH: Union Park Press.

13. BarMedia 1987 [website]. (2012). Retrieved February 6, 2015, from http://www.barmedia.com/pages/ amo/archive.htm#BACKBAR

14. Ibid.

15. The brew. (2009, May 1). *Nightclub & Bar Magazine.* Retrieved December 2012 from http://www .nightclub.com/the-brew/the-brew-may-2009

16. Therrien, M., & Ramirez, R. R. (2000). *The Hispanic population in the United States: March 2002.* Current Population Reports, P20-535. Washington, DC: U.S. Census Bureau.

17. Ahorre.com [website]. (2015). Retrieved February 6, 2015, from http://www.ahorre.com/compartido/

18. U.S. Census Bureau. (2015). State & country QuickFacts: USA. Retrieved February 6, 2015, from http:// quickfacts.census.gov/qfd/states/00000.html

19. *U.S. Hispanic Consumers in Transition*

20. Ibid.

21. Ibid.

22. Ahorre.com [website]. (2015). Retrieved February 6, 2015, from http://www.ahorre.com/compartido/

23. Mauricio Gaston Institute for Latino Community Development and Public Policy. (2004). *Advancing the Latino agenda*, p. 1. Boston, MA: Author.

24. Torres, A., & Chavez, L. (n.d.). Latinos in Massachusetts: An update. Retrieved February 6, 2015, from http://scholarworks.umb.edu/gaston_pubs/104/

25. CensusScope. (2000). Massachusetts ethnic and racial heritage. Retrieved February 6, 2015, from http://www.censusscope.org/us/s25/chart_ancestry.html

26. Census 2000, Boston Neighborhood Profile.

27. Ibid.

28. Mauricio Gaston Institute for Latino Community Development and Public Policy. (2004). *Advancing the Latino agenda*, p. 1. Boston, MA: Author.

29. Melnik, M. (2011, November 29). Demographic and socio-economic trends in Boston: What we've learned from the latest Census data. Retrieved February 6, 2015, from http://www.bostonredevelop mentauthority.org/getattachment/83972a7a-c454-4aac-b3eb-02e1fddd71e3/

30. Mishra, R. (2006, July 6). Record rainfall favors mold, health officials warn. Retrieved February 6, 2015, from http://www.boston.com/news/local/massachusetts/articles/2006/07/06/record_rainfall_favors_ mold_health_officials_warn/

Wiosna Association

Dominika Salwa, PhD,
assistant professor at Cracow University of Economics,

Malik Representative Poland

Artur Zipf, MA/Dipl. Psych.
associate partner, Head of Malik Poland[1]

Introduction

Four closely related and complex issues are relevant for every organization, whether it is business for profit, nonprofit nongovernmental organizations (NGOs), or public institutions: vision/mission, strategy, structure, and culture. Regardless of the direction of your organization, a manager needs to master these issues. One mistake in any of these areas can cost you and your organization time and can mean spending significantly more effort in moving toward success.

This case study focuses on the description of the development and structural transformation of the Wiosna Association—one of the three biggest and most well-known NGOs in Poland. Wiosna's potential was enormous. There was a high will to create value for society and a team with an enormous engagement to succeed, coupled with a set of challenges (e.g., financial or structural problems) that NGOs typically face. Wiosna's vision has the power to change the hearts of human beings—and this is something worth living or even fighting for.

Figure 1	Jacek Stryczek, Founder and Chairman of the Wiosna Association

SOURCE: Photo provided by http://www.wiosna.org.pl/.

The Starting Point

It is the late summer 1999, and Jacek Stryczek, a tall, fit guy who is usually dressed in sportswear, is riding his old bicycle around the main square in Cracow. As always, he is deep in thought. A very creative and active individual, Jacek finds it difficult to relax, but this is what keeps him looking forward to what can be done to make this world a better place to be.

Tons of ideas are keeping his mind busy and running around his head faster than he can ride his bicycle—and Jacek is passionate about cycling. He constantly kept thinking about the following questions: "What is it that really bothers the people who come to see me? What is their heart saying? Where do their problems come from?

What do they really need?" According to Jacek, "So many people open their soul to me, and all I can give them is a few short words of advice. That's already something, but it's too little to really make a difference in their daily lives."

Jacek is someone who always tries to find a solution when analyzing the issue at hand. Very focused on his vocation, he tries to go beyond what others do and think. Some might be even taken back by his provocative and, at times, almost insurgent attitude.

On one occasion, this Catholic priest arranged the opportunity to confess right in front of a famous shopping mall—at Christmas time—to make shoppers aware that there is more to life than just Christmas and shopping. He always wanted to reach out to people and listen more closely to their needs instead of waiting for them to come to see him. He was the one who took the initiative, who reached out and offered his hand. He soon discovered that this was not enough, except for generating interest by the media for one day.

Then the thoughts running around in his head finally came together. "I've got it! There is something to it! I know it for sure," he kept repeating to himself. "The people who come to me, whoever they are, whatever they do, have two main things in common, even if they are not completely aware of it. The first one is a need for spirituality and to surpass oneself. The second is a need to support others. I want to take those needs further. This will be my field of activity."

As he had learned from his previous actions, he could not do it alone. Strength is to be found in a group. But how to get started and what could be realistically done? All he had was a strong will, a more or less clear idea of what he wanted to achieve, and a group of students he met with every Thursday—one of many Christian academic societies.

Jacek shared his vision with those young students and asked them to help him bring his idea to fruition. The students agreed, feeling that together, there was real power to do something really good and precious. The spirit of action and the group dynamic started to take off with a shared vision; this and the strength of impact would become one of the strongest aspects of this informal team brought together through Jacek.

With the first snow, before Christmas time, the students met with poor families living in the area southwest of Cracow and asked them about their needs. This gave them the information they needed to be able to respond adequately.

The first calls made to friends and people who were open enough to help resulted in a package for Christmas for those in need. They learned that the gifts needed to be new, not old; new items showed respect to human decorum, despite one's personal and financial situation. This aspect changes both the giver and the receiver.

Thirty packages were handed out in 2001. "I will never forget the faces of those who received the gifts; they had tears in their eyes," said Ewa, one of the students who took part in the initiative. "This was also important to me; it is something that has changed me personally," she added. This first face-to-face initiative gave many people a new outlook on the world and their way of living.

Moving Forward

The idea of the face-to-face initiative became a kind of project in itself and started to expand. A need for better coordination of the event became critical. It became clear to everyone that the primary need was to develop a more formal structure to the actions taking place.

In February 2001, a team consisting of Jacek, Ewa, Beata, Iwona, and 11 other members signed the founding articles, creating the *Stowarzyszenie Wiosna* (Spring Association). It was later registered under number 00000 50905 in the Polish register of companies and associations

Figure 2	The logo of the Wiosna Association and Wiosna's Most Well-Known Brands, *Szlachetna Paczka* (Noble Parcel) and *Akademia Przyszłości* (Academy for the Future)

SOURCE: Photo provided by http://www.wiosna.org.pl/.

(KRS). The nerve center for coordination of the association's activities was established at one of the flats where Ewa was living. The company used several logos, as indicated in the logos in Figure 2.

A dozen people started to work on the face-to-face campaign, changing its name first to Christmas Parcel and finally to Noble Parcel. Ewa coordinated all the volunteers. A lot of hard work and long hours went into managing operations in those early days. To make phone calls, Ewa had to go outside, close to her block, to one of the many kiosks. Mobile phones, still a new technology in Poland, were expensive and not yet in use in everyday life in 2001.

Acting under a clear identity, the Wiosna Association provided solutions to many formal problems, but new challenges soon started to appear. Noble Parcel grew from 30 families in 2001 to 100 in 2002. The number of volunteers rose threefold to 33 people. The flat became a major problem in 2002: the challenging conditions, too little space to work, noise, and internal difficulties working together started to put people's nerves on edge and slow down the work being performed. The uncomfortable working conditions made it important to find a larger office. Jacek and Ewa searched to find something, but limited funds made this difficult.

Then there was a ray of light. Marcin, a volunteer who worked for one of the biggest companies in Poland, decided to ask his boss for a room for Wiosna. The company agreed to the idea. In 2003, Wiosna had its own office that was big enough with space to work; it started with one room and ended with three. This was a breakthrough for Wiosna: Extraordinary growth of over 100% started to be the norm. In the period of 2002–2004, the number of volunteers grew sixfold from 33 to 200, while there was a fivefold growth in the number of packages from 100 to 510. The whole organization consisted of three full-time employees and around 200 volunteers.

This rate of growth needed support, not only at an organizational level but also at an operational and financial level. If Wiosna could not find the necessary funds for its internal organization, there would be no way to survive.

Jacek finally decided to ask his friends for financial help, believing that people wanted to support initiatives that made sense. He understood that some people had money and wanted to help, but did not have time to do it themselves. In 2004, Jacek created a "Club 100" that connected his friends with people who understood the idea behind Wiosna's intelligent way of providing aid. Due to their financial help, Wiosna was able to survive. The problem of financing would, however, arise again a couple of times in the future. The financial problems Wiosna encountered caused the employees to be open-minded and look for assistance from a wide range of sources. They applied for and obtained grants from the City of Cracow and from the Norwegian Funds and carefully monitored the European Funds.

First Successes

The foundation for Wiosna's Noble Parcel was finally in place. The system allowed donors to choose the family they wanted to help and the volunteers that were looking for families. Everyone saw the outcome of the time and effort invested. This was a solid basis to start implementing new ideas that were occurring all around. This was especially important, given that the Noble Parcel did not yet totally fill the societal needs.

The key success factor of the Noble Parcel was meeting on a multilayered level. Donors physically met those who needed support, becoming engaged in the whole process. First, volunteers identified families that needed help. Then, a message would be posted on the Internet so that a donor could choose right from the outset who they wanted to help. They could choose either a family or a single person, and the amount of support was calculated based on the description of the family's needs. The donor then took care of buying the things required. Sometimes, donors organized themselves as a group of up to 30 people to collect money and buy the goods.

"I will never forget the face of the family to which we brought a Noble Parcel. The six children of a single mother were so happy to see new gifts—jeans, a football, a fridge, a vacuum cleaner. They were so grateful—it was unforgettable," said Mat, one of the donors, after organizing the package.

The success and growth of the Noble Parcel made Wiosna's staff think about another initiative. Jacek clearly wanted to extend the parcel initiative outside Cracow to the rest of the Voivodeship and even throughout Poland. At first, even his own staff did not believe this vision to be real. Slowly they understood and started to think about how it could be achieved. The solution was at hand, as hope, will, and commitment grew.

Another thing that was needed was to extend Wiosna's power to change the unchangeable—the human mentality: the way people think, feel, and act. It became clear that to change the world, the mindset of the individual needed to be changed. Influencing the human mentality through actions and projects as well as publications and essays in the media became an important issue for Jacek and Wiosna.

Helping families once a year with the Noble Parcel was not enough. The Noble Parcel was a starting point to help people believe that change is possible. While this would be hard to achieve, when you saw the children in those families, there was hope. These children were mostly open-minded, but no one believed in them. Some had learning difficulties and probably had never heard a good word said about them. They were usually withdrawn and needed positive support.

In 2003–2004, Wiosna started to arrange individual meetings with children from families who received Noble Parcels. This work needed to be more specifically structured. Jacek asked Ania—the current human resources director, but that time, a young Polish language teacher connected to the students' group—to prepare a substantial plan for this project.

The resulting plan, based on close individual collaboration between volunteers and the child throughout the school year, was soon in place. The idea finally materialized into a bigger project called the *Akademia Przyszłości* (the Academy for the Future).

Starting in 2003–2004, from one school with 30 children and 15 volunteers, the Academy for the Future became one of Wiosna's leading projects. The value of the first project was estimated to be 37,500 PLN (Polish złoty). Within 11 years, it increased to 1.7 million PLN.

The work of Noble Parcel and the Academy for the Future was based on volunteers. Wiosna's staff and volunteers quickly discovered the potential of these young people. Once the needs of the market were identified, Wiosna, together with other associations, organized meetings and conferences. The goal was to gain a specific knowledge of the potential and the kind of needs to make the most out of that potential. Sharing knowledge made it possible to create standards, expectations, and responsibilities within the setup of the organization.

Wiosna knew that to be effective and efficient, every solution needed to be designed in a systemic way. Wiosna's core competence and abilities were created by building a systemic approach and putting in place the right tools for action. Over time, this became one of the key success factors in Wiosna's performance.

This strong growth caused financing to be a significant problem. Wiosna's team started to look for every opportunity to obtain the funds needed. In 2004–2005, Wiosna won grants to further expand its projects. The Polish Ministry of Employment and Social Policy's *Fundusz Inicjatyw Obywatelskich* (Citizen Initiatives Fund) supported the Noble Parcel. The Academy for the Future received seven grants from different sources. However, as the projects continued to grow, additional financial resources were required. Grants started to be taken more seriously, with one person designated to be responsible for that area. With Poland's accession to the European Union in 2004, a lot of opportunities started to open up. There was the possibility of obtaining grants not only from the Polish government but also from European Funds.

External Growth

In 2006–2013, Wiosna continued to grow rapidly. At the end of 2006, they moved into new premises (150 sq. m) on ul. Starowiślna in Crakow, the first of their relocations. At this time, there were four full-time employees and almost 740 volunteers. In 2008–2009, a new project was launched: the Leaders of Wiosna. Its goal was to standardize the qualifications of volunteers and employees and determine their ability to manage a team and achieve results. The project for 30 people took two years; after the training, seven individuals decided to work for Wiosna.

In 2010, a new department for projects and development was created mainly to focus on fundraising to secure Wiosna's activities. An extension of the Wiosna's reach was planned. As part of the development of the Noble Parcel and Academy for the Future, Wiosna provided systemic qualifications and know-how to enable people to change, develop, and help each other. This led to the launch of three more projects focusing on the topic of unemployment: *Telekariera* (Tele-career) in 2010 and *Absolwent idzie do pracy* (Graduate Goes to Work) and *50+ Dojrzali, Potrzebni, Kompetentni* (50+ Mature. Valuable. Competent) in 2013. Tele-career was designed for disabled people, Graduate for humanities alumni, and 50+ for people over 50 years old who needed to work and were long-term unemployed. These three projects had a value of nearly 8 million PLN in 2013. Financing began with a grant to start the implementation. Getting a grant is not easy, as competition between applications is high. While Wiosna thought it had the necessary competences in place to apply, it needed to organize itself internally to be able to undertake the grant successfully.

While an idea is a good starting point, the success factors include hard work in implementing the idea and obtaining financial resources. In 2010, the question of "to be or not to be" occurred once again.

Jacek risked the last of his money to secure more funds. He put his trust in an initiative proposed by Kuba, a young creative director, who for over a year had been working on developing the department for public relations (PR) and marketing. Kuba, due to his extensive network of contacts, was able to get access to Jerzy Dudek—one of Poland's top goalkeepers, who was at the time playing for Real Madrid—and encouraged him to donate a Noble Parcel. Using the last of the funds at Wiosna's disposal, Kuba flew to Madrid to make a video clip featuring the Real Madrid team (including Cristiano Ronaldo, who was a very well-known figure in Poland as well) donating a Noble Parcel as well. The film was a real hit. It was shown in the Polish media and received extensive recognition. This excellent idea kicked off a new phase of development in Wiosna; through its partnerships with celebrities, Wiosna was able to create a new brand and wider brand recognition throughout Poland.

| **Figure 3** | Sports Celebrities Promoting Wiosna (from left to right): Jerzy Dudek, Robert Lewandowski, Natalia Partyka |

SOURCE: Photos provided by http://www.wiosna.org.pl/.

Many people began to recognize the value in Wiosna's system of providing help and even celebrities started to support the effort. By the middle of 2014, Wiosna had contacts with about 80 celebrities, including Adrian Zieliński (winner of an Olympic gold medal in London, weightlifter), Julia Kamińska and Basia Kurdej Szatan (Polish actresses), and even Pope Benedict XVI and the Polish presidential couple (Bronisław and Anna Komorowski) supported Wiosna. Ania and Robert Lewandowski (Poland's most well-known striker, who plays in the Bundesliga for Bayern Munich) gave a public show of support by organizing a Noble Parcel and later by contributing donations collected at their wedding, which funded several dozen student report index cards for the Academy for the Future Children.[2]

Krystian, PR coordinator, indicated that "in general, celebrities play an important role in the building of Wiosna's PR. We take care of them. They are the 'face' of our winning identity. Such celebrities are examples of how to win, how to fight for one's own future. It is not easy but, step by step, everybody can be a winner in the end. And celebrities are evidence of that."

In the meantime, Wiosna continued to develop very personal and extensive contacts with business people who supported Wiosna in different ways (financial, cobranding, knowledge sharing, information technology [IT] systems). There were well over 50 companies that collaborated on an ongoing basis. Jacek commented, "I love people who are successful in business; I love millionaires, especially those with open hearts." He knows these people have the influence not only to impact change but also to generate funds, to provide the know-how, and to support and share the association's values. Wiosna managed to multiply each 1 PLN invested by six times. Jacek published items regularly in newspapers and created a blog: the Blog for Millionaires: Present and Future. In appreciation of his work, in 2012, Jacek received an award from the Polish Business Council for outstanding results in the category of Social Activity. In 2013, he was appointed as Magellan of the Year winner in a business contest that looks for people similar to Magellan, making a significant difference in today's society.

At Wiosna, Kuba received the title of Marketing Director of the Year in 2013 as the culmination of campaigns (Social Campaign 2011 for *Real'na pomoc: Szlachetna Paczka* in 2010), initiatives (Best Initiative 2011: "100% from 1%"), and a series of other awards won by his team (PRoton Award in 2011).

2013: Facts and Figures

At the end of 2013, Wiosna had two strong brands, 63 employees, over 10,000 volunteers, and several proven systems (a training system, a volunteer system, and a concept for personal change). Wiosna had won grants for the Noble Parcel and the Academy for the Future for a cumulative value of 3.5 million PLN; had 2,000 regular donors; received over 1.9 million PLN in support from companies; had 711 publications in newspapers and 2,891 publications on the Internet; and had 318 appearances on television, 7,291 appearances in social media, and 761 appearances on radio (see Graphs 1, 2, and 3).

Graph 1	The Noble Parcel in Numbers in 2013

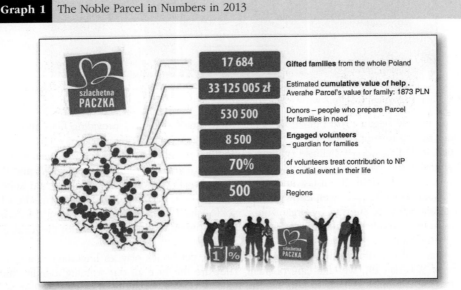

SOURCE: Data from the Wiosna Association

Internal Paralysis

While moving to third place in the rankings of the most well-known NGOs was a nice validation of Wiosna's work, its internal organizational system seemed to be overloaded. There was a lot to do. In the 10 years of Wiosna's rapid growth, many processes had been implemented and had grown rapidly as well. Like every fast-growing organization, Wiosna needed to rethink its growth and the structure in place.

"Now we need to organize differently; we need internal reorganization, otherwise our current structure will paralyze us. We need to rebuild our ship," said Jacek at a management meeting in the beginning of 2013.

Each of the 10 leadership team members of the main divisions agreed, having felt the problems for a longer period of time. Although almost every meeting lasted over two hours, a feeling of low output remained, creating a need for further meetings. The meetings were often interrupted—things

| Graph 2 | Growth of Academy for the Future in 2013 |

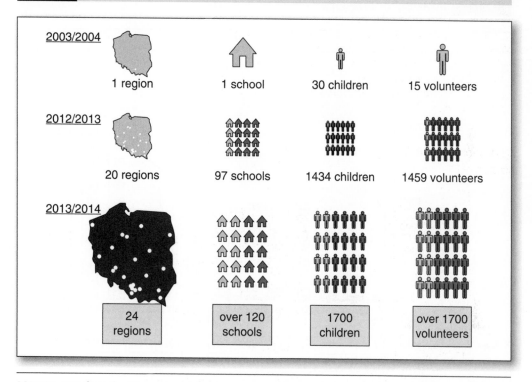

2003/2004			
1 region	1 school	30 children	15 volunteers
2012/2013			
20 regions	97 schools	1434 children	1459 volunteers
2013/2014			
24 regions	over 120 schools	1700 children	over 1700 volunteers

SOURCE: Data from the Wiosna Association

were interfering, and too many working parties and teams were involved. There was a need for a larger number of assistants and coordinators; jobs turned out to be non-jobs. Constant discussions about trans-divisional working seemed to indicate a solution.

While employees and managers focused on Wiosna's ideas and values, they all felt overloaded at the same time. The staff replacement factor was quite high (20%).

Critical for keeping that crew together were Jacek's strong values, which he had embedded in the hearts of the people who helped to create such a strong culture of dedicating time and effort to something as meaningful as Wiosna. The basis for Jacek's philosophy and vision was the WIO personality, a combination of *Wspólnota Indywidualności Otwartych* (Community of Open Individuals)—individuals who fought for ideas, made decisions, took responsibility, and created something; they were creators who challenged themselves. They all believed that openness is written in love, particularly if one opens oneself up to others; this became the starting point for change.

While everyone in Wiosna was WIO, everyone who collaborated with Wiosna was also WIO, as Jacek didn't want to collaborate with people who were not WIO. Once he had a meeting with the CEO of one of Poland's biggest companies to get funds for development. After one hour of waiting in a corridor, he said, "I do not want to collaborate with him. He is too proud; he is not WIO." Jacek simply left the office. The approach Jacek decided on did not allow for compromises.

The strategy and structure of Wiosna worked because of the culture that was created. Jacek saw some problems occurring and started to look for solutions. "Find me someone who can help

| Graph 3 | Growth of Employment and Volunteers of the Academy for the Future and the Noble Parcel, 2001–2013 |

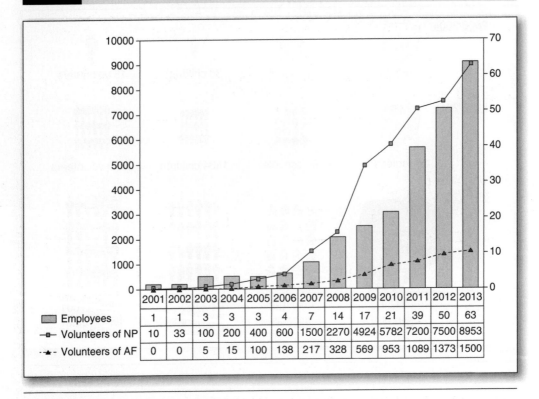

	2001	2002	2003	2004	2005	2006	2007	2008	2009	2010	2011	2012	2013
Employees	1	1	3	3	3	4	7	14	17	21	39	50	63
Volunteers of NP	10	33	100	200	400	600	1500	2270	4924	5782	7200	7500	8953
Volunteers of AF	0	0	5	15	100	138	217	328	569	953	1089	1373	1500

SOURCE: Data from the Wiosna Association

us. If no one seems to have adequate knowledge about the structure, I will create it myself," Jacek mentioned to Agata, who was responsible for coordinating the board office. To find a solution, contacts were made with companies collaborating with Wiosna. As Jacek was chosen a Magellan of the Year 2012, as mentioned above, he opened up to Malik Switzerland, a world-leading company involved in holistic general management, leadership, and governance solutions. This Swiss-based company was the patron of that contest from 2011 to 2013. First contacts between Malik and Wiosna were built, and as general management was something that Wiosna needed in the actual situation, contacts were established and intensified.

Key leaders of Wiosna took part in the first workshop, and an agreement was reached on the structural issues and the general management approach to be adapted, along with the accompanying strategy, structure, and culture that made up Wiosna.

Viable System Model

The Viable System Model (VSM) is a model for structure that was invented by Professor Stafford Beer, a cyberneticist who was known for his ability to create models on the basis of natural science. Carefully studying the human body and the central nervous system, he designed a system model that was appropriate for organizations that are meant to be and stay viable, flexible, and ready to change and adapt. At first glance, VSM differed fundamentally from typical organizational charts (see Graph 4).

In the workshop, the differences among A, B, C, and D were explained and discussed intensively. Typical organizational charts do not show the real functioning of a system, as they do not

Graph 4	Viable System Model by Professor Stafford Beer in Comparison to Typical Organizational Charts

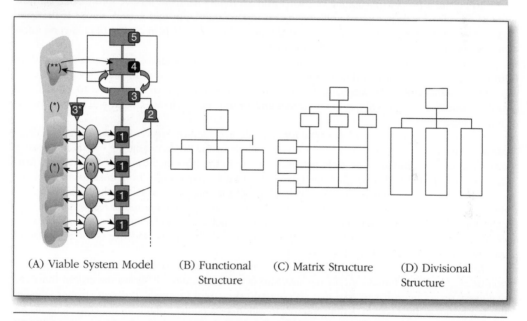

(A) Viable System Model (B) Functional Structure (C) Matrix Structure (D) Divisional Structure

SOURCE: Data from Malik (presented at the workshop on October 10, 2013)

show the power and impact of the client and the environment in which the organization operates. Conventional organization charts show the surface structure of an organization. The structures appear static and do not indicate real interconnections that allow one to understand how the organization actually functions. The VSM itself focuses on the "Deepstructure" and how an organization needs to be designed in order to function at its best, to cope with the environment in place as well as to create customer value[3] by focusing on the organization generating this value.

The Viable System Model[4] consists of five basic systems, all of which are necessary and sufficient for the viability of an organization. System 1 (S1) to System 5 (S5) need to be in place for a proper functioning of different areas in any kind of organization.

The basic element, the S1, represents the operational units. It illustrates the current organization and management and the organizational work that needs to be done to serve the chosen market segment with defined products/services that the organization is responsible for.

In many cases, organizations have more than one S1, which enables them to look for synergies within the operational forces. For example, in franchise systems, the franchise holder has to act on the basis of rules given by the franchiser on how the S1 should be organized, creating rules for a proper functioning of the organization within the S1 forces. All the rules that are created are organized in the S2. The S2 is responsible for all the rules that enable and ensure a proper functioning of the S1s. These might be rules for communication, staffing, factoring, knowledge organization, rules for behavior, and so on.

The S3 illustrates all the items that are needed to secure a friction-free operative management. Its representatives are responsible for the proper functioning of the S1 and S2, ensuring that the S3 achieves and maximizes its desired purposes within a defined environment and secures a proper allocation of all relevant resources (time, money, people, assets). In practice, the chief operational officer leads this function alongside a minimum number of people responsible for the S1 results.

To ensure a proper functioning of the S1 and S2, the S3 needs to receive information on how the S1 is really doing (not necessarily relying on reports only). For that reason, the S3 is designed as and accomplishes the role of a kind of real-time auditor. The S3 is in charge of collecting information, not corrective action within the organization.

Systems 1–3 are therefore responsible for the current functioning of the organization and for fulfilling the tasks for which the organization was created. They cover all the relevant issues of operative management. However, to function properly, each organization needs to look ahead and ask questions: How will our environment and/or the clients change? What will be their needs in the future?

For that reason, the S4 is responsible for strategic management issues. It ensures that the organization invents, creates, and responds to future needs of the environment. Its role is forecasting, investigating, and examining possible activities for the future (this might include innovations, markets, or both in a defined area). The time perspective of that system varies from business to business.

The last crucial system is the S5, which keeps all the other functions together. The S5 covers the normative management both within and outside of the organization and is responsible for the cohesion of the whole organization. It is a result of the behavior and feeling of personal affiliation of employees. The S5 needs to professionally balance the short-term perspective of the S1 (present) and the long-term perspective of the S4 (future).

In the case of the VSM, one can use it either for diagnosing the viability of an existing organization or as a reference framework for the structure of an organization. It shows the crucial functions that every organization has to take into account and design for its needs. It doesn't matter whether this is a business organization, a nonprofit organization, or a public institution, the core elements for good functioning of a whole system are always the same: the five systems that need to be mastered in a specific way to allow the organization to execute its best purpose described (see Graph 5).

A long-term viability of an organization of any kind is based on the principle of recursion. This means that each S1 represents all S1–5 systems parameters in order to remain viable.

Wiosna Structural Diagnosis

The basic information on the VSM caused Wiosna's core people to intensify their reflection about its structural issues (Graph 6). Until now, it was seen as a functional/matrix structure interconnected with projects. In addition to the perception that Wiosna did not function properly, it was difficult to exchange views about the way the whole organization was functioning. The current structure and its units (see Graph 6) needed to rethink its functions in accordance with the whole organization, instead of optimizing the tasks and duties of each unit.

After being given a set of reflecting questions alongside the VSM, Jacek and the leadership team began to perceive themselves in a more transparent way: "Now I understand my function in accordance to the whole—Jacek wants me to be responsible for S3 for a more flexible functioning of the Wiosna system," said Agata, who was at that time the newly recruited coordinator of the board office.

Graph 5 VSM: A Description of the Five Systems and Their Interplay

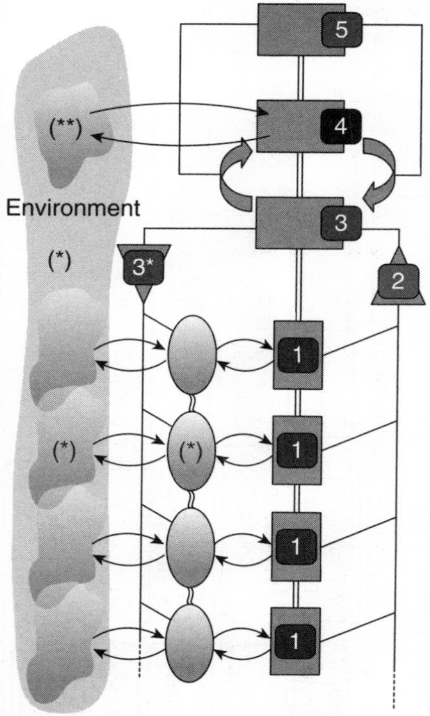

System 5:
Normative Management
Ensures values, identity, mission, vision and basic principles

System 4:
Strategic Mangement
Ensures the success in the future. Choses strategic options, invest in future success.

System 3:
Operative Management
Ensures the proper functioning of the organization in its present state, takes care for improvements and current success.

System 2:
Coordination
Functions that are responsible for coordination of the autonomously acting units (S1).

System 3*:
Audit
Collects information from operative units (S1) working with and for the client (S1) to be able to improve operational management and better adapt to the environment.

System 1:
Operative Units
Autonomous Units that serve and support and depends on certain part (clients/segment) of the market (environment). The number of S1 depends of the number of market segments which needs to be served differently.

Environment
Everything that influences the functioning of organization, especially clients.

SOURCE: Adapted version based on data from Malik

Graph 6 Current Structure of Wiosna

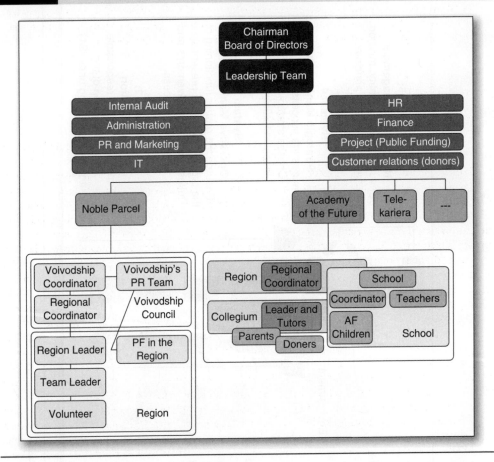

SOURCE: Data from the Wiosna Association

Jacek was inspired by the different perspective that the VSM offered and started to reflect on market issues. Besides "the big picture" of Wiosna's organization and management, key organizational blockages became clear to the leadership team.

From a functional perspective, it became clear that Jacek was the driving force and ruled the game, as he was the brain of the organization and the only driving force in the S5. He also played a main role in the S4 and S3 as well as in the S2, as their rules were defined by the top level. Jacek's intention was to slowly withdraw his strong presence from the S3, giving his people more responsibility for making their own decisions. Crucial topics needed to be managed more independently by more people.

The VSM revealed and unlocked some facts about the concept of responsibility within Wiosna. It enabled the leadership team to think in terms of their functions and to consider which decisions needed to be taken in accordance to their specific contribution to the whole. It became clear that specific roles and responsibilities for each of the TOP leaders and their departments needed to be established in the S1–S5 logic.

Right after the workshop, Jacek decided that Wiosna would implement the core aspects of the VSM. Agata was appointed to take responsibility and initiative for the structural change ahead of Wiosna.

Artur appreciated Jacek's approach to speed up the VSM implementation in a self-guided, responsible way. Malik, from this point on, took on the role of a sparring partner for further organizational developments that were carried out by representatives of the Wiosna team.

Identification of Markets and Setup of Key Structural Ideas

Wiosna's top leaders started to discuss all the structural issues in the logic of the VSM and began to rebuild Wiosna's organizational structure. A first key decision was the reduction of people in the S3 function to five. This enabled faster decision making and shorter and more result-oriented meetings.

A few weeks later, Jacek, in his S4 responsibility, prepared a presentation on what he saw as Wiosna's markets and relevant environment. He examined 11 core markets in which the organization operated. They were (1) an ideas market, which was always important to Jacek personally and that aimed to change the mind of society; (2) a direct material-aid market for families in need, through which Noble Parcel operated; (3) a children's direct-aid market, which focused on children who needed attention and had the Academy for the Future to fulfill that gap; (4) direct aid for the unemployed market, focusing on young or older people who wanted to work but had problems with finding a job, which was supported by Wiosna's projects (Tele-career, Graduate Goes to Work, and 50+ Mature. Valuable. Competent); (5) a grants market, which opened the space and possibility for NGOs such as Wiosna to obtain financing; (6) a business-to-business market for those companies that wanted to socially engage, collaborate, and support NGOs; (7) a financial aid market for those who wanted to share finances and donate to Wiosna's work; (8) a media, communications, and brand-awareness market, with all the PR actions building social trust toward Wiosna's activity and actions; (9) a market of good-hearted millionaires, decision makers, and celebrities who were influential and had the power to influence others through their behavior; (10) an employee market, made up of all those who were looking for a job and were potential employees of Wiosna; and (11) a volunteer market (usually made up of young people who want to do something) that shared time and skills to get experience. Jacek also thought about a twelfth relevant market: a services and sales market, as Wiosna had started to think about opening e-shops for some of their gadgets.

For the first time, Wiosna gained clarity concerning its markets. Based on this segmentation, the leadership team and Jacek started to derive functionally motivated consequences to the internal organization that were discussed and decided upon. Key insights of Wiosna were based on the VSM. This are summarized on Graph 7.

Based on her new assignment, Agata began to incorporate the VSM. Being responsible for auditing (S3)—what was really important for further development within Wiosna—she encouraged feedback loops within Wiosna concerning processes as well as people who had tasks to fulfill. She consciously accessed information to improve the functioning of the company as well as to make contributions by donors easier. Agata, with the support of the leadership team and Jacek, organized Wiosna's viability on a management system level, practically reshaping the organization by using information that had been collected in advance to check on the level the principle of recursiveness that was in place within Wiosna.

The challenge became clearer as people began to understand that they needed to put departmental thinking aside for the sake of a better interplay in the markets outside Wiosna. Another core insight was understanding that different people in the organization could and partly needed to serve several functions (e.g., S5 & S4; S1, S2, & S3). The discussion focus changed from optimizing

Graph 7 A Brief Look at the Wiosna VSM

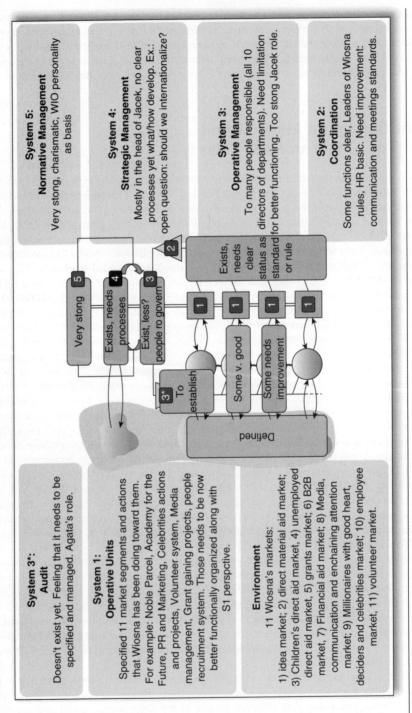

System 5:
Normative Management
Very stong, charismatic, WIO personality as basis

System 4:
Strategic Management
Mostly in the head of Jacek, no clear processes yet what/how develop. Ex.: open question: should we internationalize?

System 3:
Operative Management
To many people responsible (all 10 directors of departments). Need limitation for better functioning. Too strong Jacek role.

System 2:
Coordination
Some functions olear, Leaders of Wiosna rules, HR basic. Need improvement: communication and meetings standards.

System 3*:
Audit
Doesn't exist yet. Feeling that it needs to be specified and managed. Agata's role.

System 1:
Operative Units
Specified 11 market segments and actions that Wiosna has been doing toward them. For example: Noble Parcel, Academy for the Future, PR and Marketing, Celebrities actions and projects, Volunteer system, Media management, Grant gaining projects, people recruitment system. Those needs to be now better functionally organized along with S1 perspective.

Environment
11 Wiosna's markets:
1) idea market; 2) direct material aid market; 3) Children's direct aid market; 4) unemployed direct aid market, 5) grants market; 6) B2B market, 7) Financial aid market; 8) Media, communication and enchaining attention market; 9) Millionaires with good heart, deciders and celebrities market; 10) employee market, 11) volunteer market.

SOURCE: Elaboration done by the authors based on data from Malik

departmental issues to what the function of a specific department for a certain market was and what it needed to offer in terms of a specific customer value to be generated and taken care of by the different market segments. Discussing these kinds of questions began to show its first effects. Wiosna's people start to discuss decisions that needed to be made from a market-oriented perspective. This more radical customer-driven way of thinking led to organizational adaptions and a more functional point of view in which different departments understood themselves as part of a value chain that needed contributions from different systems in order to create, keep, and develop customer value. Today, all functions and departments are reviewed in order to align their activities in a meaningful way (e.g., controlling/finance, HR, project organization, IT, etc.).

What does it mean for the HR department to recruit the right people for Wiosna from the volunteer market? From an S2 perspective, the HR department needs (in addition to their function in hiring the right WIO people) to run the personnel development and administration in the entire organization in a consistent, coordinated way to help the organization speed up relevant personnel decisions. Based on the examples given, Wiosna moved a decisive step forward in creating a more viable and therefore more robust structure that allowed it to further realize its vision of making the world a better place by changing society's mentality continuously.

Today, Wiosna has started to professionalize its leadership team and management system consciously by providing objectives to responsible key people that are aligned with the identified market opportunities and needs. The discussion, based on the VSM logic on how to align the organization, has been kicked off and a higher maturity level of what the organization is capable of implementing was achieved in a first crucial step.

There is a lot of work still to be done, and the good news is that Jacek and his leadership team are fully aware of this. Wiosna is facing—as a consequence of its tremendous success and constant ambition over the years—deep changes as Jacek and his leadership team aim for sustainability and viability in all they do; the ambition of the people that are creating Wiosna on an everyday basis makes one confident to believe that they will manage the upcoming challenges successfully.

NOTES

1. This case is based on the real story of the Stowarzyszenie Wiosna (Spring Association), and its collaboration with Malik Switzerland, that offered their concepts to Wiosna in order to support the further organizational development of this highly ambitious NGO. It draws upon the well-proven managerial knowledge of Malik Switzerland and Fredmund Malik's books on management and leadership as relevant sources for inspiration. For more information, see http://www.wiosna.org.pl and http://www.malik-management.com. The authors would like to thank the Wiosna Association and Malik Switzerland. At Wiosna, special thanks go to Jacek Stryczek, founder and chairman of Wiosna Association, as well as to Agata Brataniec, Anna Żaczek, Anna Woźniak, Anna Wilczyńska, and Krystian Stopka for their critical input and long interviews. In the case of Malik, special thanks go to Fredmund Malik, founder and chairman of Malik Switzerland, as well as to Peter Worth, Hannes Timischl, and Peter Pattis for their support.

2. The Academy for the Future student report index cards are part of the Academy for the Future idea, allowing students to keep a record of their successes and their results while working with their tutors. Funding an index card provides a student access to the Academy for the Future and provides support for the volunteer tutor.

3. For Wiosna, *customer* means donors, donators, families in needs, celebrities, media, alumni, and members of the 50+ group.

4. Adapted from Malik, C. (2010). *Ahead of change: How crowd psychology and cybernetics transform the way we govern*. New York, NY: Campus Verlag.

Sedo.com

Christian Koropp and Dietmar Grichnik

*When starting a company, it is probably the right thing not to think about an exit at all
and instead simply focus on growing the company, but it is at least a valid question to ask
yourself once a year.*

—Tim Schumacher, CEO of Sedo

Introduction

On a lukewarm spring evening in 2006, Tim Schumacher, Ulrich Priesner, Ulrich Essmann, and
Marius Wuerzner, the founders of Sedo GmbH,[1] sat together at a Boston restaurant to discuss the
future of their organization. Sedo, a German company with offices in both Germany and the United
States, had experienced enormous growth in the 7 years since its inception in 2000 and had become
the world's leading online marketplace for domain names. Despite this success, the company's
founders were faced with a challenging decision. They had invested all their private wealth in the
company, and were now contemplating the benefits of moderating their personal risk by partially
divesting from "their" business.

Background

Sedo—an acronym for "search engine for domain offers"—was born from a youthful endeavor of
Tim Schumacher, Ulrich Priesner, and Marius Wuerzner. The three knew each other from their
school days when they developed a soccer management simulation called Offensiv. They sold this
game over the Internet, and bought the domain name offensiv.de to support it.

After finishing school, the three young men attended university in different parts of Germany.
Tim Schumacher studied business administration in Cologne. Ulrich Priesner studied computer
engineering in Mannheim. Marius Wuerzner studied history and philosophy in Freiburg. The time
commitment needed for their studies ended the Offensiv project. The three friends, however, still
owned the domain offensiv.de. It was at this time that they asked themselves: "What can we do
with this unused domain name?" The idea to develop a marketplace for used domain names was
born and they spent hour after hour outside of their studies to bring their idea to fruition.

AUTHORS' NOTE: This case study was prepared by Christian Koropp under the supervision of Professor
Dietmar Grichnik. It is based on publicly available data and on a personal interview with Tim Schumacher, CEO
and cofounder of Sedo, in May 2007.

SOURCE: © Christian Koropp/Dietmar Grichnik 2007.

In September 1999, the three students created an official partnership to formalize their endeavor and launched their first website to garner feedback from the Internet community. The industry's first offer/counteroffer system enabling domain name buyers and sellers to negotiate directly with each other was now a reality. Despite a lack of marketing, it did not take long for users to begin registering their used domain names.

In early 2000, the young entrepreneurs decided to invest more of their time and money into the business. They booked banner advertisements on websites and cultivated relationships with the press. This occurred at the height of "Internet hype," leading to an overwhelming response from the media and the Internet community. The contacts they gained during this time were invaluable: potential business partners, investors, and future competitors.

One of these competitors was Ulrich Essmann, a medical student working on a project similar to Sedo. He had already acquired the sizable customer base that Sedo lacked. After assessing Sedo's potential, Essmann decided to join the Sedo venture. The Sedo founders, now including Essmann, quickly began negotiations with potential investors.

Negotiations were arduous, as the dot-com crisis was now in full effect. The men persevered, however, and in February 2001 they succeeded in finding a major investor. United Internet, AG[2] (together with their subsidiary 1&1 Internet, AG), at that time Germany's largest registrar for domain names, took a minority stake in the newly founded Sedo GmbH. With a strong and experienced investor backing them, Sedo began offering services in all areas of domain name trading, still not yet foreseeing the tremendous growth ahead.

Sedo's Ownership Structure

Significant changes in Sedo's ownership have occurred in the organization's short history. The first major change was a conversion from the original founded partnership to a limited partnership, Sedo GmbH. The second major change occurred when United Internet AG bought 41% of Sedo GmbH for nearly €400,000 while also providing a shareholder's loan. The remaining 59% of shares was still owned by the four founders. This was preserved as a strategic move by both parties.

At the beginning of 2004, United Internet implemented its call option that was agreed upon in the 2001 investment package. As previously arranged, United Internet bought an additional 10% of Sedo's shares for €575,000 (United Internet, 2004). This deal made the company's four founders minority shareholders of their own business. Despite the restructuring, the purchase did not change the everyday functioning of the business. With the new investment, Tim Schumacher, Ulrich Priesner, Ulrich Essmann, and Marius Wuerzner were even more motivated to realize Sedo's global potential.

Only 15 months later, in April 2005, United Internet restructured its own company portfolio. The 51% stake of United Internet and another 1% from one of the founders' holdings were sold to AdLink Internet Media AG, a public, but majority-owned subsidiary of United Internet,[3] for €14.3 million (AdLink Internet Media, 2005). This sale caused some major changes for Sedo's management team. AdLink's company was much smaller than United Internet's, which increased the attention on Sedo and its growth. AdLink provided Sedo with more support but also insisted on greater management intervention. Nevertheless, the entrepreneurial spirit of the founders remained unscathed. Innovations to guarantee Sedo's future success would continue to occur.

The Domain Market

Every company that wants to succeed needs a reasonable and memorable brand name. In the age of e-business and the Internet, companies also need memorable domain names. The market for domain names (domain market) is divided into a primary market and an *aftermarket,* or secondary market.

The primary domain market is the market where new domain names are registered for the first time, using the "first come, first serve" principle. Market partners are the users who want to register a domain name (registrants) and the accredited domain issuers (registrars). The price for a new domain is a standard registration fee, usually only a few dollars.

As most of the promising domain names were already registered, there was a need for a market to buy and sell "used" domain names. This is the domain aftermarket. Transactions in this market are much more complex than primary market transactions. Many changes in the aftermarket regarding transaction procedure, market structure, and market growth have emerged in the last 10 years due to the development of domain name marketplaces like GreatDomains, Afternic, and Sedo. These marketplaces have simplified the domain selling process by reducing relevant transaction costs. For example, search and information costs are reduced by the marketplace's meta-search engine and domain name databases.

Domain aftermarket development has been rapid and unstable. The annual growth rates of the market were tremendous until the beginning of 2000. Then, because of the dot-com crisis, the prices for domain names decreased rapidly along with the total volume on the domain aftermarket. This slump leveled out in 2003, and the domain aftermarket enjoyed a strong rebound—the market volume increased by double-digit rates. By the end of 2006, the total number of aftermarket transactions increased to $96.9 million (www.dnjournal.com).

The structure of the domain aftermarket has changed significantly since Sedo entered the market. In 2000, two companies—Afternic and GreatDomains—dominated the market. The dot-com crisis detrimentally affected these organizations and wiped out the market. Once the crisis ended, the market's growth attracted many smaller competitors leading to today's highly competitive market (see Table 1). Despite this increased competition, Sedo has been the world's leading domain aftermarket since 2004, with a market share of nearly 40%. Predictions of the domain aftermarket's future are highly uncertain and it is likely that today's leaders will not be industry leaders 5 years from now.

Nevertheless, the aftermarket's growth is predicted to be positive. There are greatly underserved markets throughout the world, namely in the emerging countries throughout Asia and Eastern Europe. Millions of people will gain Internet access during the next 10 years. This increase in users will inevitably increase the demand for new and used domain names.

Valuing a Domain Name

The most important issue for domain name vendees and vendors is the determination of the domain name price. As long as a domain name is unregistered, its intrinsic value is equal to the registration fee. But, once that domain name is registered, the resale value is determined by various factors:

- General domain name demand
- Market power distribution
- General economic conditions
- Existence of similar domain names
- Political, regulatory, and sociocultural forces
- Brand name eligibility
- Traffic-generating potential[4] (largely dependent on the consumers' ability to remember, recognize the domain name, but also includes the names' descriptive power, length, use of common misspelling or mistyping, and its top-level domain, or TLD[5])
- Pricing mechanism (usually auction system, offer/counteroffer system, or a combination of both)

Table 1 Market Share for Domain Sales Above $2,000

Marketplace	2004%	2006%
Sedo	41	39.9
Pool	18	1.1
Afternic	10	4.6
GreatDomains	8	–
Moniker DS	8	5.4
Snapnames	7	18.9
Enom's Club Drop	6	0.9
Namewinner	1	–
Moniker TRAFFIC	–	7.9
Pvt Sale	–	14.3
BuyDomains	–	4.1
Forums	–	0.2
Other	1	2.7

SOURCE: www.dnjournal.com.

In 2004, a new method for determining domain value arose in the industry. This method, called "domain parking," connects idle domains with banner advertisements related to the domain's name. Every time a web user accidentally visits the idle domain, the website generates advertisement revenues through pay-per-click fees, generating up to six-figure dollar revenues each month. Aside from the revenue generation potential, this tool establishes a solid track record of revenues and traffic potential for the idle site that simplifies its future appraisal.

Today, domain names are increasingly viewed as assets. Professional domain investors who create domain portfolios own most of the domain names. The prices paid for domain names increased as the aftermarket became more successful. The majority of domain name sales are below $2,000; however, select domain name sales reach seven, or eight figures (see Table 2). Sedo's most profitable deal was the brokerage of Vodka.com for $3 million. Sedo brokered the deal between a private U.S. domain holder and the buyer, Russian Standard Vodka Company. Once purchased, Russian Standard used the domain to successfully enter the international vodka market.

Sedo's Business Model

The founders created Sedo to replace the highly fragmented domain name aftermarket. The heart of Sedo's services is a specially developed search engine and database that, by 2007, contained more than 8 million domain names. In addition to its searchable online marketplace, Sedo introduced an

Table 2 Top Sales Prices in the Domain Name Aftermarket[6]

Domain Name	Year	Price
sex.com	2005	$ 12,000,000
porn.com	2007	$ 9,500,000
business.com	1999	$ 7,500,000
diamond.com	2006	$ 7,500,000
casino.com	2003	$ 5,500,000
asseenontv.com	n.a.	$ 5,000,000
altavista.com	1997	$ 3,250,000
loans.com	2000	$ 3,000,000
wine.com	2000	$ 3,000,000
vodka.com	2006	$ 3,000,000
creditcheck.com	2007	$ 3,000,000
creditcard.com	2004	$ 2,750,000
tom.com	2000	$ 2,500,000
autos.com	1999	$ 2,200,000
express.com	2000	$ 2,000,000

SOURCE: www.dnjournal.com.

escrow service to protect their clients from fraud within domain name transfers. This was an important service addition as fraud was prevalent in other marketplaces.

To facilitate domain name pricing, Sedo additionally launched a domain name appraisal service based on scientific valuation.[7] Sedo also established a domain brokerage that provided expert negotiation services for domain name buyers or sellers. To generate alternative sources of revenue, the company developed a domain-name parking program, earning revenues from advertisements on idle domains.

Sedo began by operating on the small local domain name aftermarket in Germany, but the four founders had international aspirations. Since its founding, internationalization had been a cornerstone of Sedo's business strategy. The 20 nationalities represented on Sedo's staff displayed the organization's commitment to diversity. The company's network of localized websites included Sedo.com, Sedo.us, Sedo.co.uk, Sedo.de, Sedo.fr, Sedo.dk, Sedo.it, Sedo.nl, Sedo.se, Sedo.at, Sedo.ch, Sedo.jp and Sedo.kr. In addition to the local websites, Sedo offered content in four languages: English, French, Spanish, and German.

In 2004, Sedo opened a second office in Boston, Massachusetts. This was the most significant step toward globalizing the brand and allowed Sedo to grab a firm hold of the U.S. domain market.

With an office in Boston, Sedo was able to satisfy U.S. customer demands by facilitating faster bank transfers and more efficient customer service.

Despite its internal innovation efforts (product diversification and internationalization), Sedo also used external strategies such as horizontal integration to foster their first priority: growth. Sedo acquired GreatDomains, a former competitor that specialized in premium domain name auctions. In addition, Sedo built partnerships with major companies along the entire domain name value chain: top registrars in Europe, the United States, and Asia; domain financiers like Domain Capital; and advertising agencies such as Google AdWords.

Sedo's revenue model is based on three major columns:

- *Domain trading:* For every sold domain, Sedo charges 10% of the selling price, at least €50 (for most TLDs); the additional use of the brokerage service runs €69 for the handling fee.
- *Domain parking:* Sedo earns up to 50% of the parked domain name's advertising revenues, depending on the size and negotiating power of the domain name owner.
- *Domain appraisal:* Sedo charges €29 for a standard appraisal and €49 for a premium domain name appraisal. While an important service, its contribution to total revenue is negligible.

The Business Model's Challenges

Despite Sedo's success, there are several challenges that jeopardize the organization's growth. The law rarely protects product and service innovations in the area of Internet applications and this lack of legal protection allows the competition to benefit from Sedo's advancements. A consequence of this void is that most domain name trading marketplaces offer virtually the same services. Furthermore, marketplace designs are often similar. For example, compare the layouts of sedo.com and afternic.com. The opportunities to stay unique and ahead of the market are fast fading, and it is exceedingly difficult for consumers to differentiate between the available marketplaces and their level of quality.

In the last 2 years, competition in the domain name aftermarket has grown rapidly due to the low barriers to entry. Many small companies have taken advantage of the opportunity to enter the market and hope to capitalize on the success of Sedo and its competitors. The existing EBIT (earnings before interest and taxes) margins of the domain name aftermarket are endangered and will presumably decrease in the nearer future.

Sedo's revenue model and the key numbers presented in Table 3 reveal another challenge. Sedo's revenues, and the majority of its profits, are generated by one product: their domain parking service. This single-product dependency is likely to cause challenges for Sedo if competition in this market niche increases and EBIT margins decline.

Sedo's Advantages

Throughout its development, Sedo's greatest advantage was its customer-centric service offerings. In the early 2000s, the uncertainty of the existing auction systems and the prevalence of fraud in the established marketplaces were noticeably dissatisfying domain name customers. These imperfections led Sedo to introduce a pricing system on an offer/counteroffer basis that allowed buyers and sellers to negotiate directly. In addition, they eliminated the danger of fraud by developing a domain escrow service. Even today, Sedo is the only player in the aftermarket to have offices located in both Europe and the United States. This physical presence has proven important for

Table 3 Key Numbers in Sedo's Success Story

	2000	2001	2002	2003	2004	2005	2006	2007[a]	2008[a]
Revenue	€100,000	€500,000	€635,000	€2,000,000	€7,570,000	€20,780,000	€41,000,000	€62,100,000	€80,400,000
Direct Gross Profit	n.a.	n.a.	n.a.	n.a.	n.a.	€8,000,000	€19,600,000	€27,900,000	€35,800,000
Employees	3	8	15	22	50	80	120	150	180
Transferred Domains	n.a.	n.a.	n.a.	1,927	1,927	10,989	17,850	30,000	50,000
Average Domain Price	n.a.	n.a.	n.a.	€1,416	€1,402	€1,661	€1,720	€1,700	€1,700
Domain Sales Volume	n.a.	n.a.	n.a.	€2,728,632	€7,594,634	€18,252,729	€30,702,000	€51,000,000	€85,000,000
Domains in Database	n.a.	100,000	400,000	800,000	1,600,000	3,000,000	6,000,000	10,000,000	15,000,000
Parked Domains	no service	no service	50,000	400,000	500,000	1,000,000	2,000,000	3,500,000	5,000,000

SOURCE: Tim Schumacher, CEO, Sedo.
[a]Projected.

gaining positive press, attracting potential partners, and increasing its customer base. Sedo is the only true multilingual and IDN-ready marketplace.[8] The Sedo team's technical background is another major asset. The technical heart of Sedo's service is the world's largest domain name database, containing 8 million domain names listed for sale, and its meta-search engine. The research and development department is constantly innovating current and future service offerings. Recently, Sedo became the first marketplace to offer financing programs for high-value domains.

November 2006

On that lukewarm spring evening, the four founders sat together late into the night and discussed the prospect of selling a portion of their shares. By the end of the evening, they came to a unanimous decision—they would each sell half of their shares, equaling 24% of all company shares. However, the more difficult decision was deciding to whom they would sell the shares.

AdLink, already a major investor, was an eager prospect. But the founders also considered other investors, particularly private equity companies that were attracted by Sedo's fast growth and future potential. The decision-making process was not as easy as it had been in 2001, when United Internet acquired 41% of Sedo's shares. It took the founders 6 months to reach a decision and, ultimately, it was their intuition and past experiences that allowed them to come to a consensus. Tim Schumacher, Ulrich Priesner, Ulrich Essmann, and Marius Wuerzner decided to sell their shares to their current investor, AdLink, despite higher offers from other bidders.

AdLink increased its stake in Sedo to 76% for nearly €35 million in cash. Today, the four founders still work at Sedo in top management positions. They all hope to remain with the company as it continues to grow and realizes its potential.

CASE QUESTIONS

1. How did Sedo's market value develop from 2000 to 2006?

2. To what extent was the 2000 exit strategic for the founders and the investor, AdLink?

3. Was the 2006 exit a bargain, fair valued, or overpriced? Take into account that Sedo's estimated EBIT was €16 million and average EBIT multiples range between 5.5 and 8.1 for companies in the IT industry.

4. How can Sedo's management team sustain the company's current market position in the future?

NOTES

1. "GmbH" is a legal form in Germany comparable to an LLC in the United States.

2. The abbreviation "AG" indicates a corporation.

3. AdLink Internet Media is—like United Internet—publicly noted on the Frankfurt Stock Exchange (Ticker Symbol ISIN DE0005490155), but United Internet owns 82% of the shares, with a small 18% free float remaining.

4. Within this context, traffic means the frequency of visits to a website, measured by the amount of "page impressions" or "unique visitors."

5. Top-level domains are the domain extensions indicating the class of organization behind the website (e.g., .com for commercial organization or .edu for educational organizations) or the country where the website owner is located (e.g., .de for Germany or .cn for China).

6. It should be noted that prices are often not published.

7. The approach was drawn from Tim Schumacher's master's degree thesis, *Price Formation in the Trade of Internet Domain Names.*

8. An internationalized domain name (IDN) is a domain name that can contain non-ASCII characters used in languages such as Arabic or Chinese.

REFERENCES

AdLink Internet Media. (2005). *Annual report 2005.* Montabaur, Germany: Author.

Schumacher, T. (2002). *Price formation in the trade of Internet domain names.* Unpublished master's thesis, University of Cologne, Germany.

Sedo. (2005). *2004 record year for Internet domain trader* [Electronic press release]. Retrieved from www.sedo.de/presse/presse_190105.php4?tracked=&partnerid=&language=d

Sedo. (2007). *Sedo domain market survey 2006* [Electronic press release]. Retrieved from www.sedo.de/presse/presse_260307.php4?tracked=&partnerid=&language=d

United Internet. (2004). *Annual report 2004.* Montabaur, Germany: Author.

Cross-Border Sponsorship

Gregory Stoller et al.[1]

Sports sponsorship gained prominence in the 1970s in the United States (U.S.). According to Benoît Seguin, at the University of Ottawa, Canada, as television and radio licenses increased in the 1970s, "competition between advertisers to attract consumers' attention was fierce." [2] As originally coined by Tony Meenaghan in the *International Journal of Advertising* in 1991, sponsorship is defined as "an investment in cash or kind, in an activity, person or event (*sponsoree*, or athlete being sponsored), in return for access to the exploitable commercial potential associated with that activity, person or event by the investor (sponsor)." According to sports sponsorship expert, IEG, what originally began as a means to attract advertisers across the four major U.S. professional sports leagues and their teams is now an industry of over $2.46 billion (Exhibit 1). The trend of sponsorship not only has expanded outside of U.S. markets but also now regularly involves cross-border sponsorship, where a country uses a spokesperson that is not one of its citizens. For example, Turkish Airlines recently used basketball star Kobe Bryant to endorse its expanded seating capacity and good food.

Exhibit 1 Sports Sponsorships in the Four Major US Sports Leagues[1]

Corporate Partners of the Four Major US Pro Sports Leagues			
League	**Sponsor**	**Category**	**Start of Relationship**
MLB	Anheuser-Busch	Alcoholic & nonalcoholic malt beverages	1980
	Bank of America	Banking services	2004 (1997 for MBNA affinity card)
	Bayer Advanced Aspirin	Pain relief	2011
	Firestone	Tires	2010
	Frito-Lay	Salty snacks	2006
	Gatorade	Isotonic beverages, energy bars	1990
	General Motors/Chevrolet	Foreign & domestic vehicles	2005

(Continued)

Exhibit 1 (Continued)

Corporate Partners of the Four Major US Pro Sports Leagues			
League	**Sponsor**	**Category**	**Start of Relationship**
	InterContinental Hotels Group/Holiday Inn	Hotel & resort	2006
	MasterCard	Credit card/payment system	1998
	Nike	Athletic footwear & athletic eyewear	1998
	One A Day/Bayer	Multivitamin	2008
	Pepsi Cola	Beverage (nonalcoholic & non-isotonic)	1997
	Procter & Gamble/Gillette and Head & Shoulders	Men's and women's grooming products	1939
	Scotts	Lawn care & grass seed	2010
	Sirius/XM	Satellite radio network	2004
	State Farm	Insurance	2007
	Taco Bell	Quick-service restaurant	2004
NBA*	Adidas	Apparel/footwear	2002
	American Express	Credit card	2010
	Anheuser-Busch InBev	Beer (alcohol & nonalcohol malt beverages)	1998
	AutoTrader.com	Online auto retailer	2006
	Bacardi	Rum	2010
	BBVA	Banking	2010
	Cisco	Information technology & networking solutions, digital camcorders	2007
	The Coca-Cola Co.	Soft drink/juice/flavored beverages	1986
	Electronic Arts	Video game software	2002
	Gatorade	Sports & energy drinks	1984

Corporate Partners of the Four Major US Pro Sports Leagues			
League	**Sponsor**	**Category**	**Start of Relationship**
	Haier America	High-definition TVs & consumer appliances	2006
	Hewlett-Packard	Personal computers, printers, & IT services	2008
	Kia Motors	Automotive	2008
	Nike	Footwear	1992
	Right Guard	Antiperspirant, deodorant, & body wash	2008
	Sirius XM Radio	Satellite radio	2005
	Spaulding	Basketballs	1983
	State Farm	Insurance	2010
	T-Mobile	Wireless service provider & handset	2005
	Taco Bell	Quick service restaurant	2009
NFL	Anheuser-Busch InBev	Official beer	–
	Barclays	Official credit card	2010
	Bose	Official home theater system	2011
	Bridgestone	Official tire sponsor	2007
	Campbell's Soup	Soup, canned pasta, tomato food sauces, salsa	1998
	Castrol	Motor oil	2011
	Dairy Management Inc.	Dairy, milk, yogurt, cheese	2003
	FedEx	Worldwide package delivery service	2000
	Frito-Lay	Salted snack/popcorn/peanuts/dips	–
	Gatorade	Isotonic beverages	1983
	General Motors	Car & passenger trucks	2001

(Continued)

Exhibit 1 (Continued)

Corporate Partners of the Four Major US Pro Sports Leagues			
League	**Sponsor**	**Category**	**Start of Relationship**
	IBM	Computer hardware, software, IT services	2003
	Marriott	Official hotel	2011
	Mars Snackfood	Chocolate & non-chocolate confectionery	2002
	Motorola	Wireless telecommunications equipment	1999
	National Guard	U.S. armed forces	2009
	Papa John's	Pizza	2010
	Pepsi	Soft drinks	2002
	Prilosec	Heartburn medication	2005
	Procter & Gamble/ Gillette; Head & Shoulders; Vicks	Grooming products, fabric care/air care, household needs	2009
	USAA	Official military appreciation	2011
	Verizon	Wireless telecommunication service	2010
	Visa USA	Payment systems services	1995
NHL	**North America**		
	Bridgestone	Official tire	2008
	Cisco	Official technology partner	2008
	Compuware	Global application performance partner	2009
	Cybex	Preferred fitness equipment	2010
	Enterprise	Official rent-a-car	2009
	EA Sports	Official video game	1994
	Las Vegas Convention & Visitors Authority	Official gaming destination	2009
	Palms Hotel Las Vegas	Host hotel of the NHL Awards	2008

Corporate Partners of the Four Major US Pro Sports Leagues			
League	**Sponsor**	**Category**	**Start of Relationship**
	Panini	Official trading card	–
	Pepsi Co./Pepsi, Gatorade, Aquafina, Frito-Lay	Official soft drink, energy drink, water and juice	2006
	Reebok	Official authentic outfitter	2003
	Sirius/XM	Official satellite radio	2005
	Starwood Hotels	Official hotel	2009
	Ticketmaster	Official secondary ticket provider	2007
	Upper Deck	Official trading card partner	1990
U.S.			
	Discover	Official credit/charge/debit card	2010
	Geico	Official insurance partner	2010
	Honda	Official U.S. automotive partner	2008
	McDonald's	Official quick-service restaurant	2009
	MillerCoors	Official beer	2011
	Verizon Wireless	Official wireless service provider	2006
Canada Only			
	Bell	Official wireless and wireline telecommunications provider	2008
	Canadian Tire	Official home improvement retailer	2010
	Hershey's	Official chocolate, chocolate bar, gum, candy, and confectionary partner	2009
	Kraft	Official cookie, cracker, gelatin, pudding, ground & instant coffee, peanut butter, cheese, cream cheese, mayonnaise, salad dressing, compartment snack, and convenient meal	1989

(Continued)

Exhibit 1 (Continued)

Corporate Partners of the Four Major US Pro Sports Leagues			
League	Sponsor	Category	Start of Relationship
	Pepsi	Official beverages, isotonic sports drinks, savory snacks	2005
	Scotiabank	Official retail bank, financial services provider and affinity card provider	2007
	Tim Hortons	Official quick-service restaurant (coffee, breakfast, & donut) partner	2011
	Visa	Official payment card, credit card, and payment system	2008
	Molson Coors	Official beer	2011
*Marketing partners as of the June NBA Finals			

[1]Major pro sports sponsorships to total $2.46 billion in 2011. (2011, September 26). *IEG Sponsorship Report.*

SOURCE: Retrieved March 2012 from http://www.sponsorship.com/IEGSR/2011/09/26/Major-Pro-Sports-Sponsorships-To-Total-$2-46-Billi.aspx. Reprinted with permission of Mr. Mike Maggini, via telephone and email confirmation on 5/2/12.

As Mr. Tanaka began reviewing his marketing plan for the second half of 2012, he wondered to what extent his Japanese company should continue the trend of other Japanese firms, such as Phiten, in using non-Japanese athletes to pitch their products.

Sponsorship Overview

With the growth of sponsorships over the last few decades, some argue that sponsorships now should be considered part of the promotional mix along with publicity, public relations, sales promotions, personal selling, and advertising. When the number of television and radio networks began to grow in the 1970s, some began to question the continued effectiveness of traditional advertising routes. As a result, sponsorships emerged and began to grow during this time period, as they were considered effective at a lower cost. Additionally, sponsorships were considered different from traditional advertising because audiences with an "association" element thought of their perception separately.[3]

Companies and organizations began to set objectives for sponsorships to justify return on investment (ROI). Three types of sponsorship objectives have been identified. The first is broad corporate objectives. The second is marketing objectives, including brand promotions and sales promotions. Finally, media objectives have been identified, including reaching target markets and obtaining cost efficiency. Overall, some argue that sponsorships are utilized to generate additional sales with the goal of enhancing profitability, while others believe that corporations attempt to achieve multiple objectives with the use of sponsorships.[4]

The vast increase in sponsorships over the past decades points to the success of sponsorships since their introduction. Moreover, there has been an increase in the number of sponsorship opportunities that companies and organizations have taken advantage of. A marketing team must now carefully take into consideration how sponsorships can be integrated into its promotional and communications strategy.[5]

There is a stark contrast between traditional advertising and sponsorships. Advertising intends to "exploit emotion" in individuals, whereas sponsorship intends to "connect with the emotion" inherent in the product or brand that is being sponsored. An association between the sponsor and sponsoree is created that enhances the relationship beyond the basic promotional value found in traditional advertising. Sponsorship attempts to persuade consumers in a more indirect manner than advertising.[6]

Sponsorships are extremely prominent in sports relative to other areas. For instance, there is significantly more investment in sports sponsorships than the next largest area of sponsorship investment, the arts. The demographic for the arts is different from sports, including a smaller group of older and more affluent people. Art events attract less media coverage and publicity than sports. With the exception of music, arts appeal less to the mainstream commercial market.[7] Individual music artists tend to appeal to a specific group of people rather than a large mass audience. In fact, sports have 75%–80% of total sponsorship investments, while arts account for only 10%–15% of sponsorship investments.[8] Total sponsorship expenditures have exceeded well over $15 billion.[9]

There are several reasons why sponsorships mainly are found in the sports area. Sports provide a flexible communication vehicle. In addition, sports and athletic "heroes" are commercially driven phenomena. Finally, consumers are extremely interested in sports and sporting events, as they provide a leisure activity that differs from their daily work routines.[10]

Sports sponsorships can transcend the increasingly accessible communication channels, which began with cable and have now additionally moved to the new Internet technologies. Sports sponsorships can target either a niche audience or a larger demographic, which may span a range of demographic and psychographic profiles. Furthermore, sports sponsorships can reach international audiences due to their ability to transcend cultural, lingual, and geographic boundaries. Whether in the United States or internationally, sports sponsors tend to aim for a broad audience reach in an attempt to better gain brand and product awareness.[11]

History

Sponsorship in sports can be traced back to the ancient Greek athletic and arts festivals, which the wealthy could sponsor to enhance social standing. Additionally, those in the Roman aristocracy could support or own gladiators.[12] Sports marketing emerged in the 1870s when cards of baseball stars appeared in cigarette packs.[13] Modern sports promotions became prevalent during the 1896 Olympics with the placement of advertisements in the official programs for the event. The first recorded sponsorship for the United Kingdom (UK) occurred in 1898, when the Nottingham Forest soccer team endorsed the Bovril beverage company.[14] For the 1928 Olympics, Coca-Cola purchased product-sampling rights. During the Berlin Olympics in 1936, Adi Dassler provided shoes to sprinter Jessie Owens.[15]

Sports sponsorships increased significantly beginning in the mid-1970s. Specifically, the largest increase in sports sponsorships occurred between the 1976 Montreal Olympics and the 1984 Los Angeles Olympics, as sporting event promoters reacted to the losses that Montreal suffered while holding the Olympics. Organizers of the 1984 Los Angeles Olympics gained approximately $200 million in sponsorships, with the event reaching 2.5 billion people in 156 countries.[16] Sponsorships for the 1988 summer and winter Olympics totaled $350 million. For the 1996 Summer Olympics, the 14 major sponsors paid approximately $40 million each.[17]

At the 2008 Beijing Olympics, sponsorships came in from both the Western countries and from China and the rest of Asia. In the coming years, we can expect to see a battle for sponsorships in emerging nations, including China and India. Established brands such as Nike and Adidas will be competing against local sports brands, such as the Chinese sports manufacturer Li Ning. For example, Li Ning signed Yelena Isenbyva, a Russia pole-vaulter, for $2.5 million per year in 2008. Isenbyva had been signed with Adidas prior to this. The deal made her the highest-paid track and field star worldwide. Also, in the English Premier League (EPL), Far Eastern brands such as EPL clubs, Mansion Casino, and Chang Beer Kuomo Tyres have gained a significant share of sponsorship agreements.[18]

Trends in Sports Sponsorship

There have been some subtle, and recent, changes in trends relating to sports sponsorships. For instance, as new and different sports gain popularity, the opportunity has arisen for sponsorships in these sports, such as darts. In another trend, sponsorship rights holders slowly have begun moving away from selling all possible revenue opportunities, including stadium naming rights as well as the right to be official partners for financial services, alcohol, soft drinks, sportswear, TV, and utilities. People have begun to feel that the emotional connection was being abused, and as a result, clubs, teams, and events now typically have fewer sponsorship partners.[19]

Some organizations even have begun donating their sponsorship revenue to charity. For example, the English soccer organization Aston Villa FC donated its shirt sponsorship to the ACORNS charity. By demonstrating that it is a responsible organization, it has attracted even more sponsorship opportunities.[20]

Cross-promotion also is gaining popularity as an effective sports sponsorship option. Cross-promotion sponsorships occur when one company shares a sponsorship with another company or a different strategic business unit within the same company. In addition to allowing companies to share the total cost of the sponsorship and/or promotional execution, companies can utilize existing business relationships as well as test the relationship of potential future business opportunities. In certain situations, a weaker company can "piggyback" on the strength and position of a stronger company. There is also the potential of a pass-through cross-promotional agreement in which a company, such as a grocery store, can pass some or all of its sponsorship costs to product vendors in its stores. An example of a successful cross-promotion sponsorship is Got Milk and Kellogg's sponsorship of NASCAR.[21]

Sports organizations now must look for innovative ways to attract corporate sponsors. For instance, the minor league baseball team the Dayton Dragons created what it calls the "world's largest outdoor billboard," which is 240 feet long by 6 feet high. Rather than using the traditional method of cluttering the billboard with upwards of 50 different advertisements from sponsors, the sign is backlit and shows one of the team's major sponsors wall-to-wall for a half inning. The billboard rotates every half inning and shows another sponsor to the standing-room-only crowd.[22]

International Sports Sponsorships

International sports sponsorship deals are prominent in today's market. At the start of the 2012 Olympic Games in London, the International Olympic Committee confirmed that nearly $900 million of sponsorship revenue was in place, and they hoped total revenue would climb over $1 billion.[23]

Additionally, with major professional sports sponsorships totaling $2.46 billion in 2011, companies and sports leagues have continued to take advantage of international sports sponsorship opportunities.[24] International sports sponsorships can be found in baseball, basketball, football, hockey, soccer, golf, and tennis, among other sports.

These deals also mirror the globalization of every one of the U.S. sports leagues in the past decade. Ranging from a low of currently under 5% non-U.S. active players in the National Football League (NFL) to a high of approximately 80% in the NHL, sponsors, fans, and the media now have a robust and heterogeneous demographic athlete pool with which to work.[25]

The National Hockey League (NHL) has a number of international sponsors. In 2008, Japanese automaker Honda signed a three-year deal to become the official vehicle of the NHL in North America. The deal is Honda's first sponsorship in the "big four" American sports. Honda was the official sponsor of the 2009 NHL Winter Classic and 2009 NHL All-Star Game.[26] Labatt, a Canadian beer company, is the official sponsor of several American NHL teams, including the Buffalo Sabres, Carolina Hurricanes, Columbus Blue Jackets, New York Islanders, and Pittsburgh Penguins, as well as the NFL's Buffalo Bills.[27]

Major League Baseball (MLB) has a number of international sponsorship programs in Latin America and Asia. Pepsi has been the official soft drink of the MLB in Latin America since 2002. Additionally, MasterCard has been the Official Worldwide Sponsor of the MLB since January 2001. In Japan, Kellogg's is the Official Breakfast Cereal, Kolkeya is the Official Salty Snack Provider, Komatsu is an Official Sponsor, NIT is the Official Telecommunications Provider, Sato Pharmaceutical is the Official Nutrition and Invigoration Drink, and Nikko Cordial is the Official Financial Services and Securities Provider. E.Sun is the Official Banking and Financial Service Provider in Taiwan. In Latin America, Anheuser-Busch is the Official Beer in Panama and Puerto Rico, Banco BHD is the Official Bank in the Dominican Republic, DIRECTV is the Official Direct Broadcast Satellite Pay Television in Venezuela, Gillette is an Official Sponsor in several Latin American countries, Maltín is the Official Malt Beverage in Venezuela, and Presidente is the Official Beer in the Dominican Republic.[28]

Companies sponsor individual athletes in countries other than their own as well. Phiten, a Japanese company that produces necklaces for the purpose of soothing one's body, sponsors a number of U.S. athletes. These include MLB players Josh Beckett, Tim Lincecum, Joba Chamberlain, Jon Lester, Randy Johnson, Clay Buchholz, Justin Verlander, Curtis Granderson, Justin Morneau, Brandon Webb, C.J. Wilson, and Dustin Pedroia, as well as golfer Sergio Garcia, marathon runner Paula Radcliffe, basketball player Carmelo Anthony, German ice hockey player Otto Keresztes, and softball player Jennie Finch.[29]

There are a number of instances of U.S. athletes sponsored by international companies in golf and tennis. Golfer Phil Mickelson is sponsored by the English bank, Barclays.[30] Golfer Tiger Woods held a sponsorship by Swiss watchmaker TAG Heuer, but he was dropped from the company in August 2011.[31] Russian tennis star Maria Sharapova is sponsored by both TAG Heuer and French mineral water producer, Evian.[32]

In basketball and football, further examples of U.S. athletes who have endorsed companies in countries outside of the United States exist. For example, Li Ning, a Chinese athletic company, sponsors National Basketball Association (NBA) player Shaquille O'Neal.[33] Also, NBA player Kobe Bryant starred in a commercial for Turkish Airlines.[34] NFL quarterback Tom Brady appears on the Australian clothing company UGG's website.[35]

There are also international athletes sponsored by countries other than their own. Li Na, a Chinese international tennis star, is sponsored by the U.S. ice cream company Haagen-Dazs.[36] Andy Murray, a Scottish professional tennis player, signed a five-year deal with German athletic clothing company Adidas.[37] English soccer player David Beckham will be electronics company Samsung's company ambassador for the 2012 Olympics.[38]

Sponsorship Marketing Strategies

Basketball

Turkish Airlines has established a prominent mass-media sports-marketing strategy through several sponsorship agreements across different sports categories with highly reputed teams, sport associations, and celebrity players, notably NBA superstar Kobe Bryant, who the airline enlisted as its "Global Brand Ambassador."[39]

At the time of the two-year deal in December 2010, Bryant had been named Most Valuable Player (MVP) of the NBA finals for the past two years. He also had won five NBA championships, been the NBA scoring champion twice, and was a key player in the USA Basketball Men's National Team that won the gold medal at the Beijing Summer Olympics in 2008.[40] Bryant is the highest-paid player in the NBA, with a salary slated to increase to $30.5 million per year by the 2013–2014 season after signing a three-year, $83.5 million extension with the Lakers in April 2010.[41] Bryant was ranked 14th on Forbes' "Celebrity 100," a list of the 100 most valued stars in the world, in 2011.[42]

Such impressive numbers illustrate how no player in the league has leveraged his global popularity quite like Bryant. He is perhaps the most popular basketball player overseas. As such, he is in demand as an endorser for a variety of products apart from basketball apparel and shoes.[43] In 2010, he earned about $24 million in product endorsements—more than any other NBA player.[44]

Tapping Bryant especially for its "Globally Yours" campaign directly reflected that Turkish Airlines was seeking to become more competitive by aggressively promoting its image as a global brand with a global vision.[45] Turkey's state-run airline is one of the fastest growing and most profitable in Europe.[46] Passenger traffic grew 17.1% in 2010, prompting the airline to add 42 new planes in 2011.[47] As the fourth-largest network carrier in Europe, Turkish Airlines was rapidly expanding its presence in the United States when it selected Bryant.[48]

The airline used Bryant to publicize the start of its nonstop flights from Los Angeles to Istanbul, the only such service from the West Coast. The longtime, venerable face of the Los Angeles Lakers organization thus appeared in TV, movie, billboard, print, and online advertisements in more than 80 countries in 2011.[49] Though Bryant was heavily featured in this worldwide advertising campaign, special attention was given to his home country, with the first commercials and billboards appropriately launching locally in Los Angeles.[50] The campaign focused on the United States, the Middle East, and the Far East (Asia Pacific), where Bryant is known to have a massive fan base. Indeed, Bryant is the most revered athlete in China. He makes annual trips there in support of Nike, another one of his many corporate sponsors, and (unsurprisingly) received the loudest cheers at the 2008 Olympics.[51]

Following Bryant's humorous and lighthearted TV advertisement in which he trades jobs with the onboard chef, Turkish Airlines released another campaign titled "Passenger Portraits," a series of portraits created by New York-based artist Craig Redman.[52] The portraits covered the full line of the airline's sponsorships so that it could address the people in all of the countries that it services.[53] While the portraits were displayed in major airports and magazines (such as *Newsweek*) around the world, only Bryant's face was seen across the U.S.[54] To better reach out to its target audiences and thus increase its customers, Turkish Airlines used its extensive roster of cultural symbols in their corresponding countries of origin—the portraits of FC Barcelona players were exhibited in Barcelona, whereas the Manchester United player portraits were exhibited in Manchester, and so on.[55]

American Football

To increase market share in the footwear industry and solidify its status as a complete "lifestyle" brand, UGG Australia has sponsored the New England Patriots' quarterback Tom Brady, one of the most visible athletes in the United States, since November 2010.[56] The company's partnership with Brady is part of its UGG for Men campaign, a multimedia marketing initiative that kicked off in a particularly appropriate fashion: UGG debuted its first-ever broadcast commercial during the nationally televised *Monday Night Football* game of the Patriots' season opener against the Miami Dolphins—a clear appeal to American male football fans, which previously had not been UGG's primary clientele. The TV commercial, called "Steps," showed Brady traipsing about town in Los Angeles in various UGG shoes from the Fall/Winter 2011 men's collection, played out to the music of hip-hop artist Mos Def.[57] Like its fashionable yet masculine celebrity face, UGG's "Steps" was an effort to show men the comfortable yet manly side of the company.[58] The 30-second spot also launched across online digital media platforms, including ESPN.com, CBS.com, Pandora, Hulu, and YouTube, in advance. Along with TV and online content, the campaign has included print advertisements in publications such as *GQ, Esquire, Details, ESPN the Magazine,* and *Men's Journal* as well as billboards and "tall walls" in Boston, New York, and Los Angeles.[59] In the first billboard, Brady showed off the calm, cool, and collected demeanor for which he is known on the field.

UGG made a calculated move to build consumer awareness among men, and its strategy with Brady aligns with its long-term objective of diversifying its product offerings and increasing the total number of men in its target demographic. Even though UGG originated as a sandal brand geared toward male surfers, the brand became best known as a women's line and developed a rather "girly" stigma.[60] The last decade has seen double-digit sales growth in the women's line, but sales of the men's styles grew more slowly, and public perception of the brand reflected this fact.[61] With Brady as the focal point of the company's marketing plan, however, UGG hoped to change that misconception to a great degree.

Yet UGG's choice to endorse Brady was mainly a bid to increase its male market presence and customer base primarily in the United States, home to the NFL. Since its target market was American, not Australian, men, UGG did not use an Australian sports star, which most likely would not be known to the general U.S. populace. Brady's celebrity has given UGG an all-American makeover so that it more effectively can market Australia's sheepskin shoes in the U.S.[62] (See Exhibit 2 for more detailed background on selected sponsorship marketing strategies.)

| **Exhibit 2** | More Detailed Background on Sponsorship Marketing Strategies |

American Football

The company bet on Brady to convince the masses that the UGG brand is both fashionable and "macho" enough for men. Believing that Brady represents the modern man, UGG Australia president Constance X. Rishwain is convinced that the attractive California native can help reposition the UGG name. Despite his high-profile marriage, the fact that he had just signed a $72 million contract extension, and his widespread metrosexual crossover appeal to women, Rishwain believes that Brady—perhaps because he was an underdog second-to-last-round draft pick who later went on to win three Super Bowls—still comes across a "normal guy" that can convince men that UGG shoes are cool shoes worn by cool guys.[1] Brady has an impressive set of credentials and is well respected as a player; the quarterback holds numerous records and accolades for his game-time performances. By enlisting such a successful athlete, family man, and philanthropist who regularly participates in charity events, UGG presumed that its commercial endorsement would appeal to a new generation of men—and help enhance its own reputation in the process.[2]

(Continued)

Exhibit 2 (Continued)

With only about 10% of sales of the UGG brand currently going to men and children, this change in image to a more masculine, rugged look is in part a transformation and modernization of the brand and also a line extension (the introduction of slippers, urban shoes, and outdoor boots) into a relatively uncharted segment of the shoe market.[3]

Building off of the fall 2011 UGG for Men launch and the spring 2012 campaign, UGG opened a UGG for Men flagship store on June 6, 2012, in New York. Located on Madison Avenue and connected to the current UGG Australia store, it is the first dedicated UGG for Men location in the world. Brady's highly publicized appearance at the grand opening of the men's store helped push the men's brand further into the spotlight.[4] This tactic is in line with the UGG retail store segment currently being the main focus of management's plans for future expansion due to higher margins.

Women's Tennis

After Li's semifinal win was watched by as many as 65 million viewers in China, Haagen-Dazs saw a prime opportunity to gain traction in a sport achieving higher levels of viewership, for exposure becomes more valuable.[5] The company's investment paid off, as about 116 million people in China went on to watch her victory in the French Open final, a record for a tennis match that is up there with the opening ceremony of the Beijing Olympic Games in 2008 and a larger audience than the Super Bowl this year, which was a record in the U.S.[6]

Li's on-court success has made her a household name in the world's fastest-growing major economy, making her very enticing for any Western company looking to break into the Chinese market—a market that has proven extremely difficult for big brands to crack.[7] Besides linguistic and cultural barriers, the Chinese government has stymied attempts of foreign brands to make an impression on their consumers in the past. Far from trying to limit Li's appeal, however, Chinese authorities have looked to her as an ambassador for the country, with China's all-important state media fully embracing her success. In fact, Li was plastered across the front of the official Communist newspaper, *People's Daily*, a privilege almost always reserved for the most senior leaders.[8]

---

[1]Cancer Council, Cancer Institute NSW, & Melanoma Institute Australia. (2014, January 13). NSW skin cancer campaign targeting men aged 50 and over. Retrieved February 2015 from http://gp.cancer.org.au/editorial-entry/nsw-skin-cancer-campaign-targeting-men-aged-50-and-over/

[2]Deckers. (2010). Corporate responsibility update. Retrieved June 2012 from http://www.deckers.com/wp-content/uploads/Deckers-Update-pdf3.pdf

[3]Deckers. (2012). Investor relations. Retrieved June 2012 from http://www.deckers.com/investors (Accessed June 2012)

[4]Brady brings UGGs to midtown Patriots locker room. (2012, June 6). *New York Post*. Retrieved June 2012 from http://www.nypost.com/p/entertainment/fashion/patriots_brady_helps_open_ugg_men_r3ydydsSarQBSJdU36HxcK

[5]Rossingh, D., & Ying, T. (2011, June 5). Li's French Open victory may boost Chinese market for tennis. Retrieved May 2012 from http://www.bloomberg.com/news/2011-06-04/li-na-accomplishes-dream-with-china-s-first-tennis-major-at-french-open.html

[6]Badenhausen, K. (2012, May 28). One year after French open triumph, Li Na is a global icon. Retrieved May 2012 from http://www.forbes.com/sites/kurtbadenhausen/2012/05/28/one-year-after-french-open-triumph-li-na-is-a-global-icon/

[7]Rossing, D. (2011, July 31). Li Na nears Sharapova with $42 million in endorsement contracts. Retrieved May 2012 from http://www.bloomberg.com/news/2011-07-31/li-na-nears-top-earner-sharapova-with-42-million-in-endorsement-contracts.html

[8]Branigan, T. (2011, June 18). Li Na, a singular lady leading China's long march to glory. *The Guardian*. Retrieved May 2012 from http://www.guardian.co.uk/sport/2011/jun/19/li-na-china-wimbledon-2011

Golf

Phil Mickelson signed with Barclays in 2008 when he was the number-two golfer in the world. Given such an achievement, and the constant publicity that comes along with it, the deal called for him to wear the Barclays logo on the chest of his golf apparel, make corporate appearances on the firm's behalf, and be involved with advertising and marketing campaigns. His arrangement with the bank, with which he was already a client prior to the deal, came a mere month after the then-two-time Masters champion signed a three-year endorsement agreement with another New York-based financial services firm, KPMG.[63]

Mickelson's sponsorship marks yet another golf-related investment for Barclays, which is particularly strategic, given that golf often is considered the "banker's sport of choice." The firm also sponsors the Barclays Scottish Open on the European Tour, the Barclays Singapore Open on the Asian Tour, and The Barclays, the first tournament in the PGA Tour playoffs for the FedEx Cup. Barclays also has an endorsement deal with British golfer Darren Clarke to more easily market to those in its home country.[64]

An integral part of Barclays' golf sponsorship with Mickelson is drawing a parallel between the way he overcomes challenges out on the golf course to the way Barclays helps its corporate clients overcome challenges in business. One example is the manner in which Mickelson was able to refocus and adapt after he and two members of his family faced and overcame serious health issues.[65] Such values and leadership traits are perceived as shared between Mickelson and Barclays, serving not only as the foundation that guides his Hall of Fame career but also, in effect, the firm's success in the United States. The sponsorship proved positively symbolic for Barclays in another respect—after previous blow-ups in multiple Majors (Barclays is the current owner of Lehman Brothers' assets), Mickelson (Barclays) was able to dominate.

Men's Tennis

Although Adidas is a German-based company, its sponsorship deals give it global coverage and awareness. Second only to Nike in the sports goods market, Adidas sponsors a number of athletes from all around the world, including tennis star Andy Murray.[66] Formerly associated with the English brand, Fred Perry, sportswear (since 2004), the UK's top male singles player now is signed with Adidas. Beginning in January 2010, with the Australian Open, Murray began promoting the Adidas brand. The world's number-four player wears an Adidas tennis shoe named The Barricade as part of his contract, touting the company's reputation for advanced research.[67] Unlike Fred Perry, which is sold on a much more exclusive basis, Adidas tennis attire and footwear is widely available in every country. Murray (and/or general tennis) fans easily can buy The Andy Murray Competition apparel and Barricade footwear at retailers worldwide.

Murray replaced the current number-one-ranked tennis player, Novak Djokovic, as an Adidas spokesperson. Djokovic has since been formidable, winning multiple Grand Slam titles and building a huge global following in the process. While Murray has yet to hit such mesmeric heights, Djokovic's Serbian nationality means that his base of supporters does not extend as far as the UK's Murray; there is a larger market to which to sell products in the UK than in Serbia.[68] Adopting a long-term perspective, the payoff to Adidas if Murray becomes the first British player in decades to win Wimbledon (or any Major championship) could go far beyond that with Djokovic, which may have been what pushed Adidas to go with the Scot rather than the Serb. Given the immense popularity of tennis in the UK, Murray's appeal would reach out not only across his homeland but also globally, especially given his prolonged delay in capturing his first Grand Slam.[69] Despite commentators such as CNBC's Darren Rovell believing that Adidas' "move to drop Djokovic for Andy Murray will be one of the biggest mistakes in their history," Djokovic's relatively small home market of Serbia is not one of significant importance to the Adidas brand.[70]

Women's Tennis

Haagen-Dazs' sponsorship of Chinese tennis star Li Na is the first athlete endorsement deal for the premium ice cream maker. Haagen-Dazs signed Li after she became the first Asian, male or female, ever to reach a Grand Slam singles final.[71] After her breakthrough results at the 2011 Australian Open, she rose to a new career-high of number seven in the world, which was the highest ranking ever for a Chinese player in the history of the World Tennis Association (WTA) and second-highest ever for any Asian player.[72] The U.S.-based ice cream company then reaped even greater rewards when Li became the first Asian woman to win a Grand Slam title. Since her victory at the French Open in 2011, Li not only climbed to number four in the rankings but also became a national hero, gaining more than 2.5 million fans on Weibo, China's equivalent of the banned social network, Twitter.[73] Within four minutes of her win, Li's fans took to social media and sent her 300,000 messages on her website.[74]

Sponsors are drawn to tennis because tennis fans are usually a wealthy demographic with more disposable income to spend. But Li is doubly attractive because of the opportunity to reach 1.3 billion consumers in China, where there is a growing middle class that is becoming increasingly confident and brand-conscious, and gain brand presence. Prior to signing Li, Haagen-Dazs had been searching for an inlet to Chinese consumers, and Li—despite more recent losses on tour—offers the company that.[75] With Li's help, it pioneered the growth of ice cream parlors, which now appear in all major cities and serve as evidence of a growing popularity with luxury brands.[76]

Though the Haagen-Dazs deal is global, it is largely focused within China, given that Li has become a countrywide favorite.[77] Haagen-Dazs has used Li's image in print advertisements and PR activities, such as company-sponsored events, and enlists her for store visits all over China and in select cities around the world.[78] In addition to her sports achievements, what draws Haagen-Dazs to Li is her perceived fashionable sensibility as well as her romantic story with her husband/coach, Jiang Shan, which coincides with Haagen-Dazs' self-projected brand image. Li's laughter-filled journey to the Australian Open final included some affectionate teasing of her husband's snoring. She said that she could not sleep the night before the match because her husband snored so loud.[79]

Since tennis is such a global sport, Li will be an important asset for Haagen-Dazs not only in China but also in Chinese communities around the world, positioning the company well for a potential huge payback.[80] With her likeable personality, humor, and charismatic appeal (and the fact that she can speak English), Haagen-Dazs believes that, as its spokesperson, she has the ability to transcend her sport and eventually make it out on to the global stage.[81]

Response to Advertising Campaigns

Basketball

When Turkish Airlines announced that it had hired Kobe Bryant as its new official spokesperson, backlash erupted, sparking protest among Armenian Americans in Los Angeles and nationwide. Many outraged fans took to radio and social media sites, threatening to boycott Lakers games and Bryant merchandise unless he immediately backed out of the contract.[82] Reality TV star Kim Kardashian, who is of Armenian descent and the sister-in-law to Bryant's then-teammate Lamar Odom, mounted a Twitter campaign seeking for Bryant to dissociate himself from the airline. She also tweeted to her followers to ask U.S. House of Representatives Speaker Nancy Pelosi to schedule a new vote on House Resolution 252, the Armenian Genocide Resolution, which officially would recognize the genocide. Some Armenians then called on Bryant to show remorse by using his fame to support the resolution.[83]

California has 600,000–700,000 Armenians, with a heavy concentration in southern California and more than 100,000 in the greater Los Angeles area alone. This large, and vocal, Armenian population in Los Angeles—many of them ardent Lakers fans—furiously objected to Bryant's latest deal due to the airline's close connection to the Turkish government.[84] For years, Armenian Americans have demanded that both Turkey and the United States recognize the early 20th century killings of nearly 1.5 million Armenians in what was then the Ottoman Empire as *genocide*, a term that the Turkish government has continually rejected. The Turkish government denies that those deaths resulted from genocide, maintaining that people became casualties of the civil unrest during the collapse of the Ottoman Empire.[85] Given the Turkish government's 49% stake in Turkish Airlines, diaspora groups said that they felt betrayed by Bryant's deal, suggesting that he had accepted "blood money."[86] The Armenian National Committee said that for many people in the community, Bryant's advertisements directly translated to an endorsement of the Turkish government.

Every news outlet in the region aired coverage of the story, including the local FOX affiliate, whose newscast featured reactions from local Armenians.[87] Also, at the Lakers' next game in Toronto after Bryant's deal was announced, the team was met with about 30 protesters from the city's Armenian community, holding signs that read "Kobe: Do the Right Thing" outside of the Raptors' stadium.[88]

American Football

Judging by some of the recent feedback, even after endorsing Tom Brady, UGG still has a fair amount of male skepticism to overcome if it wants to reclaim its image as a men's brand. The announcement of Brady's endorsement caused mixed reactions among sports commentators, as pundits jokingly questioned UGG's level of endorsement quality in the masculinity department. On ESPN's *SportsNation*, for example, Colin Cowherd said that Brady is "hip and urban; he can sell anything to anybody." But Michele Beadle responded with, "The only thing I have a problem with is [UGGs are] very girly. I know men are starting to wear them more, but I still equate UGGs with California girls in denim shorts."[89] Given that the brand has become (in some circles) a punch line at the end of a joke about ugly shoes, even those who love Brady, and/or his wife, found it difficult to take seriously the idea of anything making UGG shoes cool.[90]

AP sports writer Jimmy Golen also was unconvinced of UGG's new appeal, saying that Brady was the wrong ambassador to boost the brand's image among men. The football icon always has been more of an iconoclast when it comes to style, with choices that have turned him into the target of some (mostly) good-natured teasing. He is often poked fun at for his marriage to super-model Gisele Bündchen and once-flowing Justin Bieber-esque haircut, and he was photographed for a glossy men's magazine cradling a goat in his arms and caught goofily dancing at Carnival in Brazil sporting a ponytail—looks not necessarily associated with the "manly man" one might picture stomping around in a pair of boots made for the rough and rugged.[91]

The immediate reactions to Brady's "Steps" commercial on Twitter were mixed as well, according to UGG Assistant PR Manager Lindsey Di Cola: Some were pleased and impressed, while others described Brady using certain unpleasant and derogatory terms.[92] UGG decided to measure response by posting an extended 60-second version of "Steps" on YouTube a week before unveiling it on live TV. The video helped build up a decent amount of anticipation (it generated more than 200,000 views on YouTube), but the TV spot itself was instrumental in drawing men on to its website and Facebook page, destinations designed to showcase and allow consumers to purchase the brand's full line of men's products. Combining TV and online video in an integrated marketing strategy helped UGG to increase its following on both Facebook and Twitter.

Conclusion

Mr. Tanaka previously had been contacted by a U.S. sports agency representing one of basketball's premier athletes. Since Mr. Tanaka's company was performing extremely well financially, signing a multiyear sponsorship commitment with the agency would be seen as another routine marketing budget expense. Strategically, however, it could be a masterstroke in terms of returning his company's products to prominence in the eyes of his customers. He envisioned a multimedia campaign involving television, radio, social networking, and in-person appearances. More importantly, Mr. Tanaka had spent the last six months completing extensive due diligence through a multifaceted approach: This included investigating his competitors in the Japanese market; the reputation of the agency that contacted him; and the athlete's past positive history, both on and off of the basketball court. Of course, part of Mr. Tanaka's research focused on how much the Japanese public admired this athlete as well as the country's love for that sport. It was now no longer a matter of "if" Mr. Tanaka's company would move forward but rather "when." He looked forward to meeting the agency's staff in Tokyo and then traveling to the United States to sign the deal. The year was going extremely well so far, and this new deal might indeed be the one to keep that trajectory going strong.

NOTES

1. This case was researched, and prepared, by James Holland, Steve Wise, Kate Grogan, Alison Hart and Nancy Tow under the supervision of Boston College Professor Gregory L. Stoller as the basis for in-class discussion and debate rather than to highlight either effective or ineffective handling of management situations and/or decision making. This case was prepared entirely from existing, publicly available sources.

   Copyright © 2012. No part of this case study may be reproduced, stored in a retrieval system, used in a spreadsheet, or transmitted in any form or by any means-electronic, mechanical, photocopying, recording, or otherwise-without the permission of the author. This includes but is not limited to adaptation, reproduction, and distribution in any manner or medium now or hereafter known or invented.

2. Segun, B. (2008, March 14). "Sponsorship in the trenches": Case study evidence of its legitimate place in the promotional mix. Retrieved March 2012 from http://thesportjournal.org/article/sponsorship-in-the-trenches-case-study-evidence-of-its-legitimate-place-in-the-promotional-mix/

3. Segun, B. (2008, March 14). "Sponsorship in the trenches": Case study evidence of its legitimate place in the promotional mix. Retrieved March 2012 from http://thesportjournal.org/article/sponsorship-in-the-trenches-case-study-evidence-of-its-legitimate-place-in-the-promotional-mix/

4. Segun, B. (2008, March 14). "Sponsorship in the trenches": Case study evidence of its legitimate place in the promotional mix. Retrieved March 2012 from http://thesportjournal.org/article/sponsorship-in-the-trenches-case-study-evidence-of-its-legitimate-place-in-the-promotional-mix/

5. Segun, B. (2008, March 14). "Sponsorship in the trenches": Case study evidence of its legitimate place in the promotional mix. Retrieved March 2012 from http://thesportjournal.org/article/sponsorship-in-the-trenches-case-study-evidence-of-its-legitimate-place-in-the-promotional-mix/

6. Segun, B. (2008, March 14). "Sponsorship in the trenches": Case study evidence of its legitimate place in the promotional mix. Retrieved March 2012 from http://thesportjournal.org/article/sponsorship-in-the-trenches-case-study-evidence-of-its-legitimate-place-in-the-promotional-mix/

7. Farrelly, F. J., & Quester, P. G. (n.d.). Sports and arts sponsors: Investigating the similarities and differences in management practices. Retrieved February 12, 2015, from http://2014.australiacouncil.gov.au/__data/assets/pdf_file/0018/38304/031219_Strategic_Planning_-_Sports_and_Arts_Sponsors_-_Investigating_the_Similarities_and_Differences_in_Management_Practices.pdf

8. Ibid.

9. Statista. (n.d.). Sponsorship spending in North America from 2007 to 2015. Retrieved March 2012 from http://www.statista.com/statistics/196848/north-american-sponsorship-spending-since-2007/

10. Farrelly, F. J., & Quester, P. G. (n.d.). Sports and arts sponsors: Investigating the similarities and differences in management practices. Retrieved February 12, 2015, from http://2014.australiacouncil.gov.au/__data/assets/pdf_file/0018/38304/031219_Strategic_Planning_-_Sports_and_Arts_Sponsors_-_Investigating_the_Similarities_and_Differences_in_Management_Practices.pdf

11. Ibid.

12. Pope, N. (n.d.). Overview of current sponsorship thought. *Cyber-Journal of Sports Marketing*. Retrieved April 2012 from http://fulltext.ausport.gov.au/fulltext/1998/cjsm/v2n1/pope21.htm

13. The history of sports marketing. (2011, April 18). Retrieved April 2012 from http://www.freshbusinessthinking.com/business_advice.php?CID=&AID=8869&PGID=&Title=The+History+Of+Sports+Marketing

14. Pope, N. (n.d.). Overview of current sponsorship thought. *Cyber-Journal of Sports Marketing*. Retrieved April 2012 from http://fulltext.ausport.gov.au/fulltext/1998/cjsm/v2n1/pope21.htm

15. The history of sports marketing. (2011, April 18). Retrieved April 2012 from http://www.freshbusinessthinking.com/business_advice.php?CID=&AID=8869&PGID=&Title=The+History+Of+Sports+Marketing

16. The history of sports marketing. (2011, April 18). Retrieved April 2012 from http://www.freshbusinessthinking.com/business_advice.php?CID=&AID=8869&PGID=&Title=The+History+Of+Sports+Marketing

17. Pope, N. (n.d.). Overview of current sponsorship thought. *Cyber-Journal of Sports Marketing*. Retrieved April 2012 from http://fulltext.ausport.gov.au/fulltext/1998/cjsm/v2n1/pope21.htm

18. The history of sports marketing. (2011, April 18). Retrieved April 2012 from http://www.freshbusinessthinking.com/business_advice.php?CID=&AID=8869&PGID=&Title=The+History+Of+Sports+Marketing

19. The history of sports marketing. (2011, April 18). Retrieved April 2012 from http://www.freshbusinessthinking.com/business_advice.php?CID=&AID=8869&PGID=&Title=The+History+Of+Sports+Marketing

20. The history of sports marketing. (2011, April 18). Retrieved April 2012 from http://www.freshbusinessthinking.com/business_advice.php?CID=&AID=8869&PGID=&Title=The+History+Of+Sports+Marketing

21. Masteralexis, L. P., Barr, C. A., & Hums, M. A. (Eds.). (2009). *Principles and practice of sport management* (3rd ed.). Burlington, MA Jones and Bartlett Learning. Retrieved April 2012 from http://

books.google.com/books?id=tiheH6mu-DAC&pg=PA338&lpg=PA338&dq=history+of+sports+sponso
rship&source=bl&ots=AIHF6avVXS&sig=PeEGU7wszjUzVRNNhwJcPv3aFLA&hl=en&sa=X&ei=MDVd
T9iRNOK70AHGqoXLAg&ved=0CG8Q6AEwBw#v=onepage&q=history%20of%20sports%20
sponsorship&f=false

22. Masteralexis, L. P., Barr, C. A., & Hums, M. A. (Eds.). (2009). *Principles and practice of sport manage-ment* (3rd ed.). Burlington, MA Jones and Bartlett Learning. Retrieved April 2012 from http://books
.google.com/books?id=tiheH6mu-DAC&pg=PA338&lpg=PA338&dq=history+of+sports+sponsorship&
source=bl&ots=AIHF6avVXS&sig=PeEGU7wszjUzVRNNhwJcPv3aFLA&hl=en&sa=X&ei=MDVdT9iRN
OK70AHGqoXLAg&ved=0CG8Q6AEwBw#v=onepage&q=history%20of%20sports%20
sponsorship&f=false

23. Hughes, C. (2010, August 17). Sports sponsorship is alive and well . . . if only you know where to look. Retrieved April 2012 from http://www.theuksportsnetwork.com/sports-sponsorship-is-alive-and-well-if-only-you-know-where-to-look

24. Major pro sports sponsorships to total $2.46 billion in 2011. (2011, September 26). Retrieved April 2012 from http://www.sponsorship.com/IEGSR/2011/09/26/Major-Pro-Sports-Sponsorships-To-Total-$2-46-Billi.aspx

25. Marc. (2010, March 1). The most global U.S. sport. Retrieved April 2012 from http://mkcohen.com/the-most-global-u-s-sport; List of foreign NBA players. (n.d.). In *Wikipedia*. Retrieved April 2012 from http://en.wikipedia.org/wiki/List_of_foreign_NBA_players; Gaines, C. (2011, November 17). Sports chart of the day: The international origins of NFL players. *Business Insider*. Retrieved April 2012 from http://articles.businessinsider.com/2011-11-17/sports/30409298_1_military-bases-american-samoa-pro-football-reference-com; 2011 opening day MLB rosters feature 234 foreign-born players. (2011, April 1). Retrieved April 2012 from http://mlb.mlb.com/news/press_releases/press_release
.jsp?ymd=20110401&content_id=17248920&vkey=pr_mlb&fext=.jsp&c_id=mlb

26. Lefton, T. (2008, October 6). Sponsorships help NHL jump-start new season. Retrieved April 2012 from http://www.sportsbusinessdaily.com/Journal/Issues/2008/10/20081006/This-Weeks-News/Sponsorships-Help-NHL-Jump-Start-New-Season.aspx

27. Labatt Brewing Company. (n.d.). In *Wikipedia*. Retrieved April 2012 from http://en.wikipedia.org/wiki/Labatt_Brewing_Company

28. MLB International. (2014, June 20). Retrieved April 2012 from http://mlb.mlb.com/mlb/international/sections.jsp?feature=mlbi_sponsorship

29. Phiten. (n.d.). In *Wikipedia*. Retrieved April 2012 from http://en.wikipedia.org/wiki/Phiten

30. Phil Mickelson [website]. (2013). Retrieved February 2015 from http://philmickelson.com

31. Buteau, M. (2011, August 8). Tiger Woods is dropped by TAG Heuer from watch endorsement. Retrieved April 2012 from http://www.bloomberg.com/news/2011-08-08/tiger-woods-dropped-by-tag-heuer-from-watch-endorsement-deal-as-rank-falls.html

32. Badenhausen, K. (2014, August 12). The world's highest-paid female athletes 2014. *Forbes*. Retrieved Aril 2012 from http://www.mariasharapova.com/sponsors.aspx

33. Stoningon, J. (2012). Woods no longer #1 in Businessweek power rankings. Retrieved April 2012 from http://www.msnbc.msn.com/id/41340335/ns/business-us_business/t/woods-no-longer-busi
nessweek-power-rankings/#.TzV95JhOHgQ

34. Geran, P. [styleiconPKG's channel]. (2012, February 26). *Kobe Bryant Turkish Airlines commercial.* [YouTube video]. Retrieved April 2012 from http://www.youtube.com/watch?v=gxdW7fnY3jo

35. UGGAustralia.com [website]. (2012). Retrieved April 2012 from http://www.uggaustralia.com/media/ugg-media,default,pg.html

36. Li Na—Haagen-Dazs. (2013). Retrieved April 2012 from http://www.sportseasia.com/portfolio/li-na-%E2%80%93-haagen-dazs/

37. Andy Murray. (n.d.). In *Wikipedia*. Retrieved April 2012 from http://en.wikipedia.org/wiki/Andy_Murray

38. Benson, R. (2011, May 4). Samsung announce David Beckham will be the company's ambassador for London 2012 Olympics. Retrieved April 2012 from http://www.goal.com/en-gb/news/2931/go-global/2011/05/04/2470164/samsung-announce-david-beckham-will-be-the-companys

39. Jahad, S. (2010, December 17). Backlash against Kobe Bryant's endorsement deal with Turkish Airlines. Retrieved June 2012 from http://www.scpr.org/news/2010/12/17/21992/Kobe-turkish-air/

40. Kobe Bryant. (n.d.). In *Wikipedia*. Retrieved June 2012 from http://en.wikipedia.org/wiki/Kobe_bryant

41. Harvey B. (2010, December 15). Kobe's Turkey ties ire L.A. Armenians like Kardashian. Retrieved June 2012 from http://www.bloomberg.com/news/2010-12-15/kobe-bryant-s-sponsorship-by-turkish-airlines-provokes-l-a-armenians-ire.html

42. The world's most powerful celebrities. (2011). Retrieved June 2012 from http://www.forbes.com/celebrities/

43. Kobe Bryant. (n.d.). In *Wikipedia*. Retrieved June 2012 from http://en.wikipedia.org/wiki/Kobe_bryant

44. Jahad, S. (2010, December 17). Backlash against Kobe Bryant's endorsement deal with Turkish Airlines. Retrieved June 2012 from http://www.scpr.org/news/2010/12/17/21992/Kobe-turkish-air/

45. Kucukerdogan, R., Zeybek, I., & Ekin, V. (2011, July). The global advertising of a local brand in terms of analyzing the visual content: Turkish Airlines Globally Yours advertising campaign. *The Turkish Online Journal of Design, Art and Communication*. Retrieved June 2012 from http://www.tojdac.org/tojdac/VOLUME1-ISSUE1_files/v01i106.pdf

46. Harvey B. (2010, December 15). Kobe's Turkey ties ire L.A. Armenians like Kardashian. Retrieved June 2012 from http://www.bloomberg.com/news/2010-12-15/kobe-bryant-s-sponsorship-by-turkish-airlines-provokes-l-a-armenians-ire.html

47. Rovell, D. (2010, December 13). Kobe Bryant to endorse Turkish Airlines. Retrieved June 2012 from http://www.cnbc.com/id/40641746/Kobe_Bryant_To_Endorse_Turkish_Airlines

48. Kucukerdogan, R., Zeybek, I., & Ekin, V. (2011, July). The global advertising of a local brand in terms of analyzing the visual content: Turkish Airlines Globally Yours advertising campaign. *The Turkish Online Journal of Design, Art and Communication*. Retrieved June 2012 from http://www.tojdac.org/tojdac/VOLUME1-ISSUE1_files/v01i106.pdf

49. Rovell, D. (2010, December 13). Kobe Bryant to endorse Turkish Airlines. Retrieved June 2012 from http://www.cnbc.com/id/40641746/Kobe_Bryant_To_Endorse_Turkish_Airlines

50. Kobe Bryant signs two-year deal to endorse Turkish Airlines. (2010, December 13). Retrieved June 2021 from http://www.sportsbusinessdaily.com/Daily/Issues/2010/12/Issue-64/Sponsorships-Advertising-Marketing/Kobe-Bryant-Signs-Two-Year-Deal-To-Endorse-Turkish-Airlines.aspx

51. Badenhausen, K. (2012, January 25). The top-earning NBA Players. Retrieved June 2012 from http://www.forbes.com/sites/kurtbadenhausen/2012/01/25/the-top-earning-nba-players/

52. Knight, C. (2014). Craig Redman & passenger portraits. *A&H Magazine*. Retrieved February 2015 from http://www.aandhmag.com/craig-redman-passenger-portraits/

53. Kucukerdogan, R., Zeybek, I., & Ekin, V. (2011, July). The global advertising of a local brand in terms of analyzing the visual content: Turkish Airlines Globally Yours advertising campaign. *The Turkish Online Journal of Design, Art and Communication*. Retrieved June 2012 from http://www.tojdac.org/tojdac/VOLUME1-ISSUE1_files/v01i106.pdf

54. Carr, J. (2012, June 14). A whole different kind of "Kobe face." Retrieved June 2012 from http://lak ers.ocregister.com/2012/06/14/a-whole-different-kind-of-kobe-face/73133/

55. Knight, C. (2014). Craig Redman & passenger portraits. *A&H Magazine*. Retrieved February 2015 from http://www.aandhmag.com/craig-redman-passenger-portraits/

56. Deckers. (n.d.). [news releases]. Retrieved February 2015 from http://ir.deckers.com/phoenix .zhtml?c=91148&p=irol-news

57. Deckers Outdoor Corporation. (2010, November 30). UGG® Australia announces partnership with Tom Brady. Retrieved February 2015 from http://ir.deckers.com/phoenix.zhtml?c=91148&p=irol-newsArticle&ID=1501097

58. Horney, B. (2011, October 26). Tom Brady: Man enough to change UGG image? Retrieved June 2012 from http://www.thepostgame.com/blog/style-points/201110/tom-brady-man-enough-change-uggs-image

59. Deckers. (n.d.). [news releases]. Retrieved February 2015 from http://ir.deckers.com/phoenix .zhtml?c=91148&p=irol-news

60. Horney, B. (2011, October 26). Tom Brady: Man enough to change UGG image? Retrieved June 2012 from http://www.thepostgame.com/blog/style-points/201110/tom-brady-man-enough-change-uggs-image

61. Williams, C. C. (2012, June 4). UGGs still have legs. Retrieved June 2012 from http://online.barrons .com/article/SB50001424053111904081004577436541280590490.html#articleTabs_article%3D1

62. Thompson, A. (2011, September 14). American football star Tom Brady features in UGG boot TV advert. *Herald Sun*. Retrieved June 2012 from http://www.heraldsun.com.au/entertainment/us-foot ball-star-tom-brady-features-in-ugg-boot-advert/story-e6frf96o-1226136577755

63. Show, J. (2008, March 12). Money player: Mickelson signs multi-year deal with Barclays. Retrieved June 2012 from http://www.sportsbusinessdaily.com/Daily/Issues/2008/03/Issue-120/Sponsorships-Advertising-Marketing/Money-Player-Mickelson-Signs-Multi-Year-Deal-With-Barclays.aspx

64. Barclays. (2015). *Newsroom*. Retrieved February 2015 from http://www.newsroom.barclays.co.uk

65. Phil Mickelson. (n.d.). In *Wikipedia*. Retrieved June 2012 from http://en.wikipedia.org/wiki/Phil_Mickelson

66. Adidas. (n.d.). In *Wikipedia*. Retrieved June 2012 from http://en.wikipedia.org/wiki/Adidas

67. Andy Murray drops Fred Perry, signs five-year deal with Adidas. (2009, November 4). Retrieved June 2012 from http://www.sportsbusinessdaily.com/Daily/Issues/2009/11/Issue-38/Sponsorships-Advertising-Marketing/Andy-Murray-Drops-Fred-Perry-Signs-Five-Year-Deal-With-Adidas.aspx

68. Buddell, J. (2013, June 7). How the Wimbledon final was won. *ATP World Tour*. Retrieved February 2015 from http://www.atpworldtour.com/News/Tennis/2013/07/27/Wimbledon-Sunday2-Djokovic-Murray-Final.aspx

69. Wilson, B. (2011, February 1). Andy Murray can still be sponsorship winner. Retrieved June 2012 from http://www.bbc.co.uk/news/business-12314656

70. Rovell, D. [Darren Rovell]. (2012, January 27). adidas' move to drop Djokovic for Andy Murray will be 1 of the biggest mistakes in their history. [Tweet]. Retrieved June 2012 from https://twitter.com/darrenrovell/status/162894090571223040

71. Kaplan, D. (2011, February 8). Tennis player Li Na will endorse ice cream brand Haagen-Dazs. Retrieved May 2012 from http://www.sportsbusinessdaily.com/Daily/Morning-Buzz/2011/02/08/Li-Na.aspx

72. Anich, G. (n.d.). Li Na's craving for Chinese and Haagen Dazs. Retrieved February 2015 from http://www.palmspringslife.com/Palm-Springs-Life/Desert-Guide/March-2012/Li-Nas-Craving-for-Chinese-and-Haagen-Dazs/

73. Coonan, C. (2011, June 13). Li Na's win to give China's sports marketing industry a boost. Retrieved May 2012 from http://www.thenational.ae/thenationalconversation/industry-insights/media/li-nas-win-to-give-chinas-sports-marketing-industry-a-boost

74. French Open win likely to turn to gold for Li Na. (2011, June 6). Retrieved May 2012 from http://www.cbsnews.com/2100-500202_162-20069269.html

75. Burkitt, L. (2011, October 3). Li Na still a winner after crashing out of China Open. *The Wall Street Journal*. Retrieved May 2012 from http://blogs.wsj.com/chinarealtime/2011/10/03/li-na-still-a-winner-after-crashing-out-of-china-open/

76. 19th FHC China 2015 [website]. (n.d.). Retrieved February 2015 from http://www.fhcchina.com/en/index.asp

77. Kaplan, D. (2011, February 8). Tennis player Li Na will endorse ice cream brand Haagen-Dazs. Retrieved May 2012 from http://www.sportsbusinessdaily.com/Daily/Morning-Buzz/2011/02/08/Li-Na.aspx

78. Anich, G. (n.d.). Li Na's craving for Chinese and Haagen Dazs. Retrieved February 2015 from http://www.palmspringslife.com/Palm-Springs-Life/Desert-Guide/March-2012/Li-Nas-Craving-for-Chinese-and-Haagen-Dazs/

79. Li Na shocks Caroline Wozniacki to reach Australian Open final. (2011, January 27). Retrieved February 2015 from http://www.thenational.ae/sport/tennis/li-na-shocks-caroline-wozniacki-to-reach-australian-open-final

80. Kaplan, D. (2011, June 20). Mercedes endorsement won't be last for Li; 'We could do 25 deals,' agent says. Retrieved May 2012 from http://www.sportsbusinessdaily.com/Journal/Issues/2011/06/20/Marketing-and-Sponsorship/Li-Na.aspx

81. Branigan, T. (2011, June 18). Li Na, a singular lady leading China's long march to glory. *The Guardian*. Retrieved May 2012 from http://www.guardian.co.uk/sport/2011/jun/19/li-na-china-wimbledon-2011

82. Sinco, L. (2010, December 15). Kobe Bryant's deal with Turkish Airlines outrages Armenian Americans. *Los Angeles Times*. Retrieved June 2012 from http://latimesblogs.latimes.com/lanow/2010/12/lakers-kobe-bryant-turkish-airlines-armenian.html

83. Harvey B. (2010, December 15). Kobe's Turkey ties ire L.A. Armenians like Kardashian. Retrieved June 2012 from http://www.bloomberg.com/news/2010-12-15/kobe-bryant-s-sponsorship-by-turkish-airlines-provokes-l-a-armenians-ire.html

84. Harvey B. (2010, December 15). Kobe's Turkey ties ire L.A. Armenians like Kardashian. Retrieved June 2012 from http://www.bloomberg.com/news/2010-12-15/kobe-bryant-s-sponsorship-by-turkish-airlines-provokes-l-a-armenians-ire.html

85. Watson, I. (2010, December 20). Armenians denounce Kobe Bryant deal with Turkish Airlines. Retrieved June 2012 from http://edition.cnn.com/2010/SPORT/12/20/turkey.kobe.bryant.deal/index.html

86. Aghajanian, L. (2011, May 9). Armenia: Kobe Bryant getting heat for Turkish Airlines endorsement. Retrieved June 2012 from http://www.eurasianet.org/node/63446

87. Helin, K. (2010, December 16). Kobe Bryant endorses Turkish Airlines, Los Angeles Armenian community protests. Retrieved June 2012 from http://probasketballtalk.nbcsports.com/2010/12/16/kobe-bryant-endorses-turkish-airlines-los-angeles-armenian-community-protests/

88. Benitah, S. (2010, December 19). Kobe Bryant's Toronto appearance met with protests. Retrieved June 2012 from http://www.cp24.com/servlet/an/local/CTVNews/20101219/101219_kobe_bryant/20101219/?hub=CP24Home

89. Can Tom Brady's endorsement make UGG brand seem more manly? (2010, December 1). Retrieved June 2012 from http://www.sportsbusinessdaily.com/Daily/Issues/2010/12/Issue-56/Sponsorships-Advertising-Marketing/Can-Tom-Bradys-Endorsement-Make-UGG-Brand-Seem-More-Manly.aspx

90. Krupnick, E. (2011, September 9). Tom Brady's got a new UGG commercial (VIDEO). Retrieved June 2012 from http://www.huffingtonpost.com/2011/09/09/tom-bradys-uggs_n_955394.html

91. Golen, J. (2011, September 12). Brady steps out in UGG endorsement deal. Retrieved February 2015 from http://sports.espn.go.com/espn/wire?section=nfl&id=6962780

92. Horney, B. (2011, October 26). Tom Brady: Man enough to change UGG Image? Retrieved June 2012 from http://www.thepostgame.com/blog/style-points/201110/tom-brady-man-enough-change-uggs-image

Trimo

Brane Semolic[1]

Trimo History

Trimo was founded in 1961 under the name *Kovinsko Podjetje Trebnje* (Trebnje Metal Company). The company was completely restructured and rebranded as Trimo during the national privatization program that occurred in Slovenia during the mid-1990s. Slovenia had been part of the former socialist Yugoslavia until 1990, when the country disintegrated into several independent nations. Slovenia is now a democratic multiparty society. Trimo became a publicly owned company in 1994.

A Summary of Trimo's Product History

In 1974, Trimo began manufacturing thermally insulated plates with polyurethane filling. Thirteen years later, the company turned to manufacturing construction plates filled with mineral wool. And in 1989, it began manufacturing containers. Trimo's first anti-noise fences were manufactured in 1995, while the TPO Dom roof was first presented in 1996. The following year a new technology was developed for the manufacturing of fire-resistant panels. In 2002, the TrimoFORM roof represented an innovative approach to the installation of residential roofing systems because it was marketed to individual customers. In the following year, a new line of TrimoTERM fire-resistant facade panels was launched. As of 2001, a comprehensive approach had been applied to the development of Trimo's new products, technologies, and systems, which led to a range of new products in roofing, facades, prefabricated steel constructions, and decorative elements entering the market (see Figure 1). With the start-up in 2006 of a new development-innovation center, the Trimo Institute, the company entered its next development phase.

Leadership

One of the most important drivers within the company is Tatjana Fink (see Figure 2). She joined the company immediately after graduating from college in 1980. She began in the controlling department; later she was promoted to director of the finance, sales, design, and commercial divisions. In 1992, she was promoted to general manager of Trimo.

Under her leadership, Trimo flourished and became one of the most successful manufacturing and construction companies in the region. Tatjana Fink has received numerous awards from

AUTHOR'S NOTE: Sources for this article included the general manager's response to a company questionnaire, and the Trimo website (http://www.trimo.eu/).

SOURCE: Used by permission from Brane Semolic.

| Figure 1 | A Trimo Installation for the Rossman Company in Germany |

SOURCE: Trimo.

| Figure 2 | Tatjana Fink, Trimo's Award-Winning General Manager |

SOURCE: Trimo.

national and international professional associations. She was named the most powerful and influential female manager in Slovenia in 2006. The next year, she was selected as the most respected manager in Slovenia. Throughout her time as director, Trimo has also received much recognition in its different fields of activities.

Trimo Quality

In 1993, the company acquired the ISO 9001 Quality Certificate, and in 2000, the ISO 14001 Environmental Certificate. The Slovene Committee on Business Excellence granted Trimo its award on behalf of the Republic of Slovenia. This is the highest state honor given to recognize the maintenance of high standards in the quality of products, services, and operations due to the development of knowledge and innovation. Trimo also has placed great importance on the health and safety of its employees. In 2003, the company was awarded the OHSAS 18001 Certificate in recognition of their hard work to ensure safety on the job. In 2004, the European Foundation for Quality Management (EFQM) recognized Trimo for excellence in the industry, and 3 years later Trimo was a finalist for the 2007 EFQM award.

The Trimo Business Network and Its Dynamics

The first foreign subsidiary of Trimo was established in 1990. By the end of 2006, Trimo had 14 subsidiaries, 7 representative offices, and 8 agents in relevant markets. Trimo's story of development, which was primarily Europe oriented, began in 1992 with the motto, "Satisfied customers make the largest profit." Every year, this motto was updated to support and modernize the foundation of Trimo's operations. The 2007 motto, "Innovation for sustainable growth and development," exhibited a new development leap. Trimo is now an international company employing over a thousand people, selling in more than 50 world markets, and manufacturing in Slovenia and abroad.

Comprehensive customer relationship management (CRM) and the establishment of long-term partnerships with all target public groups is a key strategy for Trimo. The company has established strategic partnerships with customers, investors, suppliers, architects, designers, specialists, and others by segmenting its public groups, offering relationships adjusted to their requirements, and organizing work procedures tailored to customer needs. Trimo assesses each of its target groups' satisfaction levels to gain feedback to improve future products, services, and processes.

Trimo's Key Competencies and Strategic Orientations

Trimo strives to ensure complete solutions in the field of prefabricated steel buildings, roofs, facades, steel constructions, and containers. The company's customers are offered efficient and integrated solutions from the very first concept proposal to the final construction, thanks to Trimo's knowledge, research and development, design, advanced technology, and top-quality building materials.

Trimo's main advantages are its clear vision and strategy, capital strength, ambitious and innovative employees, and its extensive marketing and sales network. The company's key competencies are represented by its advanced construction technologies, solutions to complex client problems, quality products and services, and its profound individual and organizational competencies.

At Trimo, special consideration is given to the individual competencies of employees. Employees are encouraged to develop their communication skills, innovation capabilities, teamwork, and self-management. This is how new technical, specific, process, and company knowledge is developed throughout the organization. Throughout the learning process, motivation, creativity, responsibility, and ethics are of utmost importance. Continuous development of competencies by Trimo employees results in added value for all of its customers.

Balanced company growth and development are ensured by the adherence to its development plan, the introduction of new products, and pursuing the company's marketing objectives. These objectives include maintaining the existing and the entering of new strategic markets. For Trimo, an important factor in developing new products is cooperation with independent experts from companies, institutes, and universities, which contributes to its knowledge-creation and innovation abilities as is indicated in the TrimoTERM panel installed in the EUROPARK (see Figure 3).

| **Figure 3** | Trimo Product and Installation at the Europark Shopping Mall in Slovenia |

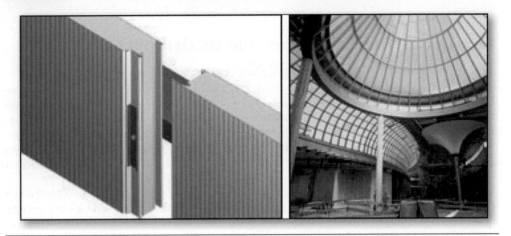

SOURCE: Trimo.

Construction Industry

Overview

Trimo operates and generates sales from its products and solutions in the construction sector. The construction market is divided into three segments: residential buildings, nonresidential buildings, and infrastructure construction. For Trimo, the most important segment is the development of nonresidential buildings in Europe. In 2005, the size of the European nonresidential building market was estimated at €400 billion. Its largest subsegment was the construction of industrial facilities, followed by commercial and business facilities. Construction of storage facilities is currently on the rise, especially in Eastern Europe and Russia. The nonresidential buildings market in Eastern Europe is increasing by 6% a year, on average, and due to substantial investments in these markets, this growth rate can also be projected into the future.

According to the micro-segmentation of the construction sector, Trimo is a competitor in the global market for insulation sandwich panels. This is part of the construction mezzo-market of roofs and facades. Insulation sandwich panels are a modern alternative to the classical construction of roofs and facades using concrete, wood, and other materials. Insulation panels differ according to the type of filling. The insulation panels with the largest market share in Europe are filled with polyurethane; however, the use of panels made of mineral wool and extruded polystyrene (EPS) is increasing due to stricter safety legislation.

The entire European panel market is estimated at 140 million square meters, of which 15% to 20% is mineral wool panels. Trimo is the leading European manufacturer of this product. The predominant European manufacturers of PU panels, and Trimo's major competitors, come from Italy, Great Britain, Germany, and France. The strongest markets for insulation panels in Europe are France, Great Britain, Germany, and Spain. Italy is the largest exporter of insulation panels to the European markets.

By providing comprehensive solutions in the field of prefabricated steel buildings, Trimo creates its competitive edge in relation to its competitors. In the European construction market, the top five companies are Vinci, Skanska, Bouygues, Hochtief, and Ferrovial. These major market players are not direct competitors with Trimo because Trimo also serves as their supplier for many projects. With this in mind, Trimo considers the following companies its main competitors: Rukki, Kingspan, Paroc, and Metecno.

Trends in the Construction Industry

Growth in the construction sector is largely dependent on economic trends and investments in the private and public sectors. In the Western European market, the growth of the construction sector is expected to continue at a relatively slow rate. According to projections, this rate will ultimately decrease as interest rates are expected to go up and thus negatively influence credit and loan operations. The interest rate increase will slow consumer spending and lead to less investment in construction projects. In the Western Europe construction market, the fastest growth is expected in the field of building renovation.

Compared to Western Europe, the booming markets of Central and Southeastern Europe represent a great business opportunity. All development prospects and expectations are oriented toward these markets, which are predicted to generate the largest profits in the European construction business through 2010. Market development is focused on the following regions:

1. The markets of new EU member states (i.e., the Czech Republic, Poland, Hungary, and the Baltic states), which together attained a mere 4.5% of the European construction market share in 2004. Growth rates in these markets will be much faster than in Western Europe (5% to 6% a year on average). Growth is expected to level off slowly in this region by 2009.

2. The markets of Southeastern Europe (i.e., Bulgaria, Romania, Croatia, Bosnia-Herzegovina, Serbia, Montenegro, and Macedonia) together constitute just 1.3% of the European construction market. They maintain a fast growth rate that is strongly supported by the programs to move toward EU membership. Growth in their construction market is projected to be in the double digits.

3. The Russian states represent only 3.5% of the European market share in construction. This market, however, is currently in a building boom, thanks to new money coming in from oil and gas reserves. These natural resources have turned Russia into a magnet for foreign investors. The construction growth rate in Russia is expected to exceed 20% a year. Apart from Russia, Belarus and Ukraine are also considered very attractive markets.

Figures 4 and 5 compare the size of the construction sector in 2004 and 2006 in Southeastern Europe and the former Soviet nations. The fastest growth is predicted for the Russian market, followed by Romania, Croatia, Serbia, and Ukraine.

Keys to Success for an Industry Branch

The success of an industry branch strongly depends on the overall economic situation in a particular market. Key factors for the success of an industry branch are the following:

- Fast economic growth
- Substantial foreign direct investment

Figure 4 Value of Construction Output in Southeastern Europe

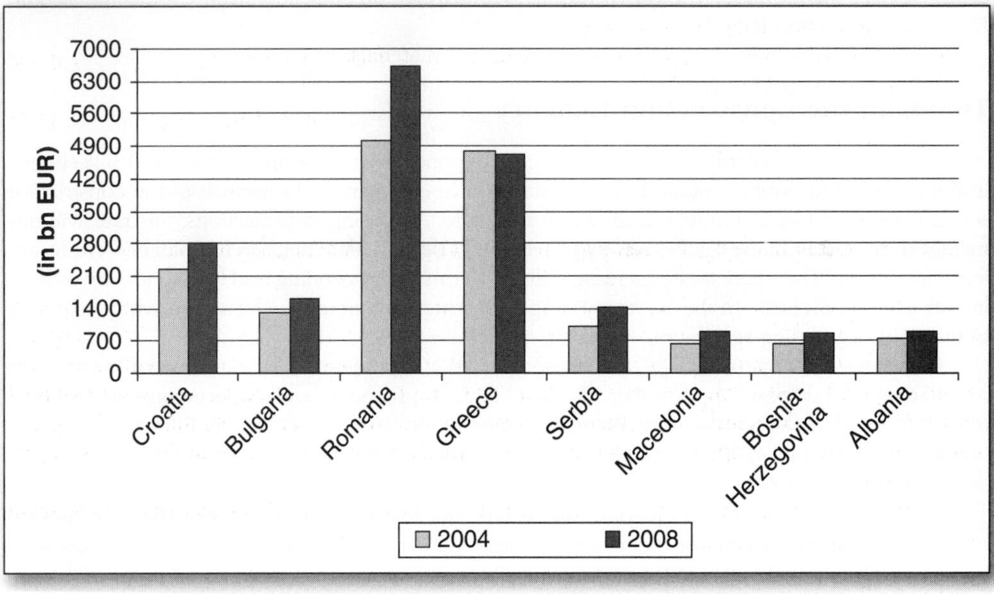

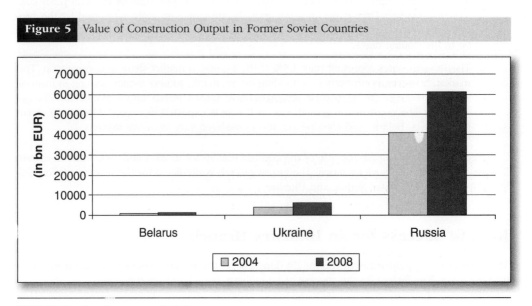

SOURCE: Croatian Government Statistics.

Figure 5 Value of Construction Output in Former Soviet Countries

SOURCE: Croatian Government Statistics.

- Development programs supported by the EU, the European Bank of Reconstruction (EBRD), the European Industrial Bank (EIB), and the World Bank
- Ability to ensure comprehensive solutions in the field of construction
- Strong R&D and technical support
- Launching of new products (new construction materials, new types of construction, speed and ease of assembly, etc.)
- Systematic implementation of customer relations management (CRM) in particular target segments (architects, investors, etc.)

Trimo's Marketing Strategy in Southeastern Europe

Trimo's marketing strategy in Southeastern European is aimed at becoming the leading European company in the provision of comprehensive prefabricated steel building solutions. The company has successfully gained recognition in the Southeastern European market by providing innovative, high-quality, and comprehensive solutions for fireproof roofs, facades, and nonresidential construction. The company focus here is trained on assuring quality solutions, fulfilling the needs of its clients, completing its projects in a timely fashion, and constantly improving its customer support.

Trimo's strategy for entering the Southeastern European markets is divided into three main parts:

1. Marketing:

- Approach clients
- Acquire new clients
- Follow strategic clients
- Follow foreign investors
- Set trends in the field of facades
- Expand market network
- Enter new markets
- Increase market share
- Increase regional sales distribution channels

2. Research & Development

- Increase innovation
- Joint development with suppliers and clients
- Transfer technology and technological knowledge
- Develop products that are catered to the market/target groups
- Market new products with a higher added value

3. Production and Purchase

- Market comprehensive solutions
- Use local sources for purchase of raw materials
- Acquire a less costly work force
- Lower transportation costs
- Find local manufacturers

Trimo's marketing strategy is pursued through the effective use of different tools and steps in market communication. Its strategy is oriented toward producing effective business plans for each region Trimo enters and by raising the company's reputation and recognition within the target markets. The business plans are oriented toward long-term, two-way relationships, strengthening the Trimo brand, supporting sales, and ensuring access for new products and services in new markets. Trimo supports these efforts by giving presentations at specialized trade fairs and for target groups such as architects and investors, advertising in trade magazines, and placing promotional articles and TV advertising.

Because of the size of the Southeastern European market, the expansion and development of the Trimo sales network is carried out by establishing local sales companies and hiring local sales representatives. This ensures that marketing communication is as effective as possible because it is country/region specific.

Trimo and the Croatian Market

Marketing Strategy for the Croatian Market

The Trimo network is based on a unified organizational culture and the high standards it holds for its projects in all markets. The business model for the Croatian market is based on overall corporate strategy, but is targeted specifically to the local market situation, local buyer characteristics, and the development of the local branch.

In 2001, Trimo established Trimo Građenje Ltd. in Croatia (*građenje* is the Croatian word for "construction"). Trimo Građenje's headquarters were located in Croatia's capital, Zagreb, which continues to grow and has more qualified personnel than in the rest of the country. In 2006, the Croatian branch had 14 employees working in sales, project planning, assembly, and imports. Trimo Građenje works closely with the parent company, Trimo.

The Croatian company has successfully established its position in the market. Trimo Građenje organized presentations for architects and investors in Croatia's larger cities (see Figure 6), to continue its networking efforts and increase its brand recognition. The Croatian subsidiary also participated in a construction fair in the town of Split, where it acquired many new and important contacts, extending its network to all regions of Croatia.

Trimo Građenje informs its market about innovations through advertising in specialized magazines. The company also increases its recognition and innovation opportunities through cooperation with local universities and their faculties of civil engineering in Zagreb and Split. For example, the company holds competitions for students in these local universities. Trimo also holds organized visits to its construction sites and the company headquarters in Trebnje, Slovenia, for fourth-year students in civil engineering.

The Marketing Situation, Market Structure, Target Clients, Risks, and Opportunities

Construction is one of the most important industry sectors in Croatia. It alone represents approximately 15% of the Croatian annual gross domestic product (GDP). This fast growth in the construction sector was spurred by the increasing flow of net foreign investments. The growth occurs in the large concentration of construction companies present in the market—the top 10 companies (according to income) account for more than 30% of the entire Croatian construction

Figure 6 Trimo Građenje Took Its Marketing Efforts to Such Croatian Cities as Osijek, Rijeka, Zadar, and Zagreb

market. The main foreign companies in the Croatian construction market are Bechtel, Strabag, and Bouygues (through a joint venture with Bina Istra).

Residential construction holds the largest share and represents approximately 40% of all construction activities in the Croatian market. Nonresidential construction and infrastructure construction are gaining value. At first, the growth of nonresidential construction increased due to the restoration of old tourist attractions, but today the number of new buildings in this sector is growing. The construction of shopping centers and logistics centers, and investment in business premises is becoming increasingly essential to the Croatian economy (see Figure 7). Croatia's pending accession into the EU is also providing a significant impetus for the construction and upgrade of nationwide infrastructure.

Croatia is one of the biggest markets in Southeastern Europe and one of five essential markets for Trimo. As mentioned previously, the road to Trimo's success was paved by strong relationships with clients built upon satisfying clients' needs efficiently and effectively. Trimo Građenje successfully cooperates with existing strategic partners and continues to acquire new clients and potential strategic partners in the Croatian market. The company's target clients and respective partners include investors, architects, project planners, engineering companies, construction companies, assembly companies, licensed partners, tradesmen, and agents.

Figure 7 The GETRO Shopping Mall Under Construction in Croatia

SOURCE: Trimo.

Trimo Građenje's key advantages in the Croatian market lie in its complete solutions, which are praised by clients, architects, and project planners alike. Trimo's roof assemblies and facades are highly regarded as clients have recognized the quality proven by the many acquired certificates. Trimo Građenje has the additional advantage of being able to offer engineering services, which include project planning, assembly, transport, and construction work. There is strong competition in the Croatian market coming from Italy, Austria, the Czech Republic, and other countries, and the local competition has an increasingly strong position. Nevertheless, Trimo is confident that it will be able to sustain its market share.

The risks for Trimo in the Croatian market are increased local and foreign competition, unsolved economic and political issues, and the unpredictable environment as a whole. There are numerous opportunities in the Croatian market that the company recognizes and builds into its strategic and annual activity plans. It is very clear to Trimo that the need for flexibility and ensuring individual solutions is increasing. Trimo's clients are becoming more demanding, the competition is stronger, and it is vital that the company prepare to react in time to reap the benefits of the changing market conditions. Company results are indicated in Table 1.

| Table 1 | Key Financial Performance Data for Trimo Građenje, 2003–2006 (in euros) |

	2003	2004	2005	2006
Net Sales Revenue	6,272,774	10,466,736	13,171,008	16,729,997
Net Profit	93,172	72,635	217,940	249,335
Assets	2,740,716	4,085,951	5,112,387	9,411,116
Financial Liabilities	0	0	0	0
Average Number of Employees	8	7	11	14

SOURCE: Trimo.

CASE QUESTIONS

1. Describe the nature of the European panel industry in terms of size and characteristics.

2. Explain the trends in the European construction industry.

3. What are the critical factors for success in this industry?

4. Why is a business network so important for the Trimo Company?

5. How does Trimo develop and maintain its competitive advantage?

6. What are the main characteristics of the Trimo marketing strategy in Southeastern Europe?

7. Describe the Trimo marketing strategy for the Croatian market.

8. Why did Trimo establish Trimo Građenje in Croatia?

9. What is the role of Trimo Građenje in the Trimo Company?

NOTE

1. Brane Semolic is the director of INOVA Consulting; Professor of Project, Technology Management and Entrepreneurship; Head of Project, Technology Management Institute; Faculty of Logistics, University of Maribor, Slovenia.

UniMed and EduMed

Omar M. Zaki

In April 2004, Dr. Michael Zachary and his son, Oscar Zachary, were faced with a critical go or no-go decision. The no-go decision would close an almost 3-year chapter on a vested effort to create a world-class global telemedicine network, which by that point seemed to be unfeasible based on their efforts and capabilities alone. The go decision, however, could potentially create a new business prospect that would help them recapture their investment.

They sat and discussed the new opportunity that was brought to them: teaming up with new business partners who would help facilitate the creation of a new business entity through securing tangible projects in continuous medical education with major multinational pharmaceutical companies.

Dr. Zachary: What do you think Oscar? This is finally an opportunity for us to make our investment into UniMed back and at least break even after all this effort and money spent.

Oscar: But it's a completely different business concept, model, and market strategy than what we've been focused on for the last 3 years. Plus, I'm not sure if I'm comfortable with the idea of partnering with these folks just yet; do you trust them?

Dr. Zachary: Well, I've worked with Ahmed on a separate project before, and the guy is pretty knowledgeable about this market and how to take advantage of its growth opportunities. Plus, he doesn't give me a bad feeling when we discuss ideas, and in fact seems to be a real trustworthy guy. I don't know the other guys very well, but my feeling is they're OK since they came through Ahmed.

Oscar: I don't know, we would be putting all of our relationships and expertise on the line, and who knows what we might lose if something goes sour. I'm almost ready to just say let's pack up for now what we've got, get back to the drawing board, and seek out some stronger financial backing to get the web portal going. That's the real goal here, isn't it? This educational conference stuff just doesn't seem to be what we were trying to do.

Dr. Zachary: I agree with you, but look at it this way: It's a way for us to put to use all the research and relationships we've built thus far and at least see how it works. Although it won't be patient-related services, we will still be providing some benefit to the medical community through these education projects, and we can build some credibility at the same time. Who knows, maybe it's what will lead us to making UniMed a reality instead of a dream down the road.

SOURCE: Used by permission from Omar Zaki.

The Telemedicine Industry

History of Telemedicine

Telemedicine is the practice of rendering medical diagnoses, advice, opinions, education, and even participating in surgery over long distances through current technology and telecommunication applications, without the physical presence of a doctor or patient being required. The idea of performing medical examinations and evaluations through the use of telecommunications is not new. Shortly after the invention of the telephone, attempts were made to transmit heart and lung sounds to a trained expert who could assess the state of the organs; however, poor transmission systems made the attempts a failure. Although it may seem that recent interest in telemedicine can be attributed to advances in the Internet and telecommunications, the truth is that telemedicine has been around since the 1960s, when astronauts first went into space. In fact, NASA built telemedicine technology into early spacecraft and spacesuits to monitor astronauts' physiological parameters. Other milestones mark telemedicine's journey to where it is today.

- 1906: ECG Transmission—Einthoven, the father of electrocardiography, first investigated the use of electrocardiogram transmission over telephone lines.
- 1920s: Help for Ships—Radios were used to link physicians standing watch at shore stations to assist ships at sea that had medical emergencies.
- 1955: Telepsychiatry—The Nebraska Psychiatric Institute was one of the first facilities in the country to have closed-circuit television in 1955. In 1971, the Nebraska Medical Center was linked with the Omaha Veterans Administration (VA) Hospital and VA facilities in two other towns.
- 1967: Massachusetts General Hospital—Telemedicine was established in 1967 to provide occupational health services to airport employees and to deliver emergency care and medical attention to travelers.

Evolution of Telemedicine: A Global Perspective

In the past, access to quality medical care has been restricted both within and between countries by geographic limitations, the inconsistent distribution of physician specialists, and limitations of existing technology. Although telemedicine has been successfully deployed in several countries and in numerous large-scale projects already, recent advances in telecommunications and technology have shown promising opportunities for explosive growth and the ability to provide the highest-quality health care throughout the world.

Limitations to the widespread implementation of telemedicine technologies were imposed by bandwidth, because the transmission of images and interactive video imaging demanded robust communications support. Those barriers have been steadily falling away, however, allowing telemedicine to become a realistic, cost-effective, and timely solution to the problems caused by inconsistent access to health care specialists. Telemedicine has successfully expanded the remote delivery of health care expertise from a broader range of medical specialties and applications, although the various specialty areas are at differing levels of sophistication and acceptance. Examples of those that have been successfully deployed include teleradiology, telecardiology, teledermatology, telepathology, and continuous medical education for health care professionals.

The Benefits of Telemedicine

Telemedicine has allowed for real-time consultations across great distances—whether between physicians, between facilities, or between patients and physicians. High-quality medical care is not delayed by the time required for travel. Not only is the quality of care improved in its timeliness, but the patient is not subjected to the additional stress of long hours of travel and being away from the support of home, family, and friends. With current advances in technology and the growth of tele-medicine equipment, software, and service providers, new lines of telemedicine have emerged, such as home care, mobile medical units, and connected rural health centers, which are making medical expertise more readily accessible and simultaneously cutting down on a myriad of health care costs.

Beyond the technology, however, there are many lessons learned from previous telemedicine programs and efforts. Without adequate investment in infrastructure development, quality programs, and careful vendor selection, contracting, and management, the potential benefits to be gained from the use of technology may fall short of expectations. Although physicians have become enamored with the concept of telemedicine, there are different demands in the provision of services to wide geo-graphic areas, and the benefit of an experienced support team becomes critical to the success of a telemedicine project, both in terms of the quality of services offered and maintaining financial viability.

Telemedicine is a reality today and represents the future of how quality health care services can be provided on a global scale. The advantage rests with those countries possessing the ade-quate communications infrastructure, funding, and innovation. To that degree, therefore, health care access will still be unequally distributed worldwide.

Health Care in the Middle East

History

The Middle East health care market is a very complex one because it is constituted by a number of individual nations each with its own laws, policies, regulative bodies, economies, infrastructure, demographics, and history. Countries such as Egypt, Syria, Jordan, and Saudi Arabia have traditionally been considered major medical markets in the region due to their historical medical academic sys-tems, extensive medical infrastructures, and large market sizes. Thought leaders tend to come out of these markets, making them medical service destinations for many other nations in the region that are close by and have a similar native tongue. Other nations such as Lebanon, Tunisia, Libya, and the Gulf states (Qatar, Bahrain, Kuwait, United Arab Emirates) are still considered either primitive or very young with regard to their capacity for medical services and expertise.

With expanding populations and the emergence of new policies for health care restructuring, nations such as the United Arab Emirates, Qatar, Saudi Arabia, Kuwait, and Bahrain are investing a great deal of money, time, and effort to build and expand their health care infrastructures and capacity to serve their people better, in addition to promoting health care tourism in the region. The reality though is that Western medical care is still far superior in its quality and outcomes, and remains the most trusted destination for those who have the capacity and ability to travel.

The 9/11 Effect

Among the most devastating events to ever occur on U.S. soil were the terrible attacks on New York City, Pennsylvania, and Washington, D.C., that occurred on September 11, 2001. This set of unfortunate events had a definite negative effect on the international patient care market. Before 9/11, many large medical institutions in the United States relied heavily on international patients;

for many, 20% to 40% of their profits came directly from international patients. Patients would come to the United States to take advantage of the great medical services available, and get checkups, diagnoses, and additional treatments or services that they required.

This was a great source of income for U.S. health care and the general economy for two main reasons. First, the sheer volume of patients continually coming to the United States to receive treatment provided a steady base of tourism and spending in the country. Second, the reason international patients are so valuable is that they are generally dollar-for-dollar, cash-basis patients, unlike domestic Medicaid/Medicare patients who pay around $0.40 to the dollar. In other words, institutions receive full payment for services provided to international patients instead of government or insurance-subsidized payments. The events of 9/11 changed everything for these facilities.

After 9/11, the inflow of international visitors decreased dramatically. Visas were harder to come by. Fears led many potential patients to consider other options before coming to the United States to receive medical treatment and diagnosis. Travel declined and was sometimes made too difficult. This opened the floodgates for telemedicine.

Telemedicine: A Natural Fit

Telemedicine solved problems for both the patient who wanted superior medical service and the domestic medical institutions that had lost so much revenue post-9/11. By allowing international patients and medical practitioners to send x-rays, digitized records, and other medical tools across the world in real time, telemedicine instantly connected patients to the great medical institutions in the United States. This process cut costs and time, and it gave both sides the opportunity to overcome problems triggered by 9/11. Through telemedicine, medical institutions would be able to change their business processes slightly and still gain revenue from these international patients who were no longer making the long trip to the United States. Telemedicine had become a natural fit and solution for everyone involved. All that was needed was a company to connect the patients and doctors in the Middle East with the medical prowess of the U.S. medical system. UniMed saw telemedicine's natural fit and sought to capitalize on the opportunity through having a first-mover advantage in the region.

Building a Network

The UniMed Concept

International patients have been coming to the United States and Europe for diagnosis and treatment for many years. In the last decade, increasing numbers of U.S. medical institutions have created programs specifically to serve the needs of international clientele. UniMed's mission was to dramatically improve medical services for patients residing in the Middle East by making Western medicine readily accessible. The concept was spawned through Dr. Zachary's experience managing international patient divisions at leading hospitals in the Washington, D.C., area and the effect he personally witnessed on the international patient business shortly after 9/11.

UniMed's business concept was to combine telemedicine capabilities with a world-class network of medical institutions and physicians to create an efficient, market-leading medical service portal for Middle Eastern patients seeking Western medical services. By providing access to an extensive network of medical institutions through telemedicine technology, UniMed sought to offer second opinions, e-consulting, and patient referral management services for the patients who are able to choose to travel overseas for medical diagnosis and treatment (see Figure 1). Patients' medical files and images would be digitally sent to consulting physicians for review and diagnosis

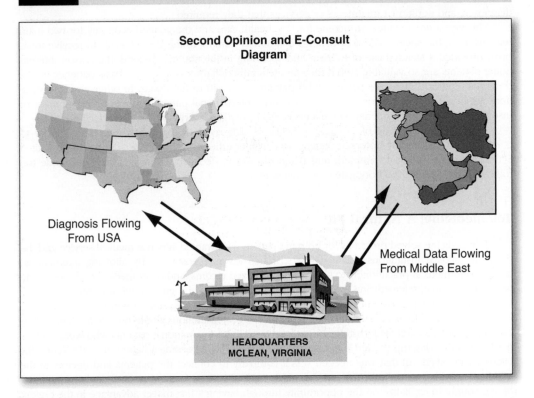

| Figure 1 | Patient Information and Service Flow |

Second Opinion and E-Consult Diagram

Diagnosis Flowing From USA

Medical Data Flowing From Middle East

HEADQUARTERS MCLEAN, VIRGINIA

(see Figure 2). Additionally, by having an extensive network of health care constituents, UniMed would be able to offer targeted marketing services for hospitals and physicians who want ready access to these high-margin, high-dollar medical patients.

The Value Proposition

UniMed's first guiding principle was that well-informed patients can and should make their own decisions regarding their health care. UniMed thus took responsibility for helping patients to become informed, get access, and develop reasonable expectations of the process ahead to fully understand the capabilities of participating institutions and physicians, and the associated costs. UniMed's second guiding principle was to ensure a positive experience for the patient. Medical problems are traumatic and the uncertainty of dealing with the unknown makes them more so. The UniMed team was committed to working quickly and effectively on the patient's behalf while being a good and empathetic listener. This was considered a global solution-selling concept for the health care industry, because it was a highly customized service for patients and providers alike. UniMed planned to offer the following services: e-consultation, second opinions, and referral management services.

E-Consultations

Patients or their physicians submit questions to Western physicians via e-mail at the satellite UniMed office. The requests are processed, forwarded, and tracked as indicated in Figure 3.

Figure 2 Transactional Flow of Patient Files

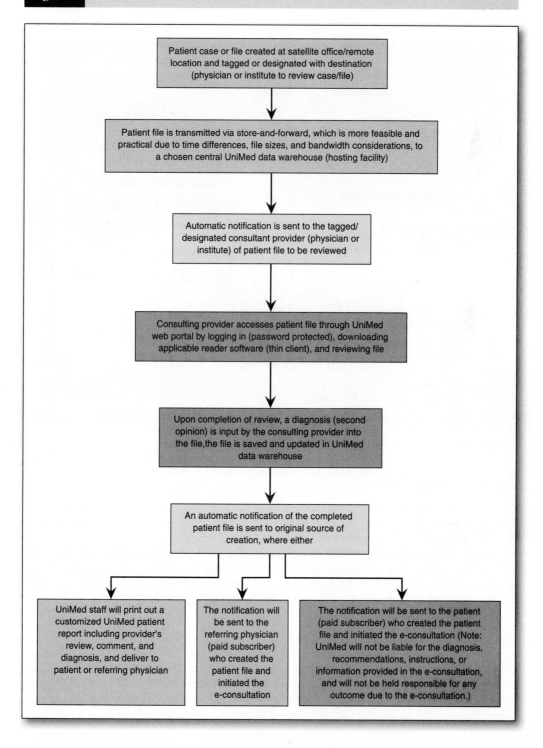

Figure 3 Sample Telemedicine Interface Used by UniMed Personnel

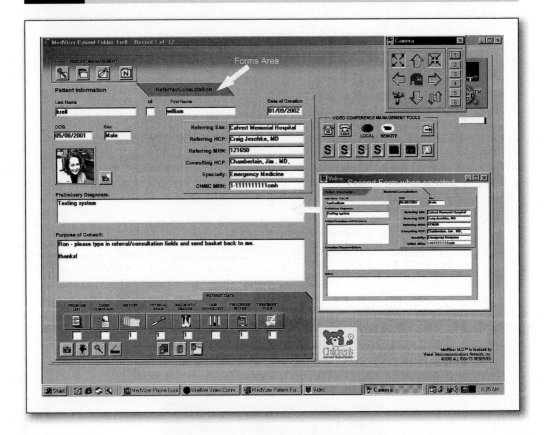

Responses are received, the patient is notified, and the response is then delivered. Assistance is available in understanding and interpreting the response. A fee of US$50 is charged for electronic consultations.

Second Opinions

Patients or their physicians submit medical records for second opinions from Western physicians via the telemedicine workstation at the satellite UniMed office. This typically requires scanning and digitizing the patient's medical records unless the digitized files are brought or e-mailed to the satellite office. Second opinions generate an average of US$400 in fees.

Referral Management Services

Patients who are able to choose to travel outside the Middle East to obtain second opinions or surgery begin their process with an examination of their options at the UniMed office. The staff provides all the options that fall within patients' parameters so that they can make the best decision.

Once a patient makes an informed decision, UniMed processes the referral to the participating institution and provides whatever level of support the patient desires on an a la carte basis. Management fees are a flat rate of US$150, in addition to a percentage-based brokerage fee to the institution or physician where the patient is referred.

The benefits of telemedicine as practiced by UniMed include:

- Access to advanced medical resources
- Avoiding the time and expense of travel when telemedicine is an appropriate alternative
- Accelerating the time it takes to connect the patient with a Western physician
- Patients make well-informed decisions based on their own criteria
- Cost-effective services due to UniMed's negotiated arrangements with PPOs, medical institutions, and technology partners

The Early Stages of a Start-Up

UniMed, LLC, was founded by Dr. Zachary and his son Oscar in early 2002, and headquartered in Washington, D.C. The company was based on a functional structure that would maximize the skills and talents of individual consultants and advisers in the early development of the company. The initial strategy was to establish two satellite offices in the Middle East, one in Egypt and one in the United Arab Emirates, as wholly owned subsidiaries owned by the parent UniMed, LLC, and then open additional satellite offices as the company grew. This strategy was based on studies done by both Dr. Zachary and Oscar on establishing a business in those two countries. The offices were to function as patient centers that would process medical documents and records for second opinions and e-consultations. Those two locations were chosen initially as the starting point for UniMed because of their market attractiveness, such as available resources (e.g., staffing, infrastructure); relatively low mobilization costs, especially in Egypt; and market factors, such as demand and growth, and even government tax incentives in Egypt that were available to companies marketing Internet-based services to help promote information and communications technology (ICT) sector growth.

Relationships Are Everything

UniMed was positioning itself as an innovative service that it was hoped would lead to high-margin business. Building relationships was vital to the success of UniMed. Being a start-up company spawned many challenges for UniMed, many of which would prove extremely difficult to overcome. Because UniMed was a new entity in a new industry, the dynamics of building the necessary relationships was different from that of other companies. There were many barriers to entry that UniMed would have to overcome if it was to be successful.

Building the company required intense dedication and a keen feel for the needs and wants of both the customers and the doctors. One of the most difficult obstacles would be raising capital. Without money, the company had no chance of getting off the ground. Gaining access to resources and information were also big barriers to entry for UniMed. There was no existing network set up for this type of service, and there were no tried-and-tested structures to model the company after. The concept was new within a relatively young industry in itself that still had not formalized standards and protocols. The software and equipment providers had not been prepared for this type of service model and much customization and creativity were needed to develop the ideal application service provider (ASP) solution.

The telemedicine industry was not like any other industry. The Internet industry, for example, had an established structure and form, making it possible to follow standards and protocols that had already been set. To gain the necessary support and create a solid network, the founders of UniMed had one choice: to build a network from the ground up bit-by-bit, ensuring each brick in the foundation of the network was sturdy and meshed well with the overall corporate objective. To build a global network of providers and customers, many key relationships and strategic alliances had to be formed; and because the concept was new, the founders of UniMed had to sell the idea.

Much of UniMed's success would come as a direct function of how well it could provide credibility to the service, industry, and business it represented. It had to attract some of the greatest medical institutions and doctors in the world to buy into the idea and therefore help create the credibility it so greatly needed. Names such as Partner's Healthcare, Johns Hopkins, and Cleveland Clinic were industry leaders and sought-after medical destinations for the potential customer base UniMed was targeting. Institutional partners like these would help UniMed get off the ground by leveraging their reputations and experience.

To start the process of building a network, Oscar decided to join the American Telemedicine Association and attended its annual conference in 2002 in Los Angeles. The conference exposed him to the major players in the industry, both companies and individuals, and provided him with tremendous knowledge on the latest developments in the industry. Through the conference, Oscar was able to gain valuable insight and direction from leaders in the telemedicine world and to embark on building the initial relationships that would prove to be vital to UniMed's success.

One such relationship was made with a pioneer in the industry named Dr. Saunders. Dr. Saunders was an accomplished physician and was considered the godfather of telemedicine because of his long-standing involvement, contributions, and impact on the industry. Oscar attended Dr. Saunders' lecture during the conference and was amazed at how he painted such a simple yet compelling picture of the value and benefits of telemedicine. Immediately after Dr. Saunders' presentation, Oscar approached him and discussed with him the idea for UniMed, which Dr. Saunders thought was excellent. They both realized that their offices were very close to each other in Washington, D.C., and scheduled a meeting to discuss the possible business opportunities, paths to follow, and resources required for implementation. Dr. Saunders had extensive relationships and clout in the industry, so without hesitation Oscar retained his services as a chief adviser to UniMed. Immediately, Dr. Saunders began to facilitate introductions that Oscar pursued in an effort to develop needed relationships.

These initial contacts were very good starting points for UniMed. They opened the doors to forming key partnerships with leading medical institutions like Partner's Healthcare and Johns Hopkins, in addition to technology vendors that could help develop web-based solutions for the company. Through these medical institutions, UniMed would be able to cover every major medical specialty and gain the prestige and credibility that would be needed for the start-up of the company.

The Chicken or the Egg?

Client Buy-In or Provider Buy-In?

UniMed's next task was to gain support and buy-in from prospective patients and physicians who would like to use this type of service. Because much of the Middle East used public-sponsored health care services through government and military coverage, the first logical path to pursue was getting the buy-in of the decision makers, and therefore financers, of all the patients traveling abroad for health care services. By the beginning of 2003, UniMed had built several solid industry relationships and had access to many of the resources required to set up a solution. The military in Egypt and the United Arab Emirates were the first two pieces of the puzzle for linking the Middle East with U.S. medical doctors and facilities.

The challenge at this point, however, was that UniMed still did not own its own solution yet. Because it was still only a start-up with limited financial resources, it lacked the significant capital necessary to put the middle part of the solution, the software and hardware, into play. Additionally, it was still only Oscar and Dr. Zachary who were running the show, wearing all hats. Eventually, they would need to build a competent team of managerial, technical, and administrative staff both in the United States and the Middle East for the service model to be operational.

To initiate the process, the plan was to set up a project with the military in either country and have them pay for the consulting and building of the first system. The prospects all thought it was a great, innovative, and desirable solution for the region; but no one wanted to be the first to take a leap of faith with this new idea, and the bureaucracy was astounding. Furthermore, Oscar and Dr. Zachary began to experience the politics and corruption inherent in doing business in the region. For instance, because no legitimate business was yet established with a potential patient base in the region, exclusive contracts still could not be set up between UniMed and the medical institutions in the United States. This then led to some prospective customers in the Middle East wanting to bypass UniMed and go directly to the medical institutions and technology vendors themselves.

Pilot Project

After a little over 2 years of marketing and trying to build a project base that would warrant investing into a system and organizational structure UniMed would require to deliver the service, an opportunity and idea came up to test the concept. The founders obtained the medical records of 20 real patients through Dr. Zachary's extensive relationships with the medical industry in Egypt and sought to use them for a pilot project. They developed a relationship with an independent doctor/computer programmer who claimed to have an open-source electronic patient record (EPR) solution and virtual data center, and had expressed interest in being a part of UniMed's growth. He offered to build a model for the entire company, based on an initial retainer fee to keep the pilot project going, and upon user and provider acceptance, gain equity in the company as it developed its project base.

Oscar and Dr. Zachary wanted to test the concept they had worked so hard on for over 2 years. Piloting the concept by sending real medical records to 5 independent doctors they had strong relationships with was the only way for them to make sure it worked. If they could gain end-user (physicians and patients) acceptance of the system and business model, they would be sure to capture real business and patient transaction flow. The unfortunate outcome, however, was that UniMed was again faced with another example of corruption and deceit with the doctor/computer programmer, who conned the founders by taking his retainer and providing UniMed with a useless, nonfunctioning software solution. UniMed was back to square one again.

End of the Rope

Half a million dollars and 2½ years after the birth of a company and concept, there were still no tangible projects or visible success stories. There were continuous costs to maintain the offices in the United States and Egypt, consultants and advisers, and other expenses, which were becoming too much. Oscar began feeling the frustration of carrying the company's weight all on his shoulders, and started to think he could not continue doing everything on his own anymore. Both he and Dr. Zachary were becoming disheartened with the progress of the company.

After all the trials and troubles, corruption, and deceitfulness UniMed faced, Oscar decided to return to the United States and take a step back from the entire project. With money running out and relationships quickly fading, he felt there was no real way to continue. He started his own job search and agreed with Dr. Zachary to continue attempts to build UniMed on a part-time basis, scaling back all the activities to save on costs. After a couple of months of searching for new work, Oscar was about to accept one of two job offers he had received.

Opportunity Knocks

Just as Oscar was considering new employment, he received an interesting call from his father. Dr. Zachary had just met with a gentleman in Abu Dhabi, named Dr. Ahmed, who had previously worked with him on a medical education project sponsored by a large pharmaceutical entity in collaboration with the hospital Dr. Zachary managed at the time. When Dr. Ahmed heard about what UniMed was attempting to do, he thought it was an amazing concept and had an epiphany. He knew he could use this type of technology in the pharmaceutical industry to train and educate medical doctors in the Middle East, which was a requirement now with recent ethical guidelines in the industry, but was exceedingly difficult to do with quality content after the reality of 9/11. After 9/11, it had become challenging to train and educate doctors because many U.S. and European doctors that had previously come to the Middle East to speak were reluctant to do so now because of fears and anxiety over the geopolitical situation in the region. Additionally, the Middle Eastern physicians who used to travel to the United States for training had more difficulty doing so after 9/11 because of problems with visas and rising travel costs. This ultimately caused major problems for the pharmaceutical industry, making it difficult to maintain the fruitful relationships with health care professionals that allowed the companies to market their products.

Simultaneously, health care in the Middle East was undergoing major restructuring and process and quality improvements, including the implementation of educational requirements for physicians to maintain their licensing in an effort to help raise the standards of care. Pharmaceutical companies were under pressure to keep doctors happy and provide educational opportunities for the doctors through their extensive marketing budgets. Video and web-based communications from the United States, which UniMed specialized in for medical purposes, would help to reunite doctors and the medical sector in the Middle East to those of the Western world for an exchange of best practices and information.

EduMed Is Born

Faced now with a new opportunity to leverage their knowledge and relationships, Dr. Zachary and Oscar considered taking on this new possibility to develop a business slightly different in its objective from UniMed, but nonetheless viable in itself. Dr. Ahmed proposed involving two other associates of his, who he considered influential in the pharmaceutical industry, and proceeded to facilitate a meeting in April 2004, bringing together his associates, Dr. Zachary and Oscar, to discuss the idea and potential for the market. Dr. Zachary, Dr. Ahmed, and his associates discussed starting a new business entity based in Dubai, named EduMed, which would develop, market, and execute continuous medical education (CME) projects (Figure 4) using the same technical and academic resources UniMed had developed relationships with. They sought to create a successful profit-generating business by securing tangible projects that could be facilitated through the industry relationships of Dr. Ahmed and his associates. Meanwhile, Oscar sat and observed during the meeting without much involvement, listening to the new potential business partners' suggestions and ideas, with a bit of skepticism based on his previous experiences.

Figure 4 Typical EduMed CME Project Structure

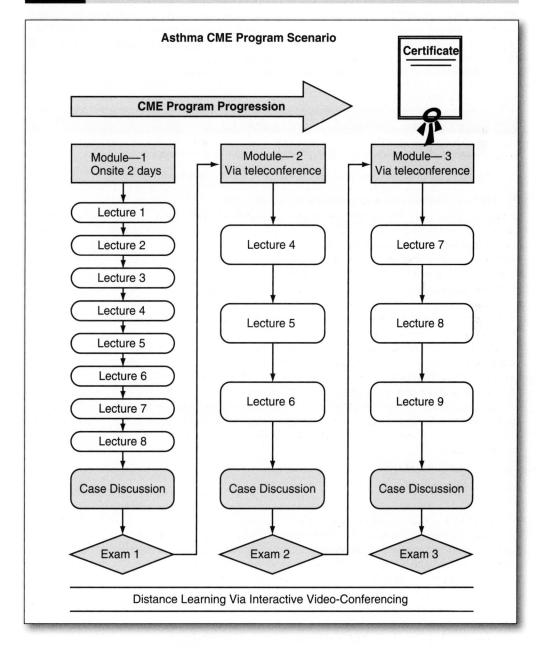

Asthma CME Program Scenario

CME Program Progression

Certificate

| Module—1 Onsite 2 days | Module—2 Via teleconference | Module—3 Via teleconference |

Module—1: Lecture 1, Lecture 2, Lecture 3, Lecture 4, Lecture 5, Lecture 6, Lecture 7, Lecture 8, Case Discussion, Exam 1

Module—2: Lecture 4, Lecture 5, Lecture 6, Case Discussion, Exam 2

Module—3: Lecture 7, Lecture 8, Lecture 9, Case Discussion, Exam 3

Distance Learning Via Interactive Video-Conferencing

Oscar knew there would be many similar potential pitfalls to what UniMed faced, but the majority of them would be new due to a shift in the market focus and strategy for acquiring the business EduMed would pursue. There was no way to know if EduMed could have a better fate than UniMed, and there was still a sense of attachment and almost parental protection that was felt by both Dr. Zachary and Oscar with regard to letting UniMed's inner core be exposed to these new business partners. The fact remained, however, that UniMed was still not generating any revenue on its own, and for the sake of recapturing the vast investments made into the company, Dr. Zachary and Oscar both realized that EduMed was a necessary endeavor. By 2005, EduMed had secured 12 CME projects throughout the Middle East with many multinational pharmaceutical companies as clients, and the founders had finally recouped their investment in UniMed.

CASE QUESTIONS

1. What are the key market factors that drove UniMed's business model?

2. What were some of the core elements in creating the UniMed business?

3. What was UniMed's value proposition?

4. What were some of the challenges UniMed faced?

5. What was the dilemma with EduMed?

6. What were the opportunities with EduMed?

7. For EduMed to be a success, what seemed to be required?

Veconinter, CA

Gregory Stoller & Jeremy Bass[1]

Introduction

During the late 1980s, while Leonardo Brea was working in New York City for a Venezuelan Maritime Shipping Carrier in an administrative management position, he had an idea that even his closest friends and colleagues said was laughable. "'Don't go through with it, Leonardo, since you won't even recover the cost of traveling down to Venezuela for your presentation,' [they said]" Leonardo recalled with a grin. Leonardo envisioned that his idea would drastically change how demurrage would be handled within the marine shipping industry and, to date, it has. The concept behind demurrage is to charge consignees (importers and/or exporters) a fee for the additional days they held on to containers (metal boxes used to ship goods) greater than the stipulated amount agreed upon in the shipping contract, known officially as a *Bill of Lading* (B/L). (See Exhibit 1 for definition of this term as well as others common to the industry.) The additional fee is known as *demurrage* (if the fee is incurred while the container is at the port) or *detention* (if the fee is incurred while the container is in the possession of the consignee). Today, Leonardo's concept has nearly revolutionized the Latin American marine shipping industry such that demurrage and detention (D&D) is now an important source of added revenue for shipping carriers rather than just a commercial tool to gain clients. It often determines whether the operations for a carrier are profitable or not.

By 1988, Leonardo had over 15 years of experience in the international maritime industry, having been an officer in the Venezuelan Navy, a deck officer in the Merchant Marines, and an Intermodal Equipment Control Manager at a now-defunct Venezuelan shipping carrier. In addition, while working in New York City, he obtained his master's degree from the State University of New York (SUNY-Fort Schuyler Maritime College) in Maritime Transportation Management. Having come from a modest background, Leonardo had finally obtained financial and professional stability by the time he was working in New York City. However, he saw an unmet opportunity in the industry and decided to take advantage of it full throttle, resigning from his position as manager. Like most entrepreneurs, Leonardo faced the harsh reality of necessary cash flow to get his idea up and running. In addition, he would need to convince any shipping carrier to give him the opportunity to provide the service. However, *unlike* many entrepreneurs, while currently living in New Jersey, he was pursuing his idea in his home country of Venezuela. Leonardo would need to leverage his experience, contacts, discipline, and innovative thinking across time zones and international boundaries to attempt to build a multimillion dollar enterprise from the ground up.

If any economic law currently prevails in Venezuela, it is the risk-return relationship. Though Venezuela is an extremely risky country in which to invest, if it is done correctly and carefully, then the return to that investment can be substantial and expeditious. But there are always risks. For example, despite having built a successful corporation that spanned 2 decades and had survived throughout arguably the most volatile economic and political eras in Venezuelan history, Venezolana de Control

Exhibit 1 Case definitions

Bill of Lading (B/L): A document issued by a carrier acknowledging that specified goods have been received on board as cargo for conveyance to a named place for delivery to the consignee, who is usually identified.[1]

Equipment Interchange Receipt (EIR): A document transferring a container from one carrier to another or to/from a terminal.[2]

Demurrage: Ancillary cost that represents liquidated fees for delays. Occurs when the vessel is prevented from the loading or discharging of cargo within the stipulated time.[3]

Detention: Ancillary cost that represents liquidated fees for delays. Occurs when the vessel is prevented from the loading or discharging of cargo within the stipulated time and the container is in the possession of the consignee.

Non-Vessel Operating Common Carrier (NVOCC): Type of sea freight forwarder. Instead of using their own ships, they operate as transportation or logistics intermediaries. That is, they book space on ships and sell it in smaller quantities, consolidating freight for transport in standard containers.[4]

Twenty equivalent units (TEUs): Capacity measurement. For example, a vessel that can hold 1,000 40-foot containers or 2,000 20-foot containers can be said to have a capacity of 2,000 TEU.[5]

Container: Main type of equipment used in intermodal transport, particularly when one of the modes of transportation is by ship[6]

Stuffing: The action of filling a container with goods for import or for export

Consignee: Person to whom the shipment is to be delivered whether by land, sea, or air.[7]

---

[1]Bill of Lading. (2008). In *Wikipedia*. Retrieved December 2007 from http://en.wikipedia.org/wiki/Bill_of_Lading

[2]U.S. Maritime Administration. (2008). Glossary and dictionary: Equipment Interchange Receipt (EIR). Retrieved January 2008 from https://www.justia.com/dictionary/equipment-interchange-receipt.html

[3]Demurrage. (2007). In *Wikipedia*. Retrieved December 2008 from http://en.wikipedia.org/wiki/Demurrage

[4]NVOCC. (2007). In *Wikipedia*. Retrieved December 2008 from http://en.wikipedia.org/wiki/NVOCC

[5]Marine transportation. (2007). In *Wikipedia*. Retrieved December 2008 from http://en.wikipedia.org/wiki/Marine Transportation

[6]Ibid.

[7]Admiralty law. (2007). In *Wikipedia*. Retrieved December 2008 from http://en.wikipedia.org/wiki/Admiralty_law

Intermodal, CA ("Veconinter"), the original model upon which Leonardo's idea would be built, had lost 75% of its client base by 2005 and was struggling to find its identity and a way to redefine itself. Also, while Leonardo; his wife, Evelyn; and his oldest son, 29-year-old Francisco, who officially joined the team in 2007 after obtaining an MBA from the Boston College Carroll School of Management, were deciding the future fate of the corporation, the unstable nature of Venezuela was serving as a not-so-subtle backdrop. In addition to the risks facing any business, the country came replete with risks involving legal insecurities, an ever-increasing threat to private property, and extremely rigid labor laws. Perhaps a natural source of competitive hedge would come not from ramping up investment throughout Venezuela but rather from looking outside of the country. These markets, most of which shared the common Spanish language, would certainly be lower risk and easier to navigate—at least, on paper. However, two failed attempts to expand internationally had already dogged Veconinter to date, etched in stone in the company's institutional memory and resume.

History

Leonardo entered the D&D invoicing and collection business as an opportunity that he identified as not being met by any outsourcing provider. The main goal behind charging for D&D was not, and still is not today, the additional revenue stream that is created but rather to decrease the turnaround time it takes for a consignee to return the container itself. Since the shipping carriers' main source of revenue is the sale of ocean freight with the use of their container fleets, it is imperative for operational effectiveness to retrieve the physical boxes back from their clients as quickly as possible. On average, the goal for every carrier is to lease each of these units (also known as *stuffing*) once every 45 days. As an operational manager, Leonardo understood this concept well and enhanced the current system to motivate consignees to eschew keeping containers for more time than what was duly required. Once the shipments were received by the consignee, the device by which it was carried wouldn't have any utility to the recipient anyway.

Under this premise, Veconinter was founded in 1988 and it focused solely on this concept, which is what made it one of the first companies in Latin America to focus on this unique source of income. The theory behind D&D is relatively simple—fees are calculated by simply subtracting two dates: (1) the date of arrival of the container (defined as the date that it becomes available to the cargo owner to begin the paperwork to go through customs and clear its shipment) and (2) the date of return of the container by the consignee, usually at the same location it was picked up at. Every additional day a container is utilized by a consignee results in a daily penalty.

Veconinter opened its first office in the capital city of Caracas, the financial and economic center of Venezuela. (See Exhibit 2 for a map of Venezuela.) Among its first challenges was developing the required software to control the activities of thousands of containers, their locations, and under whose control were they in. Additionally, the code would have to determine D&D amounts depending upon each carrier's guidelines (the carrier sets the conditions for their consignees), produce invoices, and the codes' distribution (in a country where postal service is ineffective and cannot be relied on for delivery) and to develop accounting controls to keep track of all its financial operations. These functions were not commercial and therefore had to be developed from scratch.

Apart from the computer work, the company would have to recruit a trained team to operate at port level, data processing, and other administrative functions concurrently. Leonardo determined that the new company would need 19 employees (including software engineers) all working nine months prior to the distribution of the first invoice. There was little room for mistakes, as revenue was based on daily penalties; if someone made a mistake that required a day to fix, it would directly affect the firm's bottom line. However, in most businesses, a day's delay is treated as a nonevent.

As Leonardo explained,

> The market that we originally targeted was a highly specialized industry with a relatively small number of players in any given market. Overall, no more than 20–25 shipping carriers were doing business in Venezuela at any given time. This resulted in a tight-knit community amongst competitors, which could prove beneficial, or a hindrance, as word-of-mouth marketing is prevalent and reputations are made and destroyed quickly. In addition, it also meant there were a very finite number of clients Veconinter could target, so being a first mover was truly an advantage.

Exhibit 2 Map of Venezuela[1]

[1]Country maps: Venezuela (Physiography). (2007). Retrieved January 2008 from http://www.lib.utexas.edu/maps/americas/venezuela_physio-2007.jpg

From Planning to Implementation

Initially, carriers were more than skeptical about the nature of Veconinter. Most had a legitimate concern over a concept that had existed but never been truly enforced before and rightfully responded that if the idea proved successful, they would eventually not need the middleman. Operating more efficiently would render Veconinter's service offerings moot. To buttress this possibility, Leonardo knew from the beginning that he would have to employ as many outside players and factors into the business as possible, making Veconinter's elimination that much more difficult and was banking on the fact that no matter how innovative and efficient the systems of global trade companies became, unexpected daily events would always create D&D issues and the (unantici-pated) retention of shipping containers beyond their planned dates.

Veconinter's first client to sign a service agreement was a group of carriers that were organized under the Venezuelan American Association (VENAMA), which, at the time, were collectively hav-ing critical problems recovering containers that were either kept by the consignees for months or never returned at all. The problem was dire enough to motivate the carriers to gamble on hiring Veconinter. In addition, the contracting of a third-party would function as an auditor to their operations, thus increasing transparency.

During these first few years, Leonardo worked in Venezuela, trying to consolidate the company while his family continued living in New Jersey. He commuted once a month between both countries, which was not only emotionally stressful but also significantly impacted the needed cash flow to keep the operations going. In 1991, the family made the decision to move back to Venezuela to make the country the true base of operations. By 1998, Veconinter had signed just about every carrier that worked in Venezuela in its client portfolio and was collecting over $20 million a year for its clients.

After many years, Leonardo said, when recalling all initial years of a business that changed his life and the entire future of his family,

> Success came about through good old-fashioned networking and pavement pounding. But it came at a time when you had to decide either to keep yourself in a net of comfort with our existing (small) client place and proven security, or to jump and follow your instincts with all the passion and energy you knew you could put into it. If you opted for the latter, never ever look back. You can only look ahead. Getting those first few clients now seem so easy, compared with expanding the company so dramatically from small to big.

Veconinter's financial model consists of getting paid on invoices sent to consignees and charg-ing a commission for every invoice in which an amount is collected. The commission was deducted automatically from the total amount, which was then sent to the client. This approach virtually guaranteed swift payment for services rendered, as no time or energy was required to retrieve pay-ment. In addition, it showed existing and potential clients that Veconinter was willing to bear a significant level of risk by not receiving payment for any invoices they could not collect on. Hence, it was a true results-driven approach. Every container that did not incur the D&D charge was con-trolled (kept in the system and its location identified) by Veconinter's operational process, all at no additional charge.

Leonardo also implemented a security deposit concept that required every consignee to make the deposit that would cover, amongst other expenses, D&D. The idea skyrocketed Veconinter's collection rates.

Despite all of its success between 1999 and 2005, Veconinter suffered through a difficult period that saw it lose 75% of its client base due to a number of reasons (see Exhibits 3, 4, 5, and 6 for financial and operational statistics on the company):

1. The political situation in Venezuela had quickly deteriorated, driving many of its clients to leave the Venezuelan market due to perceived instability.

2. Veconinter's rapid growth had affected the quality of service provided and the volume of work outstripped the capacity to tend to it effectively and consistently.

| Exhibit 3 | Historical Data: Veconinter Collections (2002–2005) |

Collected in US Dollars			
Year	**Detention**	**Demurrage**	**D&D***	**Total**
2002	$505,192	$4,149,833	$5,363,451	$10,018,476
2003	$266,218	$1,595,914	$2,660,129	$4,522,261
2004	$346,060	$1,093,970	$2,760,579	$4,200,609
2005	$1,951,785	$750,686	$4,804,394	$7,506,866
2006	$3,003,993	$2,924,940	$1,976,311	$7,905,244
2007	$5,852,526	$6,739,275	$5,143,130	$17,734,931
2008	**$12,442,927**	**$437,855**	**$28,457,153**	**$41,337,932**
Total (Prior 2008)	**11,925,774**	**17,254,618**	**22,707,994**	**51,888,387**

Year	**Detention**	**Demurrage**	**D&D***	
2002	5%	41%	54%	
2003	6%	35%	59%	
2004	8%	26%	66%	
2005	26%	10%	64%	
2006	38%	37%	25%	
2007	33%	38%	29%	
2008	**30%**	**1%**	**69%**	
Total	**7%**	**36%**	**58%**	**100%**

*Indicates containers that incurred both demurrage and detention

SOURCE: Veconinter (reprinted with permission)

3. Seeing the level of income that Veconinter provided, many shipping lines felt that they could obtain the same level of benefit without having to invest in a third party to obtain the results. In part, this was due to the implementation of the security deposit as a method to cover D&D obligations.

4. Consolidation in the industry started to take shape. Therefore, clients became much larger and a decision to pursue a different D&D strategy meant the impact of exiting was greater.

5. New competitors entered the market, taking away a percentage of Veconinter's market share.

During this period, however, heavy investments in information technology (IT) and a new focus on improving quality were made, all of which would prove pivotal in the current status of the company. In 2001, Veconinter obtained the ISO-9001 (International Organization for Standardization based in Switzerland) making it the first maritime service company in Venezuela to obtain the certification recognizing superior quality and operational processes. (See Exhibit 7 for a copy of this certificate.) In 2007, Veconinter was recertified with a 99% compliance record.

One of these heavy IT investments involved refining Veconinter's in-house software system, Millenium. The Sequel Server-based database was specifically designed to attend the needs of D&D and allowed Veconinter a system to methodically and efficiently track literally millions of pieces of information in a timely manner and also facilitated its reporting to clients. These investments in quality control and IT proved to be the backbone of the company's resurgence in 2006, as the software was more effectively updated to reflect current business practices. Especially because Veconinter is a family-owned company, the inclusion of Francisco into the leadership team in 2007 alongside his parents had proven valuable, since sensitive information would now no longer be passed on to nonfamily members, thereby guaranteeing that the priorities, ethics, and direction of the company would not significantly change under the second generation of leadership.

Exhibit 4	Average Demurrage and Detention (2004–2007)

Net Collected per Container Mobilized (with or without Demurrage)	
Average Collected	
Year	Amount
2000	$132
2001	$116
2002	$253
2003	$210
2004	$115
2005	$214
2006	$164
2007	$268
2008	$412

SOURCE: Veconinter (reprinted with permission)

The Guts of the Business

Leonardo commented on the basics of his firm:

> The theory behind the business is rather simple. Veconinter succeeds in combining the right mix of technology, operational know-how, accuracy, and speed. In laymen's terms, Veconinter began as a collection agency. Having said that, in the 20 years of existence, we have not taken one client to court for collections, which is an unprecedented feat, especially in a country like Venezuela, where the culture for debt payment is much less developed than in the United States.
>
> For the process to work, Veconinter needs to keep track of when the allotted free time begins and ends for the importer/exporter. This is done by obtaining three key documents: (1) the Bill of Lading to determine the arrival of the container and the ship, (2) the Interchange Equipment Receipt (EIR) Out to determine the date in which the consignee picked up the container, and (3) the EIR In to determine the date in which the consignee returned the container. These three data points will function as the basis for the entire operational process.

Veconinter has discovered a relationship that works and adds value between IT and its human resources. During the first years of this decade, Veconinter began heavily investing in its IT research and infrastructure, as the lack of strong IT solutions was one reason the company began seeing its decline during the late 1990s and early 2000s. Millenium has now become an important part of the current capabilities of the company, as it has shortened invoicing time; added the capability of new

Exhibit 5 Veconinter Financial Summary (2006–2008)

Operating Income Breakdown	Revenue 2006 Bs	$	Revenue % Increase 2006/2005	Revenue 2007 Bs	$	Increase 2007/2006	2008 Bs	$	% Increase 2008/2007
Demurrage & Detention	1,451,351,128	675,047	−8%	3,389,788,361	1,576,646	134%	8,717,566	4,054,682	157%
Damage Recoveries	4,973,101	2,313	−8%	98,997,947	46,046	1891%	234,089,800	108,879	136%
Insurance Policies	396,313,886	184,332	24%	910,319,142	423,404	130%	1,402,870,700	652,498	54%
Rent	47,300,742	22,000	13%	48,343,330	22,485	2%	47,685,400	22,179	−1%
Other Income							299,182,800	139,103	N/A
Total Operating Income	1,899,938,856	883,692	−2%	4,447,448,780	2,068,581	134%	10,701,394,900	4,977,341	141%
Financial Income Breakdown									
Interest	1,696,272	789	−93%	10,063,266	4,681	493%	23,651,075	11,001	135%
Financing	533,740,011	248,251	61%	895,379,078	416,455	68%	1,839,621,700	855,638	105%
Currency Hedging	0	0	−100%	0	0	0%	0	0	
Online Membership	0	0	0%	9,963,510	4,634	0%	0	0	
Administrative	45,251,096	21,047	135%	101,099,163	47,023	123%	168,266,525	78,264	66%
Total Financial Income	580,687,380	270,087	1%	1,016,505,017	472,793	75%	2,031,539,300	944,902	100%
Total Income	2,480,626,236	1,153,780	−2%	5,463,953,797	2,541,374	120%	12,732,934,200	5,922,243	133%

SOURCE: Veconinter (reprinted with permission)

Exhibit 6 Veconinter Demurrage and Detention Revenue Breakdown by Client Type (2005–2007)

Revenue by Client Type	Revenue % 2006		Distribution	Revenue % 2007		Distribution	Revenue % 2008		Distribution
	Bs	$		Bs	$		Bs	$	
Revenue from Carriers	1,439,933	669,736	99%	2,564,374	1,192,733	76%	8,071,509	3,754,190	76%
Revenue from NVOCCs	11,697	5,441	1%	825,413	383,913	24%	2,548,898	1,185,534	24%
Total Revenue	1,451,631	675,177	100%	3,389,788	1,576,646	100%	10,620,407	4,939,724	100%

SOURCE: Veconinter (reprinted with permission)

Exhibit 7 ISO-9001 Quality Control Certificate[1]

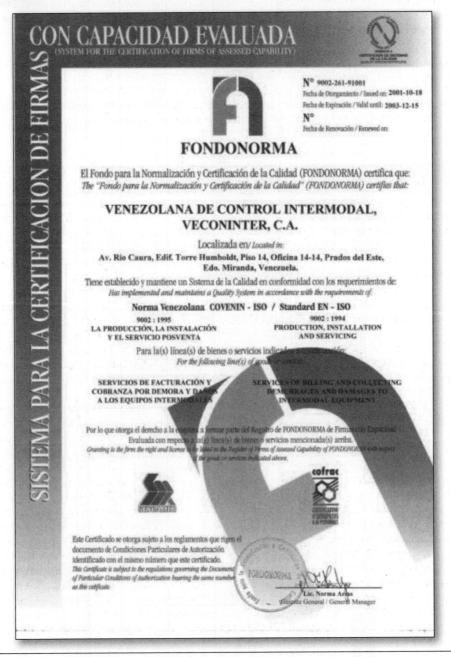

[1]Veconinter, C.A. International Organization for Standardization Certificate, 2001.

SOURCE: Veconinter (reprinted with permission)

services; and provided online capabilities for both clients and consignees to make payments, check reports and information, and make changes to profiles, amongst other features. It is proven through information that Veconinter has collected over the years that the more quickly an invoice goes out the door, the higher the probability of payment and thus the importance of faster turnaround time and accurate information. No good comes from sending an invoice with inaccurate information, as this causes additional stress to the consignee as well as damages the reputation of Veconinter as a company that lacks the controls to submit correct bills. Another obvious disadvantage of releasing erroneous invoices is that rework will be required and if payment is made, it will come in at a much slower pace. (See Exhibit 8 for a discussion of the role of IT at Veconinter.)

Relationships in the industry are pivotal. Veconinter must create and maintain strong relationships with all players in the operational process. These actors include warehouses, shipping lines,

| **Exhibit 8** | Role of Information Technology at Veconinter |

IT has also been improved to create a relationship with the consignees rather than treating them as a center of income. This recent approach has made it easier to collect, as consignees also see some benefit from the contracting of Veconinter as the service provider of shipping carriers. For example, Millenium automatically creates a notification for importers the first day demurrage is incurred and periodically thereafter, usually between 5–7 business days, though this can vary at the request of the carrier. The reminders help consignees manage the use of the container and are intended to help reduce the level of demurrage or detention they incur. Millenium also allows for interim billing for special cases where the demurrage incurred is significant (i.e., 20 days of demurrage). This helps break into more manageable pieces the debt incurred by the consignee. In addition, Veconinter offers free consulting to consignees that consistently incur significant bills in order to reduce the level of D&D they pay Veconinter on behalf of the carrier. This automated process is key in decreasing the number of units that are kept in the hands of the importer for more than 30 days.

IT also plays an important role in connecting the regional offices together as well as the clients, ports, and importers. Regional offices are important, as each office is strategically located near or at main port cities in order to reduce the time in obtaining key documentation. (See the table below for the collected amount.) On a daily basis, the B/Ls are received and the EIRs are picked up by staff at the shipping line warehouses. They are all scanned into the system for future reference. Once the information is entered into the system and an account is manually created for each container, it can be accessed by any person linked into Millenium and by the client via the web. (Clients can view only information pertinent to their operations and cannot make any changes to the information.) In addition, the offices function as locations where consignees can make payments if they do not choose to do it via Veconinter's website (the majority of clients pay at the offices). Also, each office is responsible for the invoicing and collection in their respective region. Therefore, an invoice will take much less time to arrive to a consignee location with this decentralized approach. This heavy investment in geographic infrastructure has been a competitive advantage, as Veconinter has invested in a country with volatile political and economic situations where its international clients may be hesitant to do so. Also, any local competitors would have to offer at least the same level of coverage to compete, which would require a significant up-front investment.

(Continued)

Exhibit 8 (Continued)

Today, Veconinter currently has five regional offices in addition to its headquarters in Caracas: Maracaibo, Puerto Cabello, Valencia, La Guaira, and Puerto La Cruz. It has plans to open up two more offices at port cities that are quickly growing. However, the political situation is such that even the directors of the company are looking at all their investment options before expanding their operations in Venezuela.

In its effort to automate a larger portion of the operational process, Veconinter is working with its clients to receive the B/Ls in soft copy format so an account will not have to be manually created for each container from the scanned information. This improvement would not only continue to decrease the amount of time dedicated in managing and creating each account but it would also free up a significant number of full-time equivalents (FTEs) that can focus on more value-adding activities.

Millenium produces around 15 fundamental real-time reports. These reports reflect up-to-the-minute information (contingent on information being updated on the account) that clients can use to gauge a number of key indicators ranging from the current location of their containers to the amount collected per container. Carriers can view payment behavior of their importers/exporters, which they can then use to provide credit to consistent payers and to "fire" those clients who utilize their equipment but abuse the rights provided to them in the B/L. The flexibility of the system allows for tailored reports to be designed at the request of the client. Therefore, via Millenium, literally hundreds of reports can be found that have been created according to the needs of each client.

In 2008, an innovative online Collections Follow-Up module was designed and rolled out with the objective of bringing greater efficiency to the Collections Department. The module can be accessed via a login and password from any computer with Internet access. The system evenly distributes new accounts on a daily basis and organizes the accounts such that the most delinquent accounts appear first on the list. Within this parameter, the highest-dollar debt accounts are pushed upward. If a follow-up activity has been carried out, the collector can tell the system to remove the account and have it reappear the day (specific to the hour, if need be) he or she is required to continue to work it. Since its inception in September 2008, productivity has doubled, on average.

SOURCE: Veconinter (reprinted with permission)

Amount Collected per Office 2006 vs. 2007

	2006	2007
Caracas	$976,147	$1,590,789
La Guaira	$2,779,511	$5,217,443
Maracaibo	$688,358	$1,213,404
Puerto Cabello	$2,607,660	$8,196,471
Puerto La Cruz	$416,698	$627,481
Valencia	$436,868	$889,343

cargo intermediaries also known as Non-Vessel Operating Common Carriers (NVOCCs), container warehouses, port officials, SENIAT (Venezuela's version of the Internal Revenue Service), banks, importers, and others. As important as the modifications in IT have been in improving the quality of the service Veconinter currently provides, it would be meaningless without the investment in human resources. In straightforward terms, Veconinter is a service company, and the professionals that make up the team are critical in creating the relationships.

However, as trite as the above paragraph might seem, the labor market in Venezuela is markedly different to that found in the United States and an aspect of doing business that must be considered daily. Despite the closing of thousands of private businesses during the last 10 years due to the political and economic situation in the country, finding quality candidates is still extremely difficult. This can be attributed to a number of factors:

1. There is a current "brain drain" taking place in Venezuela. Thousands of top-quality talent have left the country in pursuit of greater financial and personal stability, even if it means leaving their homeland and families behind.

2. The competition for quality candidates that remain among large transnational companies (i.e., Procter & Gamble) and smaller domestic companies such as Veconinter is now much more direct.

3. The government has attempted to increase the quantity of college graduates, which, although it has achieved its goals, is often uncorrelated with quality. There are hundreds of available B- and C-level employment candidates not suitable for the open positions.

4. In Venezuela, there are very few colleges and universities that offer specialties in maritime management or a field of study even remotely close to it. This has forced Veconinter to function as a school of learning for those candidates that it hires, usually from other fields such as chemistry, engineering, and so on.

According to Leonardo, the change in human resource strategy has been anything but cosmetic:

With the incorporation of Francisco into the company, the focus on hired talent has greatly changed. Francisco has focused on hiring the right people rather than on those who may have experience in the field. He has also encouraged us to "go younger" and look at candidates fresh out of school or with a few years of experience not necessarily in the maritime industry.

In addition, [by] strongly understanding the direct competition between large and small companies in Venezuela, he has improved the incentives for candidates to choose Veconinter, such as offering to pay for training programs (including English lessons), paying for expenses such as cell phone bills, and giving educational scholarships for those employees that desire to pursue graduate programs. We've also covered tuition fees for the employees' children and are creating a program of company ownership for those employees that meet the criteria. All of this is truly revolutionary in Venezuela for small businesses. The result has been a healthy mix of personnel that have been around since or near the founding of the company, but now with a younger generation that has also allowed a smoother transition of IT into Veconinter's daily operational activities.

Exhibit 9	Units Controlled by Veconinter Clients (2000–2008)

	Total	% Change
2000	39,591	
2001	46,314	17%
2002	32,901	-29%
2003	21,454	-35%
2004	36,473	70%
2005	34,980	-4%
2006	48,182	38%
2007	66,279	38%
2008	90,039	36%

SOURCE: Veconinter (reprinted with permission)

Other Aspects of the Sea of Change in Veconinter's Business

Critical Mass

The management of a critical mass is important for Veconinter to be able to offer competitive rates, as its fixed costs are spread over a larger container population. (See Exhibits 9 and 10 for Number of Units Controlled by Veconinter Clients and the Top 30 Container Carriers Ranked by Capacity.) For example, in Venezuela during 2007, around 64% of all containers that came into the country generated either demurrage or detention. The percentage grew to around 70% in 2008. This is the population that Veconinter will invoice and collect for its clients. Therefore, as the number of containers managed by Veconinter increases, so does the number of containers that generate D&D in absolute value terms. Since Veconinter obtains a commission for each invoice collected, the number of containers invoiced has a significant impact on Veconinter's bottom line.

Marketing

Veconinter had no formal marketing strategy until 2006. It formerly relied on word-of-mouth and reputation. Considering that its reputation was declining for a span of 7–8 years, this was an additional contributor to the decrease in business. As of 2006, Veconinter implemented a business-to-business marketing strategy focusing on its services to shipping carriers, importers/exporters, and NVOCCs. The first priority was to reestablish Veconinter as a company that offered a high-quality service at a competitive price. It was also important to revamp its image. Also in 2006, a new logo was rolled out with the goal of clearly putting an end to the past and focusing on the present and future of the company. (See Exhibit 11 for examples of the old and new logos.) In addition, a new phrase accompanied the logo that summarized where the company was heading: "A World of Solutions for the Maritime Industry." With these changes, improvements, and innovations, Veconinter wanted to relay that it was no longer a one-service company but that it now offered a gamut of solutions, products, and services that could be mixed and matched at the client's convenience. Usually such a change is met with vapid acceptance by employers and customers alike, but given the challenges and immense contraction the business had experienced, everyone at the firm hoped that all stakeholders would recognize the sincerity of these creations. Finally, a key decision was made to hire a sales director, who brought to the corporation 15 years of experience and excellent relationships within the industry that have proven pivotal to the resurgence of the company.

Advertising

Veconinter focuses on publicity through industry magazines, conference attendance, article publishing, and (to an extent) ads in major newspapers. The company also distributes marketing

Exhibit 10 Top 30 Container Carriers Ranked by Capacity

	Top 30 Container Carriers Ranked by Capacity							
		January 2000			January 2006			2000-06% Growth
Carrier	Rank	TEU	% Share	Rank	TEU	% Share	
A. P. Moeller-Maerak	1	620,324	12.0	1	1,665,272	18.2	168
Mediterranean Shipping Co. (MSG)	5	224,620	4.4	2	784,48	8.6	249
CMA CGM Group	12	122,848	2.4	3	507,954	5.6	313
Evergreen Group	2	317,292	6.2	4	477,911	5.2	51
Hapag-Lloyd	14	102,769	2.0	5	412,344	4.5	301
China Shippng (CSCL)	18	86,335	1.7	6	346,493	3.8	301
APL	6	207,992	4.0	7	331,437	3.6	59
Hanjin/Senator	4	244,636	4.8	8	328,794	3.6	34
COSCO Container Line.	7	198,841	3.9	9	322,326	3.5	62
NYK	8	166,206	3.2	10	302,213	3.3	82
Mitsui O.S.K Line (MOL)	10	136,075	2.6	11	241,282	2.6	77
OOCL	16	101,044	2.0	12	234,141	2.6	132
CSAV Group	20	69,745	1.4	13	234,002	2.6	236
K Line	13	112,884	2.2	14	227,872	2.5	102
Zim	11	132,618	2.6	15	201,432	2.2	52

(Continued)

Top 30 Container Carriers Ranked by Capacity

Carrier	January 2000			January 2006			2000-06% Growth
	Rank	TEU	% Share	Rank	TEU	% Share	
Yang Ming Line	17	93,348	1.8	16	188,206	2.1	102
HamfcLiig-Sud Group	21	68,119	1.3	17	184,438	2.0	171
Hyundai Merchant Marine	15	102,314	2.0	18	147,989	1.6	45
Pacific Int'l Lines (PIL)	24	60,505	1.2	19	134,362	1.5	122
Wan Hai Lines	22	63,525	1.2	20	114,346	1.3	80
United Arab Shipping Go. (UASC)	19	74,989	1.5	21	74,004	0.8	99
IRIS Lines	42	19,920	1.4	22	53,512	0.6	169
Regional Container Line.	33	26,355	1.5	23	48,604	0.5	84
Grimaldi (Napol)	28	35,283	0.7	24	44,363	0.5	26
Malaysian Int'l Shippng Co. (MISC)	26	41,738	0.8	25	40,543	0.4	−3
Costa Container Lines	98	4,914	0.1	26	37,480	0.4	663
China Navigation Co.	60	11,377	0.2	27	36,717	0.4	223
Sea Consortium	43	17,562	0.3	28	34,242	0.4	95
CCNI	32	26,710	0.5	29	33,799	0.4	27
SYMS	128	2,954	0.1	30	32,337	0.4	995

material (i.e., pens, notepads, etc.) to its current clients to obtain a physical presence at their business locations. Finally, Veconinter has hired a design company that has revamped its image relative to the advertising material it distributes. Word of mouth is still a very important medium to obtain new clients, as the maritime industry is an extremely tight-knit community.

The Website

Veconinter's website was revamped during 2007 to offer an additional array of services and options to its clients and consignees. In 2008, the website was translated into Portuguese and was rolled out in English during the first trimester of 2009. Its goal is to motivate consignees to perform as many transactions as possible via the web and to start to shift the dependency from the regional offices to its online solutions. For example, the improvements in IT have allowed Veconinter the capability of offering its clients and importers the option of performing financial transactions via the web, thus eliminating the necessity of visiting the regional offices. In addition, they can print out reports, purchase insurance policies, and even reutilize security deposits of one container to another, provided these deposits haven't been fully consumed.

| Exhibit 11 | Veconinter Logos |

(1988–2003)

(2004–2006)

Un mundo de soluciones para la industria Marítima (2006–Present)

SOURCE: Veconinter (reprinted with written permission)

Profit Generation

Veconinter's goal is twofold: (1) to control the largest container volume possible, as this will directly affect the level of gross income it will bring in, specifically when speaking about D&D collections, and (2) to offer other products and services to clients that will also generate additional revenue.

Leonardo acknowledged that the company was too dependent on one service and thus pushed to diversify its product portfolio. Therefore, in 2005, he began an intensive push to develop some already-existing secondary services as well as to introduce new ones into the market. The result has been a successful launch of container and cargo insurance policies that have tripled since 2005. Next, Veconinter relaunched its container damage recoveries service, which focused on collecting damage fees from consignees for containers damaged during their use in

June 2007. Though the program had been in place for six months, total collections in 2007 increased twelvefold versus 2006 and quadrupled in 2008 versus 2007. Also in 2007, Veconinter created the Container Control Department to work directly with the carrier's depot to manage the status of its units and retrieve vital information. The firm would be paid a fee for every container it kept track of and dispatched to the carrier's ships. In 2008, Veconinter expanded its collections market to other administrative expenses and ocean freight. The new service would help strengthen the client/provider bond, thus increasing the client's switching cost if it decided to pursue a different strategy.

Joint Ventures

Veconinter is planning to forge new relationships with other corporations that will fortify Veconinter's position in its industry and strengthen its product and service portfolio. In 2005, Veconinter created a very successful relationship with a prominent international insurance company to offer the Venezuelan maritime industry an insurance policy to cover damages to the container and cargo during the transportation of the cargo and the utilization of the container. The result was the introduction of a new product into the market that has not only filled a void in the market but has also diversified Veconinter's product portfolio such that clients are starting to see the company as a one-stop shop rather than a one-product provider. Finally, it has allowed Veconinter to bundle services and products and given it greater flexibility of negotiation.

In 2008, Veconinter forged another vital relationship with a world-leading container-surveying (technical inspections) company with the objective of combining marketing efforts as well as products and services to enter into new markets, capture new clients, and offer an even wider range of products to potential clients. The relationship has proven so successful that clients in two non-Latin American markets are interested in pursuing a formal relationship.

The Venezuelan Maritime Shipping Industry

Large cargo ships are generally operated by shipping lines that are considered "common carriers," since the cargo being transported can be booked by the general public.[2] The modern maritime industry can be traced back to 1956, when the first container carrier set sail from Newark, New Jersey, in 1956 and was called the Ideal X.[3] More than 70% of the $700 billion (USD) in ocean commerce are transported via liner shipping.[4] Due to greater globalization and an introduction of countries into the free market (i.e., China and India), container capacity in this decade alone has increased by 77.4% from 5,150,000 TEUs (twenty equivalent units) to 9,135,000 TEUs.[5] The shipping industry is highly fragmented, even though the top five carriers worldwide possess over 42% of the global market.[6]

In Venezuela, around 250 companies are focused on offering services related to the maritime shipping industry, specifically in the fields of shipping, warehousing, and customs. The main port cities are dispersed across the Venezuelan coast, though the two largest ports (Puerto Cabello and La Guaira) are located within a few hours of the capital, Caracas.

Venezuela is a country that has always been dependent on imports. During the last few years, the combination of restrictive government policies and high oil prices has augmented this dependency. In 1992, a total of 91,160 containers were utilized for import and export activities within Venezuela. By 2006, that number had jumped to 503,163.[7]

In the past three years alone, imports have jumped 161%.[8] However, the number of cargo ships docking at Venezuelan ports has not seen as sharp an increase. For the same period as above

(1992–2006), the number of cargo ships docking increased from 2,083 to 2,339, less than a 20% increase, an indication that ships are docking with a much larger cargo level.[9] Another indication of this conclusion is the increase in metric tons mobilized for the same period increasing from 4,981,378 to 9,060,116.[10]

The Risks and Regulations of the Venezuelan Economy

As Leonardo commented, doing business locally is anything but easy or straightforward:

> Under the direction of President Hugo Chavez, the Venezuelan economy has become much more regulated [and] controlled, and as a result, extremely challenging to run a private business. The risk of having private property expropriated, the approval of new taxes, [and] extremely rigid labor laws do not allow private businesses to perform freely, and in turn increases the risk and cost of doing business throughout the country.

According to the World Bank, Venezuela is considered to have one of the toughest environments to do business freely in the world (172 out of 178 total countries). According to the nongovernmental organization (NGO) Transparency International, Venezuela holds spot #162 out of 180 total countries in being the most corrupt country, obtaining a two out of a total 10 (no corruption).

Venezuela is one of the worst places to do business, according to "Doing Business 2008." Ten factors were taken into account:

1. Time and cost to open up a private business

2. Difficulty to obtain a license

3. Legal requirements to hire (and fire) employees

4. Private property registration

5. Access to credit

6. Protection for investors

7. Taxes

8. Exportation

9. Contract honoring

10. Private business liquidation[11]

On average, it takes 141 days to open up a business, surpassed in Latin America only by Brazil (151 days). In addition, Venezuela has the highest cost to export in Latin America at $2,400 (USD) per container. As a comparison, China's exporting cost is roughly $39 per container. Importing costs are just as high and are beaten only by Mexico ($2,411).[12]

"Doing Business 2008" also indicated that Venezuelan companies also spend the most time in preparing and paying taxes in Latin America, conducting an average of 70 transactions per year and investing 864 man-hours.

Since 2004, the exchange rate has been fixed by government order and thus is Bs. (Bolivars) 2,150/$1 (USD). The going parallel rate is Bs. 5,600/$1 as of January 2009, more than double the official rate.[13] It is extremely difficult for a private business to purchase foreign currency (i.e., U.S. dollars) at the official exchange rate. Many private businesses must revert to the parallel market to obtain foreign currency at a much higher cost. However, if private businesses are to declare foreign currency in Venezuela, they must exchange the foreign currency through the BCV (Venezuelan Central Bank) at the official rate.

The Venezuelan corporate tax rate is 34%. In addition to the tax rate, private companies are obligated to provide a certain percentage of their income to worker's compensation, safety and security, and other legal obligations. According to FEDECAMARAS, an organization that conglomerates the largest private businesses in various sectors, 55 cents (USD) of every dollar are invested into these legal obligations. They also mention that to liquidate a failed business takes four years and costs 38% of the invested amount.

In November 2007, a new tax was imposed on private businesses, forcing them to pay a 1.5% tax on every payment they make, regardless the beneficiary.[14] For example, a company would have to pay $15 to the government on a payment of $1,000 (USD). The tax was removed, however, in June 2008 due to high oil prices; it may be once again reintroduced due to the sharp fall in oil prices. After all legal obligations have been paid, on average, an investment in Venezuela will provide a yearly 6.6% return on every dollar invested, compared to over 58% in neighboring Colombia.[15]

Labor laws are extremely strict and are a reason why many foreign companies are shifting their Latin American operations from Venezuela to neighboring countries such as Colombia and Chile. Also, the Venezuelan National Assembly (the equivalent to Congress in the United States) is planning on reducing the official workweek from 40 to 36 hours, further increasing the costs for private businesses to operate.

Despite the hardships, Francisco and Leonardo have no plans to close their operations in Venezuela. As Leonardo states,

> It is evident that the atmosphere for private businesses in Venezuela has deteriorated to the point where even Venezuelan companies have decided to cease investing in their own country. We have decided to continue to operate in Venezuela for a number of reasons, both emotional and financial. We feel that though the risk level in Venezuela is greater than other countries, if you carefully navigate the waters, the returns can be significant and expeditious.
>
> Having said that, we are undecided whether to expand our operations in Venezuela or pursue opportunities abroad where Veconinter will not have to deal with as many restrictions. Our family feels it is our responsibility to continue to support the Venezuelan economy, regardless of who is governing, however, sometimes the risk level is too high to stomach—even for us.

The Future of Veconinter: Product Offerings and International Expansion Options

Veconinter has learned how to operate profitably in Venezuela even during the years with little activity. One extremely strong year was 2007, as the company's net income grew threefold versus 2006, while personnel only doubled—an indication of greater efficiency. In 2008, Veconinter net income grew fourfold in comparison to 2007. However, with the volatile situation in the Venezuelan market, where long-term planning means planning six months ahead at best, should Veconinter continue to reinvest and dedicate all its resources into its domestic market? Venezuela's dependency on imports increases yearly, however, they are directly correlated to the price of oil. Veconinter is continuously obtaining a larger market share, but there are certainly many other choices throughout Latin America. Alternatively, given its two prior failed attempts, perhaps it could or should complete more comprehensive research in advance of any other strategic moves. The next steps are anything but obvious to Leonardo:

> Veconinter now offers more than five different products and services, in stark contrast with its origins. This has allowed us to create relationships with new clients and increase our negotiation leverage, now that we can bundle various types of products and services together. Should Veconinter focus on strengthening and/or increasing the number of products we offer? I honestly have no idea. Perhaps we should instead refocus on our core service of D&D invoicing and collections.

Veconinter's reputation and brand have become much stronger during 2007 and consolidation occurred during 2008. The projections for 2009 are cautious due to the current state of the global economy. It appears that Veconinter has learned once again how to successfully navigate Venezuela's regulations, so perhaps Francisco and Leonardo should work on accelerating their growth in this high-risk market, where it is less likely that competitors will be able or willing to invest. On the downside, however, regulations are implemented so quickly in Venezuela and the economy is so volatile that the business atmosphere for 2009 may be extremely different to that which was encountered in 2008.[16]

Should Veconinter maintain their domestic operations as they currently stand in Venezuela and now focus solely on international expansion? This would require that Francisco, with the support of the team, distribute his time between the operations in Venezuela and opening offices in other new markets concurrently. The attempts of expansion internationally in 1997 (Colombia) and 2000 (Panama) were not at all successful for a various number of reasons. Despite these missteps, the opportunities outside of Venezuela are considerable for a company that operates in Veconinter's field. There are few direct competitors and comparing the Venezuelan results to those achieved abroad indicates that regional markets are not as developed as the Venezuelan market.

However, another advantage of international markets is that they deal directly with foreign currencies. Due to government regulations, the Venezuelan Bs. is grossly overvalued. Thus, the income that Veconinter produces in Venezuela is truly worth almost two-thirds less in international markets. This disparity affects the financial structure of the company, especially when decisions are made to purchase foreign currency.[17]

One final option would be to move forward with domestic investment at a slower pace to allow Veconinter opportunities for international expansion. This would provide a hedge for Venezuela's risk in the event that should more drastic measures in Venezuela take place, the company will have already begun to pursue other opportunities abroad. It would undoubtedly take longer to set up operations abroad due to the distribution of time and resources, which may allow current competitors to react to Veconinter's entrance and to fortify their operations and strategy. This might well close some of these doors in the process. Conversely, Veconinter would be protecting its position in its domestic market and once operations began abroad, the income obtained could be reinvested either in other foreign markets or in continued domestic expansion.

NOTES

1. This case was prepared by Jeremy Bass under the supervision of Boston College Professor Gregory L. Stoller as the basis for class discussion rather than to illustrate either effective or ineffective handling of an administrative situation.

2. Cargo ship. (2007). In *Wikipedia*. Retrieved December 2007 from http://en.wikipedia.org/wiki/cargo_ship

3. World Shipping Council. (2007). The birth of "intermodalism." Retrieved December 2007 from http://www.worldshipping.org/about-the-industry/history-of-containerization/the-birth-of-intermodalism

4. World Shipping Council. (2007). Liner shipping in the US. Retrieve December 2007 from http://www.worldshipping.org/benefits-of-liner-shipping

5. Alphaliner. (2015, February 11). Top 100. Retrieved February 12, 2015, from http://www.alphaliner.com/top100/.

6. World Shipping Council. (2007). Liner shipping in the US. Retrieve December 2007 from http://www.worldshipping.org/benefits-of-liner-shipping

7. Instituto Portuaria de Puerto Cabello [website]. (n.d.). Retrieved February 12, 2015, from http://www.ipcdevenezuela.com

8. Puntes, S. T., & Mayela, A. H. (2008, January 13). La economia enciende las luces rojas. *El Universal, Venezuela*.

9. Instituto Portuaria de Puerto Cabello [website]. (n.d.). Retrieved February 12, 2015, from http://www.ipcdevenezuela.com

10. Ibid.

11. Anderson, E. C. (2007, September 26). Venezuela con el peor clima para negocios. *El Universal, Venezuela*.

12. Ibid.

13. Banco Central de Venezuela [website]. (2008). Retrieved February 12, 2015, from http://www.bcv.org.ve

14. SENIAT [website]. (2007). Retrieved December 2007 from http://www.seniat.gob.ve

15. Anderson, E. C. (2007, September 26). Venezuela con el peor clima para negocios. *El Universal, Venezuela*.

16. Additional investments in Venezuela, such as the opening of two planned offices, may fortify and help accelerate Veconinter's gain of market share. But it is important to point out that for many shipping carriers and NVOCCs, Venezuela is the country where they collect the largest amount for D&D, making the nation a very lucrative market. However, the risk of nationalization, expropriation, additional taxes can completely wipe out any further investment.

17. Producing in foreign currencies with no government controls would allow the corporation to obtain the full benefit of its operations. But since Veconinter is a family business, this might require the company to implement a different organizational structure, where family members are not the final decision makers.

Index

About the Author

Robert D. Hisrich, PhD, is the Bridgestone Chair of International Marketing and the associate dean of Graduate and International Programs at Kent State University. Previously, he was the Garvin Professor of Global Entrepreneurship and director of the Walker Center for Global Entrepreneurship at Thunderbird School of Global Management. He is president of H&B Associates, a marketing and management-consulting firm he founded, and has been involved in the startup of numerous global companies.

Professor Hisrich received his BA from DePauw University, his MBA and PhD degrees from the University of Cincinnati, and honorary doctorate degrees from Chuvash State University (Russia) and the University of Miskolc (Hungary). Prior to joining Thunderbird, Dr. Hisrich held the position of A. Malachi Mixon, III Chaired Professor of Entrepreneurial Studies at the Weatherhead School of Management, Case Western Reserve University. Dr. Hisrich was a Fulbright Professor at the International Management Center in Budapest, Hungary, in 1989. In 1990–1991, he was again named a Fulbright Professor in Budapest at the Foundation for Small Enterprise Economic Development, where he also held the Alexander Hamilton Chair in Entrepreneurship. Dr. Hisrich has held visiting professorships at the University of Ljubljana (Slovenia), the Technical University of Vienna (Austria), the University of Limerick (Ireland), Donau University (Austria), Queensland University of Technology (Australia), the University of Puerto Rico, and the Massachusetts Institute of Technology.

He has authored or coauthored 38 books, including *Entrepreneurial Finance: A Global Perspective* (2015); *International Entrepreneurship: Starting, Developing and Managing a Global Venture (3rd ed.)* (2015); *Technology Entrepreneurship: Value Creation, Protection, and Capture, 2nd edition* (2015); *Advanced Introduction to Entrepreneurship* (2014); *Marketing for Entrepreneurs and SMEs: A Global Perspective* (2014); *Managing Innovation and Entrepreneurship* (2014); *Entrepreneurship: Starting, Developing, and Managing a New Enterprise (9th ed.)* (2013, translated into 13 languages); *Governpreneurship: Establishing a Thriving Entrepreneurial Spirit in Government* (2013); *Corporate Entrepreneurship* (2012); *The 13 Biggest Mistakes That Derail Small Businesses and How to Avoid Them* (2004), and *The Woman Entrepreneur* (1986). Dr. Hisrich has written over 350 articles on entrepreneurship, international business management, and venture capital, which have appeared in such journals as *The Academy of Management Review, California Management Review, Columbia Journal of World Business, Journal of Business Venturing, Sloan Management Review*, and *Small Business Economics*. He has served on the editorial boards of *The Journal of Business Venturing, Entrepreneurship Theory and Practice, Journal of Small Business Management*, and *Journal of International Business and Entrepreneurship*. Besides designing and delivering management and entrepreneurship programs to U.S. and foreign businesses and governments, particularly in transition economies, Dr. Hisrich has instituted academic and training programs such as the university/industry training program in Hungary, a high school teachers' entrepreneurship training program in Russia, and an Institute of International Entrepreneurship and Management in Russia. He has also been involved in starting and growing numerous ventures in the United States and other countries.